BRETHREN BY NATURE

BRETHREN BY NATURE

New England Indians, Colonists, and the Origins of American Slavery

Margaret Ellen Newell

CORNELL UNIVERSITY PRESS

Ithaca and London

First published 2015 by Cornell University Press

Printed in the United States of America

Library of Congress Cataloging-in-Publication Data

Newell, Margaret Ellen, 1962– author.
 Brethren by nature : New England Indians, colonists, and the origins of American slavery / Margaret Ellen Newell.
  pages cm
 Includes bibliographical references and index.
 ISBN 978-0-8014-3415-0 (cloth : alk. paper)
 1. Indian slaves—New England—History—17th century.
 2. Indian slaves—New England—History—18th century.
 3. Slavery—New England—History—17th century.
 4. Slavery—New England—History—18th century.
 5. Indians of North America—New England—History—
 17th century. 6. Indians of North America—New
 England—History—18th century. 7. New England—
 History—Colonial period, ca. 1600–1775. 8. New
 England—Race relations. I. Title.
  E98.S6N49 2015
  974'.01—dc23   2014045640

Cornell University Press strives to use environmentally responsible suppliers and materials to the fullest extent possible in the publishing of its books. Such materials include vegetable-based, low-VOC inks and acid-free papers that are recycled, totally chlorine-free, or partly composed of nonwood fibers. For further information, visit our website at www.cornellpress.cornell.edu.

Cloth printing   10 9 8 7 6 5 4 3 2 1

For Keith and Michael and in loving memory
of James J. Newell, 1923–2013

Contents

ACKNOWLEDGMENTS

Many institutions, as well as generous friends, aided in the preparation of this book. The National Endowment for the Humanities, the American Council of Learned Societies, the Huntington Library, the Massachusetts Historical Society, the John Carter Brown Library at Brown University, the John Nicholas Brown Center, the Mershon Center for International Security Studies, and the College of Arts and Humanities at Ohio State all supported my research and travel. Archivists at these institutions as well as at the Massachusetts State Archives, the Connecticut Historical Society, the Connecticut State Library, the Rhode Island Historical Society, and the Rhode Island Judicial Records Center helped me navigate court records and manuscripts. Jim and Gilda Newell, Tracy Vietze and Don Cox, and Kerry McCarthy and Andrew Fredman provided much moral support and housing during research trips in Boston, Martha's Vineyard, and Bermuda. Roxann Wheeler, Peter Wood, Joanne Pope Melish, Alan Gallay, and Stephanie Smith offered perceptive readings of rough drafts and chapters.

My biggest debt remains to my family, especially my husband, Keith Dimoff, and my son, Michael Newell-Dimoff. Both of them helped me in many, many ways—most of all by showing me what is important in life. This book is dedicated to them and to my father, Jim, a lover of history who died just as it was completed.

Note on Spelling and Dates

As much as possible I have retained the original spelling of manuscript and print sources quoted here. Early modern English writers commonly used "y" in place of "i" and "e" in words such as "it" and "them" and sometimes also employed a letter known as a thorn, written as "y," to signify the sound "th" (as in "ye" for "the"). They employed the letters u and v, and i and j, interchangeably ("have" as "haue") and utilized commonly understood contractions and abbreviations ("w^{ch}" for "which" and "Mai^{ies}" for "Majesties"). Until 1752, New England followed the "old style" Julian Calendar, in which the new year began March 25. All dates here reflect the Gregorian or modern calendar, except in a few instances in which I included both the old and new style dates separated by a slash.

Introduction

The Problem of Indian Slavery in Early America

In December 1739, Justice of the Peace Joshua Hempstead called an informal court to order in his New London, Connecticut, home. Before him was a complicated case, and he had to decide whether to dismiss it or send it to a jury trial at the county court. A man named Caesar had "deserted" the service of his master, Samuel Richards, who owned a blacksmith shop where Caesar worked. Richards filed a complaint and demanded Caesar's arrest, claiming that Caesar was his slave. Caesar did more than simply run, however; he filed a countersuit that asserted he was a free man and no one's slave. Confused wording in the Richards complaint pointed to the complexity of the issue at hand: the document referred to "Caeaser" as "a Mustee or Indian Serv[an]t," but someone had also inserted the words "a Slave" in parentheses.[1] Caesar's essential identity was at question: Was he a mustee (a biracial person of African and Indian origin) or an Indian? A servant, a slave, or a free person? What did these distinctions mean in eighteenth-century New England? Being categorized in a legal document as mulatto or mustee rather than Indian could make the difference between slavery and freedom. Rhode Island had outlawed the enslavement of local Indians, and the legality of Indian slavery remained unsettled in other colonies. But more than the question of his ethnicity was at stake in Caesar's claim.

FIGURE 1. Map of New England showing approximate locations of Native American and English settlements, ca. 1640.

Caesar recounted a very specific history to justify his freedom. His suit argued "he ought not to be holden in Service as a Slave because he saies he was born of a Squaw named Betty who was a Captive in the late Indian war & not a Slave."[2] New England colonists had forced many Indians into servitude during King Philip's War in 1675–76, including Caesar's mother, Betty. Some became slaves for life, but others received more limited sentences, at least in theory. In Connecticut, the colonial legislature in 1676 and the War Council again in 1677 determined that Indian captives who had not personally committed violent acts should be considered servants, not slaves, and freed at the end of ten years. But Betty's owners had not freed her. Instead, they held her as a slave for life and subsequently asserted ownership of her son, Caesar. As a child, Betty entered the household of New London ship captain Peter Bradley. Around the time that Betty completed her assigned term, Bradley died, and his widow, Mary, married a Long Island mariner, bringing Betty as part of the estate now controlled by her new husband, Thomas Youngs. The couple did not free Betty, and eventually Betty married one of the slaves in the Youngs household and gave birth to Caesar. Mary became a widow and remarried yet again; a now adult Caesar passed through the hands of another owner and eventually became the property of Samuel Richards. These were Caesar's legal "evidences"; he argued that under the 1676 law his mother automatically became "Manumitted & sett at Libertie" after ten years of faithful service, regardless of the inaction of her so-called owners.[3] Legally she had been a free woman before she gave birth to him, which made him free as well.

New London, where Caesar and Justice Hempstead lived, boasted more slaves than any other county in Connecticut, and people of color composed nearly 10 percent of New London city's population in 1740.[4] Enterprising residents, including modest farmers such as Hempstead, made periodic voyages to the Caribbean to buy slaves and then returned to sell them to their neighbors or to nearby New York. So many people of color served as workers on New London ships, farms, and industries that ferrymen knew they must check the passes of black and Indian passengers to ensure they were free and not runaways. Many of Joshua Hempstead's friends and fellow justices owned Indian slaves. Some were captives or descendants of captives from King Philip's War and from the earlier Pequot conflict, while others had been acquired through local court actions and purchases from other regions. Hempstead himself bought and sold Indian and African servants and slaves and employed them on his farm alongside his children and assorted free Indian and English wage workers. He condemned Indians to servitude at his Justice's Court and sold them at public auction to pay fees, fines, or restitution.[5]

In Caesar's case, however, Judge Hempstead did something surprising, given his own involvement in the African and Indian slave trade: he allowed the freedom suit to proceed. Caesar prevailed again at the trial stage and continued to live as a free man, his presence a constant challenge to owners of other Indian and African slaves in the New London area, as Richards pursued various appeals. Many Indians brought similar suits in the eighteenth century. Occasionally such freedom claims made it all the way to the Connecticut General Assembly. The magistrates hesitated to rule because they feared that freeing Indian slaves would upend the whole system of chattel slavery—both Indian and African—that underpinned the economies of towns such as New London.[6]

The stories of Caesar and the other Indians who challenged their enslavement in the eighteenth century highlight two facts: that slavery flourished in colonial New England, and that Native Americans formed a significant part of New England's slave population.[7] Popular imagination associates slavery with the colonial South or the Caribbean, not with New England, although nineteenth-century Americans knew this history well. Writers such as Catharine Maria Sedgwick, Lydia Maria Child, and Nathaniel Hawthorne featured Indian slaves as key characters in their immensely popular fiction. Names did not always match historical actors; nonetheless, the Pequots Mononotto and Owaneco march through the pages of Sedgwick's novel *Hope Leslie*. A play centering on the novel's enslaved Pequot heroine, Magawisca, even appeared in London's East End in the 1850s.[8]

Yet somehow Indian slavery virtually disappeared from post–World War I scholarship on New England. Since then historians have produced almost as many books about New England as there were English colonial residents, as Edmund Morgan famously joked. They have reconstructed the compelling narrative of the Puritan migration, the complexity of the English immigrants' rich religious and intellectual life, and the intricacies of the society and innovative economy they helped create. Many of these works stressed the uniqueness of New England culture and sought there the origins of American exceptionalism. With a few notable exceptions, though, the history of slavery in general and of Indian slavery in particular remains stubbornly absent from these narratives. We still know more about the relatively few Euro-American captives among the Indians than we do about the thousands of Native Americans who served European masters.[9] This absence is all the more surprising because Indian slavery intersects with some of the central themes of New England and indeed American history: the development of the colonial economy; the creation of legal codes; the motives behind the evangelization of Indians; the core role of households in shaping colonial society and culture; the causes and consequences of warfare with indigenous groups and imperial rivals; and the changing imperial relationship with England. Including Indian servants and slaves in the story helps illuminate all these subjects.

Within the past decade several historians have explored the phenomenon of Indian slavery in New Spain, New France, and the English American Southeast, but colonists in New England crafted regionally distinct practices.[10] There, the English acquired slaves directly through capture or legal means rather than purchasing them from other Indians, and they incorporated Indians into their households in large numbers rather than exporting most of them as a commodity to slave markets elsewhere, as in the Carolinas, or exchanging them as gifts to cement alliance, as in New France. These regional differences point to the importance of local governments and cultural norms in shaping the kinds of slave regimes colonial societies adopted. English colonists did not follow an imperial playbook when they adopted slavery, nor did the colonial setting prompt identical strategies. They made conscious decisions to exploit local Indians as a labor force.

One particularly persistent historical myth about New England is that the colonists preferred to rely on wage laborers, neighbors, European indentured servants, and their own large families for workers. In other words, the supposition is that English colonial households there simply did not need—or want—slave labor, and that what market for slaves existed was largely symbolic, based on a desire for honor and status, not economic calculations.[11] Two other myths about Indians—that they made poor servants, and that Native Americans were exterminated or pushed out of southern New England in the aftermath of King Philip's War—have further obscured the history of Indian slavery and Indians' influence on the larger New England culture and economy. In fact, the colonists sought Indian workers from the beginning of settlement.[12] And, rather than avoiding Indian laborers, the Puritan household became the locus for the most intimate kinds of cultural and material exchanges between Indians and English.

The most important religious and political figures in early New England eagerly sought Pequot captives and incorporated them into their households in large numbers as a solution to the severe regional labor shortage that coincided with the Pequot War. Men such as Governor John Winthrop recreated the manors of their former homeland with retinues of Indian dependents. Indian captives conferred more than status and honor to the English who sought them, however; they provided concrete economic benefits, and slave ownership spread quickly even to the middling ranks of society. Chief among these benefits was entry into the Caribbean trade. In the 1630s and 1640s, New England elites participated in an Atlantic world of commerce, culture, and law, and one of the emerging institutions in that world was slavery. Captive Pequots helped Boston merchants enter markets in the Atlantic and the Caribbean basin—markets in which New England Indians eventually served both as a commodity for exchange and part of an emerging labor system that produced goods for global export.

Forced Indian labor augmented the colonial workforce in important ways. Indians brought highly valued skills to New England homes and enterprises. Throughout New England before 1700, and in subregions thereafter, Native Americans represented the dominant form of nonwhite labor. They toiled in ironworks, fisheries, livestock raising, extensive agriculture, provincial armies, and other enterprises that required unusually large workforces. They also made crucial contributions to small-scale household economies, since women produced many goods for market by the mid-seventeenth century.[13] When the Reverend Peter Thacher accepted his first pulpits (in Barnstable and then Milton) in 1679–80, he added slaves—including a female Indian war captive—to the household workforce.[14] The slaves eased his beloved wife's burdens during successive pregnancies and child rearing, and just as significantly their presence allowed him to pursue merchanting and farming along with his clerical duties, increasing the family's wealth. Similarly, Joshua Hempstead found that adding Indian and African slaves and wage workers to his household, fields, and weaving, boatbuilding, and shingle-making enterprises freed him to pursue other lucrative sidelines, including public service. Many other English families could tell similar stories: elites who cemented their positions via acquisition of slaves, or aspiring colonial householders such as Caesar's putative owner, the blacksmith Samuel Richards, who used slaves as a means of climbing into that elite.

Viewed through the lens of Indian slavery and forced servitude, New England looks less exceptional than previous scholarship has suggested; it looks much more like contemporary Virginia, Barbados, Providence Island, New York, and other English "societies with slaves," to borrow Ira Berlin's description.[15] In fact, in 1641 Massachusetts Bay passed the first slave law in the English Atlantic world—in large part because authorities wanted to define the legal status of the hundreds of Pequot Indian captives they had incorporated into their households. Indian servants also prompted one of the signature transatlantic Puritan activities of the seventeenth century—the push to evangelize New England Indians. Captives taught John Eliot the Wampanoag language and served as interpreters and translators for his catechisms, and in turn captives were the initial targets of his evangelical project.[16]

Recognizing the presence of Indian slaves in colonial society forces us to rethink existing models of Indian-English relations in the Northeast. A newer generation of historians has explored the rich Native American cultures that inhabited New England before and during the era of English colonization. Some have discussed the ways in which English and Indian lives intersected in war, religion, and economic and environmental life. More often, however, interactions between colonizers and Indians are framed in the context of the fur trade or warfare, sites where only certain members of each culture confronted one another in places distant from centers of their respective populations. Indian slavery was not a "frontier" or "borderlands" phenomenon in New England, however, unlike in other regions of colonial America. Nor was it short-lived. As an institution, it flourished for nearly two centuries in some of the most densely populated areas of English North America.

The household locus of slavery meant that Indians interacted with the English in daily, intimate ways.[17] Indian women cooked for English families, made their containers and textiles, and cared for their children. Indians and English shared foodways, work methods, and technology. They attended each other's funerals, religious services, and celebrations. Servants and slaves of all ethnicities slept alongside one another and socialized during their free time. Even outside the household, English and Indians served together on diplomatic and military expeditions, and worked together in fields and aboard ship. Thus, any discussion of New England society must consider its hybrid quality—the fact that Indians, English, and eventually Africans created it jointly. Indians shaped the shared culture not merely at a distance from the English but also from within the same towns and homes. In turn, while all New England Indians felt the transformative effects of the English presence, servants and slaves faced unique pressures to adapt to English ways, for the household was the institution through which Puritan society socialized all its inhabitants—Indian and English—in expected norms.

The hybridity of New England towns and households did not preclude conflicts with the large Native American populations who remained outside the system of servitude and slavery. Historical studies that mention Indian slavery do so in the context of the major Indian wars that engulfed New England in the colonial era—generally in a discussion of the impact of defeat on indigenous populations. Here again, however, Indian slavery turns out to be a significant ingredient in colonial warfare rather than a footnote to it. If not the sole cause of the Pequot War, the taking of Indian captives quickly became one of its chief purposes, especially for leaders and soldiers from Massachusetts Bay and their Indian allies among the Narragansetts, Niantics, and Mohegans. By the time of King Philip's War, Indian fear and anger over decades of slavery loomed large among grievances that helped precipitate the conflict. Again, many English commanders—sometimes referred to as "privateers" because they operated with unique government endorsement— focused more on taking captives for profit than on other aspects of the conduct of war.

If Indian slavery helps explain colonial warfare, warfare in turn helps explain the anomalous status of Indians—enslaved and free—within colonial New England society. Historian David Eltis contends that what made American slavery unique in historical terms was that European settlers drew a rigid line between "insiders"—people like themselves who could never be enslaved—and nonwhite, mostly African "outsiders" who could be subjected to enslavement.[18] But Indians were neither insiders nor outsiders in the English colonies. Some scholars have argued persuasively that European colonizers arrived with (or quickly developed) a strong racist attitude about Indian and African difference and inferiority that made them prone to enslave these groups. But equally compelling evidence points to a more complex, evolving set of views regarding the Indians' nature and humanity.[19] Roger Williams contrasted some aspects of Indian spirituality and culture favorably with that of the colonists, noting "Boast not proud *English*, of thy birth & blood, / Thy brother *Indian* is by birth as Good. / Of one blood God made Him, and Thee & All."[20] Royal policy reinforced this recognition, at least in theory. In 1665 King Charles II formally placed Native Americans on an equal plane with the colonists as subjects of the crown.[21] Both Roger Williams and Charles II stressed that Indians were members of the same "miserable drove of Adam's degenerate seed" as the English, and thus "our brethren by nature," with the same potential to be subjects and citizens.[22]

The English Origins of Indian Slavery

A century earlier, English advocates of expansion had followed with interest the controversy within Spanish society over the rights of the indigenous peoples of the Americas, especially the public debates between Bartolomé de Las Casas and Juan Ginés de Sepúlveda in 1550 over whether a just war could be waged in the Americas.[23] Officials in Spain justified possession of the Americas by religious right (the "donation" of Pope Alexander VI), by right of discovery and conquest, and because of Indians' "natural" inferiority. The best-known proponent of this latter argument, Sepúlveda contended that even the most civilized native inhabitants of the Americas were a lower form of humanity, "by nature slaves."[24] These disputes culminated in a royal prohibition of Indian slavery in Spanish possessions in 1542.[25] Although Indians continued to be targets of enslavement and coercion within New Spain, this new legal status as free Spanish subjects sometimes protected them from enslavement by other foreign powers. Translations of Las Casas's blistering criticism of Spain's genocidal exploitation of Indians appeared in the 1580s and became a staple of Hispanophobe literature pouring from English presses during a period of intense religious, military, and economic competition with Spain.

English explorers and entrepreneurs promised to do things differently. They had to, because having contested Spanish claims to the Americas, English propagandists struggled to legitimate their own presence there. European colonizing projects all confronted the same basic ethical and legal question, which John Winthrop summarized in 1629: "What right have we to take that land, which is and hath been of long tyme possessed of others of the sons of Adam?"[26] The unilateral nature of English actions precluded a "just war" rationale—they had invaded the Indians' land, not vice versa.[27] Puritan leaders could point to their charter, which outlined the Massachusetts Bay Company's rights to any lands and resources not occupied by subjects of a "Christian Prince," and which gave the company legal jurisdiction.[28] Yet the international legal standing of such a charter was doubtful at best. They could not use religion to back their claims, as France and Spain were equally Christian.

This shaky legal foundation meant that in Plymouth, Virginia, and Massachusetts the English rested their claims in North America in part on the Indians' willingness to accept them. The Massachusetts Bay Company's instructions to the small settlement at Salem in 1629 included a strong admonition to seek peaceful relations with the Indians and to recognize their rights: "aboue all, wee pray you bee carefull that there bee none in o[u]r pr[e]cincts p[er]mitted to doe any iniurie [injury], (in the least kinde,) to the heathen people; and if any offend in that way lett them receive due Correcc[ti]on etc." When pressed by Roger Williams, John Winthrop admitted that the "good likinge of the natives" alone granted legitimacy to the Massachusetts Bay Colony's patent.[29]

Leaders such as Winthrop often portrayed the Indians as cultural inferiors. They employed words such as "barbarian" (a borrowing from the Romans, which merely meant non-Roman peoples); "savage"; "pagan"; and, more ominously, "devil-worshipper." In New England, accusations of Satanism functioned the way that the Spaniards' claims of Indian cannibalism functioned in the Americas: both charges dehumanized the native peoples and therefore justified their displacement and conquest. Some historians, notably Alfred Cave, contend the colonists became convinced that Indians and their evil needed to be exterminated by the end of the Pequot War in 1637.[30] But this language was just one of many characterizations available to the colonists. It did have legal implications, and was sometimes employed ex post facto to justify seizures of Indian land and persons. Even in times of extreme conflict, however, it was far from being the only or even the primary way that the English colonists talked about Indians.

The English colonizers' complex views also reflected the respect and fear they had for Indians as powerful diplomatic and military entities. English colonizing ventures operated in a global context, jockeying for position, alliance, and legitimacy not only vis-à-vis the Indians but also in relation to other groups within England and other European claimants in the Americas. For varying lengths of time all the colonies depended on the Indians for food, trade, information, technology, and expertise. The English presence in the region remained weak and scattered for several decades between the first attempts to settle in 1607 and the establishment of Massachusetts Bay in 1630, so they needed good relations with their Native American neighbors. Positive relations with Indian groups continued to form an important part of individual colonies' foreign policies well into the eighteenth century. Connecticut, for example, valued its alliances with the Mohegans and the Mashantucket Pequots and used these relationships in competing against other regional powers, including Massachusetts Bay.

During the Pequot War, English colonists asserted their right to Indian slaves under the doctrine of the "just war," which permitted enslavement of enemies captured in a defensive conflict. Through warfare and treaties after 1637, however, the colonists gradually claimed sovereignty over the native inhabitants of southern New England. These claims of jurisdiction regarding Native Americans sometimes pitted colonial authorities against English officials. New England Indians generally rejected any assertions of outside authority, whether from Boston or London, but as pressure mounted in the 1640s and 1650s, groups such as the Narragansetts tried to leverage imperial authorities against the more menacing local governments of Massachusetts and Connecticut. In the seventeenth century, though, the colonial governments largely directed Indian affairs in the region, and imperial authorities provided little support to their native subjects. By the time of King Philip's War, colonial declarations in Plymouth and Massachusetts called the Wampanoag, Nipmuc, Pocasset, and Narragansett Indians "rebels" and defined the conflict as an insurrection rather than a war between distinct nations.

The meanings of citizenship, state, empire, and sovereignty were all far from resolved in England itself, however, much less how these categories operated abroad or applied to other peoples.[31] English colonists interested in taking Indians' labor, land, and persons could find plenty of precedents in England's recent history. The English reconquest of Ireland in particular sparked discussion between 1550 and 1650 about rights of native inhabitants there. Some English officers and policy makers, including Sir Walter Raleigh and Sir Humphrey Gilbert, recommended separate categories of inferior citizenship for both the native inhabitants and the transplanted English.[32] During the most aggressive phases of the reconquest, commanders went even further: they declared martial law, expropriated property, and killed Irish prisoners and noncombatants. Veterans from these Irish ventures, and from equally violent encounters with the Spanish in northern Europe, brought similar tactics to North America.[33] Britain's own consolidation into a recognizable nation-state was still in process during these years of imperial expansion in the Atlantic. Part of that long transition would eventually involve a shift from "subject" to "citizen," although not necessarily for native peoples in India or elsewhere in Britain's overseas empire. At the time of the Puritan migration to New England, even the most liberal definitions of citizenship limited its privileges to ethnic English residents of England—excluding both colonists and Native Americans.[34]

Meanwhile, the colonists who extended their local governments' jurisdiction over growing numbers of Indians made the Native Americans' obligations clear, but remained silent about what privileges this inclusion might carry. Victory in King Philip's War forced colonial leaders to confront new issues of Indian citizenship.[35] Subjected through force, the Indians of southern New England became legal insiders with collective rights in land recognized in colonial law and other privileges. One of the benefits of subjecthood, commonly embodied in law after 1700, was protection from enslavement.

What happened next is a testimony to just how important Indians were to the New England economy—and how weak the commitment to Indian citizenship was. Indian labor was so valued, in fact, that neither existing war captives nor Indians imported from outside the region satisfied local demand. Despite laws explicitly designed to protect Indians, forced servitude continued into the eighteenth century. New England governments constructed a legal system that effectively channeled a substantial portion of the region's free Indians into labor for English households. Colonial courts increased the sentencing of Indians to terms of servitude and even slavery as punishment for crime and debt. This new technique of judicial enslavement added many hundreds of additional Indians to an already sizable—and reproducing—population of Indian slaves and servants in New England cities, towns, and households.

New England colonial governments also continued to conduct war against Indians on their northern borders. These wars against the Wabanaki and their allies on the eastern frontier, which began during the aggressive English roundup of refugees from King Philip's War for enslavement, raged for nearly seventy more years. In the end, the English failed to convert the Wabanaki into a source of captives. Instead, the Wabanaki proved adept at capturing English and Indian soldiers in the provincial forces. By the 1740s Wabanaki retaliation, imperial pressure, and colonists' desperate need to protect their Indian auxiliaries in the eastern wars led British and colonial authorities to redefine all New England Indians from Connecticut to Maine as subjects with the same rights and privileges as any English colonist, at least in theory. In practice, however, officials often undermined this definition for many free Indians. Despite some efforts in Connecticut to create a pathway to partial citizenship for nonviolent captives, ultimately colonial towns and governments failed to provide for a transition to free status for Indian servants, or to establish what privileges Indians would enjoy if and when they left English households. Still, Native American individuals and groups used these categories of citizen and subject to enhance their status and independence, and ultimately to challenge enslavement and other abuses.

A growing number of African slaves formed yet another source of labor in eighteenth-century New England, and soon outnumbered the bound Indian population, if not the total Native American community. Indian slavery shaped this rise of African slavery in New England in important ways. It created ties of commerce and law with the Caribbean and the Atlantic Islands that brought some of the first Africans to New England—in exchange for Indian slaves. Just as significantly, it was in the context of Indian slavery that New Englanders developed law and practice that affected Africans and Indians alike by the eighteenth century.[36]

Slavery and Servitude in Early English America

Indian servitude as practiced in New England presents some conceptual challenges to traditional definitions of slavery in North America and complicates the story of slavery's evolution. Significantly, the precise legal status of Indian workers is sometimes extremely hard to determine, and Indians could find themselves in any of a number of forms of involuntary servitude and slavery. Slavery and servitude were poorly defined terms in English America for much of the seventeenth century, and New England was no exception to this rule. Contracts, writs, bills of sale, and even legislation often used the two conditions interchangeably.

English law provided plenty of precedent for controlling the labor of individuals. During the sixteenth century, Parliament required unskilled workers to bind themselves in annual contracts, and it constrained wage growth. The English Poor Laws of 1531–1601 and the 1562 Statute of Artificers enhanced the English state's power to control—and compel—the labor of its citizens. The Statute of Artificers also expanded apprenticeship to a broad range of occupations, including farming and household labor. These changes created a legal rubric for contracted apprenticeships and indentured servitude, forms of labor that evolved rapidly and became increasingly widespread in England during the late sixteenth and early seventeenth century.[37] Apprenticeship and indentured servitude in the colonies often looked different from these English models and could become less-regulated, harsher institutions, depending on local circumstances. English law prescribed various forms of coerced labor, including galley service, "slavery" (which in this sense meant a ten-year sentence), and penal servitude outside England for vagabonds and beggars (Vagrancy Act of 1547) and for traitors. It also gave the state the right to place children in service without their parents' consent. Colonial regimes would use all these tactics and precedents against inhabitants of all ethnicities early in the period, but over time they came to target Indians, and eventually Africans, more frequently.

Ultimately, chattel slavery and freedom were at opposite ends of a broad spectrum, and many Indians occupied points along that spectrum in varying degrees of unfreedom. Slavery might be a temporary status, while servitude, as in Betty's case, might be lifelong. To complicate matters further, in the seventeenth century Indians seldom had written indentures or contracts with their English masters—a factor that distinguished them from their English counterparts. This sometimes made the ad hoc enslavement of Indians a matter of a decision on the part of an individual English colonist to define a particular Indian as a slave for the economic advantage this change brought.

English and Dutch colonizers came from the only countries in Europe where slavery and serfdom (and thus the law of slavery) had essentially disappeared by the fourteenth century. English jurisprudence drew on common law—the notion that judges decide individual cases based on precedent—rather than the heavier reliance on civil (statute) or Roman law more common elsewhere in Europe. This was significant because Roman law codified—and therefore sanctioned—an elaborate system of slavery, including the enslavement of war captives. So, there was no explicit English legislation defining slavery for colonial regimes to draw upon. This did not stop the English in America from creating robust slave codes, but it did enable some regional differences.

In fact, despite being the first to legalize slavery in 1641 in the wake of the Pequot War, thereafter New England governments consciously avoided additional legislation that clearly delimited what slavery was, how and whether heredity conferred it, and who was eligible to be enslaved. The sweeping legal codes that defined slave status in the southern and Caribbean colonies between 1661 and 1705 had their echoes in New England, where governments passed laws between 1690 and 1720 that regulated the leisure time of both Indian and African slaves and servants, categorized them as property for tax purposes, and shunted them to a different legal system for certain crimes. Yet these laws fell short of codifying slavery as an inheritable, perpetual status. In this vagueness the New England colonies departed from peers in the English Atlantic world. Colonial legislatures in New England made slavery personal, in that they left it to the individuals involved and to local communities and local police power to define and negotiate who was a slave and who was not. This was precisely because New England's inhabitants formed many of their ideas regarding race, identity, and the meaning and legality of slavery in the context of trying to find ways to bind Indian labor.

From the Indians' perspective, sometimes service in New England homes created avenues for power within their own indigenous communities, or led to profitable roles mediating relations between English and Indians in this increasingly hybrid society. In New England, the total number of Indians bound and enslaved in the colonial period likely numbered in the thousands. For the Native Americans themselves, this level of enslavement represented a significant and growing proportion of a rapidly crashing population. Enslavement was both a cause and effect of the increased integration of Native American and European society, and it heightened the pressure on Indian economies, health, family, fertility, and culture. Indians in such situations confronted difficult choices about how and whether to resist enslavement, and faced pressure to acculturate to English colonial norms. Living in English households meant acquisition of new skills—language, possibly literacy, and familiarity with animal husbandry and particular commercial trades—that might help them successfully navigate the new hybrid world of New England. But servitude also brought loss of kin ties, changes to traditional Indian gender work roles, and other cultural challenges. In perhaps the worst of outcomes, hundreds of New England Indians faced a painful diaspora as colonial authorities and individual owners sold them into voracious international slave markets. Enslaved New England Indians labored in plantations in Jamaica, Bermuda, Providence Island, the Azores, and possibly even Madagascar. They served on naval galleys in the Mediterranean and built fortifications in Morocco.

Thousands more Indians lived as free persons in eighteenth-century New England, some in English towns and others on designated "Indian town" reservations in the several colonies. These men and women performed many of the same tasks as enslaved Indians, but managed to retain independent households. Indian towns remained a potential refuge and source of community and culture for the entire Indian population, free and enslaved. In some cases, particularly as day laborers, Indians could control the terms of their employ and maintain autonomy, even though they still had to adjust to a regional economy, work life, and environment that the English had dramatically altered. They also faced various forms of coercion and demands for labor and military service from white patrons, as well as pressure to indenture their children to English families.

More seriously, the presence of Indian slavery and judicial enslavement meant that free Indians stood in constant danger of involuntary servitude. Illness, debt, an altercation, an accusation of crime, or merely collusion between local authorities and an aspiring owner might result in one's conversion to a bondservant. Moreover, once enmeshed in relations of even voluntary servitude, Native Americans might find themselves in a state of de facto enslavement, as owners sought to transform Indian wage workers and term servants into slaves. Some Indian families experienced a kind of serial servitude that bound successive generations, as Caesar's case showed: masters such as the Youngs family asserted ownership over the children of Indian servants, seeking to transform them into slaves.

Indian slavery formed an important chapter in New England's contribution to the growing racialization of Anglo-American society in the long eighteenth century. At the same time, the evolution and expansion of African slavery in the Americas affected Native Americans in dramatic ways. In terms of sheer numbers, European enslavement of Africans outpaced Amerindian slavery in North America by the mid-1700s, and this shift began in earnest in the 1690s. The English colonists showed an increasing consciousness of race after 1700, and race became a key category for determining status, legal rights, social position, residence, and citizenship. Meanwhile, the growth of the African population, as well as the literal intermixing of peoples, had an enormous impact on Native Americans in New England. New legislation lumped Indian servants and slaves (and eventually many free Indians) together with Africans in a marginalized class of people of color to the detriment of their distinct Native American identity. These shifts exposed biracial Indians (and even those who were not biracial) to enslavement, since they provided a means for would-be masters to avoid laws against Indian slavery. They had only to claim that the Indian in question was really a mulatto, as Samuel Richards had described Caesar. Categorized as mulatto, mustee, "colored," or Negro by policy makers, census takers, and neighbors, Indian servants and slaves faced a kind of ethnic erasure that contributed to the historical amnesia about Indian slavery. Even the New England abolitionist movement, which had recognized Indian slaves and servants in its advocacy efforts during the eighteenth century, focused almost entirely on the issue of African American emancipation and civil rights by the nineteenth century.[38]

This erasure of Indians from the story is ironic, because Indians such as Caesar brought some of the earliest and most successful lawsuits against slavery. These suits not only challenged the legal basis for Indian slavery; they also laid bare the lack of statutory law and reasoning behind enslavement and involuntary servitude of all kinds in New England. These suits also pointed to another result of Indian slavery and servitude. New England Indians had helped create a hybrid society, one in which they had forged myriad bonds—economic, personal, familial—with English, African, and other Indian groups in the region. Some of these bonds hurt the Indians' claims for autonomy, equal treatment, and due process in New England jurisprudence. Other communities, connections, and knowledge, however, provided Indians with the cultural and social capital to challenge the ad hoc system of slavery. Caesar won a jury trial, which meant that at least some of his white neighbors supported him over Samuel Richards, confirming that Indians could leverage social capital in colonial towns. The willingness of attorneys to take such cases also showed a growing interest in antislavery and the rights of citizens and subjects on the part of lawyers, who would become the core of a nascent abolitionist movement in New England.

The ad hoc nature of Indian slavery and servitude in New England did not soften its effects for its victims. Just as it has made the institution more obscure to historians, legal vagueness sometimes made it more, not less difficult for Indians and, later, Africans to escape slavery. Despite their leadership in revolution, New England states proved slow to end slavery in the post-independence era. With the exception of Vermont, state governments failed to define freedom in clear legislative terms, just as they had failed to define slavery clearly. As in the case of enslaved Indians in the colonial era, these failures put the onus on the wrongfully enslaved to claim their freedom. Even when the Massachusetts Superior Court ruled in 1783 that the Declaration of Rights in the 1780 state constitution had inadvertently outlawed slavery, the legislature failed to act. Similarly, Connecticut did not formally abolish slavery until 1848. In postrevolutionary New England, individual slaves had to file costly individual freedom suits or try to liberate themselves by walking away from slavery; masters had to decide whether local communities would support their claim to slaves' labor. Indian slavery helps us understand how these complicated legacies of race, slavery, and civil rights came to be.

CHAPTER 1

"Davids warre"

The Pequot War and the Origins of Slavery in New England

Capture and enslavement of Indians marked the earliest contact between English adventurers and the native inhabitants. Even before the English planted colonies in New England, they forcibly removed Indians from coastal settlements to provide labor or for sale abroad. This sporadic practice moved into a new, much more intensive stage with the outbreak of the Pequot War, the first major conflict between English and indigenous peoples in the region. The war sparked new regional military and political arrangements among English and Native Americans that facilitated enslavement. After the conflict, the colonies established legal precedents that for decades defined Indian slavery and involuntary servitude.

Many scholars have explored the causes and consequences of the Pequot War. Some have viewed it as a crucial stage in the English conquest of the Northeast, opening the way to territorial and eventually demographic expansion of Euro-American settlement. Others have stressed the demonization of Indians that accompanied the battle, and the savagery with which English forces fought. Still others have viewed it from the perspective of alliances and relations among Native Americans in the region. A focus on Indian slavery points to another way of interpreting the war, however, and of explaining the actions of Massachusetts and Connecticut military forces beginning in the summer of 1637.

FIGURE 2. Flintlock musket, ca. 1667, belonging to the Roger Williams family of Providence. Courtesy of the Rhode Island Historical Society, RHi X17 1156.

Although the Pequot War began for a variety of strategic and economic reasons, for the English and their Native American allies it quickly became a conflict whose purpose was securing captives. In the context of the war English colonists saw both an opportunity to acquire captives and a legal pretext for the enslavement of Indians. At a time when Indian and European war practices offered several possible courses of action in dealing with prisoners, especially noncombatants, the English in New England made a conscious decision to enslave Pequots. Control of the surviving captives became such a priority for colonial authorities that it generated conflict with Indian allies who helped them win the war. The colonies' postwar policy toward the region's Indians also stressed the need to protect English property rights in their Pequot captives. This made the Pequot War a crucial event in initiating and shaping a labor system that would characterize New England society for over 150 years.

Early Captivities

English explorers, for several reasons, frequently kidnapped Indians in the 1500s and early 1600s. Martin Frobisher initiated the practice during his search for the Northwest Passage; he took Inuit captives on his first two expeditions and transported them to England, where their kayaks and marksmanship excited great interest. The artist and future resident of Roanoke, John White, painted several Inuits: a man named Kalicho, and a woman, Arak, and her child.[1] For expeditions such as Frobisher's, Indians served as proof of contact with unfamiliar regions. Other European voyagers sought Indians to train as interpreters and guides. Captain George Weymouth, who visited northeastern North America in 1605, took four Wabanakis to London at the behest of Sir Ferdinando Gorges, the backer of the English Sagadahoc post established in Maine in 1607. Gorges planned a colony called Norumbega that would encompass all of northern New England; he hoped that captive Indians would become fluent in a European language, provide useful intelligence about the indigenous population and their economy, and eventually accompany future expeditions back to America. He commissioned subsequent kidnappings, including the capture of a Martha's Vineyard sachem named Epenow. Parading Indians as symbols of England's power and maritime empire as well as exemplars of exoticism became a feature of court life for more than a century, and captives served as a form of entertainment in port cities. Before turning him over to Gorges, Epenow's kidnappers displayed him as a physical marvel in London taverns.[2]

While most of these kidnappings were putatively strategic, at least some mariners aimed at acquiring slaves for resale in emerging global slave markets. Thomas Hunt, a member of John Smith's 1614 expedition to New England, captured twenty-seven Pawtuxet and Nauset Indians on Cape Cod and "carried them with him to Maligo [Málaga] and there sold those silly Salvages for Rials of eight."[3] One of these Málaga captives was Tisquantum, or Squanto, who ended up in London in the household of merchant John Slaney, and eventually accompanied a Gorges-funded expedition to Norumbega in 1618. Squanto returned to England at least one more time before making his way to southern New England—just in time to provide essential diplomatic and economic assistance to the Pilgrims at Plymouth.

Some of these early captives died of disease or wounds incurred during capture, others were recaptured by English rivals during Atlantic crossings, and still others remained in slavery in Europe. One New England Indian may have fought as a mercenary among Christian armies in their battles against the Ottoman Empire in Central Europe.[4] Still others, including Epenow and Squanto, managed to return to New England as members of English-sponsored expeditions; Epenow escaped the English and rejoined his people. As historian Neal Salisbury points out, these kidnappings by the English drove some prospective Indian allies and trading partners into the arms of the French and generated suspicion and enmity among others.[5] Ad hoc kidnappings certainly outraged the Indians and wreaked havoc on individual lives and families, but they did not represent an English policy. Hunt's "trechery" prompted criticism from John Smith and others interested in deploying Indians in the service of empire rather than alienating them or treating them as a commodity.

From Partners to Enemies: The Origins of the Pequot War

Enslavement of Indians in New England entered a new phase during the 1637 Pequot War. Understanding the run-up to war—including the rationales that English civil leaders, soldiers, and inhabitants accepted and promoted—is important because colonial authorities used a certain interpretation of events to justify tactics and aims, including the taking of captives. The Pequots, whose territory stretched between the Niantic River in Connecticut and western Rhode Island, numbered between twenty-eight thousand and thirty-two thousand by the 1610s.[6] For decades, historians argued (following Puritan accounts) that the Pequot were relative newcomers who had moved into the region from the upper Hudson River valley beginning in the sixteenth century in response to Iroquois consolidation. Archaeological and linguistic evidence suggests, rather, that the Pequots had occupied the region much longer, and that culturally and linguistically they resembled other Algonquian groups in southern New England. Several other large Algonquian groups resided nearby. Massachusett Indians owned the areas where the English planted their settlements in Plymouth, Salem, and Boston. The Pokanoket or Wampanoag occupied much of the mainland between Cape Cod and Narragansett Bay, including present-day Plymouth, Bristol, and Scituate, as well as Martha's Vineyard and Block Island. The Narragansett Indians occupied lands west of Narragansett Bay, and their sometime coalition partners, the Niantic, held territory nearby in southeastern Connecticut. West of the Connecticut River toward the Hudson, the Quinnipiac, Hammonasset, and Wappingers claimed the coast. Nipmuc villages dotted the area east of the Connecticut River in what is now east-central Massachusetts. Across the sound, Montauk, Shinnecock, and other groups occupied central and eastern Long Island. Woronoco, Podunk, Pocumtuck, and other independent Indian towns clustered along the Connecticut River.

These "tribal" identities were somewhat fluid. Intermarriage, migration, and trade linked families, and many of the larger nations apparently were themselves confederacies or alliances of smaller kin-based subgroups led by minor sachems. Puritan observers noted that several groups were tributaries of others, paying annual gifts such as wampum, and the Puritans themselves entered into such connections with local Indians almost immediately.

The colonists interpreted the tributary relationship as one that conveyed sovereignty and subjection, but such arrangements among the Indians did not imply conquest or coercion.[7] Tributary groups like the Niantics shifted their allegiance frequently, and they expected a variety of benefits to come through their association with larger communities such as the Pequots and the Narragansetts.

The arrival of Europeans and the dynamics of new trade became yet another variable in these already complex relationships among indigenous peoples. At the time of European contact, the Indians of southern New England lived in villages with near kin under the leadership of semi-hereditary sachems, mostly male but occasionally female. There is some evidence that several sachems in the region were moving to consolidate their power in the early seventeenth century through marriage, gifts, and trade, creating a more hierarchical system that Europeans fostered, but this was still a process. The approximately twenty-six Pequot village sachems exercised no coercive power over their followers. Leadership required mobilizing kin support, showing oneself a wise decision maker, engaging in persuasive oratory, and providing generous gifts that placed others under an obligation to the giver.

Already by 1620, though, French and Dutch traders had begun to change local indigenous economies, drawing Indians into new Atlantic markets for furs and stimulating regional corn and wampum trades with epicenters in the St. Lawrence valley to the north and the Hudson River/Long Island Sound regions to the west and south. The chartering of the Dutch West India Company in 1621 stimulated settlement and expansion of New Netherland, including a satellite Dutch trading post on the Connecticut River.[8] The Pequots' location made them key players in these evolving networks. The Indians generally welcomed opportunities to trade with the Europeans, although native groups in New England violently repelled a few ventures in Maine and Cape Cod, perhaps in retaliation for earlier kidnappings. Even as they pursued trade ties with the new Dutch and French settlements, the Pequots constructed two forts between 1614 and 1630.

Throughout the 1620s the Pequots enjoyed decent relations with the Dutch and dominance of regional wampum and fur trade, which gave them access to goods and weapons that cemented their regional influence among other Indians and engendered a degree of independence from the English.[9] They defeated potential rivals among the many unaffiliated indigenous communities in the Connecticut River valley and Long Island, and made these groups into tributaries. Disease had decimated coastal tribes and competitors, such as the Massachusett, who suffered greatly in the epidemics of 1616–19. The Pequots, farther in the interior, seem to have avoided European disease, at least until the devastating smallpox pandemic of 1633. The new wave of English settlement and trading activity prompted some wariness, but also interest on the part of the Indians, who viewed the colonists as potential new trade partners. Early English settlements at Plymouth, Wessagusset, and Salem appeared weak and unthreatening.

Events of the early 1630s created new challenges. The expansion of Dutch settlements at New Amsterdam likely pressured the Pequots, since Dutch traders gave nearby tribes more options for exchange, and Dutch entry into wampum manufacturing competed with Pequot fur sources and devalued Pequot wampum supplies. With Pequot permission and upon payment of gifts and tribute in acknowledgment of Pequot hegemony, the Dutch established a post at the mouth of the Connecticut River, which they opened to other tribes and towns. The Pequots apparently expected to exercise more control over other tribes' access to the post than the Dutch wanted. Tensions with the Narragansetts and Niantics over control of the upper Connecticut River trade also increased. As was often the case, involvement with Europeans became a source of internal conflict among the Pequots themselves. The Dutch also facilitated Plymouth's trade with Indians at Kennebec (in present-day Maine) by making wampum available in ways that undercut Pequot and Narragansett monopolies of this increasingly important trade good.[10]

Meanwhile, the establishment of Massachusetts Bay in 1630 signaled the onset of a decade of rapid migration and physical expansion of English presence in New England. Over three thousand additional settlers arrived in 1630–33 alone, even as the Indians' numbers dropped precipitously because of the simultaneous smallpox epidemic. While the regional European population neared twenty thousand, the Pequot themselves likely lost nearly 80 percent of their population. Decimated groups such as the Massachusett and Wampanoag began to establish clientage/tributary relationships first with Plymouth and eventually Massachusetts Bay.

Expansion of English settlement into the Saybrook and Connecticut River regions began in earnest by 1634–36. English incursions threatened Pequot access to Long Island Sound in the south and to lucrative fur trade to the north of their territory, but some Pequots saw possible benefits; these divisions led to conflict between emerging pro-English and pro-Dutch factions within Pequot society. One pro-English advocate with ties to Pequot and Niantic communities, Uncas, made a failed challenge for the Pequot sachemship. Defeated in this quest, Uncas later proved crucial to the English military alliance against the Pequots.[11] A group of Pequots attacked the Connecticut Dutch trading post in 1634 and killed several visiting Indians, which prompted a retaliatory attack that killed a Pequot sachem named Tatobem.[12]

Still, these were long-term trends, easy to see in retrospect but perhaps less apparent to the main actors on both sides in the early 1630s, who likely negotiated among several possible positions and outcomes. In the short term, the Pequot actively sought alliances and trade ties with the English as part of normal diplomacy and as a strategy to reduce their dependence on the Dutch.

Religious, social, territorial, and economic tensions also divided the English. Plymouth—smaller, weaker, and less secure in its patent—continued to rely most heavily upon Indian trade as the key element of its economy more than a decade into settlement, and furs formed an important part of the Bay Colony's remittances to England as well. Both Massachusetts Bay and Plymouth leaders sought to pursue Indian trade to the north in Maine and south in the Connecticut River valley, and their competing traders' rivalry occasionally led to bloodshed. Plymouth claimed land at Saybrook, and William Bradford offered cooperative action with Massachusetts Bay to supplant the Dutch there and farther north. When Massachusetts demurred, Plymouth traders proceeded alone and established a post near present-day Windsor in 1632. Within a few years, however, settlers from Massachusetts Bay poured into Connecticut and cut into Plymouth's fur trade profits, eventually claiming the territory for a separate colony.

Rhode Island, founded by religious exiles from Massachusetts who were soon joined by other religious dissidents from England, hosted Indian trading posts in Narragansett country, most notably one managed by Roger Williams starting in 1638. Massachusetts Bay authorities had exiled Williams on pain of death for his rejection of the bedrock Congregationalist doctrine that churches could and should admit only "visible saints" as full members. From his base in Rhode Island he engaged in a lively theological print debate with the Bay Colony's defenders, and also published the best contemporary ethnography of the indigenous peoples of southern New England, *A Key into the Language of America*, in 1643. Yet despite these sympathies, Williams remained eager to aid Governor Winthrop and Massachusetts, and provided the other New England colonies with crucial intelligence and interpreter services. Williams and the Rhode Island trading posts also played a key role in persuading the Narragansett Indians to join forces with the English when conflict with the Pequots erupted.

Many scholars have recounted the war's causes and its consequences for the Pequots.[13] These characterizations range from charges that the English waged a genocidal conflict against the Pequots to accounts that more closely hew to the colonists' own portrayal of the war as a preemptive blow by English and Indian allies to prevent the Pequots from gaining the upper hand and therefore a just, defensive war. Others have focused on material bases of the conflict, as two expanding "empires" competed over territory, trade, and resources (including a food supply under stress from climate change). Still other historians have pointed to religious and cultural differences as precipitants for conflict. Yet overarching cultural, religious, and even economic explanations fail fully to explain why the English colonists attacked the Pequots even as they maintained peaceful relations with other regional Indian powers. In fact, the colonists sought alliances with other Indian "hegemons"—economically and politically strong confederacies such as the Narragansetts—in the run-up to war with the Pequots. The Narragansetts tried to control European trade and asserted sovereignty over smaller groups of Indians using strategies very similar to those of the Pequots; yet they did not become the object of English hostility until much later.[14]

In an account designed for a public audience, John Winthrop contended that Indians initiated the violence by murdering two Englishmen: John Oldham and John Stone. Stone and Oldham had both arrived in the region in the 1620s and were among the trader-adventurers who moved among English, Dutch, and Indian communities without allegiance to any one settlement. At various times, authorities in Massachusetts and Plymouth viewed them as troublesome renegades—Stone attempted to steal a Plymouth ship from New Amsterdam—although both also provided useful services carrying livestock from Virginia and corn from Indian producers to New England colonial consumers, along with crucial intelligence. Oldham was killed off the coast of Block Island in the autumn of 1636, most likely by Narragansett Indians or their tributaries. Stone died in 1634 at the hands of Pequot and Niantic Indians who were searching for Niantic Indians whom Stone had taken captive after a botched and violent trade encounter near the Dutch trading post.

The Pequots also apparently viewed the killing of Stone, whom they associated with New Amsterdam, as an act of retribution for Dutch involvement in the murders of Tatobem and another sachem. The Connecticut River valley had become the site of tense confrontations among English settlers from different colonies, between English and Dutch traders, between Europeans and Indians, and among Indian groups, all vying for leverage in trade. As Indians with multiple options demanded higher returns and better goods, Dutch and English traders used kidnapping and hostage taking to force Indians into trade in an increasingly competitive environment—a situation that likely played a role in both the Oldham and Stone incidents.

English reactions at the time of the killings were muted. Winthrop and John Endecott agreed that Oldham had gotten what he deserved, and Massachusetts Bay leaders deferred action on Stone by contacting his Virginia protectors and inviting them to assume responsibility for avenging this death. As late as July of 1636 John Winthrop seemed inclined to blame the Narragansetts more than the Pequots for Oldham's death. By August, however, the situation had changed; English negotiators in 1636–37 and eventually the articles of war against the Pequots highlighted the deaths of Oldham and Stone as part of the justification for war, despite the lack of Pequot involvement in Oldham's death. Winthrop literally went back and rewrote his journal account of Stone's death in order to emphasize Pequot complicity.[15]

Connecticut and Plymouth traders had clear economic and territorial interests at stake in displacing the Pequots. But commentary from leaders in Connecticut, Plymouth, and Rhode Island suggests that Massachusetts Bay leaders pushed strongly for the war even before Oldham's death, over objections from English settlements closer to the conflict—particularly Plymouth governor William Bradford and Lion Gardiner at the Saybrook fort.[16] The Bay authorities had decided to remove the Pequots, and their aggressive tactics placed the other colonies at risk and so forced their hands.

Reconstructing the Indians' motivations and expectations is a more complicated task. Most of what we know about Pequot intentions and actions comes through reports from their antagonists—English mercenaries Lion Gardiner, John Mason, and John Underhill; Governor John Winthrop of Massachusetts Bay and Roger Williams of Rhode Island—and as comments by Narragansett, Mohegan, and Shawomet allied with the English against the Pequots as recorded by Williams. No evidence indicates that the Pequots wanted a total war with the English. In fact, the Pequots' own changing circumstances made sustaining relations with the English important. Reeling from population loss, the fraying of the Dutch alliance, pressure from their own Niantic and Shawomet tributaries, and Narragansett incursions into their territory, the Pequots tried to cement alliance with the English in 1634–36.

By this time, Pequot weakness, not dominance, shaped English reactions. Winthrop, speaking for Massachusetts Bay, offered trade but not a military alliance, and attempted to reduce the Pequot to tributary status via an extremely heavy wampum penalty. The Pequot council apparently refused to accept the treaty. The new sachem, Sassacus, did not pay the tribute, and the Pequots tried to enlist the Narragansetts in alliance, but the episode revealed that the region lacked a true hegemon, either English or Indian. Massachusetts Bay sought to fill that void.

Despite these tensions and Pequot retaliations, contemporary observers noted that on the eve of the first English offensive in 1636 the Pequot did not seem to expect war; they had sent a new round of gifts to the Massachusetts

Bay leadership and viewed the diplomacy as ongoing—as did some of the other English colonies.[17] Lion Gardiner at Connecticut's Saybrook fort had sent Stephen Winthrop out with a trading ship to buy corn from the Pequots only days before the Massachusetts government authorized John Endecott to launch a punitive attack upon Block Island Indians in retaliation for John Oldham's death, and then to proceed against the Pequots. Not surprisingly, the Pequots cautiously welcomed Endecott's force when it first approached the Indians' villages. The Pequots assumed the Massachusetts Bay group had arrived to trade.[18]

The English Way of War

Taking captives formed an important part of English strategy in the turn to war. The August 1636 instructions to Endecott included an exhortation to kill men on Block Island but to take women and children and "bringe them awaye," presumably back to Boston.[19] The Massachusetts General Court determined in October that a Block Island Indian named Chausop impli-cated in the Oldham attack "bee kept as a slave for life to worke" at Castle Island, a military center.[20] Control of territory and trade certainly provided additional reasons why the English and their Indian allies waged war against the Pequots, but a desire for subjects—and captives—also motivated both groups. For the English, captives became an even more central goal once the conflict was under way. The war itself helped drive these shifts in purpose and meaning. During the Pequot War, English and Indians confronted each other's concepts of justifications for war, the proper conduct of war, the treat-ment of prisoners and civilian noncombatants—concepts that were in fact fluid even within their respective cultures. For the English, during the Pequot War these concepts began to solidify into distinct policy vis-à-vis the indig-enous population of New England, in which the colonists viewed Indians as outside the protections of an emergent law of war.

New England Indians went to war for reasons that Europeans sometimes found difficult to comprehend. Indian groups often sustained multiple dip-lomatic and military approaches simultaneously in ways that expressed inter-nal divisions over approach and reflected decentralized leadership structures. Although they understood—and increasingly conducted—wars to marginal-ize rivals and to defend territorial and trade monopolies, they also engaged in short, limited wars or raids to mourn and avenge the death of loved ones (at the instigation of leading women), to take captives, and to prove bravery and reaffirm masculinity. They sought to avoid casualties and generally spared women and children, although these policies were beginning to change in the seventeenth century. They took captives for ritual torture, for ransom or adoption, and they did not sexually abuse female captives.

All these practices and customs were subject to change and pressure, however, and historians sometimes draw too sharp a contrast between the violence of European warfare and its less deadly indigenous counterpart. The conflicts in New England occurred at the beginning of an era of intensifying violence, deadlier weaponry, and chronic warfare that accompanied European incursion and indigenous competition. A decade later, north and west of New England, the Iroquois initiated an extremely violent and terrifying set of attacks against the Iroquoian-speaking Huron and against the Algonquians that included the targeting and killing of children and women as well as mass assimilation and adoption of captives.[21]

Europeans also went to war for a variety of reasons.[22] The English had their own history of limited, dynastic wars, civil wars, and wars that involved a small proportion of the elite population. Indians and English understood and accepted each other's diplomacy, which signified common ground and acceptance of Indian sovereignty. John Underhill described the Pequot "Ambassadour" with whom he negotiated as "a grave Senior, a man of good understanding, portly, cariage grave, and majesticall in his expressions."[23] Gardiner, Underhill, and Winthrop all identified qualities such as gentility and bravery on the part of individual Pequots, and even empathized with their experiences in ways that validated the Indians' shared humanity.

In some ways the initial English/Indian military incursion resembled the Indian way of war—it began as a punitive, retaliatory expedition against Block Island, ostensibly to avenge Oldham's death. But the expedition quickly directed its violence against Indians unrelated to the incident—in this case, the Pequots—and became a war in which key English leaders stressed annihilation and capture of the enemy, to the dismay of some English participants and to the surprise of many Pequots, who in February 1637 again signaled their interest in patching up the conflict.[24] This intensification of the war began even before the Indians attacked Wethersfield, Connecticut, and took captives, raided several other settlements and farmsteads, and laid siege to Saybrook fort in 1637, events that prompted a second, larger expedition of English supplemented with Niantic, Narragansett, and Mohegan Indian troops. This combined force defeated the remaining Pequots, killing approximately seven hundred, or nearly one out of four. The victors also seized the "bootie" of war, including Pequot territory, corn, wampum, household goods—and captives.

English and Indian observers described the "furious" nature of the conflict, especially attacks on two Pequot fortified villages on the Thames River housing mostly women, children, and the elderly. Both battles ended with the firing of the forts and the mass killing and captivity of combatants and noncombatants alike. John Underhill offered a vivid account of the Mystic fort attack in April 1637. After meeting resistance in the fort, he and Captain John Mason set fires augmented with gunpowder in the south and west of the town, and stationed their men near the fort's spiral entranceways. Pequots trying to fight their way out of the fort literally caught fire, as did their bowstrings and weapons: "Many were burnt with the fort, both men, women, and children, and others forced out, and came in troops to the *Indians* [English allies], twentie, thirtie at a time, which our soldiers received and entertained by the point of the sword; down fell men, women, and children and those that scaped us, fell into the hands of the *Indians*."[25] Underhill hinted at dissent from the "young Souldiers" over the brutal tactics, and he finished his account of the battle with a rhetorical dialogue in which he anticipated criticism of English actions: "Why should you be so furious (as some have said) should not Christians have more mercy and compassion?"[26] Roger Williams also criticized the violence against noncombatants: "Innocent blood cries out against us at Quinnihticut [Connecticut]," he noted in a letter to Governor Winthrop. In another dispatch, he mentioned that "I must reioice that . . . some of the chiefe [English commanders] at Qunnihticut (Mr. Heynes and Mr. Ludlow) are almost averse from killing women and children"—a qualified statement, which implied that other English captains were not averse at all.[27]

English forces pursued fleeing Indians for months and sought to capture or kill literally all the survivors, even after the Pequots evacuated their territory in central Connecticut and moved into regions where the English had no immediate territorial ambitions. A remnant group under Sassacus fled west to the Hudson River region and sought to bolster an alliance with the Mahican Indians there, but the Mohawks and their Mahican allies killed Sassacus and sent his hands and head as a trophy to Massachusetts Bay—an early signal that the Mohawks would play a significant role in whatever new order emerged in New England. The colonists' tactics also shifted from killing to capturing the Indians.

To understand why colonial forces waged total war and targeted noncombatants, some historians have examined contemporary English understandings of warfare and the law of war. Several hypothesize that English soldiers did not feel bound by customs of war and treatment of prisoners and noncombatants that prevailed in England. Others point to the failure of English and Pequot diplomats to create a common understanding about the rules of engagement prior to battle, such as protection of prisoners and civilians, although the Pequot clearly tried to negotiate the conduct of war with the English prior to the conflict with regard to treatment of women and children.[28] Lion Gardiner recounted a "parlie" with the Pequots. The Indians asked, through the English interpreter Thomas Stanton, "if we did vse to kill women & children." Gardiner instructed Stanton to reply with a vague threat that "they should See yt heraftr." Apparently surprised that the English would not agree to protect noncombatants, the Pequots "weare silent a small space." Accepting that the negotiations to limit the war's scope had failed, the Indians then threatened retaliation for English violations: "they said we are pequits and haue killed Englishmen and can kill them as muske-toes, & we will goe to conectecott and kill men women & children and we will take away ye horses Cowes & hogs."[29] Soon afterward, Pequot raiders took two female captives during a deadly assault on Wethersfield, where they killed two women along with seven men. But, much to the astonishment of their English antagonists and the women themselves, they did not harm the captives. The Indians eventually turned the women over to the Dutch, who restored them to English authorities.

Why did the English reject the terms of combat the Pequots had proffered and instead pursue death or captivity for Pequot civilians? One explana-tion lay in the civil leaders' and military commanders' experience of warfare and rebellion in contemporary England and Europe. Beginning in the early 1600s, European policy makers began constructing a shared understanding and even international law concerning warfare, a view embodied in Hugo Grotius's *The Law of War and Peace* (1625, 1631). At the same time, English presses issued many critical accounts of the horrendous treatment of civilians in Germany during what would become known as the Thirty Years' War, illustrated with images of plunder and torture that graphically demonstrated the effects of total war on all parties.[30] At least some New Englanders, includ-ing Roger Williams, questioned the effectiveness of war against the Indians as a tool of policy, as well as the "justness" of any conflict that pitted colonists against a people who had proved "more friendly . . . than our native coun-trymen in our own land to us."[31] In practice, however, the extent to which the law of war restrained conflicts even among Europeans remained lim-ited. In the seventeenth century, just as today, commanders identified many exceptions when it was permissible to attack civilians and sequester captives, and the New England colonists referred to some of these exceptions in their treatment of Pequots during and after the war. The Christian tradition of the just, defensive war allowed the enslavement of non-Christian captives. But characterizing the Pequot War as a just war required the construction of Pequots as the aggressors, which in turn required rearranging the timeline of the conflict itself to a certain extent—emphasizing the murders of Stone and Oldham and the Pequot attacks on Saybrook and Wethersfield while down-playing the English attacks on Block Island and the Connecticut River that preceded the latter two events. These selective strategies characterized the narratives provided in John Winthrop's journal account and correspondence and in Captain John Mason's eyewitness account of the war's origins and progress. Even contemporaries viewed such justifications as ethically suspect; as Williams pointed out, all peoples tended to "ply to windward, and wisely [cunningly] labour to maintain their Wars to be defensive."[32]

Moreover, different rules of war applied to distinct types of conflict in the 1600s. Wars against other recognized sovereign nations tended to be more limited in scope and to involve armies rather than civilians. In contrast, internal civil or religious wars, or state efforts to halt rebellion (such as Spain's war against the breakaway Dutch Republics in the sixteenth century, or, the seventeenth-century English Civil War), often proved more violent and more apt to result in civilian casualties because opponents' status was less clear. Rebels and traitors did not receive the protection of soldiers, and they could be executed—or enslaved. Similarly, during sieges in which the inhabitants of a fort or town resisted surrender (a scenario that both Pequot "swamp" battles resembled, in the eyes of participants), victorious invaders felt they could act without restraint, since by resisting, civilians forfeited any right to protection. Several key military figures in early New England's Indian wars, including John Endecott, Miles Standish, Lion Gardiner, John Underhill, and Daniel Patrick, had lived in the Netherlands and worked as mercenaries for Dutch forces in their wars of independence against Spain, so they knew these violent European conflicts firsthand.

A related, complicating issue affecting the conduct of the Pequot War was the question of sovereignty.[33] Even after the war began, none of the New England governments claimed jurisdiction over the Pequots or their ter-ritory. Winthrop, Williams, Underhill, and others viewed the Pequots and Narragansetts as political entities with independent diplomatic apparatuses, representatives, territory, and leadership structures—not as English subjects. Yet New England authorities and military leaders frequently identified Pequots as "murderers of English" and did not grant them the protective status of soldiers of a sovereign nation. In other words, alongside the language of the just, defensive war, the English simultaneously used the language of rebellion and criminality in describing the Pequot people—a conflation of Pequot with rebellious subjects under attainder, or capital criminals, that set a legal precedent for condemning Indians in subsequent conflicts, including King Philip's War. Use of both these languages simultaneously—just war and rebellion—stripped Indians of the protections that might accrue to them both as foreign combatants and as noncombatants in armed conflict. English and Indian forces routinely executed captured Pequot men rather than holding them prisoner or exchanging them, and they continued to execute Pequots associated with war activities for several years after the peace.

The Narragansetts and Mohegans acceded to this practice because it fit their notions of the proper conduct of warfare—male warriors were fair game for execution—and formed part of their strategy for incorporating the survivors into their own social and political structures. As the Narragansett chief Miantonomo told Williams, the Indians believed "if they have the sachems heads they will make the rest Narragansetts."[34] But for the English—and the Pequots—the legal categorization of Pequots as murderers or rebels had powerful long-term consequences. New Haven magistrate Theophilus Eaton seized Nepaupuck, a Pequot Indian who appeared near the settlement to trade in 1639, because of an outstanding warrant for his involvement in the attack on Wethersfield, Connecticut, during the war. A court convicted him of murder and ordered his execution, and the town displayed his severed head in the public market.[35] Even after the peace, then, Indians associated with the Pequot war effort remained in danger of enslavement or execution.

Charges of criminality and rebellion also legally identified Pequots as suitable for enslavement. English precedents existed for condemning criminals, rebels, and prisoners of war to a set term of enforced service sometimes referred to as "slavery." Grotius noted that enslavement was a lesser punishment than death for capital crimes such as murder or treason. Against the backdrop of the English Civil War, the enslavement of "traitors" and the abuse of military prisoners and civilians intensified in ways that may have influenced New Englanders, although the practice did not peak not until the 1640s and 1650s, when Parliament dispatched Scottish prisoners of war to serve as indentured servants in New England, and sent some royalist sympathizers to the Caribbean as "slaves." During the Civil War period, local authorities in Barbados and Bermuda sentenced English settlers accused of treason to "slavery."[36]

For English persons, however, slavery in these circumstances was neither a permanent nor a inheritable status. It was more akin to indentured servitude: after serving their terms, the condemned could expect to resume the same rights and privileges of any English citizen. Moreover, almost all English "slaves" were men, while the majority of the Indians enslaved by the colonists during the Pequot War were noncombatant women and children, and these native captives faced a vastly different situation. Over the next century, what had begun as parallel processes for Indians and Europeans—being sentenced to slavery—progressively eliminated various European groups: first English were deemed non-enslavable; then Scots, Irish, and southern Europeans. These kinds of punishments eventually became limited to Indians and Africans.

Another reason that Pequot women and children did not receive the protections that sometimes accrued to ethnic Europeans in times of conflict might be that Indian work habits and sexual mores violated many European precepts regarding gender. Throughout the colonial period, commentators, officials, and legal documents expressed confusion about Indian female agency, responsibility, and femininity; they often assumed that since Indian women labored so obviously that they were part of the war effort. At other times, English field commanders and policy makers seemed not to have viewed Indian women and children as individuals or groups with distinct rights but rather as extensions or possessions of Indian men. In debating the justice of Indian enslavement with John Winthrop of Massachusetts, Roger Williams conceded that "the Enemie may lawfully be weakned and despoild of all Comfort of wife and Children, etc"—in other words, the enslavement of Indian women and children represented a "lawful" punishment for Indian men that "weakned" their martial efforts.[37] Enslavement also had an ad hoc quality that arose from the goals and actions of individual captains and ways in which New England colonial governments recruited and compensated their armies. As the first major armed conflict for the English in New England, the Pequot War set precedents that subsequent musters followed. Because of conflict with Charles I over Massachusetts Bay's right to establish an army under its charter, the armed forces were in some disarray. John Endecott marched on Block Island and Pequot country with an army of volunteers, and Massachusetts Bay hastily began to muster several regiments in the spring and summer of 1637 under an unusual organizing principle that created many captaincies, including some honorific commissions filled by non-fighting magistrates. John Winthrop proudly recorded that most officers accepted no public pay, but the many commissioned magistrates, captains, ensigns, and foot soldiers did expect compensation for their efforts. Connecticut required that each town send a specific number of recruits; they were paid a wage and also shared in the war's booty.

A Battle for Captives

Securing captives for personal use or sale preoccupied many English soldiers as the war escalated, and this desire shaped military tactics. New England governments used the promise of plunder as a means of recruiting and paying

troops, and plunder included captives. Lion Gardiner, whose Saybrook outpost was dangerously low on supplies, recommended acidly to the Endecott
expedition as it passed through en route to Pequot country in February 1637
that "if you doe not loade yor barkes with Pequits loade them with corne,"
implying that taking Pequot captives formed the mission's chief goal. The
first response of Massachusetts to the Wethersfield attack was to send veteran
mercenary captain Daniel Patrick with forty men to join the Narragansetts
in an assault on noncombatant Pequots on Block Island. Massachusetts Bay's
main expedition to Pequot country did not mobilize until June 1637, after
the first swamp battle. The Massachusetts and Plymouth recruits joined Connecticut, Narragansett, and Mohegan forces in pursuit of Sassacus and the
other surviving Pequots in their flight west and south. The Pequots sought to
shore up alliances and send women, children, and supplies to protected sites
in Long Island and western Connecticut, but these groups moved slowly, so
that English and Indian forces soon caught up with them. The English also
viewed former Pequot tributaries as fair game, and targeted Block Island,
Western Niantic, Nipmuc, and some of the smaller Connecticut groups, such
as the Wunnashowatuckoogs, taking captives as well as burning villages and
killing inhabitants. The Connecticut River area rather than the Pequots' old
territory became the main target of English settlement after the war.

From the Narragansetts' perspective (as recounted by Roger Williams),
the Massachusetts men focused their attention exclusively on taking Pequot
plunder and slaves rather than engaging Pequot warriors. Tensions over control of surrendering Pequots frayed the English-Indian alliance almost at once.
The Narragansetts captured a large contingent of over one hundred Pequots,
mostly women and children, in a cedar swamp not too distant from Mystic
that the group used as a refuge for noncombatants, called Ohomowauke, or
"the Owl's Nest." To the Narragansetts' chagrin, Daniel Patrick and Israel
Stoughton assumed charge of the captives, despite the fact that Patrick himself admitted the Narragansetts "were the chiefe Actors in the last Captiues,
and had taken all by a wile and slaine 2 before the English came." Stoughton
put all but two of the male captives—approximately twenty-two—to the
sword—and executed the remaining leaders after he no longer needed them
as guides. He divided the remaining survivors among his own troops, returning twenty to the Narragansetts and three to Massachusett Indian forces that
accompanied him. This left forty-eight captives to be remitted for sale and
distribution in Boston. The Narragansetts protested strongly to Roger Williams, charging that the English had not even participated in the battle.

Word of the first "dividence of women and children" in Boston excited
comment from several nearby English religious and political leaders in July,

including the Reverend Hugh Peter, John Endecott, and the governor of Bermuda.[38] All sought a share in the captives. While the English captains still killed Pequot men, by July and August they now seemed more open to parley and accepted Indian surrenderers, with the goal of taking captives for personal use and for sale. English troops confronted approximately two hundred Pequots who had taken shelter near present-day Fairfield, Connecticut, on July 16, in a scenario reminiscent of the Mystic swamp battle. This time, however, Thomas Stanton, Richard Davenport, John Mason, Roger Ludlow of Connecticut, Patrick, and William Trask followed more typical siege practices, offering surrender terms to the Pequots barricaded within after an initial barrage of conflict. After some negotiation, most of the men elected to stay within the swamp and fight, but nearly two hundred women, children, elderly, and a few men affiliated with Pequot tributaries whom the English were willing to indemnify all exited the swamp before battle resumed. After the English victory, these captives were also "divided, some to those of the river (Connecticut), and the rest to vs," raising the total number of Pequots captured and distributed among Europeans to over 260, along with others from area tribes.

Throughout July and August, English and Indian forces clashed over disposition of those Pequots who now streamed voluntarily into Mohegan and Narragansett camps "to bet their lives," preferring captivity among the Indians to what awaited them with the English.[39] Williams expressed concern that commanders such as Patrick were eyeing the Narragansetts themselves as possible targets in their indiscriminate thirst for captives. Several Narragansetts and other Indians from their tributary tribes kidnapped by English forces ended up in Boston among the Pequots for sale, and rumors of English designs on Narragansett civilians circulated through the region. Israel Stoughton reported that Block Island Indians confederated with the Narragansetts fled at the approach of colonial troops in August 1637 because they feared being kidnapped by their presumed allies.[40] By July, the English had indeed kidnapped five Indians on Block Island, four of whom turned out to be Niantics and one a Pequot raised among the Narragansetts who had fought alongside the English as allies on the expedition against Mystic.

In person and through intermediaries, Miantonomo and the Eastern Niantic sachem Ayanemo (later known as Ninigret) lodged numerous protests about kidnappings and the taking of ethnic Pequots who had been reared in their villages or were tied to their tribes through marriage and kinship. Despite Miantonomo's efforts, Massachusetts troops shipped at least one such young man to England.[41] Richard Davenport, one of the Bay Colony captains who took the disputed captives from the Narragansetts, confirmed that "Conetecut men have had their equall share in women and treys [Indian household goods and wampum]."[42] Patrick, Stoughton, and Davenport believed that the Narragansetts were sequestering captives and goods that rightfully belonged to them. They and other English commanders viewed Indian women and children along with other types of plunder as part of their due; "we hope to find a way to bring them in plentifully," Stoughton confidently assured Governor John Winthrop.

Soldiers claimed specific human spoils on the battlefield before remitting the majority of captives to Boston, Plymouth, Hartford, and other colonial centers for sale. Having dispatched "48 or 50 women and Children" to Winthrop in Boston for distribution, Stoughton informed the governor that "ther is one . . . that is the fairest and largest that I saw amongst them to whome I have given a coate to cloath her: It is my desire to have her for a servant. . . . There is a little Squa that Steward Calacot desireth . . . Liftenant Davenport allso desireth one, to witt a tall one that hath 3 stroakes upon her stummach thus −///+."[43] One can only speculate as to whether soldiers demanded these captives as sexual partners as well as household servants. At least one high-status female captive, Wincumbone, assumed her fate would include rape and that she would be separated from her children.[44] Overall there is little evidence that New Englanders engaged in the kind of trade in prospective wives and sexual partners that Indians and Europeans practiced in the Southwest.[45] Rather, the goal was to acquire women and children—and men and boys—to employ as household servants and to use as a commodity in regional and Atlantic trade networks.

A few colonial leaders privately questioned the killing of noncombatants and the enslavement of captives. The most persistent critic was cleric and Indian trader Roger Williams of Rhode Island, who had been exiled from Massachusetts in 1636–37 but who nonetheless served as a crucial go-between in maintaining the colonists' alliance with the Narragansett Indians. Williams was thus privy to Indian thinking on the subject of Pequot slavery and captivity; it is through his reporting that we get a sense of the Indians' perspective on what was happening to the Pequots.

In a series of letters to Massachusetts and Plymouth leaders between June 1637 and February 1638, Williams expressed ethical, legal, and strategic discomfort with Indian slavery and its consequences, although he carefully kept his criticisms private. Williams's interpretation of Mosaic law led him to conclude that identifiable Indian "murderers . . . deserved Death," but he condemned the massacre of women and children at the two swamp battles.[46] According to Williams, the Old Testament provided equivocal guidance on what to do with the survivors. "Sir concerning Captiues (pardon my wonted boldnes)," he wrote to Winthrop in July 1637, "the Scripture is full of myste-rie, and the old Testament of Types."[47] Puritan religious and civil leaders such as Williams relied on typology—the notion that the New Testament mir-rored and ultimately fulfilled certain biblical experiences of the Jews and that these "types" or analogs provided guidance for seventeenth-century Chris-tian communities—in their decision making, law writing, and other activi-ties in church and state. For some Puritans, who identified with the ancient Israelites as the chosen people of God, types were allegories or analogies; others took them more literally as historical precedents.[48] Williams conceded that Yahweh had certainly ordered the Israelites to make a "perpetuall warr" and exterminate the Amalekites, but Williams saw this as an "extraordinary" event. He urged Winthrop to follow more "ordinary" and merciful scriptural guidelines. The killing and enslavement of women and children in particular seemed to violate the teachings of 2 Kings 14:5–6 by visiting the sins of the fathers upon innocent relatives.

John Underhill, also disenfranchised and banished for his religious views during the Antinomian crisis soon after returning to Boston from the Pequot War, invoked the biblical precedent of King "Davids warre, when a people is growne to such a height of bloud, and sinne against God and man, and all confederates in the action, there hee hath no respect to persons, but harrowes them, and sawes them, and puts them to the sword, and the most terriblest death that may bee." By turning to scriptural authority rather than contem-porary understandings of the law of war for precedent, Underhill, Williams, and their contemporaries placed the Pequot War in a distinct legal context that permitted mistreatment of Indian prisoners. Yet Underhill, like Wil-liams, acknowledged how contingent and equivocal these biblical precedents were: "sometimes the Scripture declareth women and children must perish with their parents; sometime the case alters."[49] For Underhill, consultation with clergy and a shared sense of English colonists' special religious mission in New England resolved the moral ambiguities of the Pequot War in the colonists' favor.

Although Roger Williams convinced himself in the end that the English had the legal authority to enslave Indians, he thought it questionable policy from a strategic and ultimately an ethical standpoint. Having observed the effects of enslavement and competition for captives on the English–Indian alliance over the summer of 1637, Williams knew that pressure for slaves was fast eroding Narragansett trust. Enslaved Pequots would be a chronic internal security concern, and the policy would antagonize Indian allies. In his capac-ity as go-between with the Narragansetts and Eastern Niantics, Williams also became a slave catcher and slave trader of sorts. He fielded constant requests from English correspondents to monitor Pequot slaves sent as messengers, to recover particular Indians claimed by soldiers, and to track down runaways. Williams knew that pressuring the Narragansetts, Mohegans, and Niantics to return contested captives further damaged the alliance. His interviews with runaway slaves, who often reported abuse, shaped his concerns about English participation in slavery as well. Several times over the course of the summer and fall he urged Winthrop to qualify the policy of enslavement, and to substitute a middle ground—a tributary system or a finite period of servitude followed by freedom "after a due time of trayning up to labour, and restraint."[50] "Since the Most High delights in mercy, and great revenge hath been already taken," he ultimately recommended instead that the "rest be divided and dispersed . . . to become subjects to yourselves in the Bay and at Connecticut," with a limited requirement for tribute. This way the colonies would achieve sovereign jurisdiction over the Pequots and their territory and keep them from re-concentrating as a viable military force, all without upsetting other Indian groups.[51]

Still, Williams was far from an abolitionist. Indeed, he himself claimed a particular Pequot boy: "I haue fixed mine eye on this little one with the red about his neck, but I will not be peremtory in my choice but will rest in your living pleasure for him or any etc.," he informed Winthop.[52] Despite his reservations he aided English colonists in the distribution and sale of Pequot Indian captives, negotiated the return of runaways from the Indian protectors to whom they had fled, and generally facilitated the enslavement policy. He continued to serve as a conduit for recovering runaways in subsequent decades, and knowingly returned captives to abusive households, content to offer general admonishments to good care.

Only one group of New Englanders consistently created a debate over the law of war and Indian slavery—the Indians themselves. They contested with the English not only over possession of Indian captives, but also the rights of civilians, the postwar status of Pequots, and the subsequent treatment of captives among the English.

Indian groups who aided the English against the Pequots thought they had reached an understanding with their allies on the treatment of noncombatants, surrendering Indians, and captives prior to the onset of the conflict. They continued to press the English on this issue during and after the war, referring to "articles in the league" between the two groups, a formal agreement with defined parameters. Roger Williams met with Canonicus and Miantonomo, two Narragansett sachems, in May 1637 to discuss tactics and agree on a general strategy. Miantonomo recommended a night assault that would take the Indians by surprise and permit English and Indian forces to enter Pequot villages, with separate ambushes to block retreating warriors or refugees. Once the Pequots identified an English force offshore, he informed Williams, they would likely send the women, children, and elderly to the fortified village Ohomowauke (the site of the "swamp battle"). Miantonomo demanded that the English forbear killing these noncombatants and focus their energy on killing and capturing Pequot sachems. English and Indians were in agreement on killing Pequot leaders, and, indeed, twenty-four of the twenty-six most significant Pequot sachems died in battle or via execution. His position on noncombatants, however, separated Miantonomo from the English. In a report on the meeting, Williams informed John Winthrop "that it would be pleasing to all natives, that women and children be spared, &c."[53] Indians present at the Mystic battle expressed immediate disapproval about the English killing of women and children, and the disputes continued.

Disposition and treatment of captives formed another controversial issue. As allies of the English colonists, the Narragansetts, Eastern Niantics, and Mohegans shared in the division of the war's human spoils. Along with dividing survivors among the English and allied Indians, the 1638 treaty that ended the war—the "Articles of Agreement between the English in Connecticutt and the Indian Sachems," also known as the Hartford Treaty, or Tripartite Treaty—literally tried to extinguish the Pequot name, forbidding its use. Those Pequots who avoided slavery were to be permanent tributaries of the English, while the "territory formerly theirs" became an exclusive English jurisdiction "by conquest."[54] Again, Williams served as a negotiator as the colonists and Indians discussed the "dividence" of surviving Pequots.[55]

Initially, Williams reported to John Winthrop that Miantonomo "liked well" the United Colonies' plan for the Pequot captives—"that they should live with the English and themselves as Slaves." The victorious Indians even acceded to the transport of some captives to England and to the execution of male leaders. Several English commanders complained bitterly that that Narragansetts urged the English to execute the Pequot leadership and then reaped the benefits while decrying English brutality. Yet negotiations foundered over the meaning of slavery for the surviving captives, especially those who had surrendered peacefully.[56] The Narragansetts proposed that captives "be not enslaved, like those which are taken in warr: but (as they say is their generall Custome) be vsed kindly, haue howses and goods and fields given them."[57] In other words, the Narragansetts, Niantics, and Mohegans defined captivity and slavery differently from the English. The Indians balked at the notion of condemning captives to chattel slavery and potential export to the Atlantic or Caribbean. Ayanemo, the Niantic sachem, also wrangled with Bay authorities over the fate of Pequot refugees and forestalled attempts to round them up. These positions coincided with the Indians' interests, to be sure: the Narragansetts expected that many of the Pequots would settle in their country, augmenting Narragansett numbers and status. Similarly, as leaders of small, aspiring groups, Uncas and Ayanemo viewed Pequot refugees as essential human capital in their quests for power vis-à-vis the Narragansetts and other regional hegemons.[58]

The complex kinship and sociopolitical structures that organized the lives of New England Indians remain difficult to recover. We have to rely upon flawed European accounts that viewed all Indian social arrangements and political structures through the selective lens of their own experiences and preferences, and observers who remained ignorant of many details of great importance to Indian lives. Evidence suggests that chattel slavery was a relatively new concept for Indians as well as Europeans. Still, although their culture stressed reciprocity and communalism, the Algonquians of coastal southern New England understood hierarchy. New England Indians lived in societies characterized by social inequality, and status differences were becoming more pronounced in the decades immediately before and after English colonization.[59] Writing in 1645, Roger Williams noted the presence among the Narragansetts of "obscure and meane persons . . . [that] have no name"—most likely captives who lacked the relatives or clan affiliations that brought protection, status, and identity.[60] But there is little evidence that the Indians of southern New England regularly sought captives for labor, torture, or adoption in the ways that other groups such as the Iroquois or the Mississippians did. Even Uncas, the Mohegan leader whose regional power depended on his close ties with Connecticut and who coveted his share of Pequot captives, sought to place himself at the top of a network of tributary relationships with Pequot survivors, not to control completely their labor and persons. Eventually, English usages and economic goals began to reshape indigenous practices of captivity and encourage the commodification of captives, but this was a slow process whose effects remained muted until later in the century.

Like the English, the Narragansetts, Mohegans, and Niantics valued Pequot women for their potential economic contributions, but Indians also valued them for different reasons. Women headed lineage groups and kin networks, so securing women meant preserving networks that would help stabilize the integration of Pequots into neighboring Indian groups. Women could claim land rights, and although both indigenous trends and English influence were altering this understanding in favor of male lineages and landownership, it still made marriage to high-status women even more attractive to aspiring male leaders. Marriage to elite females conferred political legitimacy in regional indigenous societies. All the individual leaders who had allied with the English against the Pequots had to prove the sagacity of these choices to their followers and to possible rivals for leadership. They had to incorporate angry refugees whom they had recently fought against. The Niantics and Mohegans challenged the Narragansetts for control of former tributaries to the Pequots and also sought to fill the power vacuum created by the Pequot dispersal. Uncas, Ayanemo, Miantonomo and his uncle Canonicus, the Pequot turned English ally Wequashcook, and other aspirants to regional leadership all desired female Pequot captives and refugees—especially the children, widows, and mothers of sachems—as wives and subjects in order to help manage these transitions.[61] Uncas, Ayanemo, and Wequashcook each married relatives of Sassacus, the Pequot sachem, and Uncas eventually took additional high-status Pequots as wives.

Uncas and Miantonomo occasionally pressed the English to release, sell, or exchange particular Indian women whom they valued for kinship ties. Miantonomo tried to redeem several captives who he claimed were wives or children of sachems with ties to the Narragansetts. The teenage Pawtucket Indian John Sassamon, who was a servant in the household of Richard Callicott of Dorchester, accompanied his master in the expedition against Pequot country and served as an interpreter. Like Callicott, Sassamon claimed the right to take a Pequot captive, but his goals differed from those of his English master: he chose a daughter of Sassacus, and planned to marry her, signaling his desire for leadership among Indians rather than assimilation to English norms.

Because of the support of Connecticut leaders, who viewed him as an extremely useful ally, Uncas had great success in his negotiations with the English over particular captives. Still, English owners often resisted these offers, and insisted on keeping particular female captives even when offered other captives in exchange or compensation. It is difficult to know exactly why. Was it a level of comfort with elite status that elided ethnic difference? Sexual attraction? Or a sense of the captives' high value that attempts by Indians to regain them only confirmed? Although the English also sought control of the Pequots' former tributaries, they chose means other than the creation of kinship bonds to accomplish their ends.

There is some evidence that the English also singled out a few high-status captives for preferential treatment, if not for marriage. The colonists refused Miantonomo's offer to buy several high-status women because an even more powerful person claimed them: Governor John Winthrop of Boston. Winthrop also sought out the wife of Pequot sachem Mononnotto, who arrived in Boston "amonge the prisoners" from the Fairfield swamp battle with her

FIGURE 3. Governor John Winthrop as he appeared the year of Massachusetts Bay's founding. Miniature watercolor on vellum, in round ivory case, ca. 1630, by unidentified artist of the English school after Anthony Van Dyke. Courtesy of the Massachusetts Historical Society.

children. Mononnotto was sachem of Mystic and a close ally of Sassacus who apparently escaped death or capture after the battle there despite intense English pursuit, although he reportedly died later at the hands of the Mohawk-allied Mahicans. Wincumbone, his wife, excited different feelings among the English. Winthrop praised her "modest countenance and behavior" and credited her with having helped preserve the lives of the young English-women captured in Wethersfield, an account that John Mason confirmed.[62] Lion Gardiner identified Wincumbone as the woman who warned Stephen Winthrop and Thomas Hurlbut that the Pequots were about to ambush them during a trading session, and thus facilitated their escape.[63]

Because of both stories, Winthrop apparently treated her with some kindness, although he seems also to have asserted ownership of her and her children (Roger Williams called her Winthrop's "captive"). Winthrop occasionally used his captives as messengers and interpreters—an opportunity that several used to run away—and it is possible that Wincumbone filled that role because she surfaced in the record again two years later in Pequot/Nameaug country, "presuming upon" Winthrop's "Experimented Kindnes toward [her]."[64] Other captives would be less fortunate.

The Pequots emerged from the war a devastated but resilient people. Within a decade many survivors had regrouped and created new lives in enclaves under the jurisdiction of powerful nations and patrons, both Indian and English—led, in at least one important case, by a former captive. Indians who survived the war as captives and servants entered a wide range of positions and places in the English Atlantic. Almost all of them, a few such as Wincumbone excepted, could expect to labor at tasks their masters and mistresses set them to. The Pequot War became a war of captivity because the English—in New England, the Atlantic, and the Caribbean—wanted workers at a time when several empires were engaged in a frenzy of competitive colonial establishment and expansion that pushed labor demands beyond what the supply of European servants could satisfy.

CHAPTER 2

"I doe not see how wee can thrive untill wee gett into a stock of slaves"

Slavery in the Puritan Atlantic World

If Pequot enslavement sparked little moral, legal, or political debate among the English colonists, contemporaries were perfectly clear about its utility. Colonial governments and interested individuals offered a number of material, strategic, and social justifications for enslaving Indians over the course of the seventeenth century. Foremost among these rationales was the need for labor both in New England and in the Atlantic and Caribbean plantations where Puritans established trade and personal ties. One has only to skim contemporary correspondence to uncover scores of complaints regarding the lack of servants and the difficulty of keeping bondsmen and women. In a New World environment characterized by abundant land and few workers, many colonists recognized "that our servants will still desire freedome to plant for themselves, and not stay but for verie great wages."[1] The employment of Indians as servants or wage laborers was already so prevalent that the Massachusetts Court of Assistants stepped in to regulate the practice in 1631, calling on households with Indians to either "discharge" them or get the court's permission to retain them. Plymouth and Massachusetts Bay both prohibited cash payments to Indians in 1636.[2]

Pequot Indian captives represented a crucial source of workers at a time when colonists desperately needed them. Ultimately, neither moral nor legal considerations checked the move to Indian slavery. Even ministers closely concerned with evangelization of Native Americans seldom went on the

record against Indian slavery in the seventeenth century. Indeed, many clergymen themselves wanted Indian slaves. Writing to John Winthrop in 1637,
the Reverend Hugh Peter noted that "Mr. Endecot and my selfe . . . have
heard of a dividence of women and children in the bay and would bee glad
of a share viz. a yong woman or girle and a boy." Peter proceeded to outline
a plan for shipping additional "boyes" to Bermuda, a plan that Winthrop
later tried to carry out.[3] Reducing Indians to servitude offered a solution
to labor shortages and a means of punishing, controlling, or acculturating
local native populations. It reinforced a trend toward increased discipline for
all workers, English and Indian. The Pequot War coincided with a period
of particularly acute labor shortage in New England when political leaders
and entrepreneurs sought to tighten their grip on existing sources of labor
and find new ones. European colonists in other parts of the Atlantic world
faced similar challenges, and through personal and commercial contact with
Barbados, Bermuda, and Providence Island (a Puritan colony off the coast of
Venezuela), New Englanders knew about the labor regimes emerging there.
In the Atlantic, coercive labor practices affected workers of all ethnicities,
but Africans and Indians in particular experienced conditions and length of
service that distinguished them from European servants. Captives from the
Pequot War helped New England elites build ties with the Atlantic economy
and its emerging slave labor systems.

Servitude in Early New England

In 1637–38 no statutory law clarified the status of Indians taken during the
Pequot War or prescribed their treatment among the English. Laws regarding
slavery would not appear until Massachusetts passed the first statue in 1641.
For the first year or two of the Indians' integration into English households,
colonists typically referred to them as "captives," a word conveying a type
of legal status, or as "servant." But law and precedent already regulated the
nature of servitude for English people in New England in the 1630s. English servants typically entered into contracts. Plymouth, for example, specified a maximum term of seven years for servants, and those finishing their
term received freedom dues—land and corn if men, clothing if women,
although these could vary.[4] Any term longer than seven years automatically
made one an apprentice, a status associated with younger children, who could
also expect their freedom at age eighteen or twenty-one and who received
contractually agreed-upon training and maintenance. Any sale of a servant's
contract or assignment of his or her remaining "time" required the servant's
formal consent, or that of a parent or guardian (although magistrates also

intervened to prevent masters from freeing their servants early). These agreements specified the masters' obligations with regard to clothing, diet, maintenance and training, and usually required education for younger servants.

In contrast, New England courts did not regulate the relationships
between Pequot captives and their masters in this early period. Thus the use
of the term "servant" in this case did not necessarily carry the same sense of
mutual obligation, award, or finite framework covered in the common law.
English employers appear not to have entered into recorded legal contracts
with Indians until later in the seventeenth century, and did not always include
Indian servants and slaves in estate inventories. Existing law affected some
elements of Indian servitude—particularly when it came to punishment and
masters' rights—but the English colonists deviated from their customs when
it came to length of term, masters' obligations, and other aspects of Indian
captives' status.

The rapid entry of Indians into the labor market in other English colonies
in the late 1620s and the 1630s exposed this gap. The anomalous status of
Indians as a laboring group that occupied a legal gray area between servants
of European origins and African slaves attracted attention (and legislation
a year before the Pequot conflict) in Barbados and Providence Island, two
colonies with close ties to New England. Pequot and Manissean captives
exported out of New England in the 1630s entered an Atlantic world where
Indians already composed a significant proportion of the agricultural and
public works and infrastructure labor force. They joined Caribs and Arawaks
from the Caribbean Islands, Guyana, and Venezuela; Miskitos and members
of smaller groups raided by the Miskitos from Central America; and Indians
from northern Mexico and South America traded through Gracias De Dios,
a port on the coast between present-day Nicaragua and Honduras. Indian
captives from this western rim region also moved to and through Jamaica,
which served as a hub of the region's labor market. By the 1640s, the Dutch
in New York and the English in Virginia exported Indian captives to Curaçao,
Bermuda, and Barbados.[5]

From Servitude to Slavery in the Seventeenth-Century Atlantic

The status of Indians in many Atlantic societies changed between 1630 and
1650 from contract workers to servants, and eventually to "perpetual slaves."
Sometime around 1629–30, during a contest for control between battling
groups of Barbados proprietors, Henry Hawley, a representative of the Earl of
Carlisle, reduced to forced servitude a group of Arawaks who had voluntarily

accompanied the first English there with "divers sorts of Seeds & Roots, and agreed with them to instruct the English in Planting Cotton, Tobacco, Indigo, Etc." The Arawaks helped construct the initial settlement.[6] In 1636, now Governor Hawley and his council made efforts to distinguish between Indians and European servants by declaring that Indian and African servants and their children would henceforth be considered slaves for life unless they had formal contracts for service that specified a lesser term.[7]

In Bermuda, Indians were among the first laborers purchased by the Somers Island Company from Jamaica and the Leeward Islands, but the few surviving records suggest that most served limited terms, and that masters had an obligation to Christianize their Indian servants.[8] This notion of "Christian servitude" for indigenous peoples as an alternative to conquest, slavery, or brutal exploitation informed the views of at least some English traders and officials involved in various colonizing projects in Virginia and the islands, particularly but not exclusively Puritans. George Thorpe, an early resident of Virginia, lobbied for the creation of an Indian college there in the 1610s, raised money to send Indian children to be educated and Christianized in England, and urged acculturation through household service.[9] Thorpe's death during the Powhatan attack of 1622 derailed the Virginia Indian college project, but other individuals promoted the same ideas—though, interestingly, no one from New England. The Virginia Company sent one of Pocahontas's female attendants to Bermuda, where she married, and the company planned to send the couple back to Virginia as evangelists before the loss of its charter ended the company's involvement. Virginia authorities continued to advocate a regulated, contractual, "voluntary" servitude for Indian children in treaties with local groups such as the Necotowance in the 1630s and 1640s, although at the same time the government exported, without clear contractual limits, captives taken in the Anglo-Powhatan War. An illicit but growing trade in Indian slaves for employment within Virginia further undermined these stated goals.[10]

Even within the "wild west" atmosphere of the Caribbean in the 1630s and 1640s, as contending English, Dutch, French, and Spanish private and public forces raided one another's shipping, labor supplies, and settlements while battling local Indians and slave revolts, a few individual captains and traders made efforts to preserve from lifetime service the Indians and Africans they raided and resold. The legal status of Spanish Indians remained hazy in the wake of the "New Laws," which in 1542 had officially outlawed enslavement of Indians. Although this legislation hardly halted the flow of Indians from New Spain into the Atlantic, individual Indians used it to gain their freedom, and some Europeans viewed Spanish Indians as unenslavable.[11] When the Spanish captured a Bermudian-owned ship in 1664, they removed two Indian men, Christopher and Andreas, whom the owner Anthony Peniston had purchased in Jamaica. The Spanish captain claimed that the Indians were "the King of Spain's subjects" and therefore not liable to be sold as slaves.[12]

Some English agreed with this position and even extended the protections of subjecthood and immunity from enslavement to Africans. William Jackson, a Puritan captain who helped take the port of Bristol for Parliamentary forces, sold "divers Indians and Negroes" to "divers persons" in Bermuda in January 1645—but as servants with seven-year terms, not slaves. Jackson wrote elaborate contracts when he sold four of the "Nigroes"—including a couple and a four-year-old boy who was likely their child—to Governor Sayle of Bermuda. The man and woman were to serve for seven years, and the child until the age of thirty. Jackson specifically indemnified them all against future claims on their labor after they fulfilled these terms, with the caveat that the child would receive his freedom at thirty only if he could "make a reasonable profession of the Christian faith."[13] People of color and parents of biracial children sought baptism for their children as a means of qualifying them as Christians eligible for contracts rather than perpetual slavery. Still, the plantation owner who purchased Jackson's Indians and Africans, Governor William Sayle, also purchased laborers from the Puritan Hugh Wentworth, an agent for Robert Rich who later managed Rich's plantations on Providence Island. Wentworth dealt in all kinds of labor in the Caribbean and Atlantic, buying and selling European servants, Africans, and Indians. In the 1630s he sold African and Indian laborers to Sayle for terms of "fourscore and nineteen" years—more than a life sentence and a synonym for perpetual slavery.[14]

In Barbados and Bermuda, Indians as well as Africans also lost control of the ownership of their children to masters beginning in the 1640s unless they could purchase a replacement. Since inheritability was slavery's defining characteristic, the element that distinguished it from other forms of servitude, this shift was crucial. A 1651 marriage contract involving two Indian servants, James and Frances, belonging to two different owners, Thomas Lea and William Williams, specified that Lea and Williams would control alternate offspring. Lea sold the couple's second child in 1657 to a third party as a slave for life.[15] When Anne, an Indian woman "servant" of Simon Harding, married a free Indian, Frank Fernandes, in Bermuda in 1644, Fernandes had to promise not to "draw her away from her masters service," and signed a contract to divide their future children with Harding: "when it shall please God [to give] them children, that then [the children] are to be equally divided betwe[en] them, the first child [to be for] Symon Hardinge and the next to be [for] franck, and so to go on."[16] These arrangements borrowed legal usages common in livestock breeding, where owners of male and female animals split the progeny.

In addition, a decreasing number of sales included the kinds of limits that William Jackson put on the length of service. Virginia Bernhard calculates that between 1636 and 1650 in Bermuda, of the twenty-eight individual Indians appearing in bills of sale or indentures, only three had contracts that specified a term of service. Even when bills of sale specified length of service for Indians, these terms differed from those assigned Europeans and instead matched those given to African slaves. Governor Willem Kieft of New Amsterdam "presented" an Indian man from New York to Governor Sayle of Bermuda in 1644 for a term of ninety-nine years. By the 1640s, owners and parish officials were blocking access to baptism for African children or those of mixed-race parents.[17] Meanwhile, European servants avoided these changes in their status; company officials intervened to protect Scots prisoners of war sent to Bermuda as "slaves" and whose masters had kept them beyond their stated terms, ordering owners to indemnify the men for service that exceeded seven years.[18]

There is evidence that Indian victims and some Somers Island Company officials challenged this informal trend toward Indian slavery. Captain Bartholomew Preston of the ship *Charles* brought "30 or 40 Indians" to sell in Bermuda in January and February of 1646. Ten years later company officials asked the Governor's Council to respond to a petition from councilor and captain of the castle Richard Jennings, as well as individual complaints. Some commentators have assumed that these were Spanish Indians, but given the Anglicized names of most of them (and the Algonquian name Tomakin of one), it is plausible that they were in fact from North America—possibly New England, Virginia, or a mixture. Jennings argued that the Indians were "freeborne persons," not slaves, and therefore should they be freed or signed to contract servitude terms because "their enslavement was to the great dishonour of God and pulling down of His judgement against us." "Although we have not intention to take from any man his lawful servant," noted the company officials in their letter, "we feel obliged to relieve the oppressed and to execute justice and are ready to do what has been proposed to us." Ultimately, however, company officials in England left such matters in the hands of local leaders like Sayle and Hawley, who had already shown public and personal support for racialized terms of lifelong, heritable service for Africans and Indians. Hawley himself owned two hundred laborers of all races by 1640.[19] The matter came up again in Bermuda's assembly in 1661. The assembly agreed that the matter should be looked into and the Indians "enfranchised" and catechized but took no specific action.[20] At least some of the individuals whom Preston sold remained enslaved at the time of their death years later.

On the Puritan colony of Providence Island (organized by many of the same figures who backed the Massachusetts Bay Company), despite early efforts to limit African slavery—and to prohibit Indian slavery—the slave population exploded after 1634, and slaves outnumbered English colonists by the end of the decade. Providence Island Company officials and investors differed somewhat on the length and heritability of slave status. One eminent councilor named Samuel Rishworth, who supported the rights of English servants against company and planter exploitation, also attacked slavery vehemently as incompatible with godly aims and encouraged slaves to rebel. But in practice, by 1634 most planters expected slaves to work for life and claimed ownership of the children of non-European workers—again, a crucial distinction between slavery and servitude. Such was the demand for labor that despite two major slave revolts and the presence of a restive maroon community, the government refused to let inhabitants who left the island for any reason take enslaved workers with them because they were needed for construction of public defense projects as well as agricultural work.[21] A Captain Bell did receive permission to sell his plantation and leave with "his Indian Woman," wife, and Negroes in 1638.[22]

Possibly Bell's Indian was a New England captive. In one of the only surviving documents that mentions the Pequots, in May 1638 the company's officials warned the governor of Providence Island that "we would have the Cannibal Negroes from New England inquired after, whose they are and special care taken of them."[23] But given slave unrest, these worries seem excited by security concerns rather than humanitarian ones; company and island officials were worried about the captives fomenting rebellion or forging relationships with existing Indian and maroon communities. This is the first mention of what would become a stereotype in the English Atlantic/Caribbean correspondence and legislation in the seventeenth century: that New England Indians were particularly troublesome and prone to rebellion. No direct evidence that the Pequots (or later the Wampanoag or Narragansett) were involved in slave revolt or rebellion has appeared in colonial records, yet these official concerns resurfaced in the 1640s and the 1670s in times of slave revolt and insecurity.

The New England–Caribbean Connection

Given the number of New England colonists with direct ties to Virginia and the islands, New Englanders were likely well informed of these changes. John

Winthrop had apprenticed his son Henry to work as an overseer and agent in Barbados in 1627–28. Henry stayed there until 1629—he may have witnessed the enslavement of the Arawaks—and subsequently joined the family migration to New England. Henry described Barbados to his family, noting the presence of "forty slaves of negroes and Indians" as well as "Christian" English workers. He quickly grasped the connection between wealth and control of labor there, and saw how English landowners were perfecting their systems of labor exploitation. He demanded that his father procure "10 men" to aid in his own efforts at tobacco cultivation. Winthrop senior replied, "I sent you also 2:boyes (for men I could get none)," and his letter captured some of the confusion shared by contemporaries who only dimly understood what servitude had become in places like Barbados. The long terms that Henry desired presented a challenge for his father: "I knewe not what to doe for their binding, and they beinge but youths," the elder Winthrop reported. The limits of England's hired labor market chafed somewhat.[24]

Other Winthrop children beside Henry had personal experience with the African slave trade: John Winthrop Jr. spent time in the Levant and Deane Winthrop in Spain, both slave market centers. After a stint as a merchant in the Caribbean and Azorean networks, Winthrop's younger son Samuel became a sugar planter in the Leeward Islands. His estate, named Groton Hall after the elder Winthrop's beloved manor house in England, employed twenty-five slaves. Connections with Atlantic slavery shaped the New England colonists' willingness to turn to Indian labor, and vice versa: many of the individuals who eagerly sought Indian captives also bought African slaves as soon as they became available. In fact, early adapters of Indian captives as household slaves and servants were among the first English inhabitants to bring African slaves into their households, sometimes in direct exchange for Pequot captives.

The diaspora of Indians out of New England followed the patterns of New England's trade routes and partners, which linked the region closely to Bermuda, Virginia, Barbados, Providence Island, and eventually Jamaica after the English conquest—colonies where slavery flourished by the 1640s. Within a few years these networks included the Canaries, the Azores, Madeira, Cape Verde, and ports on the Mediterranean, as New England ships took barrel staves and fish—and local Indians—to trade for wine, which they in turn exchanged for Africans on the Guinea Coast and Barbados. Captain Powell, who ferried Henry Winthrop to and from Barbados, was a Puritan who battled against Stuart sympathizers in Barbados and also transported European laborers and eventually Africans and Indians to the island as workers—including the original Guyanese Arawaks.

William Peirce, a privateer and merchant who resided in Massachusetts, took his ship _Desire_ to sea in 1638 at a critical time in the colony's economic development. Winthrop and other leaders were deeply invested—both materially and emotionally—in the success of the voyage as a means of diversifying the region's economy beyond furs, Indian trade, and supplying new immigrants. Apparently they intended the _Desire_'s cargo for Bermuda, but the ship "miscarried" and Peirce instead plied his trade throughout the Caribbean, including a stop at Providence Island. He reported that "dry fish and strong liquors are the only comodites for those parts" that New Englanders could hope to sell, but the _Desire_ conveyed seventeen Pequot Indian captives, for whom Peirce found ready buyers. In exchange, he "bought some cotton, and tobacco, and negroes, etc., from thence, and salt from Tertugos [Tortuga]."[25] The "negroes, etc." were likely either Africans whom two English privateers had looted from captured Spanish ships, or possibly slaves involved in the May 1638 uprising that rocked Providence Island whom the governor had ordered sold off. Peirce carried this return cargo to Boston, and kept at least one woman and her child in his own household. This voyage was a public venture; these were not Peirce's slaves but rather the colony's to sell and dispose of, and the government paid Richard Davenport to house and feed them until buyers took possession.

With this voyage Peirce initiated the lucrative New England–Caribbean trade, which powered the region's economy through the American Revolution. Peirce himself made numerous return voyages until he died three years later trying to land some Massachusetts emigrants on Providence Island during the Spanish attack there. He also pioneered New England involvement in the African slave trade. Other captains followed in the early 1640s and pushed farther into the Atlantic, taking provisions and barrel staves to the Cape Verdes and Canary Islands and buying "Africoes" to sell in Barbados.[26] Word of these successful voyages spread through Boston, and in 1645 the _Rainbowe_ under Captain James Smith took a cargo of fish and staves to Madeira to pick up wine. From thence they went to Africa, where Smith, his first mate Thomas Keyser, and the crew kidnapped some Africans who approached the ship to trade, and then armed with a cannon raided the coast for more. They "assaulted one of their Townes & killed many of the people"—"neere 100" total, the crewmen later testified. They headed to Barbados to sell the cargo but eventually brought two Africans back, selling one to the lieutenant governor of Piscataqua, New Hampshire, Francis Williams.[27]

Peirce's voyage ignited a frenzy of interest in New England Indian slaves in Bermuda and the Caribbean, and in African slaves in New England.

Bermudians Patrick Copeland and William Berkeley wrote to Winthrop in 1639 and in 1648, respectively, asking for Indian captives; Berkeley wanted them for a planned sugar works.[28] Emanuel Downing, Winthrop's brother-in-law, urged a new war against the Narragansetts for the "gaynefull pilladge" of securing Indian workers.[29] Downing sounded the theme of both the necessity of bound labor and the exchangeability of Indians and African slaves:

> Wee might easily have men woemen and Children enough to exchange for moores, which wilbe more gaynefull pilladge for us then wee conceive, for I doe not see how wee can thrive untill wee gett into a stock of slaves suffitient to doe all our busines, for our Childrens Children will hardly see this great Continent filled with people, soe that our servants will still desire freedome to plant for them selves, and not stay but for verie great wages. An I suppose you know verie well how wee shall maynteyne 20 Moores cheaper then one Englishe servant. The ships that shall bring Moores may come home laden with salt which may beare most of the chardge, if not all of yt.[30]

Other voices echoed Downing's call, and the Court of Assistants discussed the possibility of a war in order to take captives "to serve or to be sent out & exchanged for Negroes."[31] Thus slavery may have played a role in the United Colonies' increasingly bellicose policy toward the Narragansetts after 1644–45.

Samuel Maverick was a likely purchaser of some of Peirce's slaves. He certainly owned three slaves by 1638, although they could have come from several sources, since he had strong connections with several colonial societies with slaves: Virginia, Barbados, and New Amsterdam. Maverick's small trading ships plied the northeastern coast and the Chesapeake in search of corn from Indian producers in the 1630s—often at a time of critical need in Massachusetts—and livestock from other European settlements. A voyage in 1635 led to a yearlong stay in Virginia, where Maverick would have seen enslaved Indians and Africans laboring in tobacco fields, and where he encountered (and purchased) ships—and possibly cargoes—returning from Barbados.[32] Judging from the knowledge of the livestock and provision trade with the Caribbean he displayed in a later memoir, Maverick entered this business as well, and his trading ties with Barbados grew during the period when Indian and African workers replaced white servants in the 1630s and '40s. Two of his children emigrated there, and he eventually sold his Massachusetts Noddles Island estate to a Barbadian and relocated to New York after the English conquest of that colony. Deane Winthrop, who inherited the elder Winthrop's Ten Hills farm, at present-day Medford, Massachusetts, added African slaves to the workforce there. Other large enterprises, such as those of Nathaniel Sylvester and Lion Gardiner in the New England offshoot colonies of Southampton and East Hampton on Long Island, also incorporated dozens of enslaved African workers by the 1650s and 1660s.[33]

Slavery Legalized in Massachusetts

Indian captivity, Indian slavery, and African slavery thus became intertwined in New England almost from the start. The Massachusetts Body of Liberties was the work of several divines and jurists, including John Cotton and Nathaniel Ward, who wrote successive drafts starting in 1634.[34] It set out the rights and privileges of the English community, which included protection against search and seizure, and the right to trial by jury, as well as the penalties for various infractions. An extensive section on servants regulated the contracting of servant labor. Section 98 of its capital laws prohibited "man-stealing" or kidnapping. But statute 91 permitted enslavement of "those lawfull Captives taken in just warres, and such strangers as willingly selle themselves or are sold to us." Slaves should "have all the liberties and Christian usages which the law of god established in Israel concerning such persons doeth morally require." Government retained the right to sentence individuals to slavery beyond this definition, though: "This exempts none from servitude who shall be Judged thereto by Authoritie." Unlike laws and customs in early Virginia, Bermuda, and Providence Island, the New England statute did not exclude Christians from enslavement. Christian conversion or baptism formed a basis for slave freedom suits through the 1640s in Bermuda, for example, before statutes closed this loophole, but no such restriction of slavery to non-Christians ever existed in Puritan New England.

This bare-bones early code, the first in English America to define slavery, remained the definition of slavery in Massachusetts, Plymouth, and Connecticut for more than 150 years. The law did not target a specific race. In fact, the General Court in 1645 determined that the two Africans brought to New England in the *Rainbowe* had been illegally enslaved. Richard Saltonstall petitioned the court to consider whether in fact the New Englanders had committed murder and man stealing in raiding the Guinea Coast. Invoking the man-stealing law, the Court of Assistants took the extreme step of demanding the return of one of the men from his purchaser, Francis Williams in New Hampshire. Officials discussed repatriating both slaves to Africa, although no evidence of their fate remains. The Rhode Island Assembly actually passed a law that prohibited racial slavery in 1652. Neither of these actions, however, stopped the importation of slaves and the forced servitude of Indians. Racialized laws aimed at controlling the behavior of enslaved and

free people of color and their interactions with English colonists would follow at the end of the seventeenth century in all southern New England governments. Similar to codes found in other colonies, these laws did not further
define slavery but rather aimed to police behavior, assembly, and access to
firearms, and to establish separate tax and legal procedures for servants and
slaves of color.

New England governments did not adopt the clear statutory definitions
of slavery, such as its heritability through the mother, for example, that other
Atlantic colonies did in the middle decades of the seventeenth century. In
New England the precise legal condition of the Indian captives and eventually of all Indian servants—their "enslavability," for want of a better term, and
indeed the heritability of slave status for children of all enslaved persons—
remained unspecified in law. New England officials chose not to carefully
define the status of any slaves, but that did not mean they eschewed slavery.
Instead, local norms and usages, and the ability of purported owners to invoke
the policing power of local officials and institutions, shaped what was possible
for the owners of captives.[35]

Historians often erroneously assume that the sugar and tobacco colonies
of Barbados and Virginia drove the development of labor law and slave codes
and practice in the English Atlantic, and that other colonies more slowly
followed suit.[36] Yet Massachusetts created precedents and strategies that influenced other regimes. After all, the English in Virginia and the Dutch in
New Netherland were emulating the New England Pequot War strategy
when they waged war against Algonquian- and Iroquoian-speaking Indians,
took captives, and consigned them to work elsewhere in North America
and the Caribbean. This became a regular practice for the Dutch under
Governor Kieft and his successor, Peter Stuyvesant. Kieft even hired John
Underhill of Pequot War fame to pursue Connecticut and Long Island Indians in 1644–45.[37]

Indian Captives and the New England Labor Regime

Another influence that shaped the framework for Indian labor—and
which Indian labor in turn shaped—was the law and practice of servitude as it applied to Europeans. The Pequot captives arrived in English
households at a moment when colonial authorities throughout the Atlantic were in the process of tightening controls on all servants and youth
labor.[38] These New England measures mirrored similar, simultaneous
efforts in Virginia, Bermuda, and the English Caribbean to control the
behavior and maximize the labor of European servants and to undermine

the position of servants of color. The Indians' presence only reinforced these trends. Between 1634 and 1641, Massachusetts courts issued harsh public punishments for servant infractions such as running away or enticing others to do so, property damage, assaulting a master, "insolence," and theft. In 1635 alone, eight servants in Boston received public whippings and other penalties; between 1636 and 1638, Salem courts sentenced nine servants to public beatings. The courts extended the period of service for offenders by weeks or even years, sometimes doubling or tripling the term owed; for burning his master's barn, Henry Stevens had his term increased to twenty-one years. The influx of Pequots certainly did not slow this process—in fact, it hastened and shaped it, and made it even more necessary in the eyes of colonial leaders.

Pequot servants encountered a regime in which government officials supported masters' discipline with state-administered punishments. In fact, the lists of justices, jury foremen, and jurors presiding at Quarterly Courts in Salem and Boston, and on the Court of Assistants, featured individuals who owned the largest number of servants, and who secured the largest numbers of Indian captives: the Winthrops, Hugh Peter, Winthrop's brother-in-law Emanuel Downing, William and John Hathorne, Israel Stoughton, John Endecott, Richard Davenport, John Humphrey, and others.[39] As government officials, these individuals used their connections to engross thousands of acres of land in the 1630s (Winthrop listed five estates in Boston, Medford, Narragansett, and Concord, plus two thousand additional acres in a 1639 draft will).[40] Multiple estates required overseers and laborers beyond the needs of the typical family farm. In addition, almost all these early figures engaged in other trading and processing ventures that relied on Indians' skills. They and other English claimants on captives engaged in diplomatic, communication, and transportation activities for which Indian labor offered significant advantages. Elites regulated labor markets in ways that benefited themselves.

The Pequots' arrival may in fact have inspired a further tightening of the system. Beginning in 1638, for particularly serious servant crimes, authorities turned to the language of slavery. In addition to being "severly whipt," a few servants were ordered by the court to be "delivered vp for a slave to whom the Court shall appoint." Five English servants received this sentence between 1638 and 1640. The court "disposed" of four, but a fifth, Jonathan Hatch, was "committed for a slave to Leift Davenport"—himself the owner of several Pequots, and the manager of the Bay Colony's slave pen.[41] This shift may have been unrelated to the Pequots, but the timing suggests that the presence of Indians, as well as the related arrival of the first African slaves in

Massachusetts and Plymouth, had begun to reshape the context of servitude and slavery for all New Englanders.

We do not know much about the mechanisms for distributing the Pequot War captives. Sandwiched between a measure directing tax collection and an order demobilizing the Bay Colony's forces from the war, a single line in the Massachusetts General Court records that "it was referd to the counsel to take order about the Indian squaws." "Disposing of ye squaws" appears in the margins.[42] There is no direct evidence that the colony sold the Pequot captives at auction for public revenue or compensation to individual English complainants, which became the custom later in the century. The distribution of captives may have followed military rank and service or social/political prominence, or both. Ministers, magistrates, and military officers—the colonists with the most wealth and political capital—acquired the most Indian servants. The reorganization of the Massachusetts militia just prior to the summer offensive against the Pequots had put civil authorities at the top of the military command chain, so that noncombatants such as John Winthrop could make a claim on prisoners based upon his commission as colonel.

Many of these individuals already owned servants. Approximately 13–17 percent of the immigrant stream to New England consisted of servants, and more than half of all households employed a servant.[43] Although some enterprising English merchants shipped children stolen from London and Bristol streets as servants, most New England households recruited their servants directly, either locally prior to migration, or on subsequent trips to England or through trusted intermediaries. Some, especially those who had acquired land and had multiple establishments, retained large numbers of servants. John Winthrop, far from the wealthiest Bostonian, employed as many as sixteen servants at five different landholdings. Even modest households viewed the presence of several servants as a necessity for completing domestic and agricultural tasks.

Crucially, by 1638 the terms of servants brought by the earliest arrivals to Plymouth, Salem, and Massachusetts Bay (and those who had removed to Connecticut, Rhode Island, and New Hampshire) had either ended or soon would, even as demand for labor, competition from other colonial outposts, and population were increasing. This was also the case in Barbados and Providence Island, settled at nearly the same time, which helps account for those societies' adoption of slavery. One historian estimates that workers' wages in New England were higher at this moment than anywhere in England or its overseas empire.[44] Civil War in England and New England's reputation for religious intolerance toward even fellow Puritans who did not strictly follow the Congregationalist model made the situation even worse; as John Winthrop complained, "warres in England kept servants from comminge to vs, so as those we had, could not be hired when their tymes were out, but vpon vnreasonable termes: & we fonde it very difficult to paye theire wages to their content."[45] This complaint helps account for the transformation of the Pequot War into a battle for captives, and also for the willingness of English households to employ Indians. By at least one estimate the proportion of English servants in the population had dropped to 8.5 percent by 1640. Assuming an English population of about 14,000 in New England, the 319 Indian captives represented less than 3 percent of the overall total, but their presence increased the potential servant pool by approximately a third. Although the ratio of men to women in early New England was much less skewed than in other early English settlements, men outnumbered women 3:2 overall and even more among the servant population. This gender imbalance has led some historians to speculate that the colonists valued Pequot women in particular to meet the dearth of female servants.[46] Still, English colonists highly valued male Indian labor, and men and boys who survived execution in the war's aftermath found employment in key households.

Several scholars who focus on labor in the Caribbean and Virginia argue that the degradation of the position of workers there—the vicious punishments, oppressive penal codes, unscrupulous extensions of time to be served, etc.—affected European servants first.[47] In this interpretation, an exploitative system was already in place by the time African slaves began to fill the labor supply. It is true that Euro-American servants experienced extremely harsh conditions and attacks on their autonomy in the late 1630s and early 1640s. In Barbados, and to a much lesser extent in Virginia, these attacks coincided with a rising plantation economy whose scale restricted economic opportunities for ex-servants and left many with severely limited prospects in freedom. Sometimes their children faced servitude as well, resulting in a kind of serial servitude over generations for some families.

Still, these servants' whiteness and, perhaps more important, their subjecthood—their identity as citizens of a Christian imperial state—gave them some legal protections and status at all stages. They could and did challenge abuses at the hands of local authorities on this basis. They managed to protect themselves and their children from perpetual servitude as a class. Irish and Scots servants in the English Atlantic had less leverage, but they still had a clearer claim to European subjecthood and citizenship than did Indians and Africans. Meanwhile, in New England, ex-servants—even ones who fell afoul of the criminal justice system as servants—faced fewer structural economic constraints as free people. They could and did become

successful citizens, voters, and officeholders. To put it another way: conditions for Euro-American servants improved over time, while those for people
of color did not.

In contrast, Indians' and Africans' ability to control the conditions of servitude, as well as their prospects in freedom, were more limited because their
claims to subjecthood and citizenship tended to be nonexistent, contested,
conditional, or local. Spain recognized some Indians as subjects and protected them, but not others; Africans in some parts of South America and
the Caribbean eventually attained a kind of local citizenship as members of
royal work crews and even acquired the status of *pueblos* with their own town
governments, but this was not the experience of most slaves.[48] Moreover, this
is not how the Body of Liberties, which limited those rights and privileges
to English inhabitants of New England, defined the Pequot captives. Contestation for control between local governments in English North America
and imperial officials in London meant that Indians' citizenship in the empire
remained an occasional question rather than a consistently implemented policy. Indians in New England would eventually gain some rights as subjects
and citizens in the late seventeenth century—but as subjects and citizens of
New England colonies, not the imperial crown. Even then, their status in
servitude and freedom remained contested. Indians interested in protecting
their own freedom and that of their kin would need to rely upon communal
membership and social capital that conferred citizenship of other sorts. This
might mean ties to a community of Indians with collective rights—resources
and land and subjecthood recognized by a colony. Or, it might mean creating social bonds within an English town—friendship, love, service, clientage,
kin—that garnered support for Indian claims of freedom.

In January 1648, John Winthrop helped the wife of a friend make a transaction. The woman, Susanna Winslow, held her husband Edward's power of
attorney when he returned to England to aid Oliver Cromwell's forces in
the English Civil War. Winslow not only played a key role in securing Parliamentary victory; he later served in the Caribbean, helping to implement
Cromwell's "Western Design" of planting English control and displacing the
Spanish. Recently, Winthrop had received a letter from an old New England
friend, Richard Vines, who had emigrated to Barbados. Vines sent the letter
via an associate, Captain John Mainfort, who came to Massachusetts hoping to purchase "provision for the belly" because Barbadians now focused
so heavily on sugar that they preferred to buy all of their food. Mainfort
purchased something else while in Boston: an Indian man named Hope.
Winthrop wrote the bill of sale himself.

Susannah sold Hope to Mainfort as a servant, not a slave. The indenture specified that Hope would serve for ten years, "according to the Orders and Customs of English servants in the said Iland, both for maintenance and other recompense."[49] Mainfort could sell Hope, but only to another English person. By limiting Hope's term and explicitly positioning him as an English servant in a Barbados English community, Winthrop and Winslow were probably trying to do what they could to protect Hope against enslavement. Still, it was 1648; since Hope was likely a Pequot captive, he had already served the Winslows for ten or eleven years. Possibly he was a child when he entered the household, and therefore the Winslows claimed him to age twenty-one or twenty-five. Just as likely, though, he was at or near the end of a typical service term when Winslow sold him to Barbados for another ten years. Even with the protections of "Englishness" that the contract gave Hope, this might entail brutal service in the cane fields. In 1640s Barbados, English identities did not always protect servants from torture and abuse.[50] We do not know whether Hope gained his freedom at the end of the ten-year term or whether he became a slave, or if Mainfort sold him to another owner, or even what kind of work he did. These were the life-and-death uncertainties that New England captive Indians faced in an interconnected Atlantic world of labor.

CHAPTER 3

"Indians we have received into our houses"

Pequot War Captives in New England Households

The lack of clarity over the Pequot Indians' legal status meant that their individual experiences varied widely, although overall they enjoyed fewer protections and benefits than English indentured servants. Some became chattel slaves, while others acquired freedom. A few gained enhanced status within indigenous communities, while others played complex roles as intermediaries between English and Indian worlds. The arrival of the Pequot captives also directly precipitated the entry of African slaves into the New England labor system, with important effects for all three groups. Yet at the same time, the Indian workers "we have received into our houses" also colonized the English, in the sense that they shaped and influenced New England material culture, foodways, technology, religious practice, and other aspects of life from within English residents' very homes.[1] The English household in New England was the locus of family and the practice of piety; it was the "little commonwealth" of patriarchal governance on which the stability of the polity rested in contemporaries' eyes.[2] It was also the main unit of economic production. Hence, Puritans desirous of exploiting Indian labor incorporated the latter into their households, and it was in these very intimate settings that Indians and English interacted.

The most powerful and influential New England leaders sought Indian captives. These individuals in turn maintained networks and affiliations that connected their captives with the powerful—and with other Indians. Indian

The South part of New-England, as it is Planted this yeare, 1634.

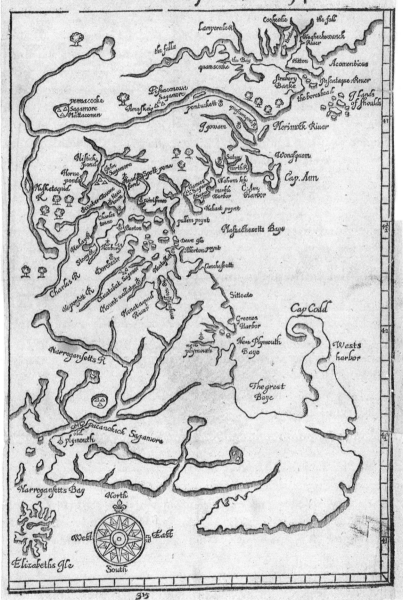

FIGURE 4. "The South Part of New England as it is Planted this Yeare 1634," from William Wood, *New England's Prospect* (London, 1634). Courtesy of the John Carter Brown Library at Brown University.

servants and slaves became ubiquitous not just in the homes of colonial leaders but in many other areas of public and private life. The Indians' presence
in homes, streets, inns, churches, stores, and fields forged a hybrid society
where Indians and Europeans came into daily contact at all social levels.
They shaped each other's lives and institutions in post–Pequot War New
England, and not just in the emerging New England culture of labor. Indians formed friendships and sexual relationships with servants and neighbors; they exchanged work and food technologies, information and tactics,
fears and confidences. Their presence prompted changes in labor law and
control. Indians attended English churches and schools, including Harvard;
they exposed English observers to Indian religious practices, funerary rites,
and other important Native American communal rituals. Captives defended
their right to continued participation in indigenous ceremony, even as their
presence prompted intensified Christian evangelization. Indians and English
raised and nursed each other's children, sharing intimate elements of their
family lives. By taking Pequot captives, English colonists did not distance
themselves from Indians but instead linked themselves to them.

The Spatial World of Pequot Captives

Historical accounts of Indian slavery often assume that the English feared the
danger of keeping Indian servants and slaves in households. Certainly, in published works New England ministers and officials discussed the importance
of maintaining separation between themselves and the Indians for reasons of
security as well as a desire for English cultural and economic unity. Plymouth's Miles Standish moved violently against a small group of European
former servants who had settled near Indians at Wessagusset in the 1620s in
part because the group assimilated to the Indians: they took Indian wives and
got their corn through trade, not cultivation. The General Court order of
1631 banning Indian servitude communicated a certain unease about social
intermixing with indigenous peoples within the household.[3] These public
pronouncements belied the fact that in practice Indians and English were in
constant contact in New England's fields and homes and on its rivers. They
dropped into each other's homes for hospitality, food, trade, and shelter when
traveling, to deliver messages, and to seek aid. They were in and out of each
other's homes so much that Connecticut authorities took pains to prevent
the kinds of accidents that happened when Indians "enter into Englishe-
mens howses, and vnadvisedly handle swords & peeces and other instruments,"
implying that this was a regular occurrence.[4] Colonial legislatures adopted
conflicting policies about allowing Indians to be armed and to serve in militia

or "train bands," and even whether English sex with Indians counted as "adultery." But owners of Pequots did not report any sense of personal danger or expectations of violence. Rather, their main concerns were acculturating the captives, exploiting Pequot labor, and preventing runaways.

Class and gender affected both the disposition and experience of Indian captives. Depending on their social class and skills, some Indians experienced conditions of service more favorable than those of typical English servants. High-status females attracted the attention of European captors and became targets of escape ploys by Indian leaders who wished to marry them and enhance their own claims to leadership. Indian men and women without key kin or skills, however, remained more anonymous, their biographies harder to recover from surviving records. Women in particular appear in the records more as objects of contestation and as bodies marked by abuse or punishment. The status of owners also mattered in shaping the experience and outcomes of servitude for Indian captives. High-status English owners could and did use their position as justice or juryman to exact public punishment upon unruly Indian servants. They also could introduce favored servants to English literacy and/or to personal networks of power that several freed Indians used to gain enhanced standing in both worlds. Higher-status households meant larger social communities of Indian, English, and eventually African servants. Poorer households had less institutional leverage to use against their servants, but also less social capital to offer an ambitious Pequot. In modest houses a captive might be the only servant or slave, and a few suggestive incidents hint that Indian women in poorer or more isolated homes faced a higher likelihood of sexual abuse.

Unsurprisingly, then, the experience of captives varied greatly across space and from household to household. Many of those who owned Pequots—Israel Stoughton, John Endecott, Richard Davenport, Daniel Patrick, John Mason, Roger Ludlow—had ties with one another that stretched back to England and/or Holland; they came from the same communities and migrated aboard ship together. The Reverend Hugh Peter, one of the original planners of Salem, would become a key figure in the English Civil War. Richard Callicott was one of several individuals authorized to engage in the fur trade under the Massachusetts Bay Company's monopoly, a list that included John Holman.[5] Winthrop's sons John Jr. and Stephen also participated in the Indian trade, and Roger Williams operated a trading post in Rhode Island. Many of these men possessed extensive experience with indigenous people as traders, negotiators, economic partners, and military opponents. Joseph Weld helped negotiate the agreement by which the Pawtuxet Indians submitted to the Bay government in 1643, and also mediated with the nearby Winnisemet. Weld, a merchant and Indian trader, operated a dry-goods store and held a permit to "draw wine."[6] He served as Roxbury's town marshal and in that capacity held Anne Hutchinson as a prisoner in his home for four months, during which time he incorporated an Indian captive into his household. Weld's brother Thomas, the Roxbury minister, brought John Eliot to assist as "teacher" for the congregation, and through this connection Eliot encountered the Indian servants who taught him native languages and assisted his evangelical work. The officers, "gentlemen, and others" of the Ancient and Honorable Artillery Company, a military and social organization chartered in March 1638 (the second corporation the Massachusetts Bay government created after Harvard), claimed captives, as did early sergeants and commanders at the newly built Boston fortifications, later known as Castle William. Several "Olde Planters" who had settled the area around Boston as agents for other trading companies and ventures before the arrival of the Massachusetts Bay Company migrants and had rendered essential assistance to the fledgling colony—a group that included John Mason, as well as non-Puritan freeholders Samuel Maverick and Rev. William Blackstone—also received Indians.

In Massachusetts Bay, households holding Indian captives clustered in Dorchester, Roxbury, Boston, and Ipswich/Salem. English newcomers created micro-communities near friends and kin from England, often those with whom they had migrated and with whom they shared business and other interests. Robert Morris, Richard Davenport, Thomas Dudley, Israel Stoughton, Hugh Peter, Joseph Weld, John Mason, and Richard Callicott lived in the Dorchester-Roxbury area, where the English erected homes in very close proximity to Indians already residing there, including the Neponset and Pawtucket.

The Neponset sachem, Chikatabut, and especially his successor, Cushnamekin, maintained close strategic ties with the Boston and Dorchester-Roxbury elite, and Cushnamekin even accompanied Endecott's military expedition to the Pequot country. Both men deeded extensive acreage to Richard Callicott, who operated a fur-trade wharf on the Neponset River in 1634, and whose land grants eventually became the town of Milton. Israel Stoughton built a gristmill on Neponset agricultural lands in 1633. Nicholas Upsall, another member of the Artillery Company, received permission to erect a wharf in Dorchester in 1637. Upsall operated an "ordinary" or inn that served as a meeting place for local officials (he was a selectman and juryman) and information clearance house.[7] Roger Williams recommended that Bostonians wishing to send messages to him leave letters at Callicott's house, "so a native might convey it," or Upsall's.[8]

Some of the families who claimed Pequot labor in 1637–38 had previously hired Indians as short-term workers and household servants. Someone with the surname Maverick—likely the Reverend Elias Maverick, a relative of the Indian trader Samuel Maverick, but possibly either Samuel himself or his minister father—removed a number of Indian orphans from their villages following a smallpox epidemic among the Pawtucket Indians who followed Sagamore John of Winnisemet. Sometime after 1633, one of these children, named John Sassamon, entered the Richard Callicott household as a servant. Sassamon accompanied Callicott (who served as commissary to Massachusetts forces) in the Pequot War and provided useful interpreter services. John Winthrop and his son John Jr. already employed Indian servants, having previously received permission in 1634 "each of them to entertain an Indean a peece, as a household servt."[9] The Winthrops sought permission to arm their male Indian servants and have them train with the newly formed militia and for them to "shoote att fowle" to furnish the family table with meat.

Several homes with Pequots, including Winthrop's, occupied the Boston High Street, later Main Street in downtown Boston. Samuel Coles, who took at least one female captive, operated Boston's first inn and tavern on High

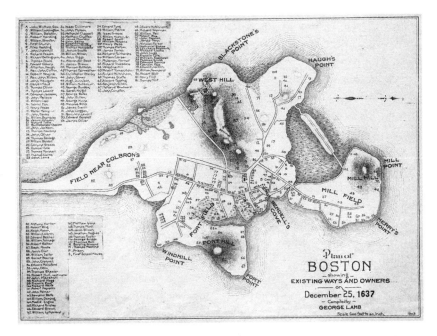

FIGURE 5. George Lamb, *Plan of Boston Showing Existing Ways and Owners on December 25, 1637* (1903). Lamb's key shows the proximity of homes with Pequot captives. Map reproduction courtesy of the Norman B. Leventhal Map Center at the Boston Public Library.

Street, across from Winthrop's "mansion house." Coles's female captive and Winthrop's Indian servants therefore lived in very public places where political meetings took place and where mariners, merchants, servants, Indians, farmers, and visiting dignitaries mingled. When Governor Henry Vane and his council met with Miantonomo on the eve of the Pequot War in October 1636 to discuss a possible alliance, they sent Miantonomo's retinue of Narragansett "sanaps" to dine at Coles's inn.[10] Coles removed the inn to the neighborhood that later became known as "Merchants' Row" near the town cove, where traders had constructed wharfage and cranes to unload ships there by 1638. There as well, he joined other owners of Pequots.

This meant that the captives entered communities and households with other indigenous people present or nearby, and whose English inhabitants had close economic and personal ties that likely facilitated continued interaction among their servants. Captive Pequots likely encountered relatives in other English households and mingled with Neponset and Massachusett Indians, not to mention visiting Narragansett, Niantic, and Mohegan diplomats who traveled frequently to Boston and Connecticut in the years before and after the conflict. Language barriers probably imposed difficulties on communication not just with English masters and mistresses but also with other Indians, free and captive. One of Richard Callicott's captives did not speak Massachusett but acquired competency in that language within a year or two of his arrival in the household, which suggests frequent mingling with local Winnisemet Indians.[11]

Some captives entered households in groups, which would have provided other social opportunities and possibly opportunities to maintain kinship ties. Richard Callicott took at least two Indians, a boy and a girl, and his Indian servant John Sassamon also requested and received another particular female captive, whom he subsequently married; presumably they both continued to live in the household for a time.[12] John Winthrop and his immediate family claimed approximately eight captives, at least five of whom lived in the senior Winthrop's home at some point: three women and two men, in addition to Indians he already employed. Others joined the household, as captives or volunteers, in the succeeding years. In a will drafted in 1639, Winthrop granted his farm "Governour's Garden," an island in Boston Harbor, along with "my Indians there," to his son Adam, indicating that he had Indians at his other properties beyond Boston—and that he viewed them as long-term servants or slaves to be bequeathed, given that his will specified no term of service.[13] The family of Indian slaveholder Edward Gibbons also had a farm on nearby Deer Island, and boats, ferries, and canoes traveled among the islands and between them and the mainland frequently. The extended Winthrop family often summered at Governor's Garden and occasionally received visits from dignitaries. Winthrop's Indian servants would have been present when Sieur LaTour, a French Acadian leader who hoped for the Bay Colony's support against a rival French claimant to the Acadian governorship, unexpectedly arrived by boat in 1643, creating fears of French invasion in Boston and a bit of panic among the household and on neighboring islands.[14] The Indian and English workforce on the farm cultivated an orchard of pear and apple trees that was a local wonder because it produced some of the finest and earliest fruit in the region.[15]

At two stories with six "chambers," Winthrop's main residence or "mansion house" was one of the largest in Boston, but as was customary, the servants all shared a single room. The sheer number of people housed there brought the home's English residents (Winthrop's wife, children living at home, sons- and daughters-in-law, and at least four of his ten to fourteen servants who lived in Boston at any given time) and its Indian inhabitants into close daily contact. English servants rolled out pallets or mattresses for sleep at night; only the married couple at the center of the household generally had a bedstead. Southern New England Indians slept on pallets or mats in single-room dwellings, so some elements of these accommodations would not have been foreign, although the particular materials and expectations of sleep behavior varied across the cultures. According to an account by Edward Winslow from the 1620s and 1630s, Wampanoag Indians commonly sang themselves to sleep; if the Pequots did so as well, one wonders how fellow servants reacted to this habit. They also practiced "the old ceremony of the maide walking alone and living apart so many days," or menstrual seclusion.[16] Judging from fines and regulations that John Eliot and Thomas Shepard imposed on Christian Indians over this custom in the 1640s, English masters and mistresses likely denied Indian women the right to engage in menstrual seclusion in the 1630s, since it would have reduced their labor and inconvenienced the household.[17] Forcing menstruating females into interaction with adult males and eating food cooked by women during menstruation violated important indigenous spiritual beliefs about the danger of contact with menstrual blood.

The geographic proximity of the Massachusetts Pequot captive community was fairly short-lived, however; the departure of several Dorchester residents to Wethersfield, Connecticut, which had helped ignite the Pequot War a year earlier, was only the first of several successive waves of out-migration in the following decade. Many Pequot War veterans supported the Hutchinson-Wheelwright faction during the Antinomian controversy, a dispute over the role of grace in human salvation that caused a political crisis in Massachusetts,

where suffrage and authority were tied to church membership. The crisis culminated in recantation by some, as well as trials, disenfranchisement, excom-
munication, and banishments for others. Many Puritans who supported the
Antinomian cause left the colony voluntarily, including John Mason, who
followed banished minister John Wheelwright to the northeastern frontier.
After John Underhill signed a petition backing the Antinomians, the Massachusetts authorities disenfranchised him in 1637. Underhill, along with Daniel Patrick, then fell further afoul of authorities because of personal behavior
and sexual improprieties subject to punishment through civil courts. They
left for New Hampshire and New Haven, respectively, before entering the
service of the Dutch at New Amsterdam.[18] William Blackstone removed to
the Narragansett country sometime in 1638.

As these religious controversies festered in 1637–38, either by choice or
under pain of banishment many individuals who claimed Indian captives
removed to communities at the fringe of English settlement. Some of these
moves brought native captives closer to large concentrations of Indians, and
potentially to groups related through marriage and language, such as the
Sakonnet region bordering Plymouth and Rhode Island (where Plymouth
Pequot War veterans received grants of land), Providence, New London, and
Hartford. Other owners took their captives north into New Hampshire and
Maine, removing them farther from kin. Richard Callicott was among several
whose fur trade interests took him to Falmouth and Saco, Maine. Those En-
glish masters who remained near the core of settlement might redeploy their
Pequot captives among several residences and newly acquired enterprises,
as Winthrop and Weld did. Hugh Peter, for example, maintained a farm in
Marblehead and sent his servant Hope there to work.

Any relocation had the potential to separate children from parents and
siblings and adults from friends and kin, beginning with the removal and sale
of Pequot, Manissean, and Montauket Indians from their homes in the first
place. For Indians the excision of individuals from kin networks and their
transfer to alien households was a form of social death.[19] Identity, lineage,
affective relationships, and economic and political life all took place within
or were defined by clan and kinship bonds. Severing those bonds created
years and even generations of turmoil and psychic stress for some Indians.[20]

In July 1637, Roger Williams thanked Winthrop for sending him the
Pequot child he had chosen from among the captives—the child around
whose neck he had tied a red scarf to mark his interest. The boy, one of fifty
captives sent by Israel Stoughton to Boston, was from a Pequot village (Sasco
or Sasquaskit) near present-day Fairfield, Connecticut, the site of the dramatic
final "swamp battle" of the war. Williams, who vowed to "endeavor his good,

and the common [good], in him," revealed a great deal of knowledge about the boy's family and genealogy garnered from the child's mother, and established to his own satisfaction that the child's father had not fought against the English.[21] Williams may have viewed his discussions with the child's mother as a form of securing permission, an unofficial indenture of sorts; he (and she) may also have felt Williams was protecting the child from transportation to Bermuda or the Caribbean, the fate of captives whose fathers stood condemned as "murderers of English." And, of course, English parents did send their children into other homes as servants and apprentices. Still, contemporaries understood that distance and absence of family members made children more vulnerable to abuse. Regardless of Williams's understanding of this relationship, he still knowingly separated the child from his mother and two siblings who remained in Boston. This separation came hard on the heels of what must have already been a terrifying experience: the battle; the surviving family's flight and capture; the voyage to Boston; and then their public sale and distribution to households.

In Plymouth, English residents maintained more spatial distance from nearby Indians but were far outnumbered by the much larger indigenous population there. Sometime-governor Edward Winslow secured at least one captive, whom he consigned with other Indian and English servants on his one-thousand-acre estate farm in Marshfield, "Careswell." Like Winthrop's Governor's Garden farm, Winslow's Careswell estate, sited on a former Indian town, employed a relatively large number of servants—as many as sixteen. They were sufficient in number that they apparently dined in a separate servants' area, rather than with the Winslow family.[22] At large estates like Governor's Garden, Careswell, the Noddles Island estate of Samuel Maverick, and Lion Gardiner's eponymous island between Connecticut and Long Island, the captives' main interactions would have been with fellow servants, both European and, eventually, African—perhaps even more than with their English masters or mistresses or other Indians. They were transferred from estate to estate as the owners' labor needs changed, or seasonally as English families moved from their urban homes to summer farms. Even as they faced shifts of residence and work patterns, however, Pequots might find other Indians nearby. Hugh Peter, William Peirce, and Emanuel Downing owned property—and Indians—in Salem and Marblehead, so their servants might have encountered one another.

At the new English settlements of Providence, Cranston, and Warwick in Rhode Island, Indian servants and English masters lived in tight quarters in bark-covered cellar dugouts and eventually modest log or frame houses. In fact, so many "newcomers" lived in wigwam-like houses that authorities in

Portsmouth and Newport passed laws in 1639 and 1642 requiring English to build homes, perhaps to distinguish them from indigenous inhabitants.[23] Other religious exiles left Boston for even more isolated residences; clergyman and Indian trader William Blackstone, for example, settled on the Plymouth–Rhode Island border (where he lent his name to the Blackstone Valley).

Indian captives residing in these places encountered large nearby populations of over thirty thousand Narragansett and Niantic Indians. These groups had resettled their own Pequot captives in villages around Narragansett Bay, possibly creating opportunities for Indians among the English to connect with other refugees and relatives. Blackstone's female captive ran away at least twice. Still other captives lived at trading posts, such as Roger Williams's at Cocumscussoc (now North Kingstown), which attracted Native American customers and diplomatic missions and served as places where captive servants and local Indians mingled. The predominance of canoe travel through familiar waterways and foot travel via Indian paths, the preferred modes of transportation for all inhabitants, offered familiar routes and possibilities for visits with extended kin.

Cultural Exchanges

Even as they faced new material realities and pressure to acculturate, free and bound Indians exposed Europeans to their social and spiritual worlds. The Narragansetts, Roger Williams reported, celebrated with weeks of feasting and dancing in August surrounding the corn harvest, as well as "*Nickommo* a Feast" that took place in December or January after a successful winter hunting season, where "they run mad . . . in their kind of Christmas feasting."[24] During the harvest festival, Williams and other fascinated English watched as upward of a thousand people lay prone under trees while powwows, or shamans, helped the assembled participants pursue healing or important spiritual experiences. Hundreds and even thousands of guests and relatives attended such gatherings in the 1630s to participate in "devotions and sports." Missionary John Eliot described the massive crowds that congregated at the Pawtucket Falls on the Merrimack River (near present-day Lowell, Massachusetts) for the fishing—and for gaming, trade, and conviviality. "Such confluences are like Faires in England," Eliot noted, and they drew English as well as Indians to engage in spiritual and material exchanges.[25] Other ceremonies, such as *kitteickauich*, required wealthier Indians in the sachem's inner circle to distribute goods and food to their less economically successful counterparts, who in turn ritually begged for aid.[26] In describing Indian ceremonies, Roger Williams found understandable analogies for these celebrations for his

English audiences—"Christmas," "sports," "devotions," aristocrats' distribution of gifts and food to the poor in rural England, in ways that confirmed hierarchy and obligation. But ministers and officials in Plymouth, Massachusetts Bay, New Haven, and Connecticut forbade the celebration of Christmas and frowned on sport since it distracted from productive labor; they remained critical of diversions that mixed folk and religious traditions.[27] The Indians' echoes of English folk traditions in some ways subverted Puritan norms and, in doing so, may have attracted Euro-American interest.

For themselves, Puritans downplayed rituals surrounding death and burial.[28] Relatives washed and laid out bodies at home or in church. Families walked the bodies to burial; ministers did not even pray over graves, and families interred relatives in simple shrouds or pine boards with little fanfare. Funerary rites were extremely important for New England Indians, by contrast. Relatives first prepared the bodies; then, flexing the bodies and orienting the dead toward the southwest, the site of "Cautantowwit his House," they placed the corpses into elaborate pits, along with burial gifts of food, tools, clothing, and jewelry commensurate with the dead person's status.[29] Next, families hosted dances and feasts that might last for as many as ten days, attended by nearby relatives and friends, and often by a large contingent of curious English observers.

Even Christian Indian converts continued to practice these burial customs rather than entirely adopting English Puritan approaches, despite pressure from ministers and colonial authorities.[30] At least one Indian soldier who fought with the English in the northeastern wars of the eighteenth century specified that he wanted to be returned home for a burial "in the Indian style." The size and richness of the accoutrements in the burial pits actually increased over the seventeenth century, according to archaeologists, which suggests that for Indians among the English these practices represented a core element of identity to be protected and even emphasized.[31] There is evidence that English masters permitted servants to attend funeral dances of kin, and English neighbors watched and commented on the Indian dances; some complained of the noise and disruption, but others came to watch out of curiosity and in some cases to honor Indian friends. When an Indian laborer on the estate of Christopher Champlin in Westerly named Peter Coyhees died, at least four English neighbors attended his funeral dances, along with Indian friends and family.[32] Captive and free Indian parents demanded the presence of children, even if they served in other households, and masters often acceded to these requests. By the turn of the century, authorities in several colonies tried to stem attendance at "Indian dances" since they interrupted work, disturbed neighbors, and "enticed [servants] to out-stay their time at such dances, and run away from their masters"—but also because they attracted an alarming number of English participants.[33] These regulations attest to the power and persistence of Indian cultural forms within servitude and the hybridity of New England spiritual and cultural life.

Work and Gender in English-Pequot Households

English and Indian material lives were not completely different. For southern New England Indians, the household formed an equally important node of family and economic production. In the decades immediately before and after the English arrival, Algonquians in the region had been moving toward a system that emphasized patriarchal households even more than in the past. Smaller leaders, or sachems, essentially anchored family bands. Families—mostly the female members—constructed and owned independent housing, although they also built commons for dining, feasts and councils, and spiritual rituals.[34] Even in fields that seemed to English observers to be undivided collective holdings, individual Indian households and families managed assigned plots, with some larger and more productive than others. Indian men interested in attaining influence knew that economic power was an important foundation of political power.[35] Like their English counterparts, aspirants to leadership sought to increase the number of people whose labor they could direct and benefit from. Polygamy offered one strategy to achieve wealth, since for Indians as well as for the English, female labor was a crucial component of household wealth production and nutrition. The Pequots and English both viewed Indian women as more economically valuable than their European female counterparts. In an attempt to discourage Pequots from attacking Connecticut English and taking captives, Lion Gardiner reminded the Indians that such tactics would "do them no good" because Englishwomen were "lazie and cannot doe thr [the Indians'] worke."[36] Indians would have found similarities in the smaller, simpler residences that English denizens lived in outside the population centers of Boston, Charlestown, and Salem. The captives would have recognized the extended-kin-based households supervised by women—their new mistresses—and the gendered assignment of tasks.

We do not know, however, how the Pequots explained their situation to themselves. For the English, servitude in households theoretically meant a kind of fictive kinship, albeit a kinship backed in law, with the patriarch standing in as a father, the mistress for mother, and the servant of age thirteen to twenty-five for their child.[37] The new fictive parents had obligations to provide food, clothing, and instruction, while the fictive child owed labor, obedience, and loyalty. In England, other communal structures and nearby kin further mediated these relationships, setting boundaries for masters and providing additional points of social identity and support for the servant. In New England, any resemblance between servitude and kinship had become even more tenuous. In English America, indentured servitude had become more of a purely economic labor arrangement in which third parties recruited and sold workers for much longer terms. Servants had fewer kin locally, and the existing institutions tended to intervene in favor of masters. For the Indians, unprotected by contracts or advocates, this situation was even more extreme and unmediated. The English gave them new names, but did not incorporate them as true kin.[38]

Many Pequots had direct experiences with captivity in other contexts, such as seeing an Indian or European captive brought into a village for torture, ransom, or adoption, all of which had occurred during the war. In a 1637 attack on Wethersfield, Pequots took two girls captive. They treated the women well, by all accounts, but resisted turning them over and only did so under pressure by the Dutch as well as the English. These women may have been intended as replacement kin or adoptees into the tribe, which helps explain the Indians' reluctance to surrender them.[39] Some male English captives in Indian hands had different experiences. Pequots captured Dorchester trader John Tilley in October 1636 when, against Lion Gardiner's orders, he left the ship to hunt waterfowl. The Indians cut off his hands and feet; he survived three days, and the Indians "themselves confessed, he was a stout man, because he cried not in his torture."[40] Sergeant Tilley conformed to Indian expectations of how a "stout man" should behave in captivity—accept the expected torture as stoically as possible. Two other members of a force Gardiner sent to protect the Saybrook colonists' corn harvest met a similar fate: the Indians "tormented" them to death.[41] The Pequots had experienced traumatic dislocation, death of near relatives, separation from surviving family members, and long travel by water and land to arrive at households—a familiar story line for the Indians' understanding of captivity, even though the particulars of arriving in a place such as Boston made it unique. It is possible that some saw the harsh enforcement of labor requirements—the whipping posts—in the context of ritual torture. But open-ended service in English households most resembled the fate of those pitiable, kinless "meane persons" whom Roger Williams had encountered in some Narragansett villages. Moreover, some elements of their situation were entirely new. Women faced unfamiliar tasks and technology such as spinning on a wheel, dairying, watching livestock, and tending gardens and fields with unfamiliar crops and techniques. Men's masculinity faced challenges, as they would be pressed into engaging in agricultural work and other activities that violated the Indians' notions of gender-appropriate work.

Unlike women, Pequot men worked in areas more removed from domestic spaces. Far from rejecting male servants, English sought out men and boys for skills that enhanced English military, diplomatic, and economic activities. The early New England economy focused on many activities, and an agricultural export economy would not develop until the second half of the seventeenth century. Many first-generation male captives engaged in warfare, trading, boating, fishing, hunting, messaging, guiding and mapmaking, and manufacturing wampum in ways that showed continuity with their pre-captivity work patterns. Like the Winthrops, Roger Williams, who had renamed his captive Pequot boy Will, petitioned Rhode Island authorities a decade later for permission to arm "his Indian" so that the man could hunt. Richard Callicott was one of several English masters who faced censure from the Massachusetts Bay government for arming or even helping Indians learn to mend guns, and Callicott perhaps trained an Indian smith. Other Indians used skills acquired through fort construction among native peoples and applied them to fortifications and the construction of stone fences for Europeans. John Eliot saw Indians as potential sawyers, "for they saw very good board and planke"; boat making, board cutting, and shingle making formed typical tasks for Indian servants.[42] Still others used their language skills to become crucial interpreters and instructors.

Haying, harvesting, and animal husbandry also became typical Indian male jobs by the 1640s and 1650s. Caring for animals at a time when this largely meant picketing them to graze, or transporting them to islands as a form of penning for the summer, or herding them into pasture and then protecting them from predators, showed some continuities with male hunting responsibilities. The fact that Indians in non-Christian communities voluntarily adopted some forms of animal husbandry in the 1660s and 1670s suggests that the Indians could incorporate raising pigs and sheep into their existing subsistence and gendered work patterns without drastic change.[43] When Benjamin Church surprised the camp of Wampanoag leader Annawon during King Philip's War in 1676 and demanded supper, the Indian courteously offered Church's troops a choice of "horse-beef" or "cow-beef" (Church chose the latter). Church brought his own salt, but proclaimed the resulting dish, cooked by Annawon's wife and thickened with pounded green cornmeal, such a "fine relish" that the Englishmen did not miss bread.[44] Indian men also sometimes pitched in with women to prepare fields or engage in heavy harvest work in Algonquian fields, so they may have had some cultural and practical preparation for the work that the English now expected them to do.

FIGURE 6. Elm burl wooden ceremonial feast bowl, ca. 1655–75, known as "King Philip's Samp Bowl." Legend has it that the bowl was a "trophy" taken from Metacom's wigwam after his death in 1676. Courtesy of the Massachusetts Historical Society.

Female servants in English households would have engaged in some types of work recognizable to Indian women, including grinding corn with mortar and pestle for several hours daily. Scholars have stressed the English colonists' desire to distinguish themselves from indigenous peoples through the importation of English grains and domestic animals, signs of their superior "civility" and "artificiality."[45] In the early decades of English presence, however, Euro-American and indigenous foodways necessarily converged because of the reliance on Indian-raised corn and Indian-hunted game. Possibly this trend became even more pronounced with Indian women's growing presence in English households after 1637. Roger Clapp recalled that the English in early Boston ate samp, a pounded corn mush with a soupy consistency (from the Narragansett word *nasàump*), prepared the Indian way, without "butter or milk." Samp formed the basis for other common foods, including cornmeal-and-squash soup, with meat and vegetables added as available. Common meat proteins for soups and roasts among Indians included venison, fowl, and fish, all of which the English consumed, though they added goat, and, increasingly, beef and pork to the regional diet. Indians would have introduced maple syrup and sugar as sweeteners. Outside of English households Indian cookery generally avoided dairy products and beef until the late seventeenth century (Annawon's feast for Church notwithstanding), although some New England Indians had begun to raise sheep and pork and incorporate them into their own cooking by then. Both English and Indians gathered and consumed large quantities of seafood and shellfish, often caught by Indians.

Indian women brought other valuable skills to English households that complemented elements of English and New England housewifery. These included identifying and gathering wild fruits and nuts for jams and cakes; baking cornmeal breads; and preserving and using medicinal plants and nursing the sick (a task that women such as Alice Winthrop supervised). They knew how to cultivate, dry, and preserve pumpkins, beans, and gourds, techniques that English households had already mimicked by the 1630s. Female Indian servants understood gardening and weeding, and they had perfected techniques for labor-saving weed and pest suppression.[46] Possibly Winthrop, Callicott, Williams, and others called upon them to prepare furs, hides, and other products of the hunt, since many English were still consigning cargoes of beaver and fox skins to England in the late 1630s and early 1640s as part of their diverse economic strategies. Contemporaries recognized Indians' skills at weaving and fiber preparation, even if they did not employ the particular materials—wool, flax, and cotton—that Europeans used. Roger Williams admired the hemp food containers that he encountered in Narragansett homes. John Josselyn raved about the beauty and utility of the clothing Wampanoag Indian women made, as well as the "Delicate sweet dishes [plates and bowls]" they manufactured and decorated. Indians made containers sized "from a dram cup to a dish that containeth a pottle, likewise Buckets to carry water or the like, large Boxes . . . spoons and trayes wrought very neatly."[47] Colonists valued such items and often mentioned them specifically among the goods they looted from Indian homes during the Pequot War. Williams noted the intricacy of design on the mats that Narragansett Indians used to cover the beds and interior spaces of their homes, and he compared them to genteel English bed hangings and curtains.[48] Indigenous women worked with hemp to make twine, thread, and containers, and with milkweed silks to make thread and wicking. Indian baskets were already a commodity valued for commercial exchange (and targeted for theft) in Boston by 1640, so the creation of storage containers was another possible occupation for female captives.

More foreign to Indian workers would be raising and processing European foodstuffs and plants such as wheat. There is no direct evidence of

FIGURE 7. Wampanoag/Algonquian basket, Rhode Island, ca. 1675. An extremely rare example of New England Indian women's weaving skills. Courtesy of the Rhode Island Historical Society, RHi X17 1685A.

Native American women being deployed in plow agriculture in this period. Cultivation of corn and grain would have been men's work with the English, violating Indian custom and undermining female roles that had profound spiritual as well as economic significance. Plow agriculture and livestock-oriented tasks such as mowing and gathering hay were unfamiliar. English assigned Indian children many tasks associated with animal husbandry—picketing and driving cattle, tending sheep and goats—which would have been completely new to them. Indian women were unaccustomed to feminine tasks of dairying, butter making, cheese making, and other activities associated with domestic animals, although already by 1638 Josselyn encountered Indian women who knew "how to milk a cow." "English" sewing—maintaining furnishings, clothing, and bed linens—differed from Indian women's expertise in fiber arts, and decorative aesthetics differed among the groups, so their learning curve was likely high in these areas. Indian women who knew such domestic arts were rare and prized enough as late as the 1730s that advertisements mentioned such skills specifically when Indians for sale could "dairy," "spin linen," "sew, card spin," or "wash, iron, bake, brew, cook."[49]

Other areas of divergence centered on the expectations of discipline and supervision in childcare. Evidence from later in the century indicates that Indian servants and slaves often cared for English children, and it seems likely that captive Pequots also faced this task. Europeans consistently highlighted Indians' tender regard for their children and the child-centered nature of indigenous family life as well as their toleration of disobedience. The lack of corporal punishment or correction of children in Native American communities made an intense impression on Roger Williams and other observers.[50] Still, Indian women may not have viewed their English charges with the same indulgence; numerous violent episodes in the late seventeenth and early eighteenth century indicate that the oppression of involuntary servitude sometimes overcame any affection Indian caregivers felt toward their English charges. Several Indian slaves, most notably Patience Boston, were tried and executed for killing English children in their care.[51] Others, including Boston, killed their own children out of depression and anger over their enslaved condition or to evade the whippings and extended terms of servitude that would follow if they were convicted of fornication.

Residing among the English meant other cultural and material challenges for the Pequot captives. Perhaps most notable was the relative sedentarism and seclusion that characterized European women's domestic life. In many indigenous cultures Indian women faced restrictions on their actions, travel, and work lives—they were not supposed to kill animals, for example; they moved seasonally but also stayed close to fields or camps while men traveled for diplomacy and hunting. Responsibilities of child rearing limited the physical mobility and roles that Indian women (as well as English women) played. Indian men filled most political and spiritual leadership positions. But Indian women controlled important economic assets, especially fields and homes. They directed certain spiritual realms and annual rituals, participated in political and military decision making, and occasionally served as hereditary sachems. In contrast, except for a few dissident communities such as the Antinomians, Quakers, and Baptists, New England authorities had severely limited women's public spiritual activities after 1637, despite their dominance as church members. English women did not participate in political or governmental life, and many spent their lives within a few miles of their households.

A few Indian women managed to transcend English notions of gender boundaries and the physical constraints of the household to work in a public capacity, in roles that Indian and English males performed more typically. At least one "Pequot maide who could speak English perfectly" served as an interpreter in English negotiations with the Narragansett leader Miantonomo. Bay authorities had summoned Miantonomo to Boston in 1640 to answer English concerns about his dealings with the Mohawks and rumors of a pan-Indian conspiracy. Roger Williams, his preferred interpreter, could not travel with him because Williams had received a capital sentence for blasphemy during the controversies of 1636–37; to avoid religious contamination, Massachusetts had passed additional legislation preventing residents of Providence from entering the Bay Colony.[52] Miantonomo rejected the services of a male Indian interpreter whom he suspected of treachery, so officials offered him the "Pequot maid." Her English skills indicate that she had been living in a local household for several years. Through her services, Miantonomo "did speak with our Committee," albeit reserving some of his "state secrets."[53]

Another woman who brushed aside expectations of female behavior in captivity was Wincumbone, the woman whom Winthrop had selected as a captive because of her presumed assistance to English forces during the war and her high status. Like male Indian captives whom the English used as interpreters and diplomats, she seems to have enjoyed significant physical freedom. She effectively escaped servitude and Winthrop's "Experimented Kindnes" by running away and returning to Pequot country. According to Roger Williams, the widow generally spoke well of the English and Winthrop's intentions, informing "all Pequts and Nayantaquits that Mr. Govrs. [Governor's] mind is, that no Pequot man should die, that her 2 sons shall ere long be Sachims there"—an optimistic take on Puritan foreign policy but not one that Winthrop had tasked her with spreading nor one that matched his intentions. What became of her children is unclear, but in 1645 John Winthrop Jr. encountered a woman he referred to as "formerly a woman of Momonottuck"—possibly Wincumbone—now married to "George," a Pequot Indian leader among the Nameaug Pequot community near New London.[54]

We have no evidence of whether Indian servants in the 1630s were expected to assume European dress, especially since this would have forced masters to incur significant expenses. According to Roger Williams, nudity was "ordinary and constant" among the Narragansetts, especially indoors.[55] Outdoors, in cooler weather men and women wore breechcloths, moccasins, leggings, and cloaks of skin, feathers, or, increasingly, English cloth. Male children went largely uncovered, and girls wore only a small "apron" until age twelve. A Plymouth court excused at least one Pequot captive servant from testifying in 1640 because she lacked appropriate clothing and footwear for the journey and court appearance. By the mid- to late seventeenth century, clothing had become the most common commodity listed in charges of theft against Indian servants, particularly women. Runaways often took multiple sets of clothes with them as well. Clothing was a valuable item, and easy to carry and to sell or exchange for food and other useful goods. The shift to wearing English clothing may have created difficulties for Indian captives, but hair represented an even more core symbol of identity for many. By the 1640s, free Christian Indians faced intense pressure to cut their hair and adopt European custom in other areas of appearance, so it is likely that captives did as well. Of all the changes he underwent, Monequassun, an early convert, "found it very hard to cut off" the long hair that he "loved."[56] Hair signaled one's gender, age, status, and tribal affiliation, so Indian men and women regarded the cutting of hair as an insult. When Niantics under Wequashcook cut the hair of several female Indians during a dispute with the Mohegans over Pequot captives, Uncas complained to Connecticut officials.[57]

While native women interacted with male English servants and masters, English women would have supervised the work of both female and male household servants closely, more so than the male heads of household. Records of Indian reactions to this intimate relationship in the 1630s and 1640s are scarce. Language and skill barriers must have made the daily encounter a complicated one. Hugh Peter actively sought a female Pequot servant to help his overstretched household in 1638. A year later, however, he begged his deceased wife's adult daughter to send Hannah, one of the family's English servants, back to his household because of his new wife's difficult pregnancy and delivery. Peter disparaged the work of their new Pequot servant, Hope, in 1639, noting "for truly wee are so destitute (hauing none but an Indian) that wee know not what to doe."[58] The Salem Quarterly Court, whose justices included fellow captors John Winthrop, John Winthrop Jr., Emanuel Downing, and William Hathorne, had sentenced Hope two months earlier to be whipped for running away and for drinking alcohol. Hope struggled to adjust to servitude in the Peter household, an experience likely unaided by her mistress's bouts of mental illness, possibly postpartum depression. A year later, "for running away & other misdemeanors," the local court sentenced Hope to be whipped again both in Boston and in Marblehead, the site of Peter's farm.[59] Similarly, in July 1640 Thomas Weld's wife had a contentious encounter with two Indian women, at least one of whom was likely a family servant, since Weld had acquired a Pequot. The exchange resulted in the Indians' prosecution at Quarterly Court, which sentenced them "to bee whiped for their insolent carriage, and abusing Mrs. Weld."[60] These and other cases of harsh corporal punishment attest not only to Indians' unhappiness with their new milieu and their resistance to captivity, but also to colonial authorities' determination to subdue their Indian servants.

Resistance and Relationships across Ethnic Lines

Captivity thrust Indians into relationships with English masters, and with English and African servants and slaves, in ways that sometimes involved friendship and cultural exchange—and sometimes violence. Lion Gardiner testified that Indian and English women working on his estate were on such intimate terms that some Indians paid English women "beads of wampum" to be wet nurses to their infants.[61] Others sought patrons among European rivals to the English. In 1646, one female captive fled her English master's Hartford home in order to avoid "publique punishment" at the whipping post for some infraction. She found a refuge of sorts at the nearby Dutch trading post on the Connecticut River, Fort Hoop (or Hope), founded a few years before the Pequot War. The tiny Fort Hoop contingent, already under severe pressure from local English communities desirous of ejecting the Dutch from their strategic outpost, resisted numerous attempts by Connecticut authorities to get her back. When an armed group tried to seize her, the fort's commissary, David Provoost, fought them off with a rapier. The English claimed that the fort's denizens kept the Indian girl for "wantonness," implying sexual exploitation, but Provoost countered that one of the traders planned to marry her as soon as she became baptized.[62] The incident became a flashpoint of rising conflict between New Netherland and the United Colonies, the New England confederacy set up in 1643. Fort Hoop could be a rowdy and even dangerous place—another commissary had killed a ten-year-old slave in an incident ruled an accident—but the company's continued insistence on protecting the Indian woman despite the risk seems to signal her ability, and theirs, to forge bonds across ethnic lines. One tantalizing reference in a letter from Governor Kieft suggested that she might have had earlier contact with the Dutch at New Netherland, possibly even in his household.[63]

In succeeding decades, Boston, Providence, Salem, and other towns hosted sites where English, Indian, and African servants and free people socialized together. Garrets, kitchens, back doorsteps, and spare rooms sometimes served as unofficial, unlicensed taverns. Mary Silverwood of Newport found herself in the middle of a court case when a slave named Indian Dick assaulted local baker John Davis in her "chamber." Silverwood had served Christmas punch and ale to a festive and diverse group of paying customers that included at least five free and enslaved Africans, as well as Dick, "Boston an Indian belongin to Mr. Peter Reby and Worwick an Indian belongin to Edward Thurston Esq.," and "some Squas" and female servants.[64] Roger Williams himself received a license to distribute "strong waters" to Indians for medicinal purposes outside his trading post, and the records are full of prosecutions of families for selling liquor by the glass or cup—smaller amounts more affordable to servants and poorer inhabitants than the barrels and bottles that spirits typically were sold in.[65]

In other cases, however, captive Indians recounted harrowing tales of mistreatment and abuse by masters and other servants. An English Pequot War veteran named Arthur Peach entered Samuel Maverick's service in 1638. Within two years Peach and several accomplices stood accused and convicted of the murder of an Indian man, and Peach became one of the first Euro-Americans executed by an English court for killing an Indian. We have no evidence that Peach engaged in conflicts with Indians in Maverick's household, but one wonders whether the violent animosity he and his comrades displayed in the murder had echoes in his relations with fellow servants. One Indian woman who suffered sexual abuse at Samuel Coles's inn escaped and ended up in Narragansett territory, where Williams recaptured her. In her interview with Williams, the woman complained "that she of all the natiues in Boston is vsed worse: is beaten with firesticks and especially by some of the Servants." She reported having been raped, and then treated as a criminal for having engaged in illicit sexual activity. James Penn, the Boston town beadle, had branded her with a hot iron in punishment.[66]

Indians in Samuel Maverick's household on Noddles Island in 1639 would have witnessed—or at least heard the commotion surrounding—a rape instigated by their master. Maverick, "desirous to have a breed of Negroes," wished two of his African slaves to have sex in order to generate children, but the woman resisted. "Seeing she would not yield to perswasion to company with a young Negroe man he had in his house; he commanded him will'd she nill'd she to go to bed to her." The woman, "a Queen in her own Country," as evinced by her bearing and the respect shown her by other household slaves, fought the man; she mourned the attack "in her own Countrey language and tune" to a shocked English visitor, John Josselyn. Josselyn noted that "this"—the sexual assault—"she took in high disdain more than her slavery, and this was the cause of her grief."[67] Not only the victims but also family members and visitors were thus privy to such violent interactions among English masters and their workers.

A few Pequot women were likely victimized sexually by their new owners, including a young captive in the home of Nicholas Simpkins. Simpkins served as the first captain of the new fort Bostonians constructed on Castle Island, but he lost this position in 1636, in part because of irregularities with his accounts. John Winthrop hinted that Simpkins was mentally unstable.[68] Still, Simpkins received a Pequot captive into his household, which included his wife Isabel and three children, and removed to Plymouth Colony. In 1640 Yarmouth authorities prosecuted him for "attempting to lye with an Indian weoman." His accuser was Jonathan Hatch, the runaway servant who had returned to Yarmouth, his father's town, to seek shelter. (Hatch himself would be sentenced to "slavery" as part of the crackdown on servants of all ethnicities.) In the end the court excused Simpkins of this crime, but also absolved Hatch of slander, suggesting that the case remained unproven, rather than a clear acquittal. We do not know whether the "Indian weoman" named in the case was his Pequot servant, but it seems significant that the court fined Simpkins for failing to bring "his Indian maide servant" to court, presumably to testify, because he claimed that she "had neither shoes nor was in health to come" and attend court in chilly December weather. Simpkins had frequent social and economic encounters of various kinds with many other local Indians—the court fined him again the following year for lending his pistol to an Indian man—so it is possible that the Indian woman mentioned in the complaint was not his servant. Still, one wonders why Simpkins did not properly equip his maidservant or allow her to testify in court. Was she a willing partner, or the victim of sexual assault, or merely a witness? Regardless, this Pequot girl faced a potentially dangerous situation with little protection or oversight.[69] Similarly, in the case of the Indian girl in Hartford who fled to the Dutch, it is impossible to tell from the surviving records whether her relationship with the trader at Fort Hoop was voluntary or involuntary.

Even as Pequots transformed the households they entered, so too did the experience of captivity confront them with sometimes life-threatening challenges and choices. They could adjust to their new roles, learn new tasks, and strive to please their masters and mistresses. They could learn English and adopt elements of their new culture. Or they could resist assimilation in various ways and seek to return to their previous lives. Meanwhile, the English had imposed a tough legal system to regulate and punish Pequots, as well as other servants and slaves. Masters and mistresses would attempt other forms of cultural colonization, including Christianization of the captives. Indian slaves exercised some choices over how to respond to these forces and to the conditions of their captivity. The variety of their responses continued to shape New England society for all its inhabitants.

CHAPTER 4

"Such a servant is part of her Master's estate"

Acculturation, Resistance, and the Making of a Hybrid Society

As Pequots entered English households, they faced choices that typically confronted captives and enslaved persons in the early modern world. Success at captivity in Indian country meant integration into the captor's society. This required that captives accept their condition and the new life presented to them, despite violence, trauma, and even torture that preceded it. It meant finding ways of gaining kin and becoming kin to others. It also required some acculturation to the dominant society on the part of the captive. Some historians have assessed the slave experience in a similar way and have noted a paradox.[1] "Success" for a slave might mean a number of different things. Securing one's own freedom and autonomy might be goals, but how best to achieve them?

The slave who acculturated enough to understand the society and system in which he or she now had to operate had some advantages. Such a person had more success at creating new social bonds to replace the ones lost through captivity. Language acquisition, knowledge of the new culture, and social networks within the community she resided in gave the slave social capital that she might parlay into either bettering her condition in slavery or possibly even making a claim for freedom. Literacy brought the ability to understand a statute or write a petition; church membership brought a spiritual fellowship with well-connected and well-disposed protectors who might provide legal help. Even a runaway might benefit from such skills and networks; several Indian captives who fled Boston to return to their home-land escaped notice because they were "dressed in the garb of servants"—they had figured out how to blend with an Indian population that had per-mission to come and go.[2] Anyone whose goal was escape would also have to consider *where*. Did she hope to return home? For the Pequots in 1637–38, home was gone, their collective name rendered illegal, and kin scattered far and wide. Yet the very act of acculturation meant at least temporarily sever-ing important bonds to one's own past, family, and meaningful ethical and spiritual universes—or, if not severing, then learning new beliefs, words, and behaviors well enough to operate in both worlds. This might make reintegra-tion into the old sociocultural system difficult. It also might erode the sense of separate identity that helped captives and enslaved persons resist their cap-tors' efforts to define them.

Pequot captives confronted all these choices and made different decisions. Some resisted by running away. Others fell victim to violence, lifetime servi-tude, and various forms of physical and spiritual abuse. Still others parlayed captivity into freedom and even leadership of postwar Indian communities: a few of these individuals had enormous influence on relations between Euro-peans and Indians in the mid-seventeenth century. Others adapted to the new realities of captivity and servitude, and accepted a measure of acculturation. Just as the Pequot War had forged new labor practices in New England, so too did the presence of captive Indian servant communities push the English to initiate the first organized evangelization and acculturation projects under John Eliot. Christianization was an ultimate form of colonization—a cul-tural colonization of Indian servants and slaves who would become emblems of the possibilities for Indians: "civilized, and in subjection to us, painfull [diligent, or taking pains] and handy in their businesse, and can speak our lan-guage."[3] Yet, by participating in this society, Indians also recast it in ways that its English leaders did not always appreciate or intend. Together, English and Indians created a hybrid society in which Indian actions and goals sometimes determined the outcomes.

Christianity and Acculturation

Indians in English households faced many new cultural pressures, but one of the most powerful was Christianization. Generally the new owners gave captives English names to symbolize their new identities. Theoreti-cally, servitude would hasten the hoped-for Indian acculturation to English ways and quickly transform the Pequots from a potential threat to orderly and even exemplary members of the community. Despite the emphasis on evangelization among the Holland Separatist community that launched the Pilgrims, and in some of the early promotional literature surrounding the Massachusetts Bay Company's program, neither Plymouth nor the new government in Boston had made much effort in this area in the early years of settlement.[4] Edward Winslow of Plymouth engaged in some missionary activity to the Pokanoket/Wampanoag and the Massachusett, and the Pawtucket Indians under Sagamore John appear to have been the target of evangelization by a few individual clergymen, including Elias Maverick. The arrival of so many Pequot captives "in our families" created a new impetus—and provided new subjects and new tools—for a more concerted effort to Christianize local Indians.[5] Ministers interested in evangelization, such as John Eliot, acquired through the 1637 captives a string of interpreters, language teachers, and translators who enabled outreach to the Massachusett, Wampanoag, and Nipmuc around Boston, Dorchester, and Springfield after 1640. Even before these more familiar efforts, however, ministers and masters focused on educating and converting the Indian servants in their own homes in 1637–38 and beyond.

Successful conversion of Pequot captives served a number of purposes. Fundamentally, it justified captivity in the eyes of many English contemporaries, in that the captives traded their freedom for tangible progress toward salvation, moral reformation, and civility. Roger Williams sounded this position in his correspondence with Winthrop and various other colonial leaders and claimants on Pequot labor. Given Williams's own moral qualms about the English right to enslave Indians, he believed that exposure to Christianity had to be at the heart of the master–Indian servant relationship; "all that haue those poore wretches," he recommended, "might be exhorted as to walke wisely and iustly towards them," leading Indians to Christianity through example.[6] He remonstrated with owners of runaways whom he suspected of abusing Indians, although this did not stop him from returning Indians to abusive households; ultimately, the importance of controls on labor and the rights of masters trumped other considerations.

By the early 1640s Massachusetts and Plymouth in particular faced scathing public criticism in England for their mistreatment of Indians and their failure to achieve any substantial Christianization. Rival settlements— English and Dutch—challenged both the hegemony and the legitimacy of Massachusetts and eventually the United Colonies by creating their own alliances and political and social alternatives. Roger Williams in Providence, the Hutchinson Antinomians in Cranston, Newport, and Portsmouth, and the Gortonists (a dissident band led by Samuel Gorton who settled in Warwick) did so by submitting themselves directly to royal protection and by initially forging relatively peaceful ties with the Narragansett Indians, even as their complaints about bullying from Massachusetts provided grist for anti–New England pamphlets from both royalist and Puritan pamphleteers in England. By successfully evangelizing their Pequot servants, Massachusetts, Connecticut, and Plymouth authorities could and did argue that they provided essential services to the Indians superior to those offered by the Dutch in New York or the English in Rhode Island and Virginia.

Other Atlantic commentators hoped that servants might return to their former communities as agents of English civility, creating a bulwark of Anglicized natives who would serve as future allies. Earlier in the decade, English friends and backers of the Massachusetts Bay Company had recommended various forms of cultural outreach. Writing about transatlantic rumors concerning the conversion of the Winnisemet leader John Sagamore "to be civilized and a Christian," Edward Howes, one of John Winthrop Jr.'s scientific associates, praised the focus on elite Indians: "soe you may thereby discouer further into the land haue more frinds and allies, and by the blessinge of god, it may be a greate meanes of civillizinge the meaner sorte."[7] Howes recommended that Winthrop take in Indian servants and teach them English, and then expand the experiment to reach more Indian children and to foster mutual knowledge and loyalty among English and Indians.

Patrick Copeland of Bermuda requested Pequot captives to aid his scheme for creating an Amerindian Atlantic to rival Dutch and Iberian inroads in the Pacific and Indian Oceans. The Scots minister had been involved with the Virginia Company, including the aborted Indian college there. Later, he served as a chaplain for the East India Company in Surat, Indonesia, and observed Dutch Protestant and Jesuit methods of education and evangelism there before taking up a pulpit in Bermuda in 1627. The Dutch and the Jesuits succeeded, Copeland noted, because they aggressively targeted elite natives and because missionaries acquired local languages and printed evangelical materials in those languages. The Jesuits also educated European children and native children together, creating a multilingual community of future missionaries, traders, and diplomats loyal to the imperial metropolis that could be deployed in other colonial ventures. Bemoaning the loss of William Peirce's load of Pequot captives to rival buyers in Providence Island, he requested that more be sent: "I wold have had a care of them to have disposed them to such honest men as should have trained them up in the principles of Religion; and so when they had been fit for your Plantation, have returned them againe to have done God some service in being Instruments to doe some good upon their Country men," Copeland assured Winthrop in 1639.[8]

A mixture of these strategies informed the early plans of the New England Company, a corporation formed in England in 1649 with the backing of the Massachusetts Bay Company to support evangelization of Native Americans. The New England Company raised money for Harvard, for Eliot's expenses and the training and salary of Indian "teachers" in the praying towns. It also provided funds for the translation and publication of catechisms and scripture into Wampanoag, for the education of Indian children, and for a public relations campaign aimed at shoring up the region's battered reputation. Although Indian servants authored these translations and facilitated early outreach services, by the late 1640s Eliot's focus was firmly on nearby free Indian populations rather than the captive/servant population. The United Colonies of New England adopted a formal policy of evangelism directed at "Indianes and Natiues among us"—that is, those living in their own villages whom the English wished to bring under the rule and ultimately the sovereignty of their colonial governments—rather than Indians living in English households. Connecticut appointed interpreter and Pequot War veteran Thomas Stanton to travel out with a minister at least twice each year.[9]

Having prompted evangelization, however, Indian servants played a declining role as helpers and targets. Whereas in the 1630s many colonists had agreed with Copeland that high-status Indian captives might be brought up to serve the English well in freedom as leaders in their home tribes (as some did), subsequently the Company recruited students from among the free population—the Nipmuc, Massachusett, and Martha's Vineyard Wampanoag—rather than the servant population. Eliot and other missionaries still focused on "noble" Indians such as Waban, the Massachusett sachem, but formerly "noble" Indians in servitude quickly lost their cachet for the English as potential converts and preachers. After 1650 the missionaries effectively left the evangelization of servants and slaves to the families they resided in. Notably, a little over a decade removed from the Pequot War, service in English households had begun to color perceptions of class and Indians' status and position in English eyes. Moreover, many servants would never become free. Copeland's optimistic vision of returning acculturated and loyal former captives from Bermuda to New England to spearhead evangelization failed to take into account the main reason for captivity—the desire for Indian labor.

Large investments in grammar school or university education of servants made little sense if Indians' labor and even their persons became commodified, or if they would never be free to lead or evangelize their communities. Certainly the Pequots sent to Providence Island were not there for a period of acculturation and Christianization. Likely they worked as slaves and were either plundered by the Spanish when they conquered the island in 1641, or evacuated along with their masters to the Leeward Islands, Bermuda, or Barbados prior to the Spanish assault. John Sassamon, one of the men who aided the Reverend Eliot's evangelization, was the only former servant of the Pequot War era among the Indians from Massachusetts and Martha's Vineyard who attended Harvard or the various grammar schools at company expense in the 1650s, and Sassamon had entered service before the war, fought alongside the English, and had become free by the time he entered the college. By the eighteenth century many servant indentures for Indian children no longer required masters to provide education and catechism. Some Indian and African servants and slaves became churchgoers, but almost none became church members before 1700.

Interestingly, the handful of girls whose education the company supported followed a reverse path: they ended up bound to service after grammar school rather than deployed as evangelists, teachers, or liaisons—possibly because of the backlash against female religious teaching in Puritan New England after the Antinomian and soon the Baptist and Quaker crises. One grammar school graduate became a servant in John Endecott's Salem household. Servitude would continue to function as a parallel form of acculturation, as ministers and authorities encouraged Christian and non-Christian Indians voluntarily to bind their children to service with English families, or even required them to do so beginning in the late seventeenth century; but the goals of such relationships for the English were not primarily religious and political but rather economic.

According to John Winthrop, the work of converting captive servants had already proceeded in earnest by early 1638, within months of the Indians' arrival. Literacy was a central component of religious competency and the practices of daily piety for Puritans, as well as a mark of civilization that the English settlers thought distinguished them from indigenous people, although not all men and even fewer women achieved it.[10] It is not clear whether Indians received instruction in local grammar schools before the 1640s. Boston had a school by 1636, Salem in 1638, Dorchester in 1639, and Roxbury in 1645; the towns had identified male and female teachers even before these dates in more informal arrangements.[11] Cockenoe, Richard Callicott's captive, had acquired reading competency in English before the Reverend John Eliot encountered him; Eliot had only to teach him to write.

Most education of captives initially took place within the household, as it did for English children. Even very young children and servants were expected to attend "the [holy] word read and expounded in our Families." Bible and catechism centered, these home reading and recitation sessions also reinforced English language skills that formed part of the captive's daily work life. Many servants and slaves later testified to the power of these home exhortations, although others "took little notice."[12] Fathers held responsibility for religious instruction, but mothers and mistresses led these weekly or nightly "family duties," and women staffed informal dame schools in Dorchester and other communities where captives lived. Indian captives also attended church and had "to give us account of the Sermons they heare" after services. Thoughtful hearing and repeating of sermons and scriptures remained central to progressing through the stages of conversion that all Puritans hoped to experience: conviction of one's own sinfulness, an affective and terrifying "sense of Gods Displeasure," and feelings of hopelessness and despair that prepared the soul for acceptance of divine grace.[13]

The acculturation project met with setbacks almost immediately. In February 1638, John Winthrop reported that "the Indians, which were in our families, were much frightened with Hobbamock (as they call the devil) appearing to them in divers shapes, and persuading them to forsake the English, and not to come at the assemblies or learn to read, etc."[14] Although Winthrop, Edward Winslow, and other leaders promoted an identification between Kiehtan/Nickommo/Cauntantowwit and the Christian god, and Hobbamock and the Christian devil, the identities of these and other supernatural beings in the Algonquian pantheon were more complex. Hobbamock was neither all bad nor all good. Associated with death, the spirit could help humans communicate with the supernatural and therefore provide insight and power to those who saw or dreamed about him. He never appeared when English were present. The search for spiritual contact with Hobbamock formed the center of some male coming-of-age rituals. Among the Wampanoag and Narragansett, young men who could see or channel Hobbamock held important positions as counselors or *pnieses* to sachems, and sometimes played important roles in battle.[15] Visions regarding Hobbamock might therefore have signaled a form of cultural resistance to Christianity and psychological regrouping on the captives' part, or the emergence of new leaders within the captive community, or even the influence of non-captive Indians and visitors from nearby communities, since sources allude to pressure from free Indians to resist Christianization. The captives may also have reacted to tensions in the English community at that moment: sightings of Hobbamock followed the banishment of some Antinomians and the disenfranchisement of others.

Despite this early resistance, according to the Puritan divines eager to report success in evangelization, "our Opening and pressing the Word upon their Consciences" had an effect: some of the earliest captives became literate, and at least a few pledged outward allegiance to Christian tenets. The stories of several captive converts appeared in *New England's First Fruits* (1643), the first in a series of eleven promotional pamphlets on the Puritan evangelical efforts collectively known as the "Eliot Tracts." Most of the later tracts highlight the efforts of Eliot, Mayhew, and others to convert Massachusett, Wampanoag, and Nipmuc Indians, and eventually to gather Indian "praying towns" at Hassanemesit, Nahanton, Gay Head (Aquinnah), and Natick.

This first publication predated these organized efforts. Its author or authors remain unknown; Henry Dunster, future president of Harvard College, is one candidate, but a more likely hypothesis credits Hugh Peter of Salem and Thomas Weld, pastor of the Roxbury Church, who were representing the colony as its agents in London. Authorship by the latter two would also account for the inclusion of captives' stories in the tract, since both men owned Pequots and therefore had intimate awareness of efforts to evangelize them. Indeed, other than the old story of Sagamore John from the 1620s, captive evangelism was all that New Englanders had to offer their international audience when describing their outreach toward local Indians. After rehashing the story of Sagamore John's interest in Christianity, *First Fruits* focused on captives and slaves as exemplary early converts: "divers of the Indians Children Boyes and Girles in our houses . . . handy in their businesse, and can speak our language familiarly; divers of whom can read English and begin to understand in their measure, the ground of Christian Religion."

Nan, "Mr. Weld's captive Indian," might have been one of the children referred to. Nan was "hopeful"—that is, had experienced signs of grace that confirmed her chance at salvation. When she died in August 1646, the Roxbury church listed Nan among deaths in the congregation, although she was not a member and the entry for her and for other Indians lacked the details included for English deaths. Another Christian Indian captive in Roxbury died a few days later: a man named Ezbon, who "having lived ten year among the English, could read, desired to know God." Both had served ten years with no sign that release was imminent, and Nan still had the qualifier of "captive."[16] Neither Nan nor Ezbon, nor any other Indian servants, were baptized or admitted into any level of church fellowship at Roxbury in the seventeenth century.

Although *First Fruits* can hardly be viewed as an unbiased account of Indian servitude, it communicated English hopes if not Native American realities. The converted Indian captives actually performed better than their English counterparts, "and being industrious in their Calling, will much Complaine of other servants' idleness, and reprove them."[17] The writer stressed the converts' newfound "love" of the English, their preference for English society over that of their former friends and relatives, and their emotional attachment to their new lives, both secular and in Christ. In this telling, Pequot servants thirsted for sermons and for household service; "convinced that our condition and ways were farre better than theirs," they "cannot indure to return anymore to the Indians." Presaging a genre repeated later in the publication series, and in the works of Experience Mayhew, *First Fruits* contained several spiritual biographies of converted servants. One young man from Salem ran away from his master, but then returned despite knowing he would receive harsh corporal punishment. Another youngster, an "Indian maid at Salem," through terror of her own damnation "grew very carefull of her carriage [behavior], proved industrious in her place, and so continued." Others visited ministers, cried when prevented from attending church, and prayed "in secret," a sign of the genuineness of their religious fervor.[18]

The account also mentions a "Blackamore maid," almost certainly a slave named Dorcas in Israel Stoughton's household, whose successful testimony of faith to the Dorchester Church led that congregation to admit her to church membership in May 1641. Stoughton owned several Pequots, and the authors of *First Fruits* credited Dorcas with working to convert Indian servants: she "hath with teares exhorted some of the *Indians* that live among us to embrace Ieusus Christ, saying how willing he would be to receive them, even as he had received her."[19]

By converting to Christianity, Dorcas and the Indian converts gave up membership in other communities—communities that focused more on maintaining their native cultures. Nearby Indians, free and captive, mocked converts, which suggests the latter may have experienced further isolation from their compatriots. Some Indians merely added the Christian god to existing systems, and continued to maintain other spiritual beliefs and ceremonials. For them, Christianization was an outer layer they could abandon in other contexts. Still, converts like Dorcas gained important patrons and supporters as well as other privileges, including time away from work. For Indians brought into households as young children, the pressure to convert and the consequences of not at least appearing to accept Christianity must have been grave.

Other advantages accrued to adult converts. Indian and African slaves appear more frequently in church records in the eighteenth century, generally as couples and families, baptizing their children and sometimes achieving degrees of church membership. Church involvement might lead to solemnizing a marriage; marriage or a child's baptism might make a master or mistress more reluctant to sell spouses or minor children of married, Christian slaves. In 1653, after nearly two decades as a slave, Dorcas was sold by her master to Aaron Cooke of Boston, and her former congregation discussed raising money to purchase her freedom. They sent Ensign Foster and two deacons first to see "what the [magistrates] could do by power"—in other words, whether she could be freed by legislative fiat; failing that, the committee was to negotiate with Cooke about the possibility of purchasing her. What legal grounds they hoped to invoke and the overall outcome of this effort remain unclear. The Roxbury church released Dorcas for membership in Boston a year later, suggesting she stayed in the latter city, presumably still Cooke's slave.[20] Church membership offered a kind of fictive kinship and status, but it seldom fundamentally altered the slave or servant's existence.

Success in a Hybrid Society

Another group of captives chose a path between assimilation and rejection of English culture. They used their time as servants to acquire cultural capital and political connections, which they then deployed for personal or collective ends. They achieved not complete autonomy but rather a degree of independence, ironically through dependent relationships in the new hybrid Indian/European world. In 1638, English forces under Richard Callicott, Daniel Patrick, and John Underhill captured a Long Island Montauket Indian who had been visiting Pequot relatives. Callicott specifically claimed him. His name, Cockenoe, signified in Algonquian "teacher" or "one with knowledge," and he confirmed its aptness through his quick acquisition of English, as well as the local dialects of nearby Wampanoag/Massachusett Indians.[21] Cockenoe served Callicott for eleven years as an interpreter and guide. Given the length of the term, he was likely a child of thirteen or fourteen when captured; although length of service was often random and dependent on the inclinations of individual masters, at least some Indians captured as children appear to have gained their freedom at age twenty-five. Cockenoe may have attended school in Dorchester; the town paid a female schoolmaster to teach children. He certainly became literate in English. Callicott eventually offered Cockenoe's aid to John Eliot, and Cockenoe helped translate English prayers, sermons, and catechisms for Eliot's oral preaching and, eventually, his printed Indian grammar and "Indian Bible." He served as interpreter during Eliot's first public evangelical efforts at preaching to the Wampanoag under Waban. Eliot recalled in 1649 that "there is an Indian living with Mr. Richard Calicott of Dorchester, who was taken in the Pequott warres, though belonging to Long Island. This Indian is ingenious, can read, and I taught him to write, which he quickly learnt. . . . He was the first that I made use of to teach me words, and to be my interpreter." By that time Cockenoe had left Callicott's household, and Eliot wondered "what use he now maketh of" his literacy skills. Eliot in fact hoped that Cockenoe would become the first Indian church member in his Dorchester congregation. He had planned to recommend Cockenoe and was bitterly disappointed when the latter chose another path.[22]

Rather than pursuing assimilation, Cockenoe chose to return to a leadership role in indigenous communities. He parlayed his training and experience into a forty-year career as an interpreter for English and Native American clients on Long Island and Connecticut, particularly the Montauket sachem Wyandanch, to whom Cockenoe became an important adviser—and a brother-in-law through Cockenoe's marriage to Wyandanch's sister. Cockenoe's name appears on numerous land deeds, treaties, and records of negotiation between English colonial leaders, individual buyers, and the Montauket Indians. Whereas Thomas Stanton had been one of the only interpreters available to English and Indians before 1645, now Cockenoe and other Manissean and Pequot captives who passed through service in English households offered other avenues for communication, diplomacy, and business with Indians. Cockenoe worked with Lion Gardiner and the New England settlements at East Hampton as a cultural intermediary and agent in land sales. Gardiner and the town offered the Montauket and Shinnecock Indians alliance and protection against the incursions of Uncas and Ninigret (Ayanemo), each of whom who sought to place the Long Island Indians and any Pequot refugees among them under his own sachemate. The United Colonies even paid Captain John Youngs to cruise Long Island Sound and prevent Mohegan and Niantic canoe attacks on the Montauket in the 1650s.[23] Cockenoe probably helped Montauket sachem Wyandanch craft his accommodationist approach to relations with local English and the United Colonies. Still, for the Montauket the strategies that Cockenoe advocated came at a very high cost. By the end of the seventeenth century, most Shinnecock and Montauket lands were in English hands.

Eliot turned to John Sassamon, Callicott's other Indian servant, who had fought in the war on the English side, for assistance with his evangelization and publication projects. Despite earlier signs of independence, such as his marriage to Sassacus's daughter, Sassamon took a different path from Cockenoe—a path of assimilation. He worked with Eliot on translations, and Eliot and the New England Company eventually sent him to Harvard in 1653 along with elite Indians from among the Massachusett and the Martha's Vineyard Wampanoag.[24] The former servant appeared to be on track to become a missionary or leader in his own right, the kind of acculturated, devout individual that Eliot and Weld had envisioned at the outset of their project. Harvard expelled Sassamon for drunkenness, however, and his career took a different turn. He became a less successful version of Cockenoe, taking jobs as scribe or interpreter for different sachems, including Metacom (Philip), the Narragansett leader. Sassamon's closeness to the English and his Christianity became a liability in these roles, and eventually his body turned up under the ice in a pond. The English ruled his death a murder and eventually executed several associates of Philip for the crime, thus inciting King Philip's War. Sassamon's story pointed to the difficulties of being a cultural go-between with no clear footing in either camp.

Other Indians moved from service in English households into positions of relative power and independence among both English and Indian communities. One Pequot man, Cassacinamon, emerged during the postwar period of 1637–38 as a member of Uncas's retinue, possibly as one of the group of Pequot captives whom Uncas had claimed as his reward. Most historians assume he had some royal kin connections because he became a leader among Pequots in the 1640s, which would have required some other legitimating factors, usually kinship networks. Williams records him as a kinsman of the Massachusett sachem Cushnamekin, though a more likely scenario is that they were in-laws related through marriage. Uncas sent him to Boston in the spring of 1638 to negotiate for the high-status female captives whom Winthrop had claimed, offering a substantial bride price.[25] Marie, Joane, and Jane were reportedly the daughters of a sunk-squaw, or female Montauket leader, who helped engineer the plan. Several regional leaders, including Uncas, Miantonomo, and Ayanemo, sought to marry one or more of them as a means of enhancing their regional influence over the Long Island Indians. According to another of Winthrop's Indian servants, when diplomacy and offers of wampum failed, on Uncas's orders Cassacinamon stayed behind and became Governor John Winthrop's "servant," "to perswade and worck their Escape" as a household insider. With Cassacinamon's help, the women escaped out the window in dramatic fashion.[26]

Marie and Jane joined Uncas's settlement, and the sachem married either one or both of the sisters, while Joane married another of Winthrop's Indian servants, Reprieve. A grateful Uncas reportedly compensated Cassacinamon for his activities with ten fathoms of wampum, although their relationship soon deteriorated. Winthrop sought the return of the runaways for over a year, but the revelation of Cassacinamon's role in their escape does not seem to have damaged his relationship with the English family, and Cassacinamon remained a servant of the Winthrops through 1645. During this period, he experienced an unusual degree of freedom. He took the name Robin and served as a diplomat and negotiator for the colony, taking messages to Roger Williams and various Narragansett and Mohegan groups.

Cassacinamon tried to use his connections in Boston to shape colonial policy toward those Pequots who had survived the war and evaded English enslavement. Despite the 1638 Hartford Treaty's insistence on terminating Pequots' identity and ties with their old lands, many of the Pequots who settled in Narragansett, Niantic, and Mohegan territory maintained a distinct identity. Indian towns and villages were often composed of scattered, smaller family-based hamlets, and some Pequots appear to have created ethnically separate enclaves within these other territories. Others avoided capture and resettlement and never left Pequot territory. Within a few years, English and other Indians began to complain that the exiled Pequots were filtering back to their former homes. Just as they had contended over Pequot captives and refugees during the war, now Uncas, Miantonomo, Ayanemo, aspiring sachems such as Wequashcook (a Pequot/Niantic ally of the Narragansetts who gathered a band in the former Pequot country of Pawcatuck), and various English governments pursued conflicting strategies toward the reconstituting Pequot communities. Each of the competing sachems wished to keep the Pequots under his personal control. New Haven and Connecticut leaders wanted to keep the Pequots from returning to their lands, where they might challenge English ownership or pose a future military threat.

Within this complex and often fraught context, Robin Cassacinamon emerged after 1640 as a leader of the newly formed Mashantucket Pequots who had settled in the vicinity of John Winthrop Jr.'s Nameaug plantation. Winthrop had extensive experience in Connecticut, having founded Saybrook as a base for Connecticut River Indian trade as an agent for the Saye and Sele family in 1636. Several English outposts courted the younger Winthrop and offered him lucrative land grants and other incentives for settlement, but he continued to serve in the Massachusetts General Court. From the court he accepted several grants that Massachusetts claimed by right of conquest over the Pequots: Fisher's Island in Long Island Sound, and another site near the mouth of the Thames River across from present-day New London, Nameaug. John Winthrop Jr.'s contemporaries jokingly called him "the Sagamore of Agawam," a reference to his estate near Springfield, but this jibe encapsulated a truth: Winthrop chose to plant at Nameaug because of, not in spite of, the presence of the Pequots. Local Indians provided crucial support, food sources, guide and transportation services, and trade opportunities. According to Winthrop, Robin Cassacinamon actually helped him choose the site for his plantation. Relationships formed via ser-

FIGURE 8.   Portrait of John Winthrop Jr. Oil on canvas by unidentified artist of the school of Sir Peter Lely or William Dobson, 1634–35. Courtesy of the Massachusetts Historical Society.

vitude proved essential to the success of both men's ventures in the coming decade.

Winthrop drew upon a variety of Old and New World models for his economic and leadership strategies at Nameaug.[27] From one perspective, Winthrop's operation resembled a Spanish *encomienda*, an estate where Indians worked for him and provided other services, including military assistance, in return for his patronage and protection from both English and Indians who claimed them as tributaries or threatened them with violence. His arrangements with the Indians also resembled informal tenancies or manorial relations. Between 1640 and 1700, Benjamin Church, Lion Gardiner, John Mason, and other military leaders followed similar paths in creating plantations that employed a mix of Indian and European subordinates housed nearby who occupied various points along a spectrum from freedom to servitude and slavery. Winthrop, Gardiner, Church, and similar figures gained title to land through conquest, cession, and agreements with Indians. They organized diverse enterprises (mining, livestock raising, farming, whaling) that deployed Indian and European labor; dispensed justice as local justices of the peace and court officials; and extended credit and goods to Indians in exchange for labor and marketable commodities.

From another perspective, though, Winthrop and later figures such as Church behaved much like other sachems who competed for power, influence, territory, and tributaries in the post–Pequot War era. His rivals included Indian leaders as well as the other English colonies that vied over jurisdiction of the former Pequot territory, particularly Connecticut. Winthrop's own comments suggest that he viewed Uncas—by now an important client of Connecticut colony—as a competitor; he complained that in some ways he exercised even less authority than Uncas. Indeed, Uncas attacked and sacked Pequot towns several times between 1646 and 1649, taking goods and "captives"—sometimes with the endorsement and even participation of English officials from New Haven and Connecticut, including John Mason and Thomas Stanton—and in the process plundered English households, cornfields, and wampum stashes at Nameaug, Noank, and Fisher's Island. This violent action on Uncas's part represented a clear signal to Winthrop and Cassacinamon of who really held regional power. Leaders in New Haven and Connecticut, worried about both the potential of Massachusetts Bay's involvement in Pequot country and the danger of a revived Pequot nation, backed Uncas in this struggle at meetings of the United Colonies of New England, the newly formed regional confederacy that oversaw collective Indian diplomacy.

In all these struggles, Cassacinamon's band aided the younger Winthrop. The Nameaug settlement attracted a stream of deserters from Uncas and the Niantics, weakening those centers and strengthening Winthrop's. The Indians made Winthrop's plantation sustainable economically. Cassacinamon helped Winthrop negotiate land transfers from local Indians in ways that incorporated indigenous peoples' expectations of continued usage rights and reflected their rituals of agreement and consensus.[28] In return, Winthrop pressed the Nameaug Pequots' case to English authorities, arguing that "if the Pequotts be not taken vnder the English, If these Indians that we must live neere be still vnder Vuncus command, there wilbe noe living for English there."[29] Even as Connecticut moved to defend the interest of its own client, Uncas, Winthrop asserted the Pequots' right to hunt and fish in nearby territories.

Cassacinamon, for his part, stressed the Winthrop connection in all his dealings with English authorities. The two brought their grievances about Uncas's "vnjustice and tyranny" before the Commissioners of the United Colonies, occasionally appearing together; each time the commissioners identified "Robin alias Casmomom" as Winthrop's current or former servant, "someone who has worked for the English." His period of servitude gave him standing that other Indians lacked. Cassacinamon also used the Pequots' ongoing work for the English at New London to excuse them from tributary service to Uncas. He took messages from Winthrop to leaders such as Roger Williams, who viewed him as a trustworthy ally and Winthrop's "man." When Uncas demanded that Cassacinamon and other Pequots accompany him on a punitive expedition to Long Island, "Robin alledged that he had promised himself to Mr. Winthrop, his former master to build him a wigwam." Similarly, Pequots hunted and fished on territory claimed by Uncas because "Mr Thomas Peeters [Winthrop's friend and the town minister] beinge ill and the rest of the Plantation wanting, wished Robin to go a hunting," and Peters issued a "warrant" as a permit.[30] Cassacinamon also presented the Nameaug Pequots as a buffer against the Narragansetts and Niantics, and as possible intermediaries with the Mohawks during periods of escalating English fears about Indian conflict in 1646, 1649, and 1655. He and his followers were key military auxiliaries during King Philip's War.[31] Indeed, through the mid-eighteenth century, Connecticut had trouble keeping the proportion of Indians in expeditions and later in the provincial forces *below* a desired target of 20 percent, so important were they to recruiters and captains.[32]

Cassacinamon and Winthrop appeared at numerous sessions of the Commissioners of the United Colonies in the 1640s and early 1650s to advocate for their common interests. In the end, Cassacinamon petitioned the commission to make him independent of Uncas and to excuse his people permanently from their tribute responsibilities to the Mohegans (and by extension to the English in general). Cassacinamon and other Pequots in these debates raised interesting questions about how long reparations should continue, a question with implications for Indian slavery. In response, the commissioners ordered that male Pequot children henceforth would not be liable for the crimes—and tribute payment—that their elders had incurred. No one at the time associated these limits on culpability with the terms that Indian slaves would serve; the heritability of the captives' bound status remained an open question. Tribute was both a tax—an acknowledgment of

English sovereignty—and a form of reparations. Cassacinamon argued that the Indians had paid two generations of reparations and should be relieved of further obligations.

In 1654, the commissioners agreed. They relieved Cassacinamon of his obligations to Uncas or "any Indian Sachem further than the Commissioners should direct"; he was to be "taken under the protection of the English and freed from tribute." The next year, the commissioners named him governor of both the Nameaug and Noank Pequots, and during the following decade Winthrop and the United Colonies granted them lands that eventually became the Mashantucket reservation. As a Pequot Indian "governor" or quasi-independent leader, Cassacinamon remained subject to the English but not to Uncas. Less than twenty years after the Treaty of Hartford had extinguished the Pequot name and banished the people from their territory, Cassacinamon had reassembled a band in their former territory and gained legal recognition and protection from the English.[33]

Another captive who negotiated a successful passage from servant to influential leader after the conflict was Jaguante (or Jacquontu) Tunkawatten, a Manissean Indian from Block Island. Evidence suggests that he may have been of elite status, related to the Manissean sachem Jacquontu, whose name he took later in life. Tunkawatten was visiting relatives among the Pequot when the English captured him. Christened "Reprieve," he became a servant of John Winthrop Sr.[34] Like Robin Cassacinamon, Reprieve appears to have enjoyed considerable freedom of movement. In autumn of 1637, he journeyed from Boston to Rhode Island, Block Island, Connecticut, and central Massachusetts over several months, gathering intelligence on Pequot survivors. Roger Williams commented on his leisurely trip, which included visits to family, friends, and female companions—behavior likely to incur serious punishment for an English servant. Rather than advising punishment, Williams merely suggested that Winthrop limit Reprieve's sojourns because contact with other Indians undermined efforts to "reform," convert, and acculturate him, "for you can not belieue how hard it is for him to escape so much evill & especially vncleanenes when he is with them."[35] Interestingly, Williams—along with other masters and observers—did not recommend isolating captive Indians from their friends and family. Instead, he urged Winthrop to encourage Reprieve's Indian friends and family to visit him in Boston, hoping that the environment would better help the servant resist temptation.

Some of Reprieve's travels were at Winthrop's behest. The Indian requested a written "word" from Roger Williams testifying to his role as Winthrop's representative, which Reprieve used as a passport to travel through the confu-

FIGURE 9.   Native American sachem, ca. 1700, artist unknown. It is thought to be the Niantic sachem Ninigret (Ayanemo) but is possibly a portrait of Robin Cassacinamon painted at his friend John Winthrop Jr.'s behest. Photograph by Erik Gould, courtesy of the Museum of Art, Rhode Island School of Design, Providence.

sion of postwar conflicts and contested territories in southern New England. Ayanemo apparently regarded Reprieve as a spy intent on helping the English recover those Pequots who had settled among the Niantics and Narragansetts; he threatened Reprieve and expelled him from Niantic country. Ayanemo also resented the Manisseans for their submission to Massachusetts Bay, since the Niantics worried that English and Narragansett policy aimed to undermine their influence by peeling off former tributaries such as the Block Islanders. Reprieve's visit coincided with a large tribute payment from Jacquontu, the Block Island sachem, to Massachusetts Bay.

Reprieve gathered intelligence for personal use and traded information with other potential patrons. In October or November 1637 he made arrangements with the Montauk Squaw Sachem to marry one of her daughters, if he could free her from captivity, a move that would enhance his claims to power within the Indian community after his period of servitude. He assisted Robin Cassacinamon in freeing the Long Island Indian females from Winthrop's Boston household. Williams reported that as a reward "for the furtherance of the business," Reprieve indeed received one of the women, Joane, as his wife.[36] One of Winthrop's other Indian servants accused Reprieve of advising the women on their escape route, recommending that they travel through Nipmuc rather than Narragansett country, "because once before escaping through the Narigansett Countrey, himselfe was sent back, by the Nariganset Sachims."[37] This earlier attempted escape indicates that some elements of his condition in Winthrop's household proved difficult, but ultimately he seems not to have viewed servitude as onerous, since he returned to Boston with a brother who voluntarily submitted to Winthrop's service. Reprieve and his brother seemingly regarded service in a high-ranking English household in the same way that elite English youths would have: as a source of potential patronage, training, and information, rather than a demeaning and exploitative relationship.[38] At least one other Indian, Oldway Necawnimeyat, expressed a willingness to enter Winthrop's service in a similar fashion in the summer of 1638. By the mid-seventeenth century Reprieve had apparently taken the name of the former sachem Jacquontu and had become one of the leaders of the Block Island Manisseans.

The experiences of Cockenoe, Reprieve, and Robin Cassacinamon illustrate that servitude in the wake of the Pequot War could be a finite experience that enhanced rather than diminished an individual Indian's status. They enjoyed autonomy, maintained kin relationships, traveled, and married, all of which made them exceptional even in comparison to English servants. For these men, captivity and service in English households provided clientage connections with prominent leaders, along with opportunities to use their existing skills and acquire new ones. All three parlayed these connections into positions of power and influence among Indians instead of remaining in English settlements. Still, they reentered Indian societies where Native American/Euro-American hybridity and interdependency were becoming a way of life. As leaders they served as brokers of ongoing English and Indian encounters, alliances, and economic relationships—including the transfer of land and sometimes sovereignty to the English.

Flight and Resistance

The success of Cockenoe, Cassacinamon, and Reprieve in navigating the new hybrid New England represented one end of a spectrum; most captives faced a reduced set of options in both servitude and freedom. A few Indians resisted acculturation and captivity altogether by running away. Indian women in particular appear frequently in the early record as runaways, and often as repeat runaways. Female servants in the households of Richard Callicott, John Winthrop, William Blackstone, and Samuel Coles all ran away in the first months and even weeks of their captivity. They sought to return to former homes, or to join relatives residing among the Narragansetts or Mohegans, a journey of fifty miles or more from Boston.

Roger Williams became the English "point man" in the recovery of runaways from Plymouth, Massachusetts Bay, and from nearby settlements in Rhode Island. In this capacity, he pressured Miantonomo and Ayanemo to help him seek out runways and to hand them over to the English rather than sheltering them. Such negotiations remained especially tricky given the competition for numbers and power among Miantonomo, Ayanemo, Uncas, and many smaller sachems, and the value of female captives. Under pressure, Miantonomo found Callicott's captive "girle" and handed her over to Williams in late August/early September 1637. Williams had returned a runaway boy to the household sometime earlier in the summer; he informed Callicott that he himself would be happy to take the children "if you be minded to put either of them away . . . Otherwise I wish you much Comfort in the keeping of them."[39] The Narragansetts found Coles's Pequot woman with a companion, an unidentified girl from Winnisemet, near Boston. They may have fled together from the city, although the Winnisemet girl identified another runaway captive from William Blackstone's household as the one who had "inticed her" to escape. This latter girl had fled to Narragansett country once before, and it is possible that Blackstone relocated to Rhode Island not just for religious freedom but to avoid losing her again. The three Boston women arrived in a Narragansett village extremely footsore and "allmost starved." Other fugitives may not have been so lucky; the Narragansetts reported that some "Runnawayes perished in the woods" during the difficult journey or as they continued to hide themselves near Providence for fear of recapture.[40]

This claim that escapees died may also have been a ruse to foil their recapture. English allies who had received official shares in captives—the Narragansetts, the Mohegans, the Niantics, and individuals such as Wequashcook—sought to increase their captives' numbers by sheltering runaways. Miantonomo had expressed a strong sense of injury over what he viewed as an unfair division of the war's booty, since he and his brother Canonicus had captured many Pequots. At a time when approximately ten runaways sheltered nearby in July and August 1637, Miantonomo and his relatives asked for more female captives, and even offered to "buy 1 or 2 from some English man." Meanwhile, when Williams pressed him to round up the runaways, the sachem responded evasively and claimed that various ritual and family obligations had delayed his efforts. Questioned about the three high-status young women who fled Winthrop's Boston home, the Narragansetts at first reported no knowledge of them and only later acknowledged the girls' presence in the area. When his followers finally brought the runaways to Miantonomo for return to the English, at least two of the women managed to escape again. Roger Williams searched for them fruitlessly over the next several years and many times got wind of their whereabouts in Rhode Island and Connecticut, but found his usual Indian allies and messengers reluctant to pursue the matter to his satisfaction. "No Indian Meanes will be able to effect their returne but that the English must fetch them," he informed Winthrop nearly a year later.[41] The other Indian women from Boston—Samuel Coles's, Blackstone's, and the unknown Winnisemet servant—were not as lucky. The Narragansetts eventually turned them over to Williams, who restored them to their owners—but not before Bay Colony authorities had all three branded on the shoulder with a hot iron, a punishment that also marked them permanently with the sign of the runaway, making future escape more difficult.

Suspicious of Indian intransigence in these matters, colonial leaders put enormous pressure on the Narragansetts, Mohegans, and other groups to return servants who ran away from the English. A series of treaties between 1638 and 1650 severely restricted the ability of free Indians to protect runaways. These measures created new questions as Pequot captives approached the end of their first decade in service: were the Indians captives, servants, or slaves, and what would that distinction entail? When agents of the United Colonies demanded the return of the captive girl who sought refuge at Fort Hoop, Governor Kieft—hardly a protector of Indians—questioned English claims about the girl's status. Kieft's comments went to the heart of the legal weakness of English claims to noncombatant Indians. "She is no slaue but a free weoman," he wrote, "because she was neither taken in war nor paid for in price."[42] The commissioners' response was succinct: "such a servant is part of her Master's estate, & a more considerable part than a beast." Like livestock—or a slave—in their eyes the Indian woman had become property without social identity or expectations of the eventual freedom and civil status that English servants could expect.

In 1647, John Winthrop Jr. received a letter through intermediaries from Captain Robert Morris of Portsmouth, Rhode Island. Morris, a former Bostonian, a member of the Ancient and Honorable Artillery Company, and a Pequot War veteran, used all his connections and social capital to get the younger Winthrop's attention; he had two friends contact Winthrop about his problem. Captain Morris's captive Pequot "maid" had run away, and he thought she was headed into Winthrop's area.

Morris's sense of personal betrayal and surprise at the girl's actions, ten years into captivity, are palpable in his letter. He had received her as pay from "the Bay" for his military service. The girl's grandfather, Sequin, was sachem of the Wangunk Indians, who had nominally supported the English during the Pequot War. Sequin's son, Sonquassen, had even brought in twenty Pequot captives.[43] But other accounts associated Sequin with an incident that directly preceded the war—the Wethersfield massacre, in which Indians killed nine English men and three women, and took the two female captives. Connecticut authorities declined to punish Sequin for these crimes in 1638. In the confusion that attended the war, however, and presumably while her grandfather and father were away fighting with the English against the Pequots, the girl had fallen into English hands, a not uncommon story. Sequin's exoneration did not procure her release. Morris still referred to the girl as a "child of death"—a biblical phrase that denoted the fact her servitude atoned for her "father's" (or in this case her grandfather's) crimes and also a reference to an English common law principle that servitude represented a lesser form of punishment than death.

According to the captain, his captive owed him her life twice over: Either because of injuries to her or illness, right after she entered his household Morris had incurred huge medical expenses, "keeping hir 2 yeares vnder the sirgens hand." She had a large cut under her eye still. Meanwhile, his family had treated her well; she had been "well kept and much tendered" by both master and mistress. The Morrises had made no effort to cut her off from her family and community, but rather "louvingly enterteyned" the girl's uncle and father, "On quassen" (probably Sonquassen, now sachem of the Sequin Indians at Hartford), and his wife on numerous occasions. Morris had even been willing to allow the girl to marry, which generally all servants were forbidden to do—possibly a marriage arranged by Sonquassen, or possibly the girl's own choice of spouse. Morris apparently offered Sonquassen a deal: to give the girl up in marriage if Sonquassen paid Morris a significant amount of wampum or purchased an African slave to take her place. This was only fair, reasoned Morris, "for they them sellves mak vs pay ransomes for oures [w]hom they tak Captiues."[44] Instead, father and uncle "inticed" the girl away to Hartford "to my gret dammeg." Now Morris's wife was "Agged and weack and is in great destres for want of a seruant." Morris's intercessors asked John Winthrop Jr. to help track down the girl. Failing that, could they grant him money "to buy a neger in her place?"

This girl's history—the questionable legal status of her captivity in the first place; her presumably affective relationship with the Morrises; her continued contact with many free relatives; and her flight after ten years of captivity— illustrates the many faces of Pequot servitude. The presumption that an African slave could replace the girl, alongside the "child of death" language, raise questions about her ultimate fate if she had stayed in Morris's household. Morris's language and actions implied that she would have been a slave for life. During the decades after the war, as colonists held some captives past the typical servant term and took new Indians as servants and slaves under questionable legal circumstances, the difference between English and Indian servitude began to widen. At the same time, English labor needs continued to grow. In the mid-seventeenth century, Indians became integrated into the English economy in many essential ways as day laborers, but with limited control over the terms of work. As the changing framework of Indian slavery and servitude reshaped Native American and Euro-American relations in New England, many individuals would see their status slowly erode by the end of the century.

CHAPTER 5

"An Indian to help in the work"

The Importance of Indian Labor in the New England Economy

In the 1640s, the New England colonies' relationships with local Indians and with each other shifted. During this period, members of the new security alliance, the United Colonies of New England—Connecticut, Plymouth, New Haven, and Massachusetts Bay—moved to assert sovereignty over the Indians in the ever-expanding areas that the English claimed. This took the form of pressure on Indians to sign treaties and cede land, as well as a tightening of tributary relations and demands for wampum or other reparations related to the war or to subsequent disputes or "crimes" against the English. The push for sovereignty had a legal component: all five colonies, including Rhode Island, slowly moved the mediation of disputes between English and Indians, and accusations of criminal activity on the part of Indians, away from diplomatic solutions and into colonial assemblies and courtrooms. These developments had consequences for the practice of Indian servitude. The labor needs that drove captive roundups in 1637 and 1638 had hardly slackened, and Indian labor remained an attractive target. Given the lack of regulation surrounding Pequot captivity, many Pequots remained servants as long as their owners declined to free them—or unless they freed themselves. The colonies moved aggressively to close off avenues for runaways in the 1640s.

Massachusetts revised its 1641 legal code in 1648, but the new Lawes and Liberties of 1648 restated the definitions of slavery offered in the previous document, which left much open to interpretation. Man stealing remained illegal, and slavery was supposed to be limited to captives in a just war, "or those who come to us" as slaves. With no active wars against the Indians, there would be no new supply of captives under the "just war" causation, although rumors of war brought threats of enslavement. The second clause left open some other possible supplies of labor—enslaved Africans and Indians from outside the region; but those, too, presumably had to be enslaved in a just war. Finally, Massachusetts had inserted a clause in the original law that did not limit enslavement to these cases, and which also gave the government the right to sentence individuals to slavery for unspecified reasons. Together, these developments pushed additional Indians into involuntary servitude and put limits on the freedoms of those already held.

Indian Relations at Mid-century

The battle for captives during the Pequot War led Connecticut, Plymouth, and Massachusetts to write controls into the treaty that ended the conflict. In a conference with the Narragansetts and Mohegans that produced the Treaty of Hartford, Connecticut officials John Haynes and Roger Ludlow made a priority of securing Pequot territory for Connecticut. After that point, however, the negotiators devised a treaty that had more to do with Narragansett and Mohegan behavior as well as English oversight than anything else. The treaty instructed the Narragansetts and Mohegans to take no action in case of "injuries or wrongs" committed by the other, but rather to seek English mediation. English decisions and English justice would be binding. The treaty also included a fugitive slave clause. After discussing the disposition of territory and captives, it noted that "it is always expected that the English Captives are forthwith to be delivered to the English such as belong to Connecticutt to the Sachems there and such as belong to the Massachusets."[1] The treaty did not stop Uncas, Ayanemo, and Miantonomo from trying to secure captives, nor did it stop the surviving Pequots from returning to their former territories under leaders such as Robin Cassacinamon. It did, however, create legal cover for the New England colonies as they pressed their case for the return of runaways.

Competition over captives and former Pequot tributaries was one of several issues that divided the Mohegans and Narragansetts during the early 1640s. Miantonomo chafed under the requirements regarding not only return of runaways but also English mediation. He complained—quite accurately, in Roger Williams's view—that the English favored Uncas in every dispute between the Indian groups, to the Narragansetts' extreme disadvantage.

Miantonomo believed that the 1638 Tripartite Treaty guaranteed the rights of Narragansetts and their tributaries to hunt in Pequot country, yet the English and the Mohegans both claimed exclusive rights. Despite the essential support that the Narragansetts had supplied to the English war effort, now they seemed less essential to maintaining the spoils of victory. Massachusetts Bay speculators had designs on territory in Narragansett Bay, and the Bay Colony also challenged the Narragansetts' hegemony by poaching several of Miantonomo's tributaries in Pawtuxet and Shawomet, whose sachems made submissions to the Massachusetts Bay government.[2] Connecticut officials backed Uncas so fully, and saw him as such a key strategic partner, that even when Massachusetts Bay authorities saw the justice of Miantonomo's grievances, they did little to ameliorate his concerns.

There is evidence that Miantonomo himself tried to step out of the constraints and animosities created by enforced English mediation. He appealed directly to the Mohegans, Niantics, Montaukets, and even the Mohawks—"all the Sachems from east to west"—to renew old alliances and create new ones in order to prevent English domination. To cement alliance with Uncas, Miantonomo proposed to marry the Mohegan's daughter.[3] It was in response to these tensions—both the Mohegan-Narragansett conflict and worries about Miantonomo anchoring an anti-English Indian alliance—as well as rising concerns over Dutch conflicts with Indians in New York and western Connecticut, that four of the New England governments formed the new military-political confederation, the United Colonies of New England, in 1643.[4] Each colony selected two commissioners, who attended quarterly meetings to discuss diplomacy, determine levies, and coordinate military action.

Miantonomo's efforts to coordinate a pan-Indian response failed. Uncas also rejected the alliance, and when he attacked Sonquassen's River Indians, the Montaukets, and other groups whom Miantonomo viewed as kin or tributaries, Miantonomo led a force against the Mohegans. Ultimately, the Mohegans prevailed, and Uncas took Miantonomo captive. After first subjecting him to treatment suitable for an elite male captive—Uncas did not torture Miantonomo, but did kill several favored captains in front of him—Uncas allegedly accepted a ransom offer from the Narragansetts.[5] Instead of freeing Miantonomo, however, he handed the Narragansett captive over to the English for a "trial." Eschewing a formal court proceeding, the newly elected Commissioners of the United Colonies and a coincidental gathering of ministers in Boston debated Miantonomo's fate in an ad hoc fashion: "all of the opinion that it would not be safe to set him at liberty, neither had we sufficient ground for us to put him to death."[6] Ultimately, at the clerics' suggestion, the commissioners handed him over to Uncas to be executed. English authorities remained present to prevent Uncas from torturing Mian-tonomo, although the Mohegan did allegedly consume a piece of the corpse's shoulder, a way of literally adopting the energy of a powerful adversary.[7]

The killing of Miantonomo made relations between the Narragansetts and Mohegans deteriorate even more, but the commissioners enforced the 1638 treaty and forbade Miantonomo's brother, Pessicus, from taking revenge. The Narragansetts decided to remove themselves from the United Colonies' oversight by submitting directly to the authority of King Charles I in 1644. Even this submission, however, stressed the Indians' consent and framed the relationship as an alliance with "that royall King Carlos and that state of ould England."[8] The Narragansetts tried to choose imperial subjecthood over being made subjects of colonial governments; such a move would have theoretically made them political equals to the other English colonies, with the crown as the final arbiter of differences among them. Charles's setbacks in the growing English Civil War rendered him a less effective partner than the Narragansetts had hoped. By 1645 the United Colonies had declared war on the Narragansetts and Niantics, and sent a force under Edward Gibbons, while Connecticut sent another force under John Mason—both Pequot War veterans. Some English welcomed the prospect of war as a way of gaining additional Indian captives.[9]

In the end, the English and Narragansetts averted open conflict, but at a huge cost to the Indians in terms of resources and sovereignty. The English imposed monetary penalties on the Narragansetts, and pushed the Nar-ragansetts' tributaries and allies to switch allegiance to the English. With Narragansett power weakening, and the crown's imperial intervention an unreliable protection, Indians mostly chose patrons from among the various English colonies when making submission or seeking protection from either other colonial or Indian threats. Uncas emerged as a stronger regional leader than ever before and a powerful advocate for himself and his own people. He parlayed the Mohegans' client status toward Connecticut into a high degree of autonomy vis-à-vis other Indians and even important English leaders such as the younger Winthrop. The Mohegans maintained a great deal of cul-tural independence and a relatively high degree of control over their own economic resources for nearly a century; Christianity made few inroads in Mohegan country. Uncas and the Niantics battled each other, and continued to pressure the now wavering Montauks and Shinnecock of Long Island for allegiance and tribute, as well as smaller bands in southern Connecticut and on the Connecticut River. Indians on Long Island, Nipmucs in central and northeastern areas, and smaller bands in Connecticut were nearly as likely to face kidnapping, forcible resettling, and even labor demands at the hands of these two groups as they were by English in the 1650s and 1660s.[10]

As for the Narragansetts, they paid a huge fine in wampum and also signed a punitive treaty with the United Colonies in August 1645 that confirmed English title to Pequot country. Pessicus had to send his son as a hostage to live in Boston.[11] As part of the treaty, the commissioners also had Pessicus sign an enhanced version of the 1638 fugitive slave act. This new measure strengthened the language from the Hartford Treaty. Now, colonists could "damadge seise & bring away any of the plantation of Indians that shall entertaine, p[ro]tect or rescue" Indians accused of crimes against the English. If any harbored runaways, both the fugitives and their Narragansett and Niantic protectors would be bound "either to serue or to be shipped out & exchanged for Negroes."[12] This language that linked Indian and African slavery echoed Emanuel Downing's 1645 recommendation that a war with the Narragansett might bring "gaynefull pilladge" and Indians to exchange for African slaves.[13]

Beyond Captives: Colonial Law and Indian Slavery

Even before this crisis, New England governments had moved independently to rethink and renegotiate their legal relationships with nearby Indians. Connecticut officials received complaints that dated from the war, such as one from Eltwood Pomery of Windsor, who charged that Pequots had stolen his horse and the Niantics had subsequently killed it. The General Court "tooke the same into serious consderacion, and [thinke] it according to their duty and good reason to protecte persons and estates of all the members of the Com[monwealth] so farr as lyeth in their power in a way of Just[ice]."[14] The elected magistrates assumed responsibility for securing restitution for Pomery, and created a committee to devise a policy that might stop the behavior and a mechanism to enforce judgments against the Indians. Roger Williams was kept busy pursuing this and other claims among the Narragansett and Niantics.[15]

There were in fact numerous occasions in which Indians and English interacted. Most of these were positive exchanges, but some also had the potential to end in cultural misunderstanding and resentment. The Massachusetts Bay General Court passed a law in 1644 requiring Indians to knock on the doors of English homes and receive permission before entering, which suggests that Indians often wandered into English homes.[16] That same year, town leaders in Portsmouth, Rhode Island, besought Indians living in the town to "depart [forthwith] to live in the woods [with their effects]."[17] Court records and depositions are full of references to Indians present in English houses, invited and uninvited. A maidservant, who accused her master's son of climbing into bed with intent to sexually assault her, testified that the boy's father tried to brush the incident aside by saying she had mistaken "David Inden or some-body ellse" for his son. David Indian was a frequent enough guest that the father, Samuel Leonard, thought this a plausible defense. Another woman in Salem, Mary Logia, testified that an Indian entered her house uninvited in the middle of the night, and she and a male servant tossed him out.[18]

Indians often assumed that they retained usage rights and hunting privi-leges for land they sold or ceded to the English, or that the English owed them continued payments and gifts as if on a lease agreement. When the Massachusett leader Cushnamekin conveyed the land that became the town of Andover, Massachusetts, he fought to protect the rights of a subsidiary band led by "Roger, the Indian" to "take alewifes [fish] in Chochichawicke River" and to keep fields already planted in corn.[19] Sometimes the English acceded to these expectations. As already mentioned, one of the sources of conflict between the Mohegan and Narragansett involved hunting rights in Pequot territory, and even though the English had claimed this territory by right of conquest, the United Colonies pushed the Mohegans to permit Nar-ragansett hunting in order to appease the latter. Even when Indians retained these rights specifically in deeds, however, as in the case of John Winthrop Jr.'s purchase of land at Tantiusques, over time individual property owners within the English plantations created bars to Indian access. English farm-ers erected fences and began sending out untethered livestock to graze to the detriment of Indian hunting grounds and cornfields.[20] When Indians burned the understory to clear or prepare their fields or to help pitch pine forests regenerate, the fires sometimes threatened English habitations. Richard Lyman filed for damages against Sonquassen's people "for burning vpp his hedge."[21] Intentionally and accidentally, Indians sometimes killed livestock they found trampling their fields and shellfish banks or encountered while hunting. Accusations against Indians for taking or riding horses, stealing sheep, taking pigs, and other such issues appear with increasing frequency in court records in the late 1640s and 1650s.

Boundaries and exclusive land rights created other problems, and charges of trespass against Indians became commonplace. Indian plantations straddled colonial and even town boundaries, creating problems of jurisdiction and ownership. Occasionally English buyers persuaded a few Indians to sign a deed that did not reflect the wishes of many Indian groups occupying the territory, so some Indians refused to acknowledge the transfers. Even for the English, the property situation remained confusing, and charges of trespass among contending claimants were frequent: overlapping deeds and battles over title generated decades of litigation and investigation. Land purchases created so much conflict, and generated so much Indian antagonism, that Massachusetts and Connecticut eventually forbade individuals from purchasing Indian land and made it a central, government-approved process. Massachusetts created a commission on Indian titles in 1652 and promised "that landes any of the Indians, within this jurisdiction, haue by possession or improuement, by subjeuing [subduing] the same, they haue just right thereunto, accordinge to that Gen: I: 28, Chap.: 9: 1, Psa: 115, 16."[22]

The court's definition of Indian possession became very narrow, however, and in no way comprehended all the territories that Indians used to harvest food. Generally the English acknowledged Indian ownership of "planting groundes or fishing places," but only if the Indians could "prove it." All other lands "shalbe accompted the just right of such English as already haue or hereafter shall haue graunt of landes fro[m] this Court & authority thereof." Fishing grounds, hunting grounds, fallow and future cornfields, and places to gather berries, tree nuts, reeds for weaving, and other materials were all essential components of the coastal Algonquian subsistence economy. As the English population grew, a second wave of displacement occurred in the 1660s as towns such as Warwick, Concord, and East Hampton began to eject Indians or prevent them from "sigging down" (building houses), "keeping stock—planting and raising crops thereon and taking firewood there from," rights that Native Americans claimed had been protected in earlier agreements.[23] The more that the English restricted Indians' access to key resources, the more economic pressure Indians experienced.

Indians also had expectations about hospitality and rent—tribute—in the form of goods and food from the English whom they had allowed to settle in their territories or to whom they had sold land for nominal fees. Gifts cemented alliance; friends expected generosity; gifts required reciprocity; and, Indians entering English households expected to be entertained and fed, just as they had helped, guided, fed, and entertained English arrivals for over two decades. Native visitors wanted to try English weapons, utensils, and tools, and to sample liquor and other interesting goods that caught their eye. Visitors might carry a bag of meal, a weapon, alcohol, or other items away. From the perspective of some English, however, these incursions could be frightening. Demanding or simply taking gifts looked like theft to English householders such as Plymouth resident William Cadman, who prosecuted an Indian named Tatamoneshkish for taking "an Ancker [about ten gallons] of liquors" out of his cellar in 1659.

A new body of laws emerged to regulate relations between English and Indians. During the Narragansett crisis, Connecticut and Massachusetts complained again about Pequots who had fought against them in the war and yet had escaped captivity or execution, and made new moves to identify and take them. Meanwhile, Connecticut, Massachusetts, Plymouth, and Rhode Island passed legislation between 1645 and 1651 that amounted to an "Indian Code"—a forerunner of the Black Codes in that they constituted a body of laws aimed at a specific ethnic group in their midst. New laws restricted the movements of free Indians within English-claimed boundaries, and, in varying ways, the relations among Indians and English.

Connecticut's revised legal code of 1650 illustrated these trends. Connecticut leaders updated their 1642 legal code in 1650 by pulling together scattered laws into a lengthy section on Indians—the longest category of any in the code. The code prohibited English from departing and settling with the Indians. It limited Indian night walking (moving about at night near English settlements) and prohibited the selling of arms to Indians or the service of repairing their firearms. Earlier, officials had given local sheriffs or town wards the right to "shutte" any Indians discovered near English habitations if they did not submit to arrest.[24] The General Court borrowed wording from the treaty with the Narragansetts regarding runaways, adding to existing language that allowed authorities to take private boats and horses in pursuit of runaway Indian servants, and to deputize citizens to aid the owner or law officers. Finally, the code asserted English legal jurisdiction over independent Indian communities. Along with establishing certain officers to oversee the communities, Connecticut, as a member of the United Colonies, claimed English rights to send armed bands to pursue and detain any Indians suspected of any crime against English persons or property. Either the Indians or their sachems would make restitution, or "the magistrates of the Jurisdiction [would] delieuer up the Indian seized to the party or partyes endammaged, either to serue or to bee shipped out and exchanged for neagers, as the case will justly beare."[25]

This language, which empowered colonists to threaten Indians with enslavement, became a tool of intimidation. Within months of the code's publication, Nameaug Pequots under Robin Cassacinamon complained that "some of the English threten to send them away to the Sugar Country."[26] A year later, representatives from Stratford asked if townsman Richard Butler could prosecute "according to the order made by the Commissioners"—and potentially enslave—an Indian named Nimrod, who he claimed stole some pigs; the General Court consented to Butler's request.[27] A decade later Connecticut leaders pressed the United Colonies for permission to enslave and

ship to Barbados four Niantic/Narragansett Indians whom they charged
with killing two Mohegans working on an English farm owned by Robert
Brewster. The commissioners approved the Connecticut request, and also
empowered Thomas Minor of Southerton in the disputed Narragansett territory to kidnap any two male followers of the sachem Shawatuck, the leader
of a small band of Indians affiliated with the Narragansetts, in retaliation for
the Indians' "detaining, Ryding and concealing his horses." Minor could sell
the men to anyone who would pay 20 pounds, and the buyers would be free
"to Transport them out of the Countrey."[28] Talk of Indian slavery was in the
air, and its application would be determined by individual colonists, communities, and policing at the local level. Indians used this language as well; even
Uncas threatened "to sell away as a slave" some Nipmuc captives whose relatives refused to pay ransom in 1661.[29] Within a few decades Indians all over
eastern North American understood what European slavery meant and how
it differed from their understanding of captivity among indigenous enemies.

Connecticut, Massachusetts, and Plymouth all created a separate legal system for processing Indians accused of crime against the English in the same
period. Noncapital Indian crimes were to be adjudged by special quarterly
courts. Eventually these were presided over by justices of the peace who
could render decisions, rather than by impaneled juries.[30] Some of the moti-
vation for this may have been humane; the Massachusetts law promised that
the justices of the peace would adjudicate Indian complaints against the
English, and also provided interpreter services for Indians. The statute also
called upon sachems to operate their own monthly courts. In a few cases,
particularly capital cases, justices made efforts to impanel Indian juries for
advice in interpreting evidence. Several scholars have argued that the Puritans
tried to achieve fairness with regard to Indian defendants and were relatively
color blind in dispensing justice to defendants.[31] Certainly, the colonists had
established a procedure for hearing Indian-versus-Indian and Indian-versus-
English disputes in court. Yet they had also empowered English individuals,
without any process, to enslave Indians accused of crimes. Moreover, the very
assertion of English jurisdiction was inherently prejudicial to the Indians.

The English presence essentially created new "crimes." Some offenses the
Indians could have avoided, such as drunkenness, although English policy
in this area was also equivocal.[32] On the one hand, authorities regulated and
restricted the selling of alcohol to Indians; on the other hand, Rhode Island
magistrates softened these regulations to permit the serving of "a dram" of
liquor "for refreshment" to Indians who worked for the English, either as
indentured or "hyred" servants. Drink got Indians into serious trouble; it
was the most common offense mentioned before 1675, either on its own or

associated with other crimes. Sometime the offenses charged against Indians were matters of interpretation, such as theft, which could be in the eye of the beholder and reflected cultural differences. But some crimes literally were unavoidable under the English-created circumstances, such as "trespassing" and livestock disputes.

Increasingly, colonial law undermined essential Indian economic activities. Leasing land, probably the most viable option for Indians interested in getting income and provisions without losing their territory, came under attack in several localities.[33] In addition, at various times between 1650 and 1680, statutes in Rhode Island, Connecticut, and Massachusetts prohibited Indians from trading with non-English Europeans, acquiring horses, killing deer, stripping bark from trees (essential for houses, mats, and boat construction), buying English boats (useful for safer whaling and trade), hunting with guns and ammunition, or even bringing pigs to town markets.[34] Some of these restrictions applied to both Indians and English, but some, such as the statutes on guns, bark, and access to public markets, targeted Indians only. When Rhode Island passed a law in 1662 giving squatters ownership rights even if they could not produce a deed or paper, they specifically excluded Indians from the notion that possession and improvement created ownership rights.[35]

Several historians have analyzed these processes within a class framework.[36] In this reading, the Indians slowly became proletarianized. But the inequity was about more than class; it was also about sovereignty and Indian ethnicity, and it implicated high-status Indians as well as poorer and more marginal individuals. Indian slavery had introduced a racial component to treatment of Indians in New England. Pequot captivity and the general language of the New England colonies' slave laws; the newer codes subjecting Indians to seizure, servitude, and slavery; and the laws that impeded the Indians' economic options, their autonomy, and their ability to respond to English land-takings and operate in the regional economy on an equal basis—all these features reinforced one another. The constant references to Barbados in legislation as a symbolic fate linked the New England Indians to an already racialized Atlantic labor system that many colonists—and some Indians—had seen with their own eyes. The punishments prescribed for New England Indians involved the seizing and marking of Indian bodies and the appropriation of Indian assets and eventually of Indian labor and that of their children. The framework of Indian captivity established in the Pequot War affected the Indians' ability to claim due process in court, access to economic resources, and other forms of citizenship within New England or in the larger English empire.

Indians and English lived in close proximity across New England. In formerly remote areas of Rhode Island, Connecticut, and central and southwestern Massachusetts, colonists were now claiming property whose boundaries and owners remained unclear or even contested. Scholars have tended to overplay Indians' lack of a sense of private property and have contrasted Indian notions of communality with English views of land as a privately held and fungible commodity.[37] In this period, both cultures understood ownership of land and other resource assets in both communal and individual (or at least familial) ways. Indians in southern New England fought other Indians over collective control of trade, resources, and territory before the Europeans arrived and had continued to do so. For example, such contests lay at the heart of the post-1638 Narragansett-Mohegan conflict. These were also personal battles, in that sachems sought individual wealth as a way of cementing their power and gave gifts to create ties of obligation among their followers. Within tribes and bands, Indians recognized particular households' rights to certain lands and produce. The English were moving toward a more individualized notion of land and property but still held many lands and resources collectively—via the "corporations" of investors who received grants from colonial governments to found towns, or through publicly held communal trusts in towns and under colonial administration.[38] Despite areas of similarity in their views on property and a mutually dependent regional economy, however, English and Indians still competed for the same territories and resources, which was bound to cause conflict. One might describe this as a shift from a model in which the English depended upon an Indian-led economy to one where the English increasingly wished to replace Indians as the English themselves developed an agriculture, fishing, and commodity-export-based Atlantic economy. Demography reinforced some of these shifts. The English population of southern New England increased to approximately 54,000 by 1670—even as the Indian population of New England had declined from 140,000 to perhaps as few as 14,000 in the same period.[39] Indigenous communities in northern New England still outnumbered Europeans, but Massachusetts and France had established growing satellite settlements in these territories as well.

Indian trade played an important role in the regional economy for decades, especially in Plymouth and the interior and the northern borderlands of Massachusetts and Connecticut, but increasingly what the colonists wanted from the Indians was their land—and the ability to exploit Indian labor directly rather than receiving its benefits indirectly via trade.[40] Indians did what they could to protect their collective and individual resources, but the growing presence of English settlers required new subsistence strategies and new types of economic interactions with Europeans beyond the fur trade in order to acquire desired English manufactures and even food. For Indians, successful economic strategies might include making and selling baskets and brooms; selling honey, maple syrup, fish, game, and other gathered foods; raising pigs and sheep; and leasing pasture and other lands to the English for rent or harvest shares in which English were the sharecroppers.

Indian Labor and the Making of the New England Economy

For a growing number of Indian men and women, subsistence in this new hybrid society also meant vending their labor directly. In the 1620s and 1630s, the colonists had settled near Indians because they relied upon indigenous people for food, technology, guides, and transportation, and because their early economy relied so heavily upon the Indian trade. By mid-century, as the English encroached on their land, some Indians moved away, but others moved toward or stayed where the English were—locating their wigwams closer to English settlements and towns (so much so that towns such as East Hampton on Long Island; Warwick, Providence, and Portsmouth in Rhode Island; and Windsor in Connecticut all regulated the practice). A friend of John Winthrop Jr. noted that when fire swept seven valuable loads of hay, it also destroyed "8 Wigwams nearby."[41]

Desire for Indian labor generated demand in the 1640s far beyond what the Pequot captives could provide. European in-migration to New England slowed to a tiny trickle after 1640. The calling of Parliament in 1642 and Puritan successes there and in the English Civil War not only removed the reason for leaving England in the first place, but also drew many New Englanders back to England to participate. The region's worsening reputation for religious intolerance and tough treatment of servants and non-Congregationalists further discouraged servant migration. A small number of Scots prisoners of war and convict laborers arrived in the 1640s, but, with a few exceptions, New England's ongoing labor pool would have to be generated from within, or from the ranks of the involuntary: slaves.

As a result, households, entrepreneurs, and entire communities sought to attract additional Indian workers in various ways. Earlier, Massachusetts authorities had forbidden colonists from "enterteyning" [hiring] Indian servants without government permission, but in 1646 the magistrates repealed the law, "there being more use of encouradgement thus then otherwise."[42] Colonial officials now wanted to encourage Indian day labor and other forms of voluntary—and involuntary—servitude. Even as Uncas complained "of being deprived of his men," John Winthrop Jr. insisted that allowing Pequots under Robin Cassacinamon to resettle Nameaug independent of their former Mohegan and Narragansett overlords would instead result in the Pequots "affording their labors and helpe for hire" to English residents.[43] Aside from his own informal tenancy arrangements with Pequots on his New London plantation, Winthrop enjoyed the day labor of Cassacinamon's Nameaugs and fielded numerous requests for Indian labor from associates. Before, his friends had asked for a few Indians to come and hunt for the pot, to take messages, to transport seeds and hay, and to perform other carriage jobs by foot or canoe. Now, they recruited Indians to guide cattle drives to coastal processing centers.[44] Mohegan Indians worked for and sometimes lived in the home of William Brewster, Robert Lay, Thomas Mason, and other inhabitants of the English settlement near their territory, helping with fencing and livestock.

Towns hired Indians to manage communal resources or engage in public works. In East Hampton (then under Connecticut's jurisdiction), after repeated failures to find adequate staff to stay on duty, the town hired Indians in 1669 to manage the town "gin," a pen and pasture system for cattle. Later the town added a second gin in Montauk, also operated by Montauket Indians, who in turn leased pasturage to local residents for a four-pound annual fee.[45] Similarly, in May 1652 the town of Warwick in Rhode Island used public monies to hire a group of Indians to build fences, paying them a fairly hefty wage of twelve pounds, ten shillings, for which the town had to levy a special tax on cattle and landowners.[46] Narragansett and Warwick Indians became well regarded as stonemasons, according to Daniel Gookin: "They are an active, laborious and ingenious people; which is demonstrated in their labors they do for the English of whom more are employed, especially in making stone fences." At least one Massachusetts Indian, named Jeremiah, gained enough metal-smithing experience that he received the nickname Tinker. Some entered military service.[47]

In other cases, private groups and individuals hired Indians as a permanent labor force for highly profitable maritime trades. East Hampton residents Thomas James, John Stretton, Thomas Diamond, and Thomas Chatfield contracted with fourteen Montauket and Manissean Indians, including the Montauket sachem Mousup, the Shelter Island sachem Wetanauhhum, and Block Island Indian Sauau, to launch a whaling venture in 1675. The English provided boats and tools, and the Indians supplied the labor, with the parties splitting the catch's profit, half to the English and half to the Indians. Ten of the men had English nicknames or aliases, and one of them, Womakauntak-kum, signed with the "alias" "Cowkeeper," a name that indicated he had previously worked for the English.[48]

This kind of long-term contract remained fairly unusual. Most Indian-English labor relationships were short, unlike the annual contracts that characterized even unskilled agricultural labor in early seventeenth-century England. Indians worked by the day at seasonal jobs for wages or in-kind payments. Daniel Gookin noted that Indians from Nantucket and Martha's Vineyard made seasonal migrations to work on the Massachusetts mainland—presumably in agriculture—and then returned to their homes with clothing, which was their largest household expense.[49] Several large landowners on Long Island Sound, including Pequot War veteran Lion Gardiner of Gardiner's Island and Nathaniel Sylvester on Shelter Island, kept running accounts with nearby Indians. Sylvester had accounts with twenty-five different people in the 1680s, twenty of which were identifiable Indians, including at least two women. Sixteen of those listed received credits for days worked, typically anywhere from one to thirty. With their labor, the Indians purchased goods such as apples, cider, rum, cotton cloth, nails, and meal. Aside from day labor, they also traded items they had gathered and manufactured for credits, including cranberries, fish, cords of firewood, canoes, and deerskins. A few transported goods and messages to New London and Manhattan.[50] Sylvester paid or credited the Indians anywhere from one to three shillings for a day of labor, the latter rate for work "at harvest," a time when English colonial workers also received premiums for jobs such as cutting hay and reaping grain or corn. These rates largely coincided with ranges that colonial Massachusetts authorities considered when they debated mandatory minimum and maximum wages for English workers in the 1670s.

These arrangements mirrored the kinds of book-debt relationships of labor and commodities that contemporary New Englanders had with one another and with local merchants, except perhaps for the prevalence of rum and cider in the exchanges.[51] Most day laborers seem to have been men; the English did not recruit Indian women for field work. When Indian women appear in accounts such as Sylvester's, their contributions resembled those made by European women in book-debt exchanges, except for the absence of dairy products. The labor and book-debt relationships involving Indians were not any more inherently exploitative than other available labor relationships for Indians or English, and perhaps less restrictive than options available to young unattached English men, whom law required to enter into service and reside in English households in the seventeenth century. Day labor allowed Indians to maintain their households and continue other economic tasks and personal, familial relationships. Although activities like whaling and seasonal work might mean long absences, so did hunting, and bands were accustomed to family units moving off for seasonal activities.

Still. Indians who worked for the English acquired new names, new skills, and new habits—including drinking alcohol. In 1672, when John Burges went looking for "an Indian to help in the work," he found the specific man he was looking for drunk at the home of John Hathorne of Lynn, along with several other Indians and English servants. When the man finally came to work, Burges testified, the Indian "was disguised with drink. He [the Indian] said 'my hed no well. No work to daye,' and that he had had one pint of liquor for which he paid a shilling at John Hathorne's."[52] Many other Indians frequented Hathorne's unofficial backyard tavern, which had been the subject of a petition from Lynn town selectmen and review by the Salem court, yet it was not shut down despite the strong restrictions on retailing liquor to Indians. Informal taverns, such as those operated by Hathorne, Peter Duncan of Gloucester, and Daniel Clarke of Ipswich, served as gathering places for young men, both English and Indian. English employers looking for day labor went to these places first; and Indians often spent newly earned cash at the taverns, drinking until drunk. As with the captive laborers, wage work required men to engage in formerly taboo agricultural tasks, although working the gin, whaling, canoe travel, woodcutting, stonework, possibly even haying matched tasks within the traditional male purview. More potentially troubling, the Indian men had now shown their value to the English in very real ways. And those Indians who came into contact with the English world of work became increasingly likely to end up bound into involuntary servitude.

Binding Indians

In 1649, a court in Providence heard a case involving two Mashpee Indians, Wesuontup and Nanhiggen, accused of stealing goods from the widow Sayers. The men did not speak English, so Christopher Hawkhurst had to interpret for them. Their depositions indicated that the two had come to Providence to work the previous day for Richard Scott. Having no place to stay overnight, they had gone across the river to sleep near where some other Indians camped. According to Wesuontup, they took a ladder from a nearby house. Then, Nanhiggen entered Sayers's home and stole a coat, three loaves of bread, tobacco, and a pipe. Wesuontup was captured quickly but escaped, then recaptured. Nanhiggen remained free, but the town issued a warrant and eventually captured him.

In his deposition and in court, Nanhiggen disputed this account and denied the theft.[53] Often, court officials were not sure whether he understood all of the witness testimony and charges against him. Nanhiggen testified that he had been busy working for William Carpenter and also looking for work with another Indian, the son of Sockanosset, the leader of a Narragansett sub-band in an area that became Cranston. At some point Nanhiggen contracted to work for Robert Coles. Nanhiggen had offered Wesuontup a subcontract of sorts for a share in the work in exchange for some wampum, but Nanhiggen claimed that Coles's wife scotched the deal because Wesuontup had a reputation as a thief. Meanwhile, Nanhiggen had also worked a few days for a Nathanael Dixings at the latter's property in Pawtuxet (Dixings, or Dickens, kept cattle), and for John Downing in Providence. During this same twenty- or thirty-day period he found time to return home to Pawtuxet, where he challenged an English neighbor named John Beirstowe who had erected a fence near Nanhiggen's plot and done unspecified damage to his wigwam in a boundary dispute. On these work trips, sometimes Nanhiggen slept in the open and sometimes in the homes of English people he knew, such as Coles.

In the end, the court convicted Nanhiggen of theft and Wesuontup of escaping custody. The court bound Nanhiggen as a servant to John Downing—a third party, and one already familiar with Nanhiggen as a worker—until he had made twofold restitution for the goods he allegedly stole from Sayers.[54] Nanhiggen went from being a free laborer and householder who controlled the nature and timing of his work relationships to an indentured servant.

Nanhiggen's case presaged many to follow in the succeeding decades. His experience illustrates some of the threads that came together to create a situation in which local governments bound autonomous Indians to service with English masters and mistresses. He lived close to the English and had apparently worked frequently in Providence and its environs. Although not an English speaker, he had work skills marketable in English towns and farms. Someone accused him of theft—for other Indians, it would be trespass, drunkenness, assault, damage to property or livestock. By the mid-1650s, all the colonies had laws in place that gave plaintiffs the right to seize individual Indians as reparation for acts of violence, theft, property destruction, missing livestock, and trespassing. As with the new labor regime in Massachusetts that the Pequot captives had faced in 1637–38, in which masters passed legislation and staffed the courts that enforced servant industriousness, Indians accused of crimes encountered plaintiffs with a vested interest in Indian labor and land who could draw on the resources of their towns—marshals, beadles, the hue and cry—to prosecute them. Other interested parties adjudicated Indians' cases as justices and jurymen, or appeared to pay their fees and bind their labor in exchange.

Backed by the legal revisions of the 1640s and 1650s, a more aggressive Providence court captured, tried, and sentenced Nanhiggen, then sold him to a third party to pay restitution and costs. In this case, the person who bought Nanhiggen's contract was a former employer who knew the man's skills. In Salem and Lynn in Essex County, Massachusetts, between 1672 and 1675, the courts heard eight cases involving Indians accused of drunkenness, theft, and assault. Some defendants had English nicknames and were well known in the towns of Lynn and Ipswich as day laborers. All but three received harsh penalties from the court—fines of five pounds plus restitution, or whippings of fifteen lashes each. "Tom Indian," also known as Thomas Robins, was a frequent visitor at John Hathorne's informal home tavern. In 1672, Simon Bradstreet accused Robins of breaking into his home, and the Salem Quarterly Court ordered the Indian "branded in the forehead with the letter B" and fined fourteen shillings. Two years later, the Ipswich Quarterly Court found Robins guilty of drunkenness and assault and ordered that if he could not pay his five-pound fine he "was to be sold to pay it." Hathorne's brother William, the justice of the peace, oversaw the sale of Robins's time to William Bradbury of Salisbury; Robins's service ended only when he agreed to serve in English forces under William Sawyer of Newbury in King Philip's War in November 1676 and Sawyer paid Bradbury for the remainder of Robins's time owed. Now the Indian would receive "wages from the country" as a soldier, although he apparently had to sue Sawyer for some of them.[55] Salem also kept several Indians incarcerated for as many as twenty-four weeks between their indictment and trial; one died in prison, and all would be charged upkeep in addition to the other fines and penalties they accrued.

Essex County was unusual in that the court was able to arrest and prosecute these defendants, in part because of their intimate connection with English people and places. The case was more complicated for Indians who resided in large, powerful, non-client communities, and even some client communities whose leaders exercised leverage and power, such as the Mohegans. Connecticut magistrates reserved the right to seek restitution for "iniuryes" (injuries) committed by members of independent sachemdoms outside Connecticut's boundaries in the "severall plantations of the Indians"—Mohegan, Niantic, and Nameaug territory, among others. If they received no satisfaction, the English could "right themselues as they may, vppon such as so meinteine them that doe the wrong."[56] In other words, these provisions made Indian leaders personally responsible for any crimes that their followers, or even people they temporarily sheltered, had committed. The language left some room for restitution and possibly Indian forms of justice, but the English defined what constituted a crime in the first place.

In places of sparser English population, and denser Indian population, the gap between English assertions of jurisdiction and the ability to enforce regulations sometimes loomed larger. Indians accused of crimes proved very elusive, and even those who were indicted escaped custody frequently—about a third of those indicted in Providence and Newport before 1676. Beginning in 1658/59, however, Rhode Island passed legislation intended to crack down on these behaviors and to compel Indian leaders to acknowledge English courts. The General Assembly of Rhode Island decreed in 1659 that any Indian convicted of theft or property damage who failed to "pay and discharge all the damages, costs, and restitutions by law due" could "be sould as a slave to any forraigne country of the English subjects."[57] The assembly recommended sale as a particularly appropriate penalty in cases where the defendants showed "insolency," suggesting that binding Indians also might serve as a means of social control.

In Providence, Warwick, and Portsmouth, Rhode Island, records of Indian arrests increased dramatically after 1659. The Providence and Newport courts heard sixteen cases involving fourteen different Indians in the succeeding decade. In several cases, sachems appeared and paid bonds to release indicted Indians before trial, and then paid the Indians' fees and restitution to secure their release. The Wampanoag sachem Wamsitta, also known to the English as Alexander, did this for Suckow, who confessed taking a sack of meal from George Layton's mill in Portsmouth. Wamsitta's deceased father Massasoit had already posted a bond, but Wamsitta, acting through his "counselor" (an Indian who presumably spoke English, "called by the English Thomas"), had to make an additional payment of wampum worth six pounds.[58] These kinds of actions not only cemented English jurisdiction but also depleted the resources available to Wamsitta. He himself faced suits for debt. Making Indians' kin and leaders collectively responsible for an individual transgression in some ways reflected Indian values and Indian justice, but English courts decided the punishments. Ninigret and Mousup (the Montauket sachem) also faced summonses and huge bond charges, but they remained out of reach for local authorities; Wamsitta was not.

The result was transfer of Indian wealth assets such as land into English hands to pay debts and increased need for money by Narragansetts and Wampanoags. When citizens of Southampton complained to the Connecticut General Court about a conspiracy on the part of some Shinnecock Indian men and a female African servant to burn several houses in the town in 1657, the General Court initially levied a staggering indemnity of £700 over seven years on the Shinnecocks, although the court subsequently reduced the award—but it also made the Montauket responsible as well. This costly penalty forced the sale of Shinnecock and Montauket lands to the English. Smaller sachems, such as Pomham and Sacanoco, had developed strategies for dealing with local Rhode Islanders who encroached on their lands: they had submitted to Massachusetts Bay's authority and offered tribute, which had complicated the town of Warwick's assertion of jurisdiction. By indicting individual Indians from their bands for robbery, however, William Arnold, William Coddington, and other powerful landowners tried to legitimate arresting and forcing Pomham and Sacanoco into court. These latter efforts failed in the short term, but they complemented more successful attempts to undermine Indian independence. Indian anger over these encroachments played a part in King Philip's War.

In this permissive environment, some colonists literally took the law into their own hands, whether they had a warrant or not, and simply seized Indians or even their children. That was the case in Rehoboth, in Plymouth Colony, in 1655, when John Woodcocke walked "into an Indian House and taking away an Indian Child and som goods, in lue of a debt said Indian ought to him." Plymouth officials did punish Woodcocke with an hour in the stocks and returned the child to the family, but the language of New England law made it unsurprising that he felt entitled to take the child.[59]

In 1660, another case in Salem shocked even Justice of the Peace William Hathorne, and signaled concern on the part of at least some English that the conflation of Indians and slavery had gone too far. It involved Mall, a young Indian girl from Nantucket.[60] John Bishop had visited the home of Thomas Macy, the proprietor of Nantucket; there, he claimed that an Indian named "Mr. Harry" inquired "if he would have a squaw live with him." Harry offered up Mall as a servant. Although Mall spoke no English, and neither did most of the Indians present at the incident, Bishop testified that Mall had consented through an interpreter to serving him for ten years, with the opportunity to end the agreement at five. Two other Englishmen present testified that they asked Harry as they left if he had "sold the squaw," and Harry replied, "yes." At some point after Bishop brought her back to Salem, she ran away toward Boston. An Indian named Harry found her at a crossroad—it is unclear whether this was Mr. Harry, although the man seemed to work for Bishop—and took her to the home of magistrate William Hathorne.

At this point, Hathorne and other parties began to examine the particulars. Bishop and Mall had no written contract or indenture. She was a minor, and no parent had consented to the arrangement. She was reluctant to return to Bishop's home, and Hathorne hinted that Bishop had sexually abused her. For Hathorne and for two other prominent Ipswich townsmen who physically prevented Bishop from recovering Mall when he showed up at the magistrate's house, these factors crossed a line. Hathorne told the Ipswich court that unlike "negroes," Mall and other Indians deserved the same legal rights that English enjoyed: "the law is undeniable that that Indian may haue the same distribusion of justice as ourselves." As Nipmuc historian Thomas Doughton points out, Hathorne put himself in the place of the girl's parents; as the father of a daughter, he empathized with Mall's plight, attesting to their shared humanity.[61] Hathorne treated Indian offenders with great sternness as justice of the peace and even sold one into bound servitude, but the age and circumstances made this case different. He held Mall equal in value to his own child. The court did not agree, however, and in September ordered her to return to Bishop's household. Mall's case shows both how membership in two communities—Indian and English—gave her some standing in protesting her enforced servitude. Yet, unlike in the case of the two Africans freed by the General Court in 1646, Hathorne could not convince most fellow English that these associations protected her from enslavement. Mall's fate highlights the fact that written indentures and protections were still absent in almost all cases involving bound Indians before 1675.

The few records that do exist suggest that masters were treating Indians differently from English servants in other ways. One result of the proximity of English and Indians was that many entered into sexual relationships. New England governments did not pass antimiscegenation laws until later in the period, and there are some examples of Indians and English marrying in the seventeenth century. But cases of fornication and pregnancy involving Indians and Africans attracted harsher physical penalties than those involving two English parties. One 1644 example involved a woman servant named Hope who likely was a New England Pequot brought to Long Island by her master Edward Howell, a Lynn resident who helped found the town of Southampton in 1640. Hope became pregnant by one of Howell's English servants, George Wood. The town sentenced George and Hope to be whipped; then, the two agreed to indenture the one-year-old boy to Howell until he reached the age of thirty. This extremely lengthy term—well past the age of eighteen or twenty-two customary for even orphan boys indentured as children—was one of several things that distinguished this indenture from agreements covering English children. Howell agreed to clothe and feed the boy, Jacob, but there is no mention of education or freedom dues, and the child disappeared from the record.[62] Nor is there any evidence that Hope ever received her freedom. Howell's son Arthur reportedly learned Algonquian from Hope, who raised him, well enough to serve as an interpreter; he himself would become the owner of Wampanoag captives from King Philip's War a generation later.

Debt—whether for court costs and fines or personal expenditure—represented another danger for Indians. Despite an early law in Massachusetts prohibiting excessive "trusting" or extension of credit to Indians, a number of cases came before the General Court in which English creditors demanded sale of Indian lands to pay off large debts. In 1654, Nanamocomuck, the son of the Pennacook sachem Passaconaway, stood bond for another Indian's court appearance over a debt with John Tinker. Authorities seized and jailed Nanamocomuck, essentially holding him ransom. In the end his brother Wannalancet agreed to sell a Merrimack River island called Wickasauke as a means of raising the forty-five pounds needed to secure the Pennacook man's freedom. Such decisions remained controversial; these manuscripts often included many depositions, as well as cross-outs, comments, and other signs of contention among the magistrates. But other than trying to protect the Indians somewhat by having the land valued, sold to a third party, or auctioned to ensure a higher price, the colony allowed several such sales to proceed in the 1650s and 1660s.[63] The Pennacooks transferred about five hundred acres to get the sixty-acre island back within the decade. Cambridge courts heard six cases of smaller amounts of debt involving Indians in the late 1640s and early 1650s; officials even hired an Indian constable just to serve all the Indian warrants. The Montauket Indians who engaged in whaling for the East Hampton investment consortium would not actually receive any of the half-share profits mentioned because they owed debts to the investors: "Wee ye aforesd Indians doe engage our selves to goe to sea from yeare to yeare at all seasonable times for these our Copartners a whale killing til wee have discharged to their satisfaction all former arrears or Debts we stand engaged to them."[64] All equipment and goods advanced to them would be added to the debt. This essentially open-ended contract bound the men to "a whaleling" for the English partners indefinitely, with all profits effectively going to the English.

Debt peonage became much more common in the late seventeenth century, and it frequently led to more formal servitude agreements. The Providence court awarded nearly thirty-four pounds to Randall Holden, creditor of an Indian named Moeallicke, to settle Holden's claim plus damages, and also charged Moeallicke court costs; this occurred at a time when a skilled artisan's wages amounted to about twenty pounds per year and a farmworker might make a shilling or two or perhaps three per day during high-demand hay mowing and reaping seasons.[65] In Providence, Indians received beatings as punishments; in one case from 1688 the court forced one defendant to whip two other convicted men.[66] In this period, though, some of the indicted Indians avoided corporal punishment by paying extra fines and had their costs and restitution paid because of English intervention and English patrons who stepped in to pay them. The early records often do not indicate what the Indians had to exchange for this assistance, but likely they paid in land or labor. By the 1680s and 1690s, such individuals would be sold to pay these debts.

This increase in the binding of defendants to servitude was not a completely racialized process. In several instances, seventeenth-century Suffolk County courts in Massachusetts ordered that English thieves, debtors, and unruly servants be sold so that the profits could be used to make restitution to their victims and their communities. In at least a few cases in Suffolk and in Rhode Island, though, courts permitted English debtors to remain at home and pay their debt over time by turning over a portion of their wages or crop rather than entering into servitude. There is some evidence of ethnic discrimination as well, in that criminal sentences against Indians in Suffolk more frequently permitted—even ordered—the sale of individuals "to Barbados" or other plantations outside New England.[67]

Between 1671 and 1676 the Newport Court of Trials for the first time explicitly linked slavery and Indian debt. Rhode Island had a law on the books that permitted seizing Indians to pay debts, and Plymouth officials passed a similar law in 1673 that permitted creditors to bind debtor Indians into terms of service.[68] In Newport, the court heard a series of cases in which Indian defendants were sold into servitude to pay for their fees, bonds, and restitution damages. Thomas Cornell accused Wickhopash, "an Indian by the English called Harry," of theft of a rapier and two yards of trading cloth. Wickhopash received an extremely harsh sentence: thirty stripes, plus four pounds in restitution to Cornell and then additional court costs. If he failed to pay within the month, the court warned, "he shall according to law be sold for a slave." Another Indian, William, who assaulted the servant of John Odlin, could be "sold as a slave by the Treasurer to Barbadoes or Elsewhere" if he failed to pay eleven pounds damages.[69] Plymouth's General Court condemned, in absentia, an "Indian, called Hoken, that hath bin a notoriouse theife," and ordered in 1674 that if captured he be sold to Barbados "to free the collonie from soe ill a member."[70] There is no evidence that Wickhopash, William, or Hoken ended up as slaves or were ever transported out of the colony. But this rhetorical environment would eventually pave the way for exportation of Wampanoag and Narragansett refugees during and after King Philip's War.

The threat of being sold out of the colony or even to Barbados, Bermuda, or Jamaica was not an imaginary bogeyman for the region's Indians. It had been a reality for the Pequots; it would become a documented reality for Narragansetts, Hassanemesits, and Wampanoags. Ships from Barbados anchored at Shelter Island, New London, New Haven, Boston, Newport, and other ports on a regular basis. The owners of Indian debt and the justices who presided over their cases were the customers and sometimes the instigators of these voyages. They bought the occasional African slave; how often did they send out Indians in return?

One Puritan captain who plied this trade, an associate of John Winthrop Jr. named Samuel Scarlet, fell afoul of Bermuda and Massachusetts authorities because of a related problem in 1648. Scarlet was a Puritan supporter at a time when Bermudans battled over whether to support royal or Parliamentary forces in England. The Bermuda Council had already fined him for bringing Nonconformist (Puritan) ministers to the island. While his ship was in harbor, in October 1648, an Indian woman "servant to a poor man" fled the island by stowing away on his vessel, the *Returne*. Once in Massachusetts, Scarlet turned her over to the General Court in Boston, but somehow she managed to escape custody again; and, "notwithstanding divers and sundry means [having been employed] both by a honord magistrates and alsoe by ye Petitioners with some considerable charges for the obtaining of her," she remained at large when Scarlet petitioned the United Colonies to relieve him of his bond in 1650.[71] We cannot be certain that the woman was from New England, but it seems likely given her choice of vessel and her ability to avoid recapture. She could have been a Pequot War captive or a recent arrival from the group vended in Bermuda in the mid-1640s. Beyond her incredible resiliency and daring, however, her story was an exceptional one: most New England Indians caught in the diaspora of servitude and slavery would not gain their freedom.

CHAPTER 6

"We sold ... 47 Indians, young and old for 80£. in money"

Enslavement in King Philip's War

King Philip's War, 1675–76, represented a
watershed in Indian-English relations and the Native American experience on many fronts. It was an existential conflict for many groups, more
so than the Pequot War, where only the Pequots and arguably the Connecticut English settlers faced serious threats. Colonial forces emerged
victorious only at great cost: Indians destroyed approximately one of seven
English towns and pushed back the boundaries of English settlement to
their mid-century limits. The violence and dislocation of the conflict
traumatized many New Englanders, both English and Indian, in profound ways; historians have linked the war, variously, to the emergence
of a vehemently non-Indian "American" identity and to the Salem witch
crisis.[1] Many English families abandoned the northern and western border regions permanently; and even after the war, those who dared resettle
their towns in Maine, New Hampshire, and central Massachusetts faced
frequent attacks. For many inhabitants, the war did not end in 1676 but
instead evolved into a series of conflicts that first pitted English against
Narragansett, Nipmuc, and Wampanoag refugees and their Wabanaki
hosts, and eventually against a loose alliance of Wabanaki, Catholic Iroquois, and French forces through 1760.

These disasters, and the early losses that the English experienced, engendered not only considerable soul-searching on the part of Puritan leaders but

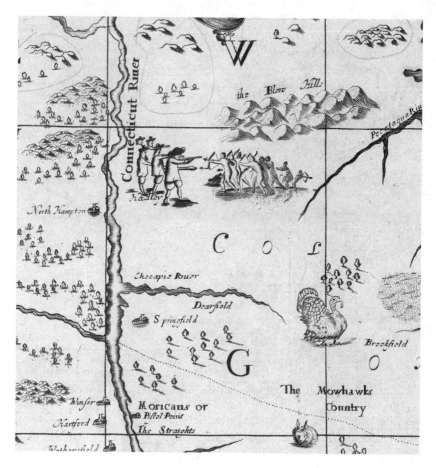

FIGURE 10.   Detail from John Seller's *A Mapp of New England* (London, [1675]). Courtesy of the John Carter Brown Library at Brown University.

also renewed imperial investigation.[2] It is not too far-fetched to say that King Philip's War prompted the revocation of the Massachusetts Bay charter in June 1684 and a shift toward new levels of imperial oversight. The revocation led to a reorganization of the New England governments. Royal agents had already legally confirmed the legitimacy of Rhode Island and New Hampshire; Connecticut emerged from a consolidation of the scattered settlements at New Haven, Hartford, Saybrook, and New London. After the war, imperial authorities further consolidated Plymouth and Massachusetts Bay into a single colony. From the Indians' perspective, the war's effects proved equally dramatic. The war hastened the demographic decline of an already stressed population through death and dislocation. The crisis sent refugees on the move to northeastern and western regions, and eventually involved the Iroquois Five Nations to the detriment of the New England Indians. The war also resolved the question of Indian sovereignty, in at least southern New England: the New England governments emerged as the controlling powers.

Most historical narratives of the war, beginning with those generated by Puritan participants such as William Hubbard, mention the captivity and enslavement of Indians. In these accounts, captivity largely forms a coda for some Indians and a marker of English victory. Putting captives at the center of King Philip's War does not completely revise our understanding of the war's progress and outcomes. It does, however, help explain the behavior of civil and military leaders on both sides of the conflict. Taking Indians formed a central preoccupation of many English participants; it also, therefore, represented a shared meme or experience for literally thousands of New England Indians.

A focus on involuntary servitude also adds a new dimension to our understanding of New England Indians' experiences during and after the war itself. At least one historian has argued that in general the English treated the Indians, both on the battlefield and thereafter, with relative restraint.[3] The extent of captivity and enslavement, however, point to a different conclusion, one that resulted more from the commodification of Indian labor and persons and the institution of slavery than from the laws of war or even civil law. Like the Pequot conflict, King Philip's War began for complex reasons but quickly became a war about captives. These were different wars, yet the outcomes with regard to captivity and enslavement proved curiously similar.

The Causes of the War

As in previous Anglo-Indian conflicts, King Philip's War arose out of a complicated mix of motives and causes. Certainly, the economic, demographic, and political pressure experienced by the region's native peoples had generated resentments. The English population of southern New England nearly tripled between 1640 and 1670, rising from 18,500 to 54,000.[4] Competition for land and other resources, coupled with colonial governments' aggressive assertions of jurisdiction and sovereignty, created many points of conflict between English and Indians. The Wampanoag leader Metacom—also known by his European name, Philip—offered a list of grievances to Rhode Island magistrate John Easton on the eve of war in June 1675 that included English trespasses on Indian territory, the damage wrought by English domestic animals on Indian planting fields and hunting grounds, and English engrossment of Indian lands through illegal land sales and manipulation of deeds. Metacom highlighted the damaging effects of alcohol and Indian debt, and the pressure Indian groups faced to accept the sovereignty of individual colonies when they were all subjects of the same English king.[5] English assertions of legal jurisdiction that brought Indians into English courts, where the asymmetries of power and unfairness of proceedings clearly favored the English, also rankled, along with the fines and debt pressure that inevitably followed. The same growing economic and spatial proximity that undermined Indian subsistence and brought Indians to work for English had also brought Indians before English courts more frequently in the 1650s and 1660s. Prosecutions for theft, debt, and drunkenness not only threatened Indians' persons but also their individual and collective wealth, since leaders drew on collective resources to pay fines and compensation and to keep the accused out of servitude.

Although Metacom did not directly refer to enslavement, at least one interested observer thought that forced expropriation of labor loomed large for the Wampanoags. Robert Mason offered a report to the Lords of Trade (as part of a case challenging Massachusetts Bay for possession of rights in Maine) in which he called such expropriation of labor "the chief if not only cause of the Indians making war upon the English." One of his agents, a Captain Wyborg, had observed hundreds of Indians working without compensation at the Boston fort, where they were "transported" for petty offenses in lieu of being whipped, then enticed into drunkenness so that new offenses would keep them "at this hard labor, many whereof had been by the practices aforesaid kept about 3 months; which barbarous usage made not only those poor sufferers, but the other Indians, to vow revenge."[6] These grievances were no mystery to anyone involved; Easton noted that the colonists "knew before, these were their [the Indians'] grand Complaints" and only hoped to resolve them without war as they had in previous decades.[7]

Indians were far from a united front on how best to respond to these issues. So many economic and social ties bound colonists and Indians together in their hybrid world by the 1670s; even Metacom raised livestock for household consumption and local English markets. As they had during the Pequot conflict, Native Americans fought on both sides of King Philip's War, and others such as the Pennacook and the Niantics sought to maintain neutrality, although that proved a difficult path to follow.

In the middle decades of the seventeenth century, Indian leaders faced intense new financial and strategic pressures. Shifting geographies of power meant that formerly dominant hegemons such as the Narragansetts now found themselves diplomatically isolated, as their former allies now paid tribute to Massachusetts, Connecticut, or various local Indian and English

KING PHILIP.

FIGURE 11.   Metacom. From Henry Trumbull's *History of the Indian Wars* (Philadelphia, 1851).

polities. The Narragansetts also encountered increasingly aggressive efforts on the part of Massachusetts, Rhode Island, and Connecticut speculators to engross their lands. The tribe eventually appealed to England about one particularly large and egregious colonial land grab, the Atherton Purchase, which involved mortgages issued under duress by leaders of the Narragansett confederation—Pessicus, Ninigret, Scuttup, and Wequanieut—to pay huge fines that the United Colonies had levied against the Narragansetts in 1660. Speculator, military official, and superintendent of the Praying Indians Humphrey Atherton purchased the mortgage from the United Colonies and then organized a land company whose shareholders included John Winthrop Jr. Atherton refused Narragansett efforts to pay the mortgage, and Ninigret (who cultivated ties with Connecticut as a counterweight to Uncas) confirmed the default in 1662, effectively delivering Narragansett lands to the Atherton Company. At the Narragansetts' behest, the Privy Council sent an investigatory commission that held years of hearings into the matter.[8] The commissioners ruled in the Indians' favor in 1665, declaring the mortgage void, but offered little enforcement to protect Indian title, and the region remained a target of English squatters and of jurisdictional competition among Massachusetts, Rhode Island, and Connecticut.

The Nipmucs, Pocumtucks, River Indians, and other groups in central Massachusetts and Connecticut also resented the encroachments and land takings of surrounding new English settlements such as Marlborough, Worcester, Deerfield, Lancaster, and Brookfield. Older settlements at Springfield and Concord also expanded, taking land and violating agreements that had guaranteed Indians continuing access to certain territory. From the 1660s onward, these Indians also faced occasional attacks and kidnappings by the Mohawk, a group with whom they had formerly maintained decent relations but whose allegiances had shifted as the Mohawks became more estranged from their regional alliance partners, the Narragansetts. Caught between English and Iroquoian pressure, Connecticut River valley Indians confronted a shrinking resource base and physical threats.

Christianization, too, engendered conflict not only between Europeans and Indians but also among Indians. It formed one of Metacom's key complaints, and he expressed concern about forced evangelization of his people and the divided loyalties of Christian Indians. In the 1670s, John Eliot and the civil guardian of the Indians, Daniel Gookin, had aggressively expanded their evangelization programs to central Massachusetts, targeting the Nipmuc and smaller Connecticut River groups. The English evangelists had many successes and installed Christian Indian constables and officers in several Nipmuc towns, but not all Nipmuc welcomed these changes, and even

Christians resented the newly imposed leadership that interfered with existing structures.[9] Metacom's complaints to Easton included forced conversion, and apparently this was a rumor from his kin in Nipmuc country. Of the southern New England Indians who rejected Christianity, only Uncas and his descendants consistently maintained internal power as well as continuing English support. Others, including the Wampanoag Metacom, the Sakonnet squaw sachem Awashunks, and Ninigret and Pessicus, had all sought cultural and political independence from the English even as their polities overlapped with English borders more and more.

Not coincidentally, these latter groups had faced confrontations with English forces in 1645, 1653, 1660, and 1671 that resulted in fines, disarmament, and/or policy directives that encroached upon Indians' control of their own lands. In 1671, Plymouth especially singled out Awashunks and Metacom for huge fines of fifty pounds and one hundred pounds, respectively, to pay for mobilization of English forces and the costs of diplomacy. Plymouth also included provisions that the Indians did not endorse but that the General Court read into law. According to these elements of the settlement, Awashunks and Metacom "submitted" to the English. Plymouth authorities had expressed their understanding of what this meant in an agreement with the Mashpee Indians that same month, in which the Mashpee promised they would "no longer be strangers and forraigners," that they would accept Christianity, and that they would enter into an agreement of mutual defense and protection.[10] This included not plotting against English, informing English of any Indian plots against the colonists, and assisting the English against any enemies. The Sakonnet and Wampanoag immediately rejected these interpretations, but the disputed agreement later informed Plymouth governor Josiah Winslow's legal decision about the fate of Indian captives. Although they had avoided outright war with the English, the Narragansetts had engaged in frequent warfare with English proxies, notably the Mohegans, and tensions among other Indian groups in the region had also erupted into warfare in the Connecticut River valley and on Long Island Sound in the previous three decades. Metacom and the Wampanoags, rather than the Narragansetts, emerged as the leader and the group who attempted to forge a coordinated Indian response to English presence and power.

Still, as in the case of the Pequot conflict, the war's scope and scale took most participants by surprise. As Easton recalled, rumors of war had circulated for decades and had never materialized, so most English and Indians assumed that a round of escalating conflicts in the early 1670s would end in a similar diplomatic solution. The English themselves remained divided, and colonial governments competed for influence in ways that allowed the

Indians some room to play them off one another. As late as 1671 Massachusetts Bay authorities perceived Metacom as generally well intentioned toward the English, or at least as someone whom they could work with, and they backed him in his disputes with the Plymouth General Court. A week before the conflict broke out, Easton and Metacom held out some faint hope for mediation.

Meanwhile, the colonists themselves had other geopolitical concerns besides the Indians. In 1674–75, Dutch privateers out of Curaçao attacked the New England coast as part of the Third Anglo-Dutch War. Massachusetts spent manpower and treasure to send its own privateers out against Dutch shipping and to patrol and protect the coast. Settlements, shipping, and fishing vessels in Long Island Sound, Maine, New Hampshire, and Martha's Vineyard and Cape Cod all faced dangers, and taking on another conflict would press their resources. New England magistrates looked askance at the colonial governor of New York, Edmund Andros, and worried that his administration represented a gateway by which imperial control might be asserted over their more autonomous governments; they even rejected his proffered aid at the onset of war. New England Indians also had reason to fear the indigenous population of New York. Although Metacom and the Narragansetts had attempted to repair relations with the Mohawks and their western New England allies the Mahicans, decline of trade and competition for tributaries in the Connecticut River valley had created a chill in relations between Iroquoia and the Indians of southern New England.[11]

As in the case of the Pequot War, a murder became a pretext for war. This time, however, the victim was not a European but rather an Indian: John Sassamon, the former Indian servant of Richard Callicott, sometime translator and assistant to missionary John Eliot, and disgraced Harvard student. Sassamon had worked as a scribe and translator for both Nipmuc and Wampanoag leaders after his dismissal from Harvard, but Metacom had become suspicious of Sassamon's loyalty and his overt evangelism. Sassamon's body appeared under the ice at a pond near Metacom's home village of Mount Hope soon after Sassamon had warned Plymouth authorities about the sachem's diplomatic outreach to other tribes. Although English authorities took no immediate action, rumors of Metacom's involvement swirled, and many English settlers and Christian Indians assumed a murder had occurred. In the spring of 1675, the Plymouth General Court accused several Wampanoags of the murder, and in June the court executed three of Metacom's chief men, despite a paucity of evidence.[12] The execution enraged many of Metacom's followers. Sassamon's cultural hybridity and questionable loyalty either to Indians or English made him a complicated pretext for a just war; his own

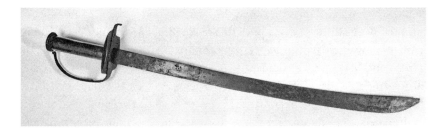

FIGURE 12. Cutlass belonging to Colonel Benjamin Church, 1650–1670. Wrought iron with maple grip, it was made in New England but has a fake English hallmark. Legend has it that this cutlass was used to kill Metacom. Courtesy of the Massachusetts Historical Society.

sister would end up as a captive servant in an English household. That Sassamon, not a European victim, prompted English intervention, and that the denouement took place in a colonial courtroom rather than a riverbank or trading post, illustrate something else about the war and its outcomes: Indians and English were now woven into the fabric of a larger New England society and economy. After the war these relations would be cemented, not severed.[13]

In retaliation for what they saw as judicial murders, as well as chronic economic grievances, some of Philip's followers raided homes in the most proximate Plymouth settlements in a targeted way, killing cattle and destroying equipment but not taking lives. Philip claimed to be unable to restrain his "young men." As fearful colonists withdrew into garrisons, Indians plundered abandoned homes. According to Easton, an English boy killed an Indian whom he saw exiting a neighbor's house, which in turn sparked a violent counter-raid that killed twelve colonists.[14] War was on in earnest by mid-July, but it remained a limited conflict mostly pitting Plymouth and some bordering Rhode Island towns against some of the Wampanoags. The Narragansetts and Niantics sent representatives to Boston for a renewal of treaty promises in July, and as late as October Roger Williams expressed hope that the Narragansetts would remain neutral.

"Privateers" and Slaver Captains: The Profits of War

Control of captives and refugees once again emerged as a crucial area of conflict between Indians and English. Deeply concerned to stave off a possible pan-Indian alliance counterpoint to the United Colonies, Massachusetts governor John Leverett had asked Roger Williams to aid in negotiations with the Narragansetts in July. The United Colonies even diverted troops from Swansea in Plymouth into Rhode Island in order to press their point. Both the Niantics and Narragansetts sheltered many refugees from the fighting, and the United Colonies pressured the Narragansett sachem Canonchet to turn all Wampanoag Indians over to the English. In the July negotiations with Narragansett representatives who did not have authority to make an agreement, Massachusetts demanded Narragansett submission, hostages, and disarmament as signs of neutrality. Massachusetts's envoys reiterated these requirements in an October 18, 1675, treaty. Backed by a military force of 120 soldiers and mercenaries, the ambassadors gave Canonchet ten days to surrender the refugees and to send Narragansett hostages to Boston. The sachem stalled, and Connecticut and Massachusetts Bay both mobilized additional troops for Narragansett country. In a sign that desire for captives once more trumped other war aims, Massachusetts Bay leaders even removed soldiers from a theater of active fighting in the Connecticut River valley to hunt for the Narragansett swamp fort that housed a large population of women and children, as well as adult males.

The English took Narragansett and Wampanoag captives along the way, creating new grievances. Some of the captives joined English forces to avoid execution or enslavement. Supplemented by these newly acquired scouts, along with "southern Indian" Pequot and Mohegan troops, the colonial force numbered over eleven hundred men, including Samuel Moseley from Massachusetts, Benjamin Church from Plymouth, and Robert Treat from Connecticut. They attacked the Narragansett swamp stronghold in December in a battle that caused many casualties on both sides. Having lost nearly a quarter of their troops in the assault, the English-Indian force, in an eerie echo of the Pequot War, set the Narragansett fort and the homes within it on fire. Many noncombatants perished or were captured, but most of their military forces survived and escaped to regroup and began attacking English towns in Rhode Island and Plymouth.[15] Now the United Colonies were at war with the Narragansetts as well.

Aggressive slaving by Massachusetts and Plymouth may also have driven the Pocassets, another group that initially remained neutral, into military alliance with Metacom in the summer and fall of 1675. Although connected with Metacom through strong kinship ties, the Pocasset squaw sachem Weetamoo continued to meet with English officials, and in June had promised neutrality. Around the same time, other Wampanoag groups and smaller sachemates "renewed their allegiances" to the English and promised to help defend English towns against Indian attack. As with the Narragansetts, however, Wampanoag refugees who moved to Weetamoo's territory soon became the target of English troops, and so by extension did her people.

Unlike the rather casual mobilizations of troops and commanders in previous conflicts, this war was different—at least initially. Colonial governments plunged into intense military preparations at the outbreak of conflict. The Massachusetts Bay General Court began by raising taxes—to be paid in money, not in kind, and with no exemptions even for soldiers themselves—in order to pay for guns, ammunition, and food supplies both for the soldiery and civilians. This was not to be a war of swords and pikes, the magistrates warned, but a deadlier conflict of "carbines," bullets, and gunpowder. The General Court published two pages of regulations delimiting the proper behavior of troops toward their officers and civilians, but gave no guidance on treatment of Indian captives. When insufficient volunteers stepped forward, impressment (a draft) of foot soldiers and cavalry followed, and the colony eventually formed two companies that Governor Leverett dispatched to Plymouth.

Leverett also turned to mercenaries—"Jamaica privateers" was one term that contemporaries used to describe these troops—with promises of captives and plunder as an incentive.[16] In an act very different from the one that established the first two companies it sent to Plymouth, the court empowered Samuel Moseley in late June 1675 to raise a group of volunteers to be paid in plunder. The General Court reached a series of agreements with the mercenary during the following thirteen months that made this arrangement even more attractive. By the summer of 1676 the colony exempted his troops from the regulations that bound the conduct of the regular Massachusetts forces but promised them aid and pensions if wounded. It freed them from garrison duty, essentially removed them from the regular chain of command or any claims on their service under other captains with other designs so they could focus on their main aims of plunder, and secured to them "the benefit that may accrew by captives or plynder yt maybe divided amongst themselves."[17] Officials even offered to help Moseley find investors to advance two months' expenses for the men—presumably in return for a share of the profits.

Moseley was a cooper by trade who had become a seafarer, possibly via his father-in-law, the shipowner Isaac Addington. He had spent some time in Jamaica, reportedly captured a Dutch prize there during the Anglo-Dutch conflict, and served as an attorney for a Jamaican privateer when the latter presented a prize in New York City. In 1674–75 during the third Anglo-Dutch War, Massachusetts Bay officials hired Moseley to patrol Long Island Sound, and in the spring of 1675 he captured two Dutch privateers out of Curaçao that were attacking local shipping. Moseley received credit for the ships and cargoes and deposited the multiethnic crews of the prize ships in the Boston jail, where they were tried for piracy. The 110-man unit that Moseley raised for his Indian campaign apparently included many individuals who would not have been accepted in regular militia units—servants, apprentices, boys younger than sixteen—and, surprisingly, several of the jailed "pirates" from the privateers he had captured in May, including Dutch, English, and reputedly renegade New England men.

Rather than tracking Metacom, Moseley and his lieutenants (including former pirate "Cornelius the Dutchman") focused more on capturing and killing Pocassets and Wampanoag refugees. Cornelius took approximately twenty Pocasset captives and killed nearly the same number, while Moseley captured some eighty Wampanoag women and children sheltering in Pocasset territory in July. By the end of that month Weetamoo had joined forces with Metacom. Moseley seems to have reaped immediate profits from these transactions. The Massachusetts treasurer John Hull recorded payments of fifty-five pounds in "cash" on August 3 to Moseley "for his sould[iers]" and entered another payment of twenty-six pounds "to captives."—in other words, Hull credited Moseley for the captives he brought in.[18] Later in August, Moseley took eight Christian Mashpee Indians captive in an early instance of what became a regular problem for Indian allies of the English— their vulnerability to capture and enslavement in an environment where Indians had become a salable commodity.

Samuel Moseley's group saw action not only in Plymouth and Rhode Island but also in the Connecticut River valley as the war expanded westward in late summer and autumn of 1675. There again, his aggression toward putatively loyal Nipmucs drove some wavering Christian Indians into Metacom's camp. Moseley and Cornelius brought in numerous captives from this area. The Massachusetts Council (the governor's advisers) sold five Indians "brought round by Cornelius" to Samuel Shrimpton at the end of September 1675.[19] Shrimpton, an Atlantic merchant and one of the richest men in Boston, owned significant properties there, including an inn, a wharf, and Noddles Island, one of Boston's harbor islands. He also had interests in Deer Island and "Long Island," other harbor islands that became combination detention camps, work camps, and slave pens as the war progressed. He sent these particular captives temporarily to work on his plantations on Noddles Island, but would purchase many others during the course of the war for work there and for export to Jamaica.

Moseley's second company, formed in 1676, fought in New Hampshire and Maine as Wampanoag and Narragansetts fleeing the war sought aid from allies there. The privateers took Nipmuc captives and raided Pennacook villages in New Hampshire during a time of nominal peace, helping to ignite a series of wars on the eastern frontier that raged for nearly six more decades. Moseley and Cornelius acquired reputations for violence toward the Indians that exceeded English norms. The troop brought several large dogs for scouting and combat, and Moseley reported to Governor Leverett in early October 1675 that after his group had interrogated a captive Nipmuc Indian woman near Springfield as to the Indians' location and intentions, "the said Indian was ordered torn in peeces by Doggs."[20] Such actions won praise from English settlers in the Merrimack Valley who wanted aggressive action toward Indians.[21]

Like their Massachusetts Bay counterparts, Plymouth Colony leaders viewed this war as a financial as well as military emergency, one that placed enormous pressure on the colony's human and material resources. Authorities there also engaged in a total mobilization of resources at their disposal, including captives. Because of its geographic proximity to the Wampanoags and the epicenter of early conflict, Plymouth confronted the issue of treatment of captives almost immediately. Josiah Winslow and the "Counsell of War" met in August 1675 regarding a "company of natives now in custody." Where the 112 "men women and children" came from remained unstated; some appear to have been Moseley's Christian captives; others were Indians taken by Uncas and his followers. About eighty were women and children whom Metacom's forces had left behind as they and the Pocassets escaped across the Taunton River to Nipmuc country in the hope of aid. The women and children had "submitted"—surrendered—to Plymouth forces under Winslow.

Rebels and Murderers: The Due Process of Indian Enslavement

The Plymouth War Council debated the status of the Indians "with serious and deliberate consideration and agitation" and concluded that most were "actors in the late rising and warr." The wording reflected the dual way in which authorities constructed the conflict: it was simultaneously a rebellion against the sovereign English governments, and a war waged by a distinct "barbarous," "heathen" enemy. In official documents, imperial and colonial leaders constructed Metacom and his allies as both foreign aggressors and traitors who had "rebelled and revolted from their obediences" and broken "covenants and agreements" entered into via treaty.[22] Echoing the language of the articles of submission that the various colonies and townships had either invited or forced Indian groups to sign in the decade before the war, the council noted that even those who had not acted directly in the violence were nonetheless "complyers" in that they did not "discouer [report] the poisonous plot" of Metacom and the other Indians.

This reasoning may have been a way of excusing the capture of the praying Indians that Moseley had seized, but it also implicated noncombatant women and children and, effectively, all Indians who did not actively take up arms with the English against Metacom. Perhaps this is what had generated the "agitation"—dissent—that Winslow referred to when describing the council's deliberations. Nonetheless, the councilors instructed treasurer Constant Southworth to find a buyer, establish a slave pen, and hire two guards to watch the captives. A few days later, on September 2, the council found another "parsell" of Indians guilty of rebellion under the same logic.[23] The fifty-seven Indians who had "come in to Sandwich in a submissive way to this collonie"—in other words, noncombatants who had surrendered— also received a sentence of "perpetuall servitude." A few weeks later the Plymouth General Court published the pay scale for soldiers. Selling Indian captives was essential to paying these wages and rewarding participants in amounts that varied by rank. Significantly, the grateful court awarded Winslow, who filled the roles of both governor and general of the forces, a bonus of "the prise of ten Indians, of those salvages lately transported out of the government."[24]

The council's blanket charge of treason against all the Indians had consequences. "Rebel" Indians did not enjoy the legal immunity that soldiers in a sovereign army did, and could be punished for the civil crimes of treason, assault, and murder, as in the Pequot War.[25] Indeed, English field commanders, war councils, and, later, local courts executed some male and female captives on these grounds. The treason charges seem also to have implicated women and children in ways that the law of war would not have, although authorities sometimes invoked scripture rather than international law in making these determinations. Captains on the battlefield and occasionally juries after the war also assigned collective responsibility to individuals not associated directly with crime.

Massachusetts Bay officials may have been a bit more guarded than their Plymouth counterparts when it came to condemning women and children, but only marginally so. In a number of cases, authorities condemned women whose only apparent crime was alleged kin relations with a soldier in Metacom's confederacy. Samuel Moseley arrested a group of approximately fifteen Nipmuc Indians and their relatives, including eleven Ohkonomesitt (Marlborough) Christian Indians, on suspicion of involvement with a recent attack on the English town of Lancaster, which had left seven English colonists dead and others, including Mary Rowlandson, captive. One of the men, a Quabaug sachem nicknamed "Great David," implicated the others after being tied to a tree, tortured, and threatened at musket point. Moseley had killed David's brother and either killed or enslaved his nephew in an almost identical interrogation some time earlier.[26]

The captain sent the men to Boston for trial, and Massachusetts Bay impaneled several juries to try a series of cases involving the Nipmucs and Pennacooks, as well as Indians from the praying towns of Wamesit and Natick. Trials took place in Dorchester, Boston, Charlestown, and Roxbury. Testimony from Indians as well as English cleared most of the accused, but nonetheless several of the men, including David, were "sentanc'd to be sold as slaves" in October 1675. By this time authorities had arrested other mostly Christian Indians (or at least Indians well known to the English) from Wamesit, on suspicion that they had fired some haystacks. Despite the lack of evidence, another jury found several of the men guilty, and magistrates sentenced them to slavery, including an Indian laborer named William Hawkings who had worked in Salem.[27] In October the treasurer sold seven Indians—"George, William, Hawkings, great David, Rouley, John Indian and Tommoquin"—to Lancelott Talbott and Joseph Smith, who received from Governor Leverett a certificate empowering them to sell the Indians "to any place out of this Continent."[28] The trial indicated that Massachusetts authorities did not consider the Indians to be foreign soldiers but rather subjects. In these early wartime cases, Indians appear to have been charged with individual crimes such as murder or arson, rather than treason.

Such efforts at legal due process for Indians in wartime met with withering attacks from both critics and supporters of the Indians. Daniel Gookin viewed the trials as a sham, and questioned the lack of evidence and the perfunctory jury deliberations. For Gookin, this treatment violated the Indians' place in New England society; having asserted their jurisdiction, the colonies owed the acculturated Indians some kind of due process: "they were subjects under the English protection"—subjects both of Charles II and of the colonial governments—"and not in hostility with us," he noted. He recorded several shoddy and biased cases in which English soldiers shot Indian civilians only to be acquitted by sympathetic juries, despite judges' instructions that pointed to guilty verdicts.[29] Meanwhile, even acquitted Indians such as Great David soon faced new charges and guilty verdicts for other crimes. Some magistrates might have shared Gookin's position, but many other English in Boston thought the opposite. They viewed trials as a dangerous charade, given the war's exigencies, and called for immediate execution of all Indian prisoners. A mob assembled at the home of Captain James Oliver, a jury member and known hard-liner who they hoped would be sympathetic to their desire to lynch the Marlborough Indians on the spot.[30]

Even more exceptional under either the law of war or Massachusetts civil law was the treatment of the accused men's dependents. At some point in the fall, Captain Thomas Henchman, another notable slaver, arrested wives, mothers, children, and dependents of the accused Nipmuc, Marlborough, and Wamesit Indians and sent them to Boston as well.[31] In early November, magistrates William Hathorne, Humphrey David, and John Wayte interrogated nine of the women about their willingness to accompany their husbands or sons into Atlantic slavery. Among them they had six children. Whether the magistrates' actions represented a wish to keep families together, or questions about the women's complicity, is unclear. At least one of the women, Sarah, whose jailed husband had actually abandoned her the previous year, knew John Eliot and mentioned the minister's name as a character reference. Another woman, also named Sarah, may have been the wife of Sampson Robin, a Nipmuc who had scouted with English forces and had helped save many English lives during the siege of Brookfield, but who had reportedly made overtures to the Narragansetts after viewing English abuses toward Nipmucs in the autumn of 1675. Sampson was not even in custody, though his brother Joseph would be sold into slavery.

The magistrates did not offer the women a choice between slavery and freedom, but rather an impossible choice between enslavement within the colony separated from family or enslavement in some unknown Atlantic destination where they might be separated anyway. They did not receive even the limited judicial reviews regarding their complicity that the men had. Five apparently did not answer the magistrates' query directly. Among those who did choose, Great David's wife Sarah agreed that she and her children would accompany her husband only "if to King Charles his countrey to the English." It seems unlikely that officials would have acceded to these conditions. Some women, including "the Squah or Wife of Will: Hawkins," declined to accompany their spouses. Others, such as "Great Davids owne Sister," agreed to accompany her husband John Umphry (Humphrey), as did the wife of Jeffery. Both women brought children with them. The magistrates used the term "volunteer" to describe their actions—effectively, in English eyes they had consented to be enslaved with their husbands—and concluded that they "shall have Liberties so to doe & be accordingly sent along with them." Hathorne ordered the other women and children sent to Brewster Island, which had become a holding pen and work camp for Indians awaiting sentencing or disposition.[32]

Other women faced arrest. William Ahaton, the Indian sachem and teacher at the praying town of Punkapoag near Boston, sought the release of a kinswoman who had been taken by the Mohegans and brought by them to

Boston in September 1675. The Mohegans had apparently tried to intercede on her behalf rather than turning her over to Connecticut or Plymouth forces. (They also interceded for the jailed Nipmucs.) Ahaton showed a familiarity with English conceptions of women's very limited public roles when he argued that her gender should protect the Mount Hope Wampanoag woman from enslavement, since it precluded her from being a political or military actor. "She being a woman whatever her mind hath been it is very probable shee hath not dun much mischefe."[33] In this case, the council agreed with Ahaton's logic and released the "old Indian squa" to his custody, but in most other cases involving younger and more valuable individuals the courts made no effort to evaluate women's engagement in the war before condemning them to servitude.[34]

Some of the language of treason that Plymouth leaders employed derived from a broadly shared Atlantic concern that had come to link Indians, Africans, slavery, and revolt. Private correspondence, depositions, and petitions suggest that an interpretation of the war as an insurrection was widely shared among the English colonial public. Recently arrived in Plymouth from England, Benjamin Batten wrote to his friend Sir Thomas Allin, comptroller of the navy, and used the term "insurrection" to describe the first weeks of the war; someone, presumably Allin's clerk, labeled Batten's letter with the notation "The rising of the Indians."[35] Allin released Batten's letter to the *London Gazette*, where it in turn shaped public consciousness in England regarding King Philip's War. New Englanders also perceived such connections. To William Harris of Rhode Island, Susquehannock attacks in Virginia were part and parcel of the "rising" in New England, evidence of a concerted insurrection with the goal of driving out the English.[36]

These terms—rising and insurrection—had other connotations in the Atlantic world of 1676, however, one associated with slave uprisings. From the perspective of London or the Caribbean, the terrifying and destructive Indian "risings" in New England and Virginia merged with conflicts involving European colonizers and indigenous people in New France, Curaçao, Surinam, St. Lucia, and the Leeward Islands and with recent slave revolts in Barbados. The governor of Barbados, Jonathan Atkins, informed the Lords of Trade that although English there indeed had experienced a devastating hurricane and a terrifying slave revolt, "they retain one advantage, they sleep not so unquietly as the rest of their neighbours in America, from whence they receive nothing but ill news of daily devastations by the Indians who increase in strength and success which spread like a contagion over all the continent from New England where they have burnt some towns and destroyed many people."[37]

Indian complicity in protecting runaways and maroon communities, as well as tensions with free Indian communities over Indian slavery and European encroachments, led Surinam's Governor Peter Versterre to crack down on the English habit of enslaving Indians there. Naval vessels had arrived to help with a final evacuation of remaining English planters in August 1675 prior to turning the province over to the Dutch, so Versterre demanded that "the free Indians that are aboard his Majesty's ships"—some hundreds, as it transpired—"may be put on shore to prevent all the mischiefs that may arise by their carrying away, from the cruelties the heathens are wont to practice."[38] The Barbados Assembly passed a law that forbade the importation of Indian slaves from New England in June 1676 because of the dual threat of insurrection and Indian anger, and even demanded that any already on the island be exported off as "being thought a people of too subtle, bloody, and dangerous nature and inclination to remain here"[39] A ship bearing New England Indian slaves, the *Seaflower*, reportedly had trouble vending its human cargo there and in Jamaica in the autumn of that year. New England Indians, it seems, had again become an Atlantic byword for rebelliousness.

Elected officials in Massachusetts and Connecticut worried that the spirit of rebellion would extend to other elements in their society, particularly servants, children, and wage laborers. One of the Massachusetts General Court's first acts after the outbreak of war was to pass a series of resolutions aimed at controlling the behavior of all three groups and to create heightened levels of surveillance. New punishments and prohibitions attended long hair in men, the wearing of "strainge fashions," "superstitious ribbons on both haire and apparel," swearing and "night walking" by servants and apprentices, "disorder and rudeness in youth," drinking, demands for high wages, and "contempt of authority."[40] As in the Pequot War era, enslavement of Indians coincided with a tightening of labor discipline for all New Englanders.

The War Council's August and September actions, and subsequent enslavement of Indians during the conflict, did not go unnoticed. Benjamin Church, who later became an enthusiastic slaver, at first thought it bad policy; he noted that many of the Indians had surrendered, and enslaving them would make others think twice about accepting English terms in the future. John Eliot and Daniel Gookin mounted even more-strenuous efforts to keep enslavement from becoming the de facto fate of captives.

Gookin was not opposed to slavery per se, or even to Indian slavery in some forms. Like most of his peers in colonial government, he was complicit in both systems. He had served in the Virginia House of Burgesses in the 1640s during a period when Virginians began to define their slave system. He participated in the Anglo-Powhatan War, during which his father, John, petitioned for and received the right to enslave Indians who attacked and damaged the family plantation at Nansemond in James City, Norfolk. As a planter there and in Maryland in his own right, Gookin was master to more than twenty indentured English servants and two generations of African slaves with the surname Warro, his "servants and vassals." Quite likely he employed Indian slaves as well, because many of his James City neighbors did. Even after moving to Massachusetts in 1644 because of his Puritan sympathies, Gookin maintained plantations in Maryland and Virginia. He presided over the execution of Susquehannock Indians who attacked and killed a slave at his Maryland plantation in 1653. Gookin sailed frequently between Boston and the Chesapeake to check on his properties and to trade in corn, tobacco, and occasionally slaves. He brought three of the Warro slaves, Maria and her sons Daniel and Sylvanus, to Cambridge with him. He apparently freed Sylvanus in 1672 without completing the formal manumission, and Sylvanus subsequently became re-enslaved with Gookin's blessing over a bastardy charge.[41]

From his position on the General Court, Gookin argued against Indian slavery on practical and legal grounds rather than offering moral absolutes.[42] He advocated for Christian Indians or those he believed could ultimately be Christianized. In New England he had become closely engaged with the missionary activities of John Eliot and the organization and administration of the seven Christian Indian "praying towns." Gookin predicted, correctly as it turned out, that enslavement at the early stages of the war would radicalize wavering and even loyal Indians, who would resent seeing kin abused. In so doing, Massachusetts Bay authorities were not only wasting souls but also valuable scouts, soldiers, and workers who could be "improved" in English service to win the war. New Englanders were enslaving Indians without regard to their guilt or innocence, giving Metacom and his allies cause to exploit fears and spread rumors that the English would enslave all New England Indians. For Gookin, the goal of protecting Christian Indians meant that all enslavement had to cease. Gookin also raised the question of citizenship and subjecthood. He stressed the United Colonies' obligations toward Indians it had rendered subjects through treaty, conquest, and annexation, and also their obligation to abide by imperial directives as subjects of King Charles II, who had instructed the English colonists to protect his Indian subjects.

The Reverend John Eliot had also raised few objections regarding slavery and Indian servitude in the past. The sheer scale of enslavement and the targeting of Christian Indians, however, roused him to protest in August 1675. He petitioned the Massachusetts General Court to stop exporting New

England Indians.[43] Eliot's arguments rested on a foundation ranging from biblical verses to practical reminders about the nature of New England's claims to Indian land and on the colony's poor global reputation. While he conceded the legality of executing particular men who had killed English, and agreed that enslavement was a lesser form of punishment, Eliot accused his fellow English of trying to "extirpate nations" by wholesale captivity. In particular, Eliot deplored the sale of New England Indians out of the country into the Atlantic slave trade, because selling Indians abroad meant giving up the chance of converting them. Such an act might hinder "the designe of Christ in these last days," a reference to some contemporaries' belief that the Indians' conversion might help bring about the Second Coming of Christ, the goal of all good Christians. Eliot reminded authorities that "when we came, we declared to the world, & it is recorded, yea we are ingaged by ye letters patent to the kings majesty, that the indeavour of the Indians conversion, not their extirpation, was our great end of our enterprize in coming to these ends of the earth." The very legitimacy of the colonists' claim to settlement in New England derived from maintaining good relations with the indigenous peoples and, ultimately, modeling Christianity for them. "All men (of reading) condemn the Spaniard for cruelty upon this point in destroying men, & depopulating the land," he noted, evoking the *leyenda negra* of Spain's destruction of the indigenous population of its territories in the Americas. The English had to find a way to convert and live with the Indians in New England; "here is land enough for them & us too." Like Gookin, Eliot also questioned enslavement as a matter of strategy. He echoed Roger Williams's comments from 1637, contending prophetically that enslavement of Indians who had surrendered peaceably "is like to be an effectual prolongation of the warre and such an exasperation of yt, as may produce we know not what evil consequences." But Eliot and Gookin were in the minority in 1675–76. In the summer of 1676 Governor Leverett issued a certificate that declared the Indians enslavable.[44] For his attempts to protect Christian Indians Gookin faced death threats from devastated colonists who confronted him in the street, "calling him an Irish Dog yt was not fathfull to his country."[45]

Other Massachusetts divines supported enslavement. Women and particularly children became transformed in their eyes into condemnable "actors" in the war via logic derived from many of the same scriptural arguments made decades earlier during the Pequot conflict. Toward the end of the war, in considering the fate of Metacom's wife Wootonekanuske and their son, political authorities consulted with several ministers, including Increase Mather, James Keith, John Cotton, and Samuel Arnold. The ministers revised the old question—should children suffer for the sins of the fathers?—that

Williams had raised forty years earlier. James Keith—who housed Woo-tonekanuske and the child to protect them from angry colonists—found scriptural evidence for mercy. In contrast, however, Mather, Cotton, and Arnold concluded that the children could be "cut off by the sword of Jus-tice for the trespasses of their parents."[46] They presented biblical precedents to support these positions, even though Arnold and Cotton admitted that "concerning some of these children it be manifest that they were not capable of being co-actors therein." In other words, the divines did not really believe that children had actively conspired in the war, but rather that they inherited their parents' culpability: an understanding with implications for the herita-bility of slave status. In giving "speciall License" to Captain Thomas Harris of the *Seaflower* to deport seventy captives to be sold abroad as slaves, Leverett specifically included women and children in the indictment of Indians for rebellion, covenant breaking, and serving as "Aidrs and Abettors" of Meta-com, so proven by "due and legall procedure."[47]

For most captives in Plymouth and Massachusetts, the outcome was the same regardless of whether they were charged with murder, treason, or wag-ing an unjust war, because the colonists justified enslavement or servitude as a merciful lesser penalty for those guilty of a capital crime. After all, as recently as the 1660s many Puritan sympathizers in England, jailed during the Res-toration of Charles II and sentenced to hang, had instead been shipped to the Caribbean—"Barbadosed," in common parlance. Legislatures considered slavery to be an appropriate punishment for treason and incorporated it into their colonial legal codes as such. Roger Williams himself seems to have abandoned all reluctance regarding enslavement by the 1670s, and he played a leading role in processing and selling Rhode Island's captives.

The Plymouth decisions on enslavement, coming as they did at the onset of war and encompassing large numbers of captives shipped abroad in a single mission, were unusual. Commanders, privateers, and soldiers from Connecticut, Massachusetts, and Rhode Island disposed of captives in a rather ad hoc way in the early months of the war. Although the Marlborough and Wamesit Indians had received trials in Boston, these were exceptional cases. Commanders such as Samuel Moseley, Peter and James Oliver, and Benja-min Church treated Indian captives as commodities and vended them to buyers as their troops moved from engagement to engagement. In part this was because of the difficulty of guarding and maintaining large numbers of prisoners, but economic motivations—the Indians did represent wages and plunder, after all—entered into commanders' calculations as well, since they could keep all the proceeds of such direct sales, rather than waiting for shares or reimbursements from colonial officials.

Sometimes soldiers simply took individual Indians that caught their fancy. Jonathan Fairbanks had volunteered under Benjamin Gibbs's command in the march to relieve the besieged town of Brookfield in August–September of 1675. The men had also been charged by the court with finding the children of Job Kattenanit, a scout and spy for the English who had left his children with pro-English Indians in what was now a war zone. In the village sheltering Job's children, Fairbanks encountered a twelve-year-old girl and promptly obtained a promise from Gibbs "that She should bee his own." Fairbanks then "tooke her up upon his horse & brought her to Quabaug," placing her with the Christian Indians there before rejoining the campaign.[48] Benjamin Church sent prisoners to central processing areas in Plymouth for recompense, but he and his men also took captives for themselves or accepted them in lieu of pay. The son of John Thaxter of Hingham accompanied Church on a raid on Martha's Vineyard in the fall of 1676 seeking Wampanoags and Narragansetts who had fled there. The group received a commission very similar to Moseley's; essentially they proposed to go and kill Indians and take captives, and Massachusetts Bay confirmed their rights to all they found. The group "tooke many Captives: and brought them to Plimoth"; but Church also "gave" Thaxter a nine-year-old boy to "keepe . . . in his famalay as a Servant."[49] Thaxter's father described the boy as not only economically useful but also as a valued member of the family in ways that implied emotional attachment, a testament to the confused and contradictory nature of Indian slavery in New England households.

Identifying legitimate targets for enslavement remained complicated, however, given the blurred lines between friend and foe. At different times Connecticut captains experimented with badges, elaborate hand signals, and other means of protecting Indian soldiers serving the English from death or kidnapping at the hands of colonists ready to shoot or take any Indian. In May 1676, the owner of a New Haven ironworks that employed many local Indians watched powerlessly as a group of vigilantes approached his forge. Angry at the death of a young boy who had been out herding cattle, the mob had remembered that several Indians labored at the ironworks. The posse grabbed two workmen as well as "one Wm Imployed by mr. wilford & some Squawes . . . and dealt harshly w[i]th th[e]m."[50] In September, wartime hysteria led the United Colonies to intern many Christian Indians in work/detention camps on Deer Island in Boston Harbor and on Long Island, ostensibly for their protection as well as for the colonists' security. Soldiers marched Christian Indians to the boats roped with yokes around their necks and hands—like slaves. Once on the desolate harbor islands, the Indians discovered that their former homes, livestock, and possessions had been looted by English neighbors and that officials had failed to prepare for their subsistence in detention. They faced starvation conditions.

Meanwhile, kidnappers raided the internment camps and stole dozens of Indians, so many that the Bay Colony magistrates felt they had to threaten prosecution of violators under the man-stealing statute in November 1675.[51] This only applied to unofficial takings; the War Council authorized several individuals to forcibly seize Indians from these sites for military and non-military tasks. Daniel Henchman drafted Indian scouts and soldiers from the harbor islands regularly, and William Brewster received permission to take Indians from the islands for forced labor on his farms.

Similarly, Indians permitted to remain in their villages in Massachusetts and parts of Connecticut had to answer daily roll calls and could be assigned to work without compensation for English overseers, as in the case of praying Indians in Nashobah. The local militia committee placed the Indians under "the inspection" of John Hoare of Concord. The committee ordered Hoare "to see they bee imployd to laibor; for their lively hood and that the country may be eased [of] expense." Hoare locked the Indians inside the workhouse each night and received permission to forcibly bind into service any Indians who refused this arrangement.[52]

Faced with a choice between internment, possible kidnapping, and death by starvation or exposure on Deer Island on the one hand, and joining the enemy on the other, some Christian Indians joined Metacom's forces. But even families of those Indians who continued to fight alongside the English remained vulnerable to capture and sale in the absence of male relatives. Soldiers such as Awaukun filed anguished petitions complaining that their children had been kidnapped and sold while fathers served in English military units.[53] Three years after the war's end, relatives of John Sassamon, the pro-English Indian interpreter whose supposed murder by Metacom had sparked the conflict, were still seeking to free Sassamon's own sister from servitude. She had been "claimed as his servant" by one John Burge, and in the end her relatives had essentially to buy her back. The Commissioners of the United Colonies recommended that Burge receive compensation in exchange for her freedom, "halfe out of the Indian Stocke as due to Sassamon for service; and the other halfe by her frinds."[54] Shifting alliances during the war, divisions within tribes, and the English commanders' practice of drafting captured Indians into colonial military service created additional confusion. Were Indians (and their families) who had doubtless killed Englishmen before changing sides subject to punishment or sale?

As Massachusetts Bay forces moved into Plymouth and Rhode Island in the autumn of 1675, soldiers bartered over Indians with fellow troops during the campaign, or sold them to civilian buyers. Captain Thomas Oliver's company took Indian prisoners daily between December 12 and 16 as they moved through Wickford, Rhode Island. On December 17, Oliver recorded that "we sold Capt. Davenport a group of 47 Indians, young and old for 80£. in money." Captain Nathaniel Davenport, who owned property in the Aquidneck area, stopped in mid-campaign to make the purchase. The companies led by Oliver, Davenport, and Moseley converged with Connecticut forces two days later and moved to engage the Narragansetts in the "Swamp Battle," where they took another 350 captives, of whom 300 were women and children.[55]

Captives as Commodities: A Changing Native American View

English colonists also received many captives from Indians themselves in the war. All the English colonies benefited enormously from the participation of crucial Indian allies. Some scholars, following comments made at the time by Daniel Gookin, have argued that public opinion remained so mistrustful of even loyal praying Indians that it became politically impossible for colonial forces to employ them in large numbers.[56] Connecticut certainly relied on Indian troops in greater numbers, yet there is considerable evidence that Indians performed essential services and supplemented English forces in important ways for all the colonies, including Massachusetts Bay and Plymouth. Both used Christian and allied Indians as scouts and soldiers in the summer of 1675, "pressing" men from the praying communities near Boston, at Mashpee, and in Nipmuc country. The Massachusetts War Council sent a company of twenty to "proul the woods south of Dorchester milton Dedham" in July 1675 and armed them with powder and shot.

In Connecticut the River Indians protected Hartford, Springfield, and other towns. The Niantics largely broke with their former Narragansett allies, first remaining neutral and then helping English forces, as did the Pequots and Mohegans. In the fall of 1675, Connecticut authorities ordered local captains to draft Indians who lived within county bounds in New London, Windham, and Hartford, as they would English inhabitants, for incorporation into joint companies—an act that assumed a kind of citizenship on the part of the Indian residents, or at least the obligations of citizenship. In some expeditions, Indians participated in nearly equal numbers to English Connecticut soldiers, as in the case of Thomas Fitch's march to Hatfield in the summer of 1676, which mustered 200 Indians and 220 English.

Often, commanders such as Plymouth's Benjamin Church offered some male captives the choice of joining his forces or being sold out of the colony.

Some Indians accepted this desperate battlefield bargain, but in order to prove their loyalty (and enhance the troops' profits), they were required to kill and bring in other Indian captives. Other Indian soldiers demanded their share of the profits. James Rumney Marsh, Zachery Abram, and Peter Ephraim brought in approximately twenty captives from Medfield in January 1677, most of whom they sent to Boston for sale. Daniel Gookin wrote on their behalf to the Massachusetts Council asking that they be recompensed at least ten pounds. Captain John Hunter (or Hunting) also captured many Indians, and even brought in his own brother-in-law, who "was sould by the Counsel." In return, Hunter received "two yards of trucking cloth."[57]

Followers of Ninigret (Ayanemo) and his son Ninigret II, Robin Cassacinamon, the Squa-Sunks sachem (a Niantic/Narragansett confederate who had sided with the English), and Uncas took captives throughout the war and received refugees. In October 1676, the General Court granted Pequot leader Robin Cassacinamon "six of the Incomers or captiues, to keep them as servants, prouided he take such as are not already enagaged or disposed by the English." Robin selected particular Indians: Nenaquabin, "an old squa wth him and his wife's vnckell Grasheacow and his wife and a pawpoose of Grasheacow, and an Indian that is sick, Sasabenewott."[58] Cassacinamon had personal ties with the Indians he chose, and he did not keep them as personal laborers or sell them. Nenaquabin resurfaced in 1700 as a Webaquasset sachem, who local English in northeastern Connecticut accused of plotting "an insurrection" because he urged alliance among different Indian groups, and they suspected him of aiding the French.[59]

Connecticut's English soldiers also took captives, perhaps fueled by the promise made after October 1675 that they could take a share according to their rank in the "plunder, both of persons and corn or estate, to be disposed by them in way of sale, so as they may best advantage themselves." The colony's government acknowledged that much "dissatisfaction" resulted when the government demobilized troops from the summer campaign without paying them wages, so Connecticut adopted a formal pay scale. Sale of captives would both fund the pay of drafted soldiers and also attract the formation of special volunteer companies that the War Council created in October under terms very similar to the ones Massachusetts Bay had offered Samuel Moseley. The government withheld its own right of first refusal in all captive sales, but promised "market price" for any captives it took from volunteer regiments.[60]

So many captives and "surrenderers" poured into Connecticut between September and February that the magistrates appointed a special commission to determine a policy. News of Plymouth's decision to export 187 Indians in

August–September had created something of a panic among Native American groups near the war zones and shifted the movement of refugees. Massachusetts Bay also began using the threat of enslavement and exportation to force wavering or neutral Indians to choose sides, which drove many Indians to throw themselves upon the tenderer mercies of other parties. Observers noted that Wampanoag and Narragansett women and children and Indians from smaller nonaligned groups made their way to Connecticut to seek shelter with Cassacinamon, and Momoho, Uncas, Squa-Sunks, and Ninigret, or to surrender to Connecticut authorities as a way of escaping enslavement in Massachusetts and Plymouth. Hunger drove others to surrender themselves or their children. The English had systematically destroyed or looted Indian food supplies in their campaigns in Narragansett country and the Connecticut River Valley in the summer and autumn, which, added to the dislocation of war, left many bands at the edge of starvation and boded ill for the coming winter and spring. Several English petitions claimed that Indians with whom they had some prior relationship simply walked up to their homes and "offered" them children.[61]

Initially the Connecticut General Assembly had left it to the sachems to oversee and resettle the refugees under their sachemates, but many English residents complained that this left Indian men who escaped from the battlefield free to regroup and perhaps renew violence against English towns. The same applied to the northeast, where Wampanoag, Narragansett, and Nipmuc refugees poured into the area north and east of the Merrimack River. At first, Massachusetts Bay relied on shaky treaties with local sachems to keep these Indians under control, but this lack "of an effectual means of disposing of them" led the General Court to commission Richard Waldron and Nicholas Shapleigh to pursue a more lasting peace. If this failed, Waldron and Shapleigh could "dispose of those Indians already come in, or that may be brought into their hands, by shipping them off or otherwise, whereby damage from them may be prevented."[62]

English commodification of Indians prompted a shift away from more traditional indigenous modes of treating captives. By the spring of 1676 Connecticut officials began to push Indian allies to bring captives to the English rather than incorporating them into their own societies. The court sent Thomas Fitch to inform Uncas that the magistrates had sold a group of his captives to one of their own, Major Edward Palmes, in May 1676. Uncas apparently resisted handing the Indians over to Palmes, a West Indian merchant and trader who served as the colony's commissary during part of the war, so Fitch had to apply additional pressure. Later that year, the General Court pressured Uncas and Ninigret to send 110 refugees to Massachusetts Bay.

Officials offered incentives for Indian soldiers to turn prisoners over to the English, including payments of two to four pounds per prisoner, "Duffils" (cloth), or two coats. They also endorsed—sometimes through legal decree— the ritual torture and/or execution of captives whom the English deemed murderers. Still, the General Assembly also permitted and even encouraged Indians to sell captives as well. Owaneco, the son of Uncas, established his own sachemate, the Showatucks, which combined Mohegans and River Indian groups. He proved a valuable ally to the English in the Connecticut River valley, and he received permission to sell captives. In January 1676 he sold a four-year-old Indian "captiue man child" to James Treat of Wethersfield "in consederation of a valuable Summe of money . . . unto the said James Treat his heires . . . And assignes for ever."[63] Owaneco had just sold the child as a slave for life. Uncas himself kept some captives and settled them within his sachemate but sold others.

Under the new policy, the Connecticut War Council established a system to try "murderers" and assign punishment—sometimes through regular court proceedings, and sometimes by merely instructing Indian allies to kill captive men—and the General Court executed several Indian men under this rule. At the same time, however, the colony offered an amnesty to Indians who surrendered, handed in their arms, and subjected themselves to colonial authority "as the Pequots, &c.," and promised to function as vassals in the future and allies in time of war. Such Indians would not be "transported out of this Country" but rather settled in reservations where they would enjoy some autonomy and have planting, hunting, and fishing rights.[64] Connecticut was the only colony that made a sustained effort to distinguish Indian "surrenderers" from "captives" (the latter being those whom they deemed complicit in the war's violence) and to protect the former from Atlantic slavery.

This May 1676 policy seems to have been a limited-time offer, however; by October of that year Connecticut offered a new and much less advantageous deal to those who surrendered by January 1677. They would be protected from exportation as slaves but would be "well used in seruice with the English where the Councill shall dispose of them" for a minimum of ten years. Children would also be removed from their parents and placed into service separately, given to counties that had received fewer Indians in the first distributions.[65] Servitude had now become the norm for noncombatants and refugees. The General Assembly modified this policy again in the spring to note that "surrenderers" who ran away or otherwise rebelled from these arrangements could be recategorized as captives sold abroad as slaves.[66] The magistrates also passed a fugitive slave law aimed at punishing nearby Indians who aided escapees, and set up a committee to oversee the capture and processing of runaways. As a result, free communities tended to turn in runaways, as when Farmington Indians "apprehended" and turned over an escaped servant man named Nuttquttheseke in April 1677.[67]

Historians have tended to focus on Indians' overall loss of status, power, and autonomy in the wake of King Philip's War. Over the course of the war, the Native American population in southern New England declined from eleven thousand to fewer than five thousand. But captives experienced an even more negative trajectory. By war's end, the efforts of Benjamin Church, Samuel Mosely, John Talcott, and other commanders had converted more than two thousand surviving Indians into English captives. Now, English towns, courts, and governments took up the task defining what the Indians' status would be in the New England that emerged from the war. Towns and central councils became dealers in Native American human capital, which they distributed to leaders, veterans, and householders, as well as to wealthy investors. Hundreds and perhaps thousands of New England households acquired Indian servants, in many cases their first non-English laborers. The regional culture had never been so diverse and multiethnic. The question was: Were these Indians servants with set terms, or slaves for life?

CHAPTER 7

"As good if not better then the Moorish Slaves"

Law, Slavery, and the Second Native Diaspora

King Philip's War brought a new generation of Indian captives—more than two thousand people—into English households and into an Atlantic diaspora. It also altered the status of all Indians—free, servant, enslaved—living in the region. Just as the Pequot War had helped frame English thinking and legislation about slavery in 1638–45, so, too, the 1675–76 war produced significant legacies in law and practice regarding involuntary servitude. Of the more than two thousand Indians reduced to servitude and slavery as captives during the war, the colonists exported approximately one-fourth into the hungry maw of global slave markets throughout the Atlantic, the Caribbean, the Mediterranean, and the Indian Ocean. This fate marked the far extreme of loss of status and autonomy for Native American victims. The rest remained within New England households to work, as auctions distributed them to households all over the region. New England was well on its way to being a "society with slaves," to quote Ira Berlin, even before the region began importing Africans in large numbers.

Significantly, the war also cemented English sovereignty in southern New England. In the 1650s and 1660s colonial governments in southern New England had asserted sovereignty over the native inhabitants but had not been fully able to enforce these claims. Now, through conquest and treaty, the colonial governments—particularly the powerful Massachusetts Bay—had come to view all the Indians as subject peoples answerable to English courts and laws.

The colonies' legal hegemony was a double-edged sword, however, since the Indians now had recourse to some of the privileges of subjecthood—notably the right of petition and access to courts. One Indian protested enslavement by saying that he was "a Native Indian [of New England] born . . . and a Freeman." He claimed membership in a hybrid New England society.[1]

English views on Indian citizenship remained undeveloped, however; only Connecticut magistrates confronted the issue of how English societies might integrate captive Indians after they completed their terms of forced servitude. Nonetheless, some captives and their relatives, as well as many Indian leaders, effectively used petitions, lawsuits, threats, and other strategies to protest enslavement and to redeem some of its victims. Some English colonists, worried about being overrun by captives, also lobbied for limits and restrictions on Indian servitude in the domestic realm. As a result, Rhode Island banned Indian slavery, at least in theory, and the other New England colonies set formal limits on the terms of Indian war captives who remained in the region, rendering them servants in law, not slaves. At the same time, however, New England governments themselves created large new constituencies for Indian servitude by spreading ownership via auctions and distributions. Localities and masters themselves subverted the few controls that protected servants from enslavement. As a result, all Indians who entered servitude during and after King Philip's War faced a high risk of remaining slaves for life and of transferring this status to their children.

Questioning a Hybrid Society

For a brief period during King Philip's War, it seemed as if the colonists might reduce their economic dependency on Indian servitude—for security reasons, if not for moral or legal ones. The very hybridity of the society that the colonists and Indians had created began to seem like a liability to colonists in the more active war zones, where suspicions extended beyond recent captives and encompassed long-standing servants, neighbors, and workers. War councils fielded petitions from local groups such as the Dorchester Selectmen and the Committee of Militia complaining that "their be severall Indians inhabiting in sundry familys in our town for the private advanteg & profit of some p[ar]ticulare p[er]sons to ye great offense & grief of ye Nighborhood. In this juncture of time when ye Indians round about us are risen up in open hostillitie."[2] Roger Williams's Pequot servant Will showed his loyalty—and the depth of his acculturation—by warning settlements about imminent Indian attacks. But years of cohabitation did not reassure all colonists about the Indians in their midst.

Class resentments inflected some of the debate over Indian labor. Some charged that wealthier New Englanders who owned Indians or benefited from their work had dragged their feet in responding to the Indian threat. Providence residents such as Mary Pray complained that the colony's "great men" failed to act because they valued Indian labor and services. According to Pray, Councilor Richard Smith "staved of[f] war with them for his porkes sake"—because he anticipated buying one hundred barrels of exportable pork from local Indians. Even after war broke out and Warwick and Seekonk faced extreme danger, some English kept as servants "those Indians that for the profit they hope to have by them . . . which may prove moer Injuury to the Contrey then all we can say wil make them sencable of." Pray singled out Henry Fuller and Joseph Wise as owners of a potentially dangerous Indian servant named "surly Tom," but she implicated all Indian workers, including Christian Indians, in her indictment.[3]

As the war expanded and the number of captives grew, other colonists questioned the keeping of adult captives as slaves in the towns. Later entry into war and lack of a colony-wide militia until well into 1676 meant that Rhode Island companies did not take the large numbers of war captives that other units did. Nonetheless, the area became flooded with captives taken by Connecticut, Plymouth, and Bay Colony troops who were anxious to exchange burdensome prisoners for quick cash. By January 1676 so many Rhode Islanders had purchased captives that Portsmouth and Providence officials interceded, giving owners six weeks "to Sell and send them off from this Towne." Many regulations targeted Indian men, but Portsmouth banned the continued employment of Indian adults of both sexes, not just men, noting that "sufferinge Such Indians to abide amongst us may prove very prejuditiall" and "apeares troublesome to most of the Inhabitants."[4] By spring the complaints pushed Rhode Island's War Council to take the extraordinary step of requiring masters of Indians over the age of twelve to send an English "keeper" or guard if their Indians ventured outside for work, and to prove that they could securely lock up their servants at night. Violators faced fines of five pounds, and the law enabled anyone seeing unattended Indians to grab them off the street or field.[5] The Plymouth court faced similar pressures from anxious town governments in the summer of 1676. In response the magistrates ordered that male Indian servants and slaves age fourteen or over be sold out of the colony.[6]

Plymouth's rush to export the 187 Indians condemned to slavery a year previously had reflected these fears, as well as concerns about the logistics of maintaining large number of prisoners prior to determining their final disposition. Already pressed to pay for the war, the colony now had to pay the guards of its own slave pen two and a half shillings apiece daily and provide some kind of victuals for the prisoners and their keepers, which drove up costs. Massachusetts Bay also grappled with the logistics of guarding and feeding the Indians held in the colony's slave pen, its island detention camps, and its prisons, not to mention calming public fears about such concentrations of potentially hostile Indians.

According to Pawtuxet planter William Harris, Connecticut companies of Mohegan, Pequot, and English soldiers in Narragansett country solved security problems by killing all adults and targeting children, women, and teens for captivity.[7] Governor William Leete's instructions to Major John Talcott in the summer of 1676 essentially instructed him to do so.[8] Perhaps because of this, or more likely because the colony was less of a battle zone, public opinion and policy in Connecticut appeared less concerned about the dangers of Indian servants. Officials there focused more on securing Indians for local servitude rather than for exportation, although Giles Hamlin captained a New London vessel that carried a cargo of somewhere between ten and twenty captives to sell in Barbados on the account of future governor Fitz-John Winthrop and other investors in the fall of 1676.[9]

If enforced, the restrictive wartime laws about keeping adult Indians would have outlawed Indian slavery in New England homes. But much of the regulatory language offered masters desirous of keeping Indian slaves and servants some room to maneuver. Massachusetts Bay's War Council issued a ban in July 1676 on the keeping of Indian servants in English towns, fining violators a hefty ten pounds. Within weeks of the order, though, the council sent a directive to militia committees and local officials exempting "Indians of known faithfulnesse to the English." Such Indian day laborers, servants, or slaves could "remain in any other English Towns, with such as shall imploy them."[10] In Rhode Island and Plymouth, petitioners had only to claim that their Indians had been younger than fourteen when they had first been made servants, or if adults that they were servants of long standing, not recent war captives. Exemptions seemed easy to obtain. When neighbors complained about an adult Indian woman in the household of Samuel Lynde of Plymouth, Lynde explained that the girl was merely very tall for her age, since her relatives—perhaps trying to protect her from exportation—had assured him she was only twelve when he purchased her. Regardless, the court granted him permission to keep her.[11]

The normalization of Indian servitude in New England made prohibitions on keeping Indians difficult. After Plymouth Colony relaxed its restrictions, individual towns such as Hingham passed local bans, but petitioners again challenged the local laws, claiming that they had purchased Indians directly from captains or at officially sanctioned auctions. When Hingham town officials fined Nathaniel Baker in December 1676 for "Entertaining and Indean or Indeans contrary to Town order," he and two other residents complained to the Plymouth Council.[12] Townspeople had been keeping Indian servants and slaves for years. The recent influx of captives merely added to an existing population, following precedents created by the keeping of Pequot captives, "which said Indians ye Petitioners hope will be no wayes prejudiciall to the towne: or disturbances to the public . . . but of great use and advantage to ye Petitioners and Neighbours."[13] Council members agreed, and Hingham's selectmen relaxed their prohibitions.

Regulating Indian Slavery

Both pressures—the sheer numbers of captives concerned and the calls for regulation—did force all four New England colonies to bring the growing population of newly captive Indians under more direct government control. Some of the ad hoc practices of the past came under new scrutiny, especially the absence of indentures or set terms of service for Indian servants. In 1677 the Plymouth court for the first time mandated that masters secure formal indentures with their Indian servants "to prevent future differences."[14] (Whether these anticipated "differences" amounted to debates among rival English claimants for the Indians' labor, or disagreements between Indians and putative masters over the nature and term of their service, remained unclear.) Local magistrates would oversee the indenture process. Indian children faced longer terms than their English counterparts, with service to end at a somewhat vague "twenty four or twenty fiue yeers of age," but at least the term would theoretically be finite and contractual, making them legal servants, not slaves. Connecticut also adopted a sliding age scale for terms of servitude for those Indians kept inside the colony and not exported. For adults, the term would be ten years, but anyone under sixteen would serve until age twenty-six. These terms were minimums, not maximums, the court warned: the magistrates retained the right to extend terms "for liberty to com[e]" and warned they could be "inlarged."[15] The general thrust of all of these measures was to replace ad hoc relationships of servitude or informal tenancies with formal sales and indentures and to define the place of Indian servants "under our Jurisdiction." Larger questions of Indian servants' future status within Rhode Island civil society remained unaddressed.

The Connecticut General Assembly was the only governmental body that considered what the status of Indians would be after these finite terms of servitude. A servant who completed his or her term had to receive a "certificate from their masters of their good seruice"—a written testimonial or freedom papers.[16] Indians with certificates would receive the designation "sojourner," a legal term that had Old Testament roots. The title of "sojourner" gave an individual newcomer the legal right to live in a town and not be warned out, but it conveyed no rights to common resources or participation in town government. Sojourners might eventually qualify for these rights and become freemen or local stakeholders—but only Europeans had done so. It is unclear whether the officials who applied the term "sojourner" to freed servants conceived of the term as a pathway to possible citizenship for the Indians. The fact that Connecticut magistrates maintained other distinctions that fellow colonial leaders did not fully embrace—between "surrenderers" and captives, for example—suggests that Connecticut authorities were in fact thinking about this issue differently.

They did not expect Indians to return to a separate and autonomous existence. Instead, they assumed that ex-servants and English would continue to create a hybrid society within the confines of English town life. The order specified that the Indians could live in English towns and "worke for themselves, they observing English laws," and the statute also included protection for the Indians, calling on English to observe the law in their interactions with the freed Indian servants.[17] Lack of a certificate would place an Indian in a difficult position of illegal residency in an English town, and might make others unwilling to recognize his or her free status, providing a coercive incentive for Indian servants to work obediently—and an incentive for masters to withhold certificates and to illegally extend the length of service. Officials tried to address the latter problem by setting up a system by which servants denied certificates without cause could "apply . . . to the authority, who shall heare his case, and grant liberty as they see cause."[18] Of course, many of the buyers and sellers of Indian captives were "the authority" in their towns, judges in courts, or key figures on the council, raising questions about what kind of hearing an Indian who had been denied his or her freedom papers would receive. This system may have in fact shaped Connecticut's elaborate pass requirements in the eighteenth century for slaves and free blacks who moved through the colony on public roads or used ferries. The plan for "division of persons" (the Indian captives) specified that they be split among the counties, and then each county committeeman would distribute them among the towns and supervise their sale at market prices "vnto such as they thinke most meete to eudicate and well nurture them." Like land divisions in New England towns, eminent residents received the largest shares, but all male heads of household received some portion. Each of the assistants received an Indian servant "for themselues freely, for their paynes," as did the committeemen who supervised the sale, which gave Connecticut's leadership down to the town level a direct interest in Indian slavery.[19]

The fact that Connecticut magistrates considered the question of what Indian servants would do upon gaining freedom suggests that they expected liberty would be the eventual outcome for most Indians. Indians' servitude would be finite, and they could enter English society as members of a recognized category of citizenship, albeit a passive one. Connecticut leaders presumed the continuation of a multiethnic society. This regional variation may have been due to the colony's relatively low number of casualties and the effective way that its Indian allies had aided the colony and therefore proved themselves reliable members of the polity.

The Connecticut law threw the lack of provisions for freed Indian servants elsewhere into sharp relief. This absence of policy on ex-servants implies that the integration of former Indian servants into English society as citizens remained controversial. It also distinguished Indian servants from those of European background, since the latter could acquire full citizenship. Increasingly, many English inhabitants conceived of hybridity not as coexistence of equals but rather as interactions mediated by institutions such as servitude—even though the continued presence of many non-slave Indians who traded and performed day labor in English towns belied this conception. And the fact was that many masters and local officials in Connecticut ignored the statutory limits on terms of Indian servitude.

After the war, townspeople in several Massachusetts and Plymouth communities expressed concern about the presence of Indians who were not servants, analogous to the ways that some Reconstruction-era southerners viewed freedmen.[20] The Massachusetts General Court received a petition from the selectmen of Dedham complaining about "ye manners and practices of ye Indians that have come in & dwell among us or neer us since the late wars." They took hundreds of deer to trade for their skins without eating the flesh "to ye great damage of the English." They refused to work "except upon unreasonable terms." Their dogs attacked English cattle. Many suspected them of theft. But more troublesome, seemingly, was the Indians' "proud and surly behavior." Free Indians did not greet English neighbors when they passed them on the road. They were a bad influence on the younger praying Indians, who had begun to question the quality of life in their own heavily regulated communities. Christian Indian leaders also complained: "They think it is much also that these Indians which of late were enemyes to the English should have such liberty . . . equall with themselves."[21] The "liberty" of Indians living in and around English towns, their social and economic autonomy, seemed threatening in postwar society. The

Massachusetts Council ordered all Indians "except apprentices and servants" to move to one of three sanctioned Indian towns or face arrest and incarceration or sale.

Authorities in several colonies also tightened what had been relatively informal and voluntary programs that placed Indian children as apprentices in English households. In June 1675, Plymouth's Council of War ordered that Indian children under English jurisdiction be removed from their families and forcibly apprenticed to English families. Massachusetts and Connecticut soon followed with laws that targeted at least some children for forcible removal, and/or offered enhanced financial incentives for families to surrender them. In the summer of 1676, Daniel Gookin bound fifty mostly Nipmuc Indian children ranging in age from three to sixteen into servitude to age twenty-four.[22] Some were war orphans, but others had living parents; siblings were divided to different masters and sent far from kin.

The most distinctive legislation of all the New England colonies aimed at regulating treatment of captives emerged from the Rhode Island General Assembly. In an oddly worded act, the magistrates in April 1676 forbade Indian enslavement *except* in cases of debt—specifically, to "pay their debts for theire bringeing up, or Custody they have received"—or "to performe Covenant, as if they had been Countreymen and not taken in warre."[23] In other words, prisoners of war were now ineligible for enslavement, but, as in the Massachusetts statute of 1641, "Countreymen" who had either agreed to serve as slaves or who had broken their covenants of submission and subjected themselves to colonial authority via treaty or agreement could be sentenced to slavery.[24] This latter category applied to just about all the Narragansetts and Wampanoags in all the other New England colonies, but Rhode Island, before the war, had defined the Narragansetts as independent in order to justify the colony's takings of Indian land via right of conquest, so ironically the treason charge was not available to Rhode Island leaders.

Instead, the Rhode Island General Assembly declared the captives to be servants. The councilors awarded militia companies who brought in captives "halfe the produce of the Indians."[25] Captive Indians would serve for nine years, except for "notorious persons duly detected or guilty," whom the colony reserved the right to remove from service, presumably to deport or execute them. Owners of such men and women would be indemnified for any losses. Finally, the colony set up a "Committee appointed to dispose of Indians" to implement the policy. As refugees and displaced Indians continued to move into English areas, mindful of "the danger of the liberty of some and the bondage of others," in October 1676 the assembly required that all Indians living in English towns—or the English employers—have a certificate identifying their status and indicating that they had passed through some official processing.[26] Any Indians who lacked a certificate would be sold into servitude, and "such [English] as entertaine them" would have to prove legal ownership.[27] Indian children could incur servitude and even enslavement to cover the costs of their "custody"—a vague way of legalizing the enslavement of children of servants or slaves without a direct statute declaring that children's status followed that of the mother, which was how Virginia, Barbados, and other colonies had defined the heritability of servitude.

Massachusetts Bay's legislators, in 1670, had already created an even more ambiguous opening for enslaving succeeding generations. In anticipation of a new printing of the colony's legal code, the court had designated a committee to review laws that needed updating. The man-stealing and bond slavery statues that defined slavery were among the laws selected for revision. Then, the court revised the revision for clarity and punctuation—but the resulting law was far from clear. It merely eliminated the word "strangers" from the statute, as in "captives taken in a just war, or such strangers as shall willingly sell themselves or are sold to us."[28] Most scholars have viewed the 1670 law as a benchmark that assured the heritability of slavery by making children born in the colony susceptible to enslavement—no longer just strangers and foreigners.[29]

But if this was the goal, other colonies (such as Virginia in 1662) had recently accomplished it with much more declarative language. Given their connections with other slave systems, Bay Colony magistrates had to be aware of this, especially since within two decades the legislature adopted "black codes" limiting the rights of Indian and African servants and slaves in virtual lockstep with Virginia and Barbados. Seemingly, Massachusetts Bay's leaders chose opacity; they chose not to say that children's status followed that of their mothers. These omissions may have reflected contention among the magistrates about encoding chattel slavery of any kind. But more likely they reflected disagreement about where Indians fit in their society, because slavery remained associated with Indians, not Africans. Approximately three thousand Indians in southern New England survived the wars, avoided captivity, and continued to live in nearby communities as free persons whose existence challenged the complete identification of Indians with slavery. Diaries and private correspondence reveal that including Indians in the new "black codes" of the late 1600s and early 1700s aroused considerable controversy within the Massachusetts leadership that was never made public.

Whatever its origins, this lack of clarity on the definition of slavery represented a conscious policy by the eighteenth century, one that officials had multiple opportunities to revisit yet elected not to. Instead, it was up to masters, individual slaves, and local authorities to contest and shape the resulting institution. As a result, multiple forms of slavery and servitude continued to coexist. From 1670 to 1677, as Anglo–New England communities faced the prospects of creating, selling, or incorporating thousands of Indian slaves, Rhode Island banned slavery while permitting it, while Massachusetts permitted slavery without fully defining its key element, inheritability. As we shall see, this vagueness permitted a variety of outcomes for Indian captives.

Creating a Master Class

The new regulatory regimes included mechanisms for distributing captives among the colonies' stakeholders. Here again, the four New England colonies pursued distinct strategies. Massachusetts Bay's handling of Indians who surrendered in the summer of 1676 concentrated captives in a relatively few hands. Colony treasurer John Hull staged two public auctions in August and September and applied the profits directly to the colony's running accounts for the war. In August and September of 1676, the colony sold over 190 Indians to various buyers in lots ranging from 1 individual to 41, while Plymouth disposed of an additional 169. "A boy" sold for three pounds; "10 Squawes, 8 papooses, & 1 man" for twenty-five pounds.[30] Women, girls, and infants represented 68 percent of the total. A few buyers, such as Samuel Shrimpton, Thomas Smith, Thomas Morse, and Simon Lynde, dominated the auctions, buying Indians both for their own use and also for export.

African slaves remained relatively rare in New England. One estimate counted 30 Africans in Connecticut in 1680 and about 150 in Massachusetts, although this number increased dramatically between 1690 and 1730.[31] In Rhode Island, African slaves formed slightly more than 5 percent of the population in 1708, the largest proportion in the region. African slaves cost approximately twenty-two pounds in Connecticut, and between ten and twenty pounds in Boston in 1690, which meant that Indians cost anywhere between a quarter and a tenth of the price of an African slave.[32] Overall, then, although the number of African slaves increased after 1690, Indian captives remained far more numerous before 1700. They offered a cheaper, entry-level investment in long-term bound labor.

Connecticut and Rhode Island officials followed a different strategy. There, local auctions made Indians available to households outside the cities that might not have had slaves or long-term servants before. Rhode Island leaders overcame prejudice and fears about keeping Indians in the colony by stressing the economic benefits of Indian servants and by decentralizing the

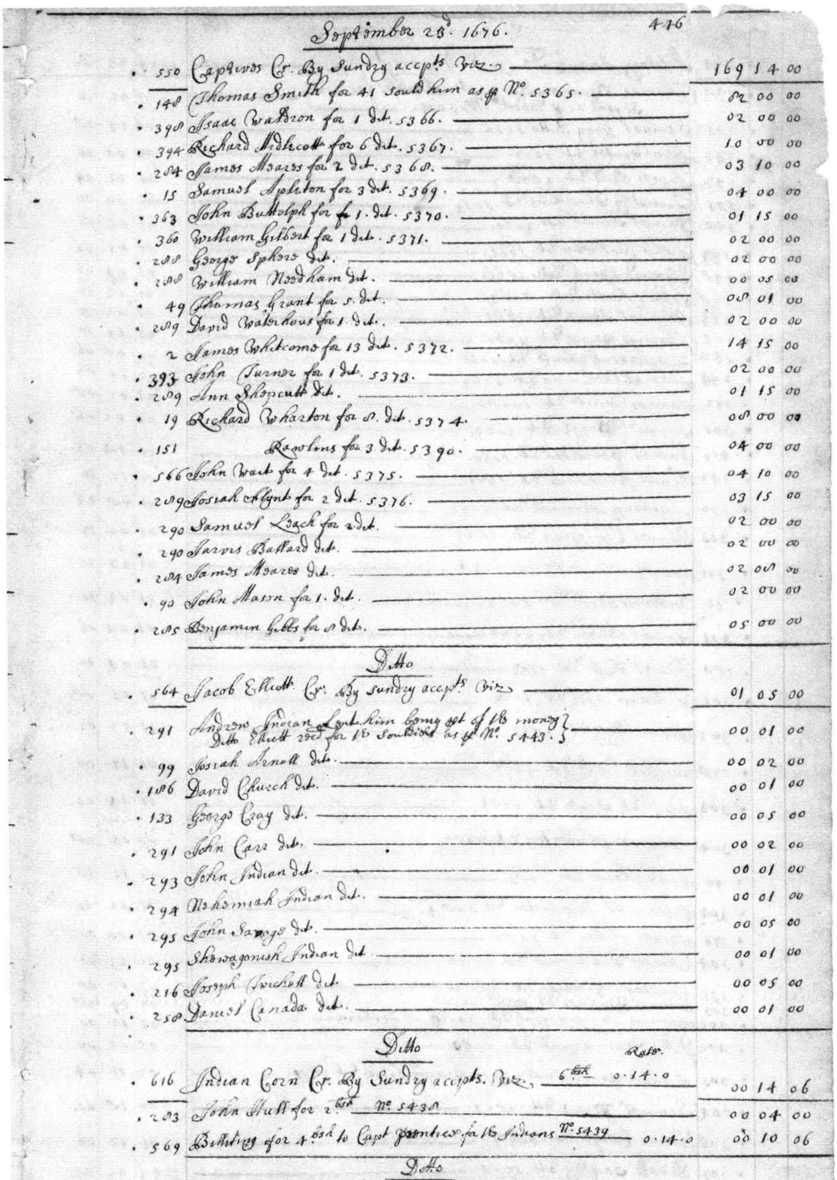

September 23. 1676. 416

550	Captives Cr. By Sundry accpts viz	169 14 00
148	Thomas Smith for 41 sould him as p No. 5365.	82 00 00
390	Isaac Waldron for 1 dit. 5366.	02 00 00
394	Richard Midlecott for 6 dit. 5367.	10 00 00
204	James Meares for 2 dit. 5368.	03 10 00
15	Samuel Apleton for 3 dit. 5369.	04 00 00
363	John Buttolph for 1. dit. 5370.	01 15 00
360	William Gilbert for 1 dit. 5371.	02 00 00
208	George Spere dit.	02 00 00
208	William Needham dit.	00 05 00
49	Thomas Grant for 5. dit.	08 01 00
209	David Waterhous for 1. dit.	02 00 00
2	James Whitcomb for 13 dit. 5372.	14 15 00
393	John Turner for 1 dit. 5373.	02 00 00
209	Ann Shapcutt dit.	01 15 00
19	Richard Wharton for 8. dit. 5374.	08 00 00
151	Rawlins for 3 dit. 5390.	04 00 00
566	John Wait for 4 dit. 5375.	04 10 00
209	Josiah Flynt for 2 dit. 5376.	03 15 00
290	Samuel Leach for 2 dit.	02 00 00
290	Jarvis Ballard dit.	02 00 00
204	James Meares dit.	02 08 00
90	John Mason for 1. dit.	02 00 00
205	Benjamin Gibbs for 8 dit.	05 00 00
	Ditto	
564	Jacob Elliott Cr. By sundry accpts viz	01 05 00
291	Andrew Indian Lent him being part of the money Ditto Eliott recd for the Souldiers as p No. 5443.	00 01 00
99	Josiah Arnold dit.	00 02 00
106	David Church dit.	00 01 00
133	George Gray dit.	00 05 00
291	John Carr dit.	00 02 00
293	John Indian dit.	00 01 00
294	Nehemiah Indian dit.	00 01 00
295	John Savage dit.	00 05 00
295	Showaganish Indian dit	00 01 00
216	Joseph Twichell dit.	00 05 00
250	Daniel Canada dit.	00 01 00
	Ditto Rate	
616	Indian Corn Cr. By Sundry accpts. viz 6 bush 0.14.0	00 14 06
203	John Hull for 2 bush No 5438	00 04 00
569	Billeting for 4 bush to Capt Prentice for the Indians No 5439 0.14.0	00 10 06
	Ditto	
616	Brass Dr. To Cambridg Towne for 20 bush as p No. 5436 4.0.0	03 00 00
433		

FIGURE 13. Record of Massachusetts Bay's second auction of Indian slaves in September 23, 1676, showing buyers and amounts, from treasurer John Hull's account book, volume 2. Courtesy of the New England Historic Genealogical Society.

Table 1   Indians sold by John Hull, war treasurer
of Massachusetts Bay, August 24, 1676 (N=66)

Adult males	5
Adult females	31★
Boys	9
Girls	14
Infants	7

★A few sales listed women and "papooses" together in a single group;
this number likely overrepresents adult women, while the infants category underrepresents infants and toddlers.

process of selling and distributing them. Officials rewarded English inhabitants who had stayed in the area during the war, and tried to assess damages
each town had incurred and to assign captives proportionately as a kind of
reparation, and similar practices prevailed in Connecticut.

Local proceedings for dividing captives were complicated pageants that
combined bloody vengeance, participatory political bargaining, and hard-
headed economic transactions. The Providence town meeting convened in
June and August of 1676 "under a Tree by ye Water side," where the freemen
chose a committee headed by Roger Williams to draft a policy regarding "all
matters concejved to belong to ye disposing of ye Jndjans now to be disposed
in ye Towne." Williams's committee recommended that the town allow individuals to keep Indian slaves and servants despite the earlier prohibitions, and
the freemen endorsed this shift. Second, the town determined which Indians
were salable. This group included the "jndians awauscug & ye women &
children yt came with him & yt may Come in." An Indian named Kewashinit, his wife and three children, his father-in-law "& ye old Woman Peter ye
Smith's mother" were also set aside for sale; the townsmen ordered them to
build themselves a shelter and "be at ye Towns dispose" awaiting their fate.
All these Indians became town property by decree. Another Indian, Chuff
(he received his nickname because of his "surliness"), was adjudged an active
"ring leader all ye War" who had done "Mischiefs to our Howses & Cattell."
"The Jnhabitants of ye Towne crjed out for Justice angst him threatning
themselues to kill him if ye Authoritie did not," so Williams convened a
hasty court that condemned the wounded Chuff "& he was shot to Death,
to ye great satisfacjon of ye Towne."[33] One can only imagine how Awascung,
Kewashinit, and their extended families viewed this scene.

Finally, Williams and the group set up a procedure that resembled the
mechanisms town corporations used to distribute land and manage other

common resources. Each head of household who had stayed in the area became a "subscriber" and had rights to certain shares in the proceeds. Tense arguments erupted over the size and number of each man's shares, but eventually they came to an agreement and appointed trusted local leaders Williams, William Hawkins, William Hopkins, and Arthur Fenner to sell the captives and to dole out share moneys. Any local who wished to buy one of the Indians could, and Roger Williams's son Providence loaded the remaining captives onto his sloop and took them to Newport for sale. The committee priced the Indians from one pound to four pounds, ten shillings, which meant that full-share subscribers each received fourteen silver shillings, some wool, and some cloth. A second sale brought even more per share.

Such town sales democratized the ownership of Indians. Of the first lot, only three buyers, including Peter Easton and John Nixen, purchased more than one Indian. Buyers could pay for Indians with wool, "12 Bushells of jndian Corne," suits of clothes, and other country commodities.[34] In Connecticut, even slaves could become owners of Indians, as evidenced by Ruth, a "Negro" woman in Thomas Stanton's household who in October 1676 purchased a twelve-year-old Indian girl "for two trucking cloth Coats, & 5 yards of painted Calico."[35] The girl's father had been shipped to Barbados. Public auctions normalized Indian servitude—especially when overseen by such trusted figures as Roger Williams. They created large numbers of colonists tied to Indian servitude, whether as sellers, buyers, or beneficiaries of collective profits, far beyond the limited networks of the seventeenth-century African slave trade.

Purchasing an Indian also brought access to the labor of relatives in more informal arrangements. Richard Arnold had numerous Indians working on his Pawtuxet farm by 1682, including his "Indian man" Sam, Sam's brother Tom, and a sister, Margaret. Sam was the only one Arnold asserted verbal ownership over (and the only one of the Indians who spoke English). The others may have been formal servants. Or, just as likely, they were free Indians who labored for Arnold because their kinsman was there. On one typical day both men worked in the fields, while Margaret and seven other Indian women did work inside the home and "celler," including "pounding" corn into meal with a mortar and pestle.[36] The presence of slave and servant labor allowed heads of households such as Arnold to pursue other important, revenue-generating tasks off the farm, such as holding public office, artisanal work, and mercantile activity.[37] Arnold worked with the men but also was free to travel for business elsewhere, and eventually he took a seat in the legislature, a sign of his increased economic success. Given the losses from the war in manpower and infrastructure, Indian labor was an important factor in the

region's economic recovery. The period between 1675 and 1730 proved to
be one of rapid population growth, economic expansion, and rising standards
of living for English New England—in part because of Indian servitude.

These very real economic advantages, combined with the public nature
of the trade in Indian slaves, however, served to undermine the few regulations that colonial authorities had constructed to distinguish between Indian
captives and chattel slaves. Devolution of control over captives to localities had long-term consequences. For example, in Rhode Island the towns
approved much longer terms of service for the Indians than the nine years
specified by the Rhode Island Assembly. Providence assigned children age
five and under to serve until age thirty; children five to ten to serve until
age twenty-eight; children ten to fifteen to serve until age twenty-seven;
and youths between the ages of fifteen and twenty to serve until they were
twenty-six. Adults over twenty would serve for eight years, or seven if they
were over thirty. Colonial officials passed a blanket statute in August 1676
that gave wartime decisions by towns and militia captains the power of law,
which meant that the colony essentially went along with local directives.[38]
This made the maximum term of servitude for captives slightly less than
twenty-eight years.

Similarly, town officials sometimes evaded rules about Indian indentures.
Portsmouth had placed the task of selling Indian captives in the hands of
former council members William Cadman and William Woddell. Woddell also served as the overseer of the poor, warning out nonresidents and
binding children of poor English families into servitude. As someone who
already traded in bound labor, Woddell merely added Indian servants to his
portfolio. Extant records have him purchasing not only many Portsmouth
captives but also Indians from other areas. For the Portsmouth captives he
purchased, Woddell used formal indenture contracts. A Pocasset woman
named Meequapew, her son Peter, and her daughter Hannah became his
"apprentices" or indentured servants. Meequapew was to serve for three years
and the children for ten. The contracts followed typical apprenticeship or
indenture forms and specified Woddell's responsibilities to clothe and feed
them, and to free the Indians at the end of the specified term. Unlike contracts he prepared for English children, however, Woddell did not promise to
educate the Indian children or to teach them skills. Nor would Meequapew's
children receive the typical "freedom dues" (such as "clothing and a cow
or a horse foal") that Woddell covenanted to give his English apprentices.
Meequapew at least kept her children with her, although Woddell could also
have sold or transferred their indentures to a third party with permission of
a magistrate—which he was himself.

Most damaging for captives, Indians traded between colonies lost the benefit of whatever regulations might limit enslavement in their previous home. Woddell bought a Wampanoag captive woman from Plymouth resident Adam Wright. Wright had purchased the woman, also named Hannah, from Benjamin Church during the war. Plymouth had permitted enslavement of captives, and Wright had a certificate stating that she had been "condemned by the Authorytie . . . to perpetuall Servitude and Slavery." He specifically conveyed these rights to Woddell via deed. Interestingly, Hannah also signed the contract, effectively consenting to the transfer and asserting "She is willing to be Servant" to Woddell "in manner and form above expressed."[39] One wonders whether Hannah spoke English or understood this transaction's implications. Perhaps she viewed becoming Woddell's slave as preferable to exportation. Having Indians and Africans consent to contracts conveying them as slaves, if not common, was not exceptional—Sylvanus Warro had signed one with Daniel Gookin—especially when the inheritability of slavery remained contested. Such endorsements indemnified masters against servants who later might challenge their enslavement, given the variation in treatment of war captives from colony to colony and even within colonies.

A master could turn a servant into a slave even without a cross-colony transaction. The Almy family of Little Compton acquired many Indians during this period. William Almy bequeathed an Indian couple and their child to heirs in his will in 1676, and his brother Job's estate included two African slaves valued at forty-two pounds and an unnamed number of "Indian servants" valued at thirty-five pounds in 1684.[40] Neither of the valuations specified the amount of time left to serve on a contract, which would have accompanied the listing of an English servant in the inventory. That omission—an increasingly common trend in wills and, beginning in the 1690s, newspaper advertisements listing Indians—conveyed the impression that the Indians were slaves for life.

The cases of two Indian children sold under such circumstances illustrate how Rhode Island and Connecticut law failed to protect Indians from slavery. Perhaps from among the surplus Indians that Providence Williams took to Newport for sale, Governor William Coddington purchased an infant boy, "a Native of their Majties. Colony of New England," whom he named Ben. When Coddington died, his will specified that Ben would receive his freedom in seven years. But his widow remarried and, with her new husband (now Ben's owner), Robert Eaves, took Ben to Pennsylvania. In the process, Ben's position changed from that of a servant with a finite, specified term to that of a slave. Ben petitioned the Pennsylvania Assembly for his freedom in 1693, noting that "yor. Pet[itione]r. Humbly conceives they can no longer

detaine yor. Pet[itione]r. in their said possession but that hee is a Native
Indian and by the will aforesaid a freeman." Ben claimed freedom on the
basis of his origins—New England, not Florida, the Carolinas, or the Caribbean; his ethnicity—native Indian, not African or East Indian; and the legal
contracts that should have assured his freedom but did not. He requested
either his freedom or a new contract specifying his remaining obligation to
Eaves.[41] Freedom suits such as this required significant social capital, and how
Ben acquired so much as a young person far from kin networks remains a
mystery. Ben was not literate. He made a diagonal mark on the petition in
lieu of a signature. Someone—we do not know who—helped him prepare
the petition and arrange a hearing of his case in Philadelphia. The outcome
of the case is unclear, but it progressed far enough that Rhode Island officials
assembled a file of papers relating to Ben's status.

Having the resources to protest his enslavement made Ben unusual. Other
captive Indians were not in a position to challenge the process. In March
1678, Samuel Rogers of New London sold an "Indian Captive girle about
Thirteene or foorteene yeeres of age" named Beck to James Loper of East
Hampton, New York. Rogers, a prosperous baker and farmer, might have
purchased the girl from one of the county auctions or from Uncas and
Owaneco, with whom he enjoyed close relations via his father-in-law, Pequot
war veteran Thomas Stanton. He sold Beck as a slave for life, declaring himself in the deed "to bee the true & Right Owner of the said girle and therefore have good & Lawfull power soe to doe."[42] Loper, a whaling entrepreneur,
had just married the granddaughter of Lion Gardiner and wanted a present
for her. He gave Beck to his "beloved wife Elizabeth" in trust for her father
to oversee "& take care that ye said Indian girle bee not sould or taken from
my said wife but be kept in her right & possession Dueringe her said naturall
life as is expressed in the abovesaid Instrumt of sale to my selfe in Case my
wife her Death: then the right for the said girle to Desend unto the Children
which we now have Living."[43] Rogers's deed turned a servant into a slave for
life; Loper reaffirmed this status in the deed to his wife, which had implications not only for the Loper children but for any future offspring Beck might
have. Slavery was the likely legacy that would "Desend unto" her children
as well.

New England Indians in Diaspora

The stories of Beck and Ben show that being resold often contributed to
the deterioration of an individual Indian's status in servitude. But the most
extreme cases of loss of status involved those New England Indians whom

colonial authorities or individual owners exported abroad during and after the war. Diaspora—the removal of people away from their ancestral lands—is a term that scholars usually associate with the transatlantic African slave trade. But New England Indians experienced their own diaspora in the seventeenth century. Hundreds of individuals became chattel slaves in places where no New England law could mediate their treatment.

As in the aftermath of the Pequot War, trade centers that New Englanders already dominated or wished to enter became the destinations of Indian captives. Despite the prohibitions on New England Indians issued in Barbados and Jamaica, owners such as Fitz-John Winthrop seemingly found buyers there, especially for small lots that formed part of the constant traffic between the two regions. In December 1676 Winthrop received word about the "bad market" for the Indians he had consigned to Nathaniel Eldred in Barbados, but in this, his second speculative slaving venture, Winthrop hoped to receive some payment in molasses, rum, and sugar.[44] Legislation issuing from destination ports in the Caribbean appears to have been temporary and symbolic, resembling the restrictions within New England. Samuel Shrimpton had purchased five slaves at the outset of war and sent one to Jamaica, although authorities made him cancel this transaction and bring the man, Joseph, back to New England. Undiscouraged, Shrimpton took advantage of John Hull's auctions in the summer of 1676. He informed his wife, Elizabeth, in July 1676, "I bought 9 [captives] the other day to send to Jamaica but I thinke to keep 3 of them upon ye [Noddles] Island." Shrimpton subsequently purchased sixteen more Indian men, women, and children, and may have exported others.[45]

Iberia, North Africa, and the Portuguese Wine Islands formed another node of trade and slavery. The Wampanoag, Pocasset, and Christian Indians condemned in the 1675 summer campaigns were among the first shipped abroad into slavery. Plymouth and Massachusetts consigned the 187 captives aboard Captain Thomas Spragg's vessel *Sampson* to be sold in Cádiz, a port on the Atlantic side of the southernmost tip of Spain.[46] Cádiz, which served as a gateway both to North Africa and to the Mediterranean, was already an important destination for New England shipping in 1675. Slightly more Boston and Salem vessels made for destinations on the Iberian Peninsula (primarily Cádiz, Bilbao, Alicante, and Oporto) and the Wine Islands (the Canaries, the Azores, Madeira, and Cape Verde) than to the West Indies in 1662–63, which may be why Spragg first tried to sell his cargo in Spain. The adventurers apparently consigned the Indians to a particular English merchant, John Mathews, who operated a trading company there and served as an English negotiator in repatriating English captives from Muslim slavery. Samuel

FIGURE 14. Samuel Shrimpton, portrait by unidentified artist of the English school, 1675. Note the slave in the background. Courtesy of the Massachusetts Historical Society.

Moseley's father-in-law, Isaac Addington, had interests in the region and may have been involved in the deal; Spragg had served as a privateer before the war in the same waters as Moseley. Merchants took timber, fish, and provisions to ports such as Cádiz; for return cargoes they could purchase salt and wine from nearby producers, or beeswax, gum, and slaves from West Africa.

A polyglot town where English, Dutch, and French merchants maintained trading houses, Cádiz had been a regional center of the slave trade since 1300. Traditionally its slave markets included Africans and South Asians, as well as "Loros," or "Browns," a group that included "Berbericos" (Muslim captives from the Barbary states and elsewhere in North Africa), Indians from the Americas, and people of other ethnicities from southern and eastern Europe and the Ottoman Empire.[47] Religion was the main dividing line between slave and free peoples, although phenotype—that is, racial appearance—began to carry increasing weight. European renegades who had converted to Islam while captive among the Ottomans could be enslaved. Dark-skinned Europeans could be at risk of illegal enslavement by privateers, although English officials did apparently free the occasional Greek or Spanish slave who could prove European and Christian affiliations. Ironically, Cádiz also formed a base of operations for English and colonial efforts to ransom Europeans from captivity among the Algerine states. Numerous mariners from New England experienced enslavement in the region throughout the seventeenth and eighteenth centuries.[48] Generally, families and communities rallied to raise the ransom money for captains and merchants, but ordinary sailors might languish for years or a lifetime. The New England Indians' enslavement met with little surprise or legal challenge in a place where ethnicity and color did not define slave status. Since demand was small locally for field or cane workers, most slaves were purchased for household use, resold to brokers throughout the Mediterranean, employed in building fortifications or public works, or taken on by one of the newer customers in the region: the English government.

English merchants had entered the Wine Islands in large numbers after 1662. Advantageous treaties with Portugal resulting from Charles II's marriage to Catarina de Braganza gave the English unique trading privileges and legal autonomy. As part of Catarina's dowry, Charles received from Portugal the port of Bombay and also the port of Tangier in North Africa in 1667 as a base from which to trade with the Levant. King Charles had become enamored of the use of galleys, and ordered two outfitted in the Mediterranean: the *Margaret* and the *Charles*.[49] Each required nearly 340 rowers. Although European states pressed men into galley service as they did other naval duties, the English appear to have viewed the brutal work of rowing the galley as a unique form of "slavery," suitable only for slave laborers or wage workers, so-called *bonovoglios*. English commanders in Tangier also needed workers to construct fortifications, and these needs sent Tangier's surveyor-general Henry Sheere and naval captain Thomas Hamilton to regional slave markets, including Cádiz.

Sometime before December 1675 John Mathews's eponymous trading company in Cádiz brokered a deal in which Spragg carried thirty of the New England Indians to Captain Hamilton for duty in the galley

Margaret. Hamilton wrote enthusiastically to the Admiralty about the Indians' abilities, finding them "very good men, and in my opinion as good if not better then the Moorish Slaves, so that if there were every year a recruit from those parts (after the galley were once manned), it might be very advantageous for his Majesty's service."[50] Hamilton was desperate, lacking money to pay the ships' builders and maintain the galley, to buy slaves, or to hire extra "Bonavolios" as supplemental rowers.

On board the *Margaret*, the Indians would have encountered excruciating conditions: not just the hard labor of rowing but also a lack of water and food due to Hamilton's shortages. Nine of the thirty Indians, "proveing wth bad usage on boord," soon died. Hamilton bewailed the general lack of food, medicine, bedding, and other basics for the crew and officers. Samuel Pepys, the naval secretary, decided to decommission the galleys in 1676 in favor of two smaller vessels with a combination of sail and human oar power, which required fewer rowers. A letter fragment from April 1676 to the Naval Office indicates that Spragg and Mathews had arranged to pick up

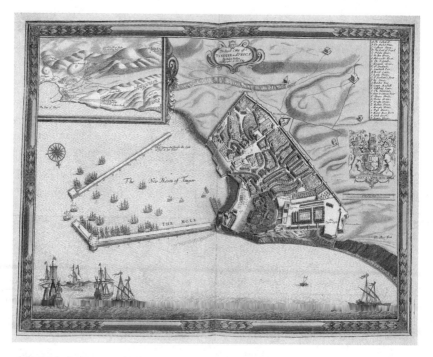

FIGURE 15. Map of Tangier with the mole, the seawall fortification that New England Indians helped construct, from John Seller's *Atlas Maritimus* (1678). Courtesy of the John Carter Brown Library at Brown University.

the remaining New England Indian galley slaves, but it is not clear for what purpose—whether to resell them or because Spragg was under pressure to return some of them to New England. From 1676 onward the English at Tangier exported now-surplus laborers to sell at slave markets all over the Mediterranean and Atlantic, including Cádiz, and some of the Indians may have dispersed through this market.

Still, at least some New England Indians remained at work in Tangier. In February of 1676/77 the Tangier naval commander conveyed approximately seventy-nine slaves to surveyor-seneral Sheere to work on building "H.Msties Mole," a project that had been under construction for nearly a decade. Sheere's plans included a deepwater harbor capable of welcoming naval vessels, protected by a massive stone breakwater, or mole, and fortifications to help foil attacks from the Barbary states. This involved dangerous and backbreaking work: mining rock by blasting with explosives, mixing the rock with cement, packing it into wooden chests, and then conveying and setting the chests of stone mix both under and above water, as well as hand dredging the harbor.[51] The slaves in "His Majesties Bagnio" (a term that conveyed both the sense of a slave pen and a POW camp to contemporaries) included men from Smyrna, Tripoli, Aleppo, Constantinople, Cairo, Rhodes, Napoli, Angola, Spain, and the Balkans. Sheere listed a group separately from the rest under the category "Indians." Ten Indians with English names appear: "Joseph Anthony Stephen John James Daniel Robin Joseph John the Father John the Sonne."[52] This group might also have included some Punkapaug Christian Indians who surrendered in the summer of 1676 but were tried and condemned in Massachusetts.[53]

The ultimate fate of the Cádiz and Tangier Indians is unclear. Like Hamilton, Sheere complained that the lack of supplies and funding meant that his slaves were malnourished and frequently sick and disabled.[54] They lacked sufficient bread for even a basic bread-and-water diet. Some survived into the 1680s, though, as evidenced by the report of an English stonemason who worked in Tangier before traveling to Boston. The man informed John Eliot that he had encountered a community of New England Indians among the workers at the mole. Eliot assumed they were slaves brought by the *Seaflower*, but it is just as likely that they were remnants of the earlier Cádiz group with some possible additions from the later voyage. In November 1683 Eliot begged Robert Boyle, then the secretary of the Corporation for the Propagation of the Gospel, to use his influence and "mediate that they might have leave to get home," either to England or New England.[55] No record of Boyle intervening in the case has surfaced. By the mid-1680s, English administrators had decided to move their base of operations from Tangier to Gibraltar, and in another dispersal civil and naval officers sold off the remaining slaves to regional markets.

According to John Eliot, the *Seaflower*, which carried some seventy Plymouth captives, had gone to Tangier because its captain, Thomas Smith, had difficulty finding Caribbean customers. Smith had stopped at Jamaica in November 1676. Although Jamaica, the main entrepôt for the Caribbean slave trade in general and the Indian slave trade in particular, remains a likely endpoint for the New England Indians, Eliot's contention that Smith took them to Tangier is also plausible. But if Smith did indeed find no market in the Caribbean, another possible destination for those captives was Madagascar, an Indian Ocean island on the southeastern side of Africa near the Cape of Good Hope. Dutch sources mention visits by an "English" ship named *Seaflower* in Madagascar in roughly 1676 and 1678–79, and at least one (unnamed) ship sailing out of Boston and planning to return there appeared in separate records in 1676. "Seaflower" was a common name for ships in this period, but the timing makes it possible that the ship captained by Thomas Smith sold New England Indian slaves in Madagascar.[56]

Madagascar was part of the East India Company's monopoly territory, but the company had not yet exploited it. Instead, the island offered captains a chance to buy slaves while evading national slave trade monopolies, such as the one held by the Royal Africa Company. About twenty-five English or English-American ships traded there between 1675 and 1692. Madagascar's Muslim rulers also welcomed trade with North Africa, with the Dutch from bases in South Africa, Mauritius, and Java, and with the Portuguese in Goa and West Africa, sending approximately six thousand slaves per year into these and other markets. English and American ships generally headed to Barbados to sell their human cargo after stopping at Madagascar. In addition to Malagasy slaves, Madagascar markets included captives from Sri Lanka, Indonesia, Mozambique, and North Africa, all of whom could be purchased much more cheaply than slaves in West Africa. Muskets and ammunition provided the main currency in exchange.[57]

Other New England Indians entered Atlantic slave markets via Fayal, one of the Azores, a chain of volcanic islands that together with Madeira and the Canaries are often called the Wine Islands or Western Islands. New England merchants, including Samuel Maverick, had been trading fish, whale oil, barrel staves, and other products to the Azores, Madeira, and the Canaries since the 1640s, and cargoes to and from the Wine Islands composed about 5 percent of inbound and outbound shipping from New England ports in the late seventeenth century.[58] The former two island chains had been uninhabited when Europeans began to settle them in the fourteenth century, and Spanish colonization had all but destroyed the indigenous population of the Canaries. Samuel Winthrop, the son of Governor John Winthrop Sr., started his career there as a nineteen-year-old clerk, and his brother Stephen shipped cargoes of provisions to Madeira.[59] Although the peak of the colonial wine trade would not arrive until the mid-eighteenth century, already by the seventeenth century the Wine Islands had become a node of Atlantic commerce that linked both hemispheres and the Old and New Worlds. Trade and people from England, Europe, Brazil, North Africa, Senegambia, North America, and Newfoundland flowed back and forth through the islands.

Given the islands' proximity to West Africa and their early role as supply stages for Portuguese and Dutch slave factories, West Indian and African slave traders often bought and sold slaves there or boarded provisions for the next leg of the voyage. Spanish treasure ships followed a route through the islands, making them attractive to both privateers and merchants seeking hard currency. Cape Verde and the Azores felt the influence of Senegambia in culture, personnel, and trade customs and products, and local markets boasted not only English linens but also African textiles and dyes for both continents' manufacturers. The Azores maintained some sugar production, although the American wine trade was in the process of supplanting this industry. As the provisioning of ships, as well as supplying slave-trade forts in Africa, and other colonies, became a more significant part of the Azorean economy, new crops from Europe, Africa, Asia, and America, including grain, sweet potatoes, tobacco, peanuts, manioc, tea, and corn, became staples of the islands' agriculture.[60] Slaves worked these plantations owned by Flemish, Portuguese, and English entrepreneurs, and many of these slaves passed through the slave market, or *pelourinho*, on the island of Fayal. As in Cádiz, aside from being employed in agriculture, slaves served in the homes of Anglo-Portuguese trading magnates or worked in other capacities in the port, including as longshoremen, mariners, washerwomen, or in the sex trades. The permanent population numbered fewer than six thousand, however, and slaves might also be reshipped to other destinations.

In a reversal of typical roles, New Englanders became customers rather than suppliers of provisions in the Atlantic in the 1670s. During King Philip's War, English and Indians alike destroyed much of the region's food supply, killing domestic animals and burning cornfields. Warfare also impeded planting and supply chains. Many Indians faced starvation, while among the English shortages of "bread for the Army," as well as for civilians, became so acute that Connecticut prohibited its merchants from exporting corn or even sending ships to the West Indies without permission, while Massachusetts forbade the outflow of any provisions other than fish.[61] Massachusetts Bay authorities commissioned several voyages to the Wine Islands to pick up corn to feed hungry English colonists. On one such trip, Bernard Trott purchased four thousand bushels of grain in Flores, another Azorean Island, in the summer of 1675, and the Massachusetts Council asked him to return in the summer of 1676 for more. Given his connections in the region, in 1677 officials gave him a different commission: to find several New England Indians who had been sold there and to ransom and repatriate them to New England.

The driving force behind Trott's commission was a kidnapping orchestrated by individuals under the command of Richard Waldron, an Indian trader based at Black Point, Maine. Waldron served as a deputy in the Massachusetts General Court and during the war had been appointed captain of the eastern settlements in New Hampshire and Maine. Sometime around August 1676, Henry Lawton, William Waldron (Richard's brother), and a Huguenot adventurer with Massachusetts roots named John Laverdure had lured approximately thirty Pennacook and Micmac men, women, and children from the Cape Sable / Machias Bay area aboard their ship on pretense of trade and diplomacy.[62] That Lawton and Waldron intended to capture slaves seemed clear to Thomas Gardner, a Pemaquid magistrate who investigated the case. Gardner complained bitterly about their "perfidious and uniust dealings," noting that they "had shackles aboard" when they sailed to Machias. Gardner perceived that the situation in Maine was already unraveling as treaty negotiations stalled. Bitter Wampanoag refugees and angry Pennacook and Penobscot Indians together attacked several trading posts and homesteads in July, taking captives.

Citing the general warrant they held from Richard Waldron to seize enemy Indians in the region, however, Lawton and the other men immediately sailed to Fayal with their shackled human cargo.[63] William Waldron was the "merchant" of record on the voyage, using a ketch named *Endeavor* leased from Simon Lynde of Boston. Lynde, among Boston's richest men, had loaned considerable sums of money to the Bay Colony to pay war expenses and had been a big purchaser of Indian captives. The *Endeavor*, built in New London by the family of its captain, John Haughton, had earlier transported slaves in the Barbados trade. Part of the profit in the venture went to two other investors: Boston merchants John Glover and John Hubbard.

Lawton, Laverdure, and Waldron had miscalculated, though, because the kidnapped Cape Sable group included an important sachem named Plagamore and his wife. Outraged Micmacs joined the war against the English and attacked trading posts and farms. Indians began harassing English fishing vessels, taking captives of their own. Even as Indian forces under Benjamin Church captured and killed Metacom and effectively ended the war in the south, within a few months Massachusetts had all but abandoned most of its northern outposts as a new conflict exploded.

Slaving was not the only cause of these conflicts, but it certainly contributed to the deterioration of relations between the English and the Wabanaki and ended the shaky truce. The previous autumn, Boston authorities—apparently mistakenly—had sold into slavery "as spyes" two emissaries from Wannalancet, although they eventually redeemed them. Meanwhile, English sailors off Machias had nearly drowned the infant son of the sachem Squando while bullying Squando's wife, and the child died soon after. Plagamore, Squando, and Wannalancet were part of the Wabanaki alliance, a group of affiliated tribes. Wabanaki neutrality proved decisive in Metacom's defeat, as Wannalancet had reluctantly refused to help the Wampanoag. Moreover, Wannalancet withheld violence in 1675 despite kidnappings and the destruction of Pennacook villages by Samuel Moseley and other privateers. He had negotiated the redemption of English captives and had even rounded up Indian captives and sent them to Boston. Now that relationship was in jeopardy. In Pemaquid, Gardner faced Indian anger and wanted Lawton and Waldron prosecuted.

Presented with these disastrous consequences, Massachusetts Bay authorities invoked the man-stealing law for the first time since 1646 and arrested all the men, including Richard Waldron, pending a full investigation. And they asked Trott for help. Trott sent his agent Samuel Turrell aboard the *Joseph Nash* for the Indians and provisions. Amazingly, Turrell managed to recover "a couple" of the Indians from Fayal in July 1677 for "one hundred Mil Res in Ready Money," but council records mention the rescue only of Plagamore and his wife.[64] According to several Portsmouth mariners who had voyaged to Fayal, a ketch had arrived from Boston—probably *Endeavor*, since the men called it "Mr. Lines" (Lynde's) ship—carrying New England Indians. Someone named Fisher had purchased approximately seventeen of them for "thirty Seven or Thirty Eight pipes of Cong Wines."[65] Another deposition mentioned a group of thirteen Indians from New England that aroused curiosity, but the ship's master and sailors would not tell the Portsmouth men the ship's name and origins or what part of New England the Indians came from.

This smaller group probably came from Prudence Island, taken in a separate man-stealing incident. In the autumn of 1675, Plymouth forces under Captains John Gorham and Matthew Fuller had moved into the Narragansett Bay area in pursuit of Wampanoags and Pocassets who had fled to the Narragansetts. Both men would participate in the Swamp Battle in December. En route, however, they took captives for profit, and in October they raided Prudence Island in Narragansett Bay over the course of a day and night and kidnapped "jack an Indian & his Squa & papoose" from the estate of William Paine. They also "surprised" other Indians on the island, including a man named Caleb staying with Jack; Jack's young brother Tom, who worked on William Allin's farm; another Indian named Tom; and other unnamed Indians. Jack and his family lived on Paine's estates but had not become formal servants until that year. They had contracted themselves to serve Paine for a year in a kind of bond for good behavior because it protected them from enslavement and capture. Paine had promised to vouch for their pro-English stance and claimed he had procured a certificate from Rhode Island authorities that they could show to other English and thereby move about the region without fear of capture.[66] But Gorham and Fuller bundled them aboard ship in the night before Paine could get certificates from Plymouth and Massachusetts Bay. The men told Paine "they had good grounds for wt they did" and refused to release the Indians, instead taking them to Plymouth, where they would "question" them.[67]

Jack and the other Indians had created bonds of usefulness and possibly friendship with their English neighbors. Five English neighbors, including William Allin and James Sweet, joined the protest. They testified that Jack was a Narragansett—a group not yet at war with the United Colonies. They noted that Jack had lived on the island for thirteen years "of[f] and on" "with sundry of the Tenants there."[68] According to Paine, Jack "planted on my land" and served as an interpreter. Seemingly, Jack and many of the other Indians on Prudence Island participated in the informal tenancy arrangements that Benjamin Church, Lion Gardiner, John Winthrop Jr., and other landowners used to create useful pools of day laborers. As in those cases, some of the other "sundry Tenants" were English. Paine was a resident, but other absentee property owners, including Roger Williams, maintained stock farms there, and all used tenant labor. Jack's family pitched their wigwam at certain seasons on what had been Narragansett land (now patented by Paine via a gift from Metacom, ironically, who also claimed the island). The family engaged in other subsistence activities and hosted kin and friends as they worked for the English.

Paine immediately wrote to Governors Leverett and Winslow to try to recover the Indians, but by then Gorham and Fuller had shipped them to Fayal.[69] Not only was Paine genuinely worried about the Indians, but he also feared Narragansett vengeance: "The Indians Conceive that I betrayed & Sould them & will not bee beat out of it here whereby I may also suffer wrongfully by their private malice & from publique." As Paine recognized, such incidents made war with the Narragansetts even more likely. Like the Cape Sable incident, the Prudence Island case prompted intervention by the General Court. But either the magistrates failed to order Trott to find the Prudence Island Indians in addition to the Machias Indians, or his agent was unable to do so. The former seems likely, since the original order only involved sufficient money to redeem Plagamore and his wife.

There is no evidence that Jack and his family ever managed to return to New England. Instead, they remained part of the eastern Atlantic slave system. Gorham and Fuller suffered no consequences, despite the fact that man stealing was a capital crime. Gorham died of fever soon after the Swamp Battle, but Fuller continued to serve and win honors and position. William Waldron proclaimed his innocence and petitioned for bail, but he faced a trial after indictment by a grand jury, as did John Haughton, the captain of the *Endeavor.* "Not Hauing the feare of God before his eyes & being Instigated by the divill in Nouember by himselfe & his partner Henry Lauton as his order wth whom he left his Colmission," Waldron, the court charged, "did vnlawfully surprise & steale away seventeen Indians men weomen & children & in yr vessel called the endeavour of Boston Barrjed & sent them to ffyall & there made sale of them Contrary to the peace of our Soueraigne Lord the king his Croune & dignity the lawes of God & of this Jurisdiction: entituled man stealing." Juries acquitted Waldron, however, and in a separate trial demanded only a ten-pound fine from Haughton. Laverdure jumped bail, took his mother's English name, and resurfaced as a trader in Nova Scotia, while Lawton and Lynde emerged with their freedom and reputations intact.

Richard Waldron, whose permissive policies inspired his brother's voyage, died gruesomely at the Wabanakis' hands more than a decade later—but not before he personally engaged in another brazen slaving venture in the autumn of 1676, including a mass kidnapping known as "Waldron's Ruse."[70] Sent by Massachusetts Bay authorities to treat with the eastern Indians out of justifiable fear that an influx of Wampanoag refugees from King Philip's War would provoke their Wabanaki kin to attack the colony's exposed eastern frontier, Waldron invited them to parley under a flag of truce. Massachusetts had borrowed Connecticut's strategy of trying to separate "surrenderers" from captives, but Waldron's application of the policy at Cocheco (now Dover, New Hampshire) undermined it from the start. Waldron's commission was to indemnify Indians against execution and enslavement (unless they had murdered English) and invite them to join English forces. Hundreds of Wamesit, Narragansett, Nipmuc, and Wampanoag men, women, and children accepted the offer and entered Cocheco, along with their Pennacook relatives and hosts, where Waldron offered them drink and entertainment in the form of war games—except that the game was real.

Instead of staging a mock battle, Waldron's forces attacked the Indians. He bragged to the Massachusetts Council that they captured "80 fighting Men & 20 Old Men & 250 women and children, 350 in all."[71] Some of the individuals who surrendered had in fact fought on both sides in what had been an extremely complex conflict for Indians with few good choices, given poor English treatment of allied Indians and the pull of kin ties among Metacom's supporters. Others were kin and relatives of men currently fighting with English forces, and still others were Pennacooks and Penobscots with whom Massachusetts authorities desperately wanted alliance. Waldron executed some of the men, enrolled others in his forces, and shipped the rest, approximately two hundred, to Boston for sale.[72]

These events, and particularly the invocation of the man-stealing statute, suggest that New England authorities did try to set some limits on the taking and enslaving of Indians. The relatively slight punishments doled out, however, point to the weakness of these interventions and of the man-stealing statute itself both in terms of enforcement and application, especially during wartime. No judges' instructions remain from the Waldron and Haughton cases, so we do not know whether authorities wanted convictions and were thwarted by juries, or whether they were content with the indictments, which demonstrated at least a public commitment against kidnapping. One could argue that the showy prosecution in this case in fact conveyed a sense that all other enslavements had followed legal procedure. Moreover, the fate of the Prudence Island group indicates that without a compelling interest, such as the threat of an unwanted war, as in the case of the Wabanaki, once Indians entered the system of Atlantic slavery authorities did not try very hard to free them. John Paine's influence and the web of relationships that Jack's family created with English and Indians on Prudence Island proved insufficient to procure the Indians' freedom.

These and many other cases illustrated a new reality: individuals and governments transformed many hundreds of formerly autonomous Indians who were neither captives nor "surrenderers"—Christian and non-Christian, allies and neutral parties—into servants and slaves. For many English, servitude had become an important way to manage the hybridity of the society that colonists and Indians now lived in. In reality, servitude was not the normative state for Indians—more remained autonomous than not—but the sheer numbers enslaved during the war precipitated a shift in perception for the English. In the eighteenth century, Indian servants would became incorporated into a subclass of servants and slaves of color, subject to distinct legislative regimes, antimiscegenation laws, and "black codes" of conduct that separated them from English and free Indians.

Meanwhile, the war had devastated much of the wealth accumulated by many Indian communities and individual households, a trend that forced servitude exacerbated. This continued transfer of Indian wealth to the English pushed more free Indians into day-labor arrangements with the English. Execution and exportation of men put additional strains on Indian household economies and communities. Female-led households would become a growing and eventually dominant phenomenon in Indian populations near English centers by the mid-eighteenth century, and eventually women and children would become targets of voracious colonial labor markets as well.

One group that did have some success in using social capital to free unjustly enslaved Indians and to ameliorate the worst aspects of the new system were Indian leaders allied with the English. Uncas, Ninigret, and Christian Indian leaders such as William Ahaton had influence, and they used it. The actions of the former two leaders appear in the record more indirectly, but Ahaton filed numerous petitions to local and colonial governments that led to freedom from captivity for several children and two women. In the aftermath of the war, interventions by Ahaton and other sachems demonstrated the continued importance of Indian leadership. They petitioned for specific laws and protections that affected both free Indians and those in servitude. Ordinary individuals not in leadership positions also had success with petitions.

In earlier conflicts, colonists had clashed with Indians whom they recognized as members of distinct sovereign nations. King Philip's War had transformed the Indians of southern New England into subjects, and the cessation of conflict meant that the large-scale enslavement of southern New England Indians had ended. "No longer forraigners and strangers," these new native subjects could not be "captives in a just war."[73] Without a hint of irony, when Mohawk allies kidnapped Natick Christian Indians in 1677, the United Colonies reacted with outrage and expressed determination to help their Indian subjects. The commissioners demanded assistance from New York's governor, Edmund Andros, in recovering "those poore prayeing Naticke Indian captives."[74] At the same time, the New England colonies faced new relationships with imperial authorities in the post-1675 era, as Massachusetts lost its charter, and all four colonies scrambled to avoid royal annihilation of their autonomous governments.[75] The colonists' treatment of the crown's Indian subjects had become a source of much interest in London, almost all of it critical. Still, many North American Indians remained outside these new civil relationships and thus remained enslavable under New England statutes. The aggressive slaving of Samuel Moseley, Richard Waldron, and others during King Philip's War had sparked an ongoing conflict with the Wabanaki alliance of northeastern New England. War captives from the southern colonies and from Spanish Florida also entered New England society, as the supply of local Indians failed to satisfy demands for bound laborers. Interactions with these groups would lead English colonists to review their own construction of what it meant to be an Indian in New England, including capacity for citizenship—or enslavement.

CHAPTER 8

"Free men subjects to the king"

The Search for Enslavable Indians in the Northeast and Southeast

In adjusting to this new world of postwar Indian relations, the colonists first turned to sources outside the region for Indian slaves. Despite these changes, local native slavery and involuntary servitude persisted and even flourished into the eighteenth century. Initially, English colonists in southern New England evaded the new barriers by importing Native Americans from other areas. Two regions in particular offered potential supplies of Indian laborers in the late seventeenth and early eighteenth centuries because intense warfare created conditions for enslavement: northern New England and the southeastern frontier of English settlement, including the Carolinas and the boundaries of Spanish Florida. English colonists incorporated captives from both sources into their homes, farms, and workshops, but in the end the search for enslavable Indians outside southern New England encountered serious challenges. Security risks and unprecedented retaliation created problems on a scale that the colonists simply had not encountered in their earlier efforts to bind Indian labor. British and indeed colonial strategic interests called for robust Indian participation in warfare as allies, so imperial officials began to criticize the practice of enslavement in unprecedented ways. By mid-century, new conceptions of Indian citizenship and subjecthood—not just for southern New England Indians, but for all Indians in the British Empire—undermined the colonists' own consensus about whom they could legally and practically reduce to servitude.

Indians to the East: The Wabanaki

One potential source of captives was the Wabanaki, whom the English called "eastern Indians": a loose alliance of groups, including the Pennacooks, Norridgewocks, Penobscot, Pemaquid, Micmac, Abenaki, and bands of Algonquians occupying a large territory that included what is now Maine, New Hampshire, Vermont, northern Massachusetts, New Brunswick, Nova Scotia, Prince Edward Island, Quebec south of the St. Lawrence, and Newfoundland. The Wabanaki also maintained ties with Iroquoian peoples living in mission settlements of Kahnawake and Quebec. Unlike the shattered Native American societies of southern New England, the Wabanaki had more or less succeeded in remaining neutral through King Philip's War. They remained quasi-sovereign, independent entities, and emerged from the conflict with their regional power enhanced and their numbers augmented by war refugees, with a population that numbered approximately ten thousand.[1] As the English sought to pursue fleeing Nipmucs, Narragansetts, and Wampanoags, and buttress their northern positions, however, tensions and open warfare with the Wabanaki followed. Warfare on the northeastern frontier erupted even as it ended in the south, punctuated by treaties in 1678, but it resumed again in earnest in 1689. Thereafter, almost continuously, northeastern North America formed a central battleground between contending empires through 1760.

As indigenous space between New France and English America, the area was strategically significant. Jeremy Dummer Jr., a colonial agent in England, called it "America's Carthage," and warned that the colonies would have no peace until the British conquered and subdued it. "Which if it be once effected," he added, "the British Empire in America will be secure & flourishing & the Crown of Great Britain may in time be as Opulent and powerful in the West Indies as the states of Holland are in the east."[2] The North Atlantic was a central node in Atlantic trade routes. Its port cities (and the rivers that linked these towns to inland resources), timber, and fishing grounds attracted traffic, and the ocean itself formed a crossroads, a kind of floating market where exchange of all kinds took place among ships without the necessity of making port.[3] Acadia, Nova Scotia, and Newfoundland abutted extremely rich fishing areas. Transporting this catch to Europe and the Caribbean, and also supplying the fishing vessels themselves with consumer goods, made the area an essential leg of Atlantic trade for New England merchants. These ports also represented the shortest transatlantic passage to Britain and northern Europe and therefore an important stop for troop movements and supplies. The Indian trade still generated profits for French and English monopoly trading companies, and trade remained crucial to imperial diplomacy with the native inhabitants.[4]

All told, "this being the Center of their Trade, & the Magazine where the Wealthy American Merchants covet to make their hoards," northeastern North America represented a vital interest for the New England governments, and they tended to support wars in the region with extensive commitments of troops and material and to urge British action.[5] For the French, the region remained equally strategic, since it protected access to the St. Lawrence River and French settlements at Quebec and Montreal. Thus, the northeast formed one theater of war in a series of grueling global conflicts that pitted some combination of France, Spain, and Bavaria against Great Britain, Austria, Prussia, Holland, and Denmark (King William's War, 1689–97; the War of Spanish Succession/Queen Anne's War, 1702–13; King George's War, 1744–48/the War of Austrian Succession), as well as the central theater in more localized regional contests (Dummer's War, 1722–27).[6] From the Indians' perspective, though, and to an extent from the colonists' perspective, these were Indian wars fought for control of territory, resources, and captives rather than for larger imperials aims. Nonetheless, imperial engagement had consequences for the English colonists and all the New England Indians in varying ways.

Despite the protection from enslavement now extended toward conquered Native American subjects in southern New England, the nearly constant warfare to the north offered another avenue for the taking of Indian captives. Massachusetts passed several acts at the onset of King William's War in 1689, in 1694, and again from 1704 to 1707 during Queen Anne's War that used the taking and selling of Indian captives—especially women and children—as a means of recruiting and paying troops.[7] Although the Wabanaki remained nonaligned, and indeed insisted that they had not made subjection to either the French or the English, the language of these recruiting bills and of the declarations of war that accompanied them deployed the same dual definitions that colonists had used against the Wampanoag and Narragansetts: it identified the Wabanaki both as foreign enemies and as insurgents—"Indian Rebells." Either definition made the Indians vulnerable to enslavement. Published scales of the price that both dead Indians and live captives of all ages and both genders would bring ranged from ten to sixty pounds. Massachusetts initially compensated soldiers at an equal rate for dead or captive Indians, but by Dummer's War in the 1720s, living captives brought slightly higher rewards. The Massachusetts Assembly passed an additional act in 1722 that offered even larger rewards for civilians and volunteers who did not receive regular army pay; such individuals would receive a one-hundred-pound reward for scalps of males age twelve and over, fifty pounds for all others, and "the benefit of the women and children prisoners under the age of 12 who are to be transported"—that is, exported.[8] These bounties continued to be part of war preparation for armies on the eastern frontier through 1760. Given this incentive structure, and also because of the logistics of transporting prisoners over such distances, expeditions seemed often to have settled upon killing Indian men, women, and children rather than taking them prisoner. So many scalps came in that in Massachusetts authorities issued stern penalties for counterfeiting or bringing in the scalps of friendly Indians nearby. At the battle of Norridgewock in 1724, Captain Johnson Harmon estimated his troops killed nearly all the inhabitants of a village that included approximately sixty "fighting men" and one hundred women and children.[9]

Still, most of these expeditions brought at least a few captives back. An Indian woman captured at Cocheco (Dover, New Hampshire) provided valuable intelligence to English troops about Indian strength in Maine in 1676, and Benjamin Church took captives on each of four assaults on Maine and Acadia between 1689 and 1695. Harmon brought four or five women and children back from Norridgewock, including the wife of the sachem Bomazeen (who himself had been taken captive on earlier raids).[10] Sometimes army officers incorporated the captives as workers in their own households, as in the case of Colonel John Gorham, who kept an Indian girl from his expedition to Nova Scotia during King George's War.[11]

Just as in King Philip's War, charges of wrongful enslavement by Indians allied with the English were common, especially in the earliest years of conflict, starting with Richard Waldron's mass kidnapping in 1676. Local Pennacook Indians had been caught up in Waldron's net as well. Wannalancet, the Pennacook sachem, complained that some of his men had agreed to assist the English in their assault on Black Point and Casco in September 1676 as a signal of goodwill, but while they were away Waldron's forces had kidnapped their wives and children at their homes in Cocheco—despite their having "life & liberty promised & ingaged"—and sold them in Boston to Thomas Deane and James Whitcomb. Daniel Gookin intervened to protect one woman, Mary Namesit, and her child: "upon motion to ye counsel she was stopt in prison & a pece of Red cloth tyed about her arme & neck." Namesit's scarlet trimmings kept her from being exported to the Azores, and the Massachusetts Council ordered Waldron to refund Whitcomb and Deane's money.[12]

Hostages taken at negotiations as well as captives from various invasion ventures regularly appeared in Portsmouth in New Hampshire, Boston,

Rhode Island, and other centers. The English required hostages at the conclusion of a treaty at Pemaquid in 1690 and again in 1692, when fifteen Indian men, women, and children "lodged" in the Boston jail in August and September, along with accused witches from Salem. One of the children, a boy, was "turned over" to Richard Short, captain of the English *Nonesuch*, whether for return or for sale is unclear.[13] Indian "spies" were brought back as captives from Saco and Pemaquid in 1695. Although the Indians made efforts to establish prisoner and captive exchanges, the colonists remained cool to such suggestions in 1690–91. Occasionally, local authorities in frontier towns such as Springfield captured Indians on raiding parties and held them. Some were incarcerated in the Boston area for long periods; the Port Royal Indians complained via the French commandant, Charles La Tourasse, that some of their countrymen had died in Boston, and they begged for the return of the remaining tribespeople.[14]

Hostages and prisoners broke out of jail with some frequency, adding to the colonists' concerns about their own security and about the loyalty of nearby Indians. In Springfield, some Indians implicated in an attack on Deerfield filed their way through prison bars, having been provided with tools by sympathetic local Indians, according to magistrate John Pynchon.[15] Several Indian hostages, including the Penobscot sachem Saccaristis, and at least one other man "taken Captive by Capt. Lovewell," escaped the Boston area in the fall of 1725. Saccaristis and his companion managed to break out of the fort at Castle William "Cloathed in English Habit of a Red Colour." They traveled northward in a stolen canoe and made it to the Merrimack River before floodwaters blocked their attempt to cross.[16]

Other captives and hostages managed to regain their freedom in more direct and conventional ways, however, because now the New England governments faced external constraints when it came to pressing Indian captives into involuntary service. Pressure from nearby colonial governments, especially Edmund Andros and his successors in New York; from imperial authorities in London and military commanders who feared alienating potential Indian allies; and, finally, from the Wabanaki themselves, all protected the northern Indians from the scale of enslavement that had afflicted the Indians of southern New England.[17]

The British Empire and Indian Citizenship

Although the strategy of appealing to their identity as English subjects—of the crown, not the colonies—had failed in the seventeenth century for the Narragansetts, the issue of Indian subjecthood and citizenship became newly relevant to the status of New England Indian captives and involuntary servants during the provincial era. Indians had a place in Oliver Cromwell's design for displacing other Europeans from the Caribbean, but his regime had paid minimal attention to North American Indian policy.[18] The Restoration of Charles II brought heightened scrutiny of all facets of the New England colonies' administration, including their treatment of Native Americans. Seen from London, the simultaneity of King Philip's War, the Susquehannock Wars that preceded and intertwined with Bacon's Rebellion, Iroquoian conflicts that threatened regions from New York to the Carolinas, and indigenous rebellions in the Caribbean all pointed to a failure of colonist-generated Indian policy and the need for closer imperial supervision. Large English populations and wealth were now at risk in North America and the Caribbean. The desire to restrict local autonomy and rationalize imperial policy played a role in the revocation of Massachusetts Bay's charter and in English efforts to restructure colonial government along more centrally directed lines via the Dominion of New England. The Glorious Revolution in England and America slowed this shift but did not entirely stop it, and the renewal of warfare in the northeast made imperial control of Indian affairs more imperative in the eyes of policy makers than ever.

Among the severest critics of the New England governments were the members of the King's Council and the Board of Trade, who asserted greater control over Indian affairs in 1691 after the new Massachusetts charter went into effect. The King's Commissioners for Plantations noted the prevalence of debt peonage and the loss of Indian lands when they sternly censured the Massachusetts General Court in 1701 for that colony's "averseness . . . to establish laws" for the relief of its Native American subjects.[19] Certainly, good relations with the Indians of southern New England had to be the starting point of successful regional policy. Royal officials and military leaders became especially interested in the fate of New England Indians when it came to the northeastern wars. For strategic reasons, imperial policy dictated an anti-enslavement stance.

Certainly, the Iroquois Five Nations (soon six) remained a linchpin of British continental policy; given the Iroquois's hegemonic stature and territorial reach, this was a necessity. And the colonists, perhaps even more than the British, remained rabidly anti-French and fearful of Catholic influence in North America. French-allied Iroquoian Catholic Indians from Kahnawake and other mission towns mounted terrifying and violent raids in Maine, New Hampshire, and Massachusetts, taking English captives, destroying farms, and pushing the northern and western boundaries of New English settlement nearly back to pre-1670 lines. The Wabanaki and their allies could impede the flow of goods and personnel down the St. Lawrence and other rivers even as far as the Hudson Bay Company's James Bay outposts—which Indians helped the French seize during the early decades of the eastern wars. The proximity of the Wabanaki to New York and the Hudson–Lake George corridor made them an important player in trade there. British officials were desperate to prevent the Wabanaki from fully embracing the French and adding to the potent Indian alliance backing Quebec, even as the French were desperate to woo them. Baron de Saint-Castin, the French governor of Acadia, had married a daughter of Penobscot sachem Madockawando, and a few Wabanaki villages began accepting Jesuits in the 1710s and 1720s.

The Wabanaki proved to be a most formidable enemy in their own right, and they presented a severe diplomatic and strategic challenge for the British and the colonists. The Wabanaki dealt serious military defeats to Governor Andros—one of his last acts as governor-general of the Dominion of New England was to lose to the Indians at Saco—and prevailed against even such successful veterans as Benjamin Church. They wreaked havoc with New England fishing and shipping, not only by attacking camps and ports as well as interrupting the fur trade, but also by taking to the sea themselves. New Englanders called them pirates, and the Wabanaki boatmen proved a match for many New England trading and fishing vessels. At first, they attacked from canoes; but by the 1720s the Wabanaki had taken so many English vessels as prizes, and managed to maintain, repair, and acquire necessary material for them, that the Indians had their own North Atlantic fleet.

In 1724 shocked Bostonians read an account in the *News-Letter* of a battle in which Indians repelled an attack by a combined New Hampshire and Boston fleet and returned canon fire with artillery of their own: "they met and engaged in a large Schooner w/ two Pateraroes or Swivel Guns, and gave them several Vollies, which the Indians briskly answered, and with a great shot, cut Dr. Jackson's Shrowds and Main sheet, and wounded him with three swan shot." Just prior, in a single offensive, the Indians had taken "11 fishing vessels, 45 men belonging to the several vessels, 22 of which were killed, 23 taken captive."[20] In what might have been an ironic swat at Massachusetts' bounty list, the Indians demanded fifty pounds for the return of each vessel, and thirty pounds for each captive. The Wabanaki were inflicting real economic damage on New England by disrupting a key industry and by taking hundreds of English captives of their own—an important form of leverage in securing better treatment and even the return of eastern Indians in English hands.

In this environment, provincial officials such as Andros of New York and Lieutenant Governor Robert Treat of Connecticut worried that New

England's well-deserved reputation for enslavement threatened to drive the eastern Indians into the arms of the French.[21] French officials such as Pierre LeMoyne d'Iberville, who led successful French assaults on Hudson's Bay, as well as the Maine and Newfoundland coasts in the 1690s, and Joseph de Villebon, the governor of Acadia, exploited native fears of enslavement by the English to recruit Indian allies, and they contrasted their own behavior with that of the English. This was disingenuous, since French colonizers trafficked in Indian slaves in Louisiana, while authorities in French Canada permitted the enslavement of western "outsider" Indians captured in war, such as the Pawnees and, increasingly, Fox and other groups from the lower Great Lakes and Mississippi Valley.[22] Nevertheless, during the 1690s and early 1700s French leaders in Quebec vociferously protested to colonial governments as well as British authorities about the enslavement of Kennebec and Pemaquid Indians as a violation of the rules of war, and they threatened to retain English prisoners if New Englanders refused to abide by the rules of prisoner exchange and return Indians loyal to the French.[23] Indians found these arguments persuasive, and the perceived threat of enslavement became part of anti-English resistance movements among other groups of Indians by the mid-eighteenth century, including participants in Pontiac's Rebellion.[24] In contrast, Villebon and Iberville cast the Indians as French subjects, citizens, and soldiers—groups protected by the laws of war and therefore immune from captivity and slavery.[25]

Native groups in northern New England and eastern Canada could make good on these threats to capture and keep English prisoners. The commodification of Indian captives happened slowly in North America. Many groups, including the Iroquois and others in the Northeast, continued to take captives for the reasons they always had: for vengeance and torture, to cement alliances, and to replace lost kin through adoption. By the late seventeenth and early eighteenth centuries, however, European centers of Indian slavery such as New England, South Carolina, New Mexico, and eventually Quebec and New Orleans—all firmly linked to an Atlantic economy of labor—had begun to alter traditional Native American rationales for warfare and captivity. Europeans' demand for Indian labor, either for internal use or export or both, began to absorb a greater share of the captive stream, creating massive, long-distance internal networks of slave fairs and markets.[26] These markets in turn affected the rationales for warfare and captive taking itself, and they created new financial incentives for Indians and Europeans to take, transport, hold for ransom, or sell captives in just about every region of North America. War bounties from colonial, French, and British governments hastened this monetization of captivity even in areas where labor demands were less pressing. For Indians whose subsistence bases and other modes of economic activity faced constant European threats, taking captives became a new source of income and trade goods.

As a result of these long-term shifts, Wabanaki, other Algonquian, and Iroquoian peoples adopted hybrid systems in which they kept and absorbed some European and Indian captives but took many more as a form of economic activity. Captives became a trade good, a commodity that brought French and English bounties, and a source of ransom money. At least some observers realized that taking Wabanaki captives merely provoked the Indians to increase their attacks on Europeans and "friend Indians" in order to take hostages of their own: "some of whome they Sell for Servants to the Inhabitants of Canada, & others they carry into the woods, & keep 'em for their own Slaves."[27] And now the English themselves faced enslavement. In newspapers and books, colonists read about devastating attacks on towns and farms in Deerfield, Saco, and Dover, where Indians killed men, women, and children and dragged the survivors back to Kahnawake, Quebec, and Acadia for sale, for labor, and (even more horrifyingly for some New Englanders) for conversion to Catholicism and absorption into new communities, be they French or Indian or both.[28] Captivity also affected the troops themselves. Both Indian and English soldiers fell prisoner to the Wabanaki and the French Indians. Indians kept Samuel Newell of Roxbury "in slavery" for four years before he managed to escape along with an Indian soldier in 1695.

Indian Soldiers in New England Armies

English military commanders and at least some provincial officials expressed concern that enslavement would hamper their efforts to recruit Indian soldiers at a time when such auxiliaries were becoming more crucial than ever.[29] During King Philip's War, New England Indians became integrated into colonial military forces in unprecedented ways, and this trend continued apace during the northeastern conflicts. For King William's War, Massachusetts first turned to Christian Indians in the praying towns of Natick and Punkapoag, paying the men one shilling in cash and eight shillings in clothing to help in the assault on Wells, Maine, in July 1689. The next month, the colony began enrolling enlistees in much larger numbers: ninety from Punkapoag and Natick under Captains Thomas Prentice and Noah Wiswall, and two hundred from Medfield and Woburn under Ebenezer Johnson and Lieutenant George Barber "to reinforce the army at the eastward."[30] During each of his four expeditions to the east in the 1690s, Benjamin Church recruited Indian troops, including an entire company he raised to attack

Chignecto in Acadia in 1697–98.[31] Mohegans and Pequots under Ben Uncas and Peter Aspinwall fought for Connecticut.

Military service brought Indian issues to the forefront of colonial and British policy in ways that had potential to improve Indians' status. Governor Robert Treat of Connecticut wrote to his counterpart William Bradstreet of Massachusetts in 1689 about the need to treat Indians better on a number of fronts. For Treat, this meant promptly paying troops and removing officers who abused them, but it also meant creating goodwill and treating all Indians more equitably by honoring treaties and leases, paying quitrents owed to tribes, and stopping the indiscriminate kidnapping and selling of Indians. Treat himself owned Indian captives; he was not advocating a ban on enslavement but rather a broader attention to the concerns of a suddenly important constituency. Army service garnered Indians respect within local communities as well. Native men who served on these expeditions, and in some cases their widows and children, successfully petitioned for pensions due to injury, years or even decades after their service, just as their English comrades did. In 1706, Ben Indian of Scituate, who had accompanied Church to Passamaquoddy, received three pounds plus an appointment as "public Sentinell" that carried forty shillings in annual wages to compensate him for disabling wounds acquired during his service. Simon Sinkaway, who lost a foot due to frostbite after a winter spent scouting for Captain George Jackson, also received supplementary monies. The General Court granted a pension to William Jeffery of Harwich in 1727 in recognition of his service at the battle of St. Georges Fort in 1724 during Dummer's War.[32]

The importance of New England Indian soldiers became clear to British military officials and cabinet officials during Queen Anne's War. Samuel Vetch (commander of the garrison at Annapolis Royal) and Francis Nicholson (leader of a planned land expedition to Canada and a maritime assault on Nova Scotia) described imperial involvement in the creation of a new provincial army in 1709. British and colonial officials intended that the provincial troops be better equipped and experience more lengthy training than the typical militia forces. They were to be uniformed troops, four hundred from Rhode Island and New Hampshire, six hundred from Connecticut, and one thousand from Massachusetts, plus others from New York and, theoretically, Pennsylvania.[33]

Vetch and Nicholson soon discovered that "all of the Governours concerned In this Land Expedition thought it absolutely for the good of Her Majesties service . . . that All the Indians, who can be raised, that are fit for Service should be encouraged to go upon this Expedition." Indians, the governors reasoned, would be much cheaper than the main provincial troops, whom the governors had to pay "foure times the pay of Europe each Man" or eighteen pence, plus provisions and a ten-pound enlistment bonus.[34] Connecticut's force consisted of eight hundred men, including two hundred Indians—25 percent of the total—and hundreds of Indians also augmented the Massachusetts troops. Benjamin Church and his son William recruited "Whaling Indians, who were very dexterous & nimble upon the water In their whaling Boats." "This Col[one]l: Church," Vetch and Nicholson continued, "who being bred up amongst those Indians, demonstrated to us the Vast use those whale Boats could be of." Nicholson was so excited about the possibilities for stealth, portage, and troop movements that the British officers committed one hundred pounds sterling on the spot to hire the Indians and thirty-five boats.[35] Indians brought a host of valuable nonmilitary skills. Connecticut leaders noted that they were "carpenters" who would build and manage canoes and take care of important logistical concerns for the army. Later land expeditions against Canada made sure to include Indians because they could make snowshoes and teach soldiers to use them.

The British failed to take Quebec, but they did take Port Royal in Nova Scotia, and Vetch and Nicholson remained pleased about their army of "Christians and Indians."[36] This language hardly amounted to an endorsement of Indian equality as citizens, but it did represent a different way of distinguishing between colonists—formerly "English"—and outsider Indians. Nicholson even asked that a detachment of New England Indians be left behind to help maintain the garrison. When he offered terms to the Port Royal garrison, however, Nicholson promised to treat the French inhabitants "with all the civility and good Manners the Law of Warr and Nations can any wise Intitule them unto" if they returned "brittish prisoners." Whether these protections applied to the Wabanaki and French Iroquois or to the New England Indians in their hands remained unclear; Indians remained outside of Nicholson's vision of Britishness.

A year later, John Hill, the British captain general and commander in chief of the 1711 Canada expedition, confirmed that Indian soldiers would prove essential to the war effort. Regular British troops were deserting in alarming numbers, "debauched" by colonists and the promise of high wages in civilian jobs. Not the first to complain about the high cost of labor in British America, Hill's British civilian superior, Secretary of the Southern Division Lord Dartmouth, expressed astonishment at the amount he had to agree to pay American soldiers and how hard it was to find enough troops. Hill considered forcibly "pressing" colonists aboard the transports to Canada, but Massachusetts governor Joseph Dudley warned against such extreme measures. Meanwhile, Hill's officers wanted to enlist "Negroes," but for unspecified reasons—likely because the men were not all free to begin with—the briga-dier regretfully decided to void the enlistments. Instead, Hill, like his prede-cessors, sought Indian enlistees. Indians were acceptable; Africans were not. The British imperial war against the French was becoming a war fought by proxy to a considerable extent, pitting southern New England Indians against northeastern Indians in large numbers.

Not all enlistees were volunteers. A sizable number of Indians who enrolled in both the provincial forces and the supplementary militias were "pressed" or forced to join. Others were servants whose masters enlisted them in order to receive their bounties and wages, in a form of servant or slave rental. Still others, such as Joseph Quasson, were former servants who had recently completed long indentures and exited servitude with no assets, isolated from former kin networks. A number of current and former Indian servants from Cape Cod joined Massachusetts forces on the 1725 cam-paign to Maine and Acadia. Often, the officers who raised the Indian troops were themselves "brokers" of Indian captives and servants—town or county officers who presided over the public "vandue" of Indians, or individuals who purchased or owned Indian indentures, such as Quasson's former master Samuel Sturgis of Barnstable—and therefore had control over Indian labor in various forms.

Noah Wiswall brought to his estate for the summer of 1689 a number of Wamesit Indians, including John Naphow and Jacob Pesaduck, who then became part of his company in an expedition during King William's War. From the Indians' point of view, service with Wiswall kept them from being jailed or sold as possible enemies. Wiswall held their debentures, however, and it is possible that he kept their wages.[37] Certainly, real profits accrued to military recruiters throughout these conflicts. Similarly, Benjamin Church received permission to settle a number of Indians on his estate in Bristol County, with the proviso that the Indians would be available for military ven-tures in the northeastern wars whenever Church wanted them, while "hee, satisfying the Indians, to haue the whole prophett of such an adventure." In other words, as commander, Church would not only receive the largest share of any plunder but also the Indians' military wages and enlistment bounties.[38]

The large numbers of Indians in the service created a new captive prob lem for the British and colonial administrators and commanders. They were not only responsible for redeeming English civilians and English prison ers of war; now, they had to find a way to protect their Indian soldiery. Since the English refused to treat enemy Indians as combatants under the law of war or as citizens under international law—a decision reaching back to the Pequot War—so too did the French and Wabanaki refuse to recognize enlisted New England Indians as soldiers. Instead, the Maquas, Wabanaki, and Kahnawake carried New England Indian soldiers into captivity, within their own tribes and in Quebec. Four Indians "in the King's service" in Kittery had experienced captivity for several years before they gained their freedom in 1695. Another Indian, named Captain John, "escaped out of the hands of the French and Indians with another briske Indian and an Englishman in Company" in 1697, only to die soon after in a skirmish on the Merrimack River; his companions were recaptured.[39] New England Indian sailors and whalemen also remained vulnerable to capture and enslavement because they lacked formal legal protections or even customary ones that guarded their status as free or indentured people. British military planners and the colonial governments realized that these policies needed revision, given their desire to recover captive Europeans and to protect the valuable manpower that Indians represented.

FIGURE 16. George I Indian Peace Medal, 1714–27. The British presented such medals to Wabanaki leaders as a sign of peace and alliance. Courtesy of the Massachusetts Historical Society.

As a result, the British—and the New England colonists—recast the Indians' role in empire. In the 1740s, with another war looming, British commanders and the cabinet ministers overseeing the colonies began to intervene more directly in New England governments' Indian policy. A series of Orders in Council chastised Massachusetts because "the Indians residing in this governmt are greatly imposed upon by some of his Majesty's English Subjects," and called on the royal governor to take action to once again address problems of debt, abuse, and land takings from Indians. The language of both the Orders in Council and the colonial responses indicated that Britons on both sides of the Atlantic had begun to incorporate Indians into their sense of British subjecthood, at least in some contexts. As treaty negotiations stalled over captive exchanges at the end of King George's War in 1749, the crown intervened to force the return and exchange of Wabanaki captives.

The Duke of Bedford informed William Shirley, the governor of Massachusetts, that George II viewed northeastern North American Indians as subjects, and therefore they were prisoners of war, not slaves or captives. Interestingly, the crown recognized the subjecthood of French-allied Indians as well, according to Bedford: "all the Indians allied to or protected by either of the two Crowns in America, who might have been made Prisoners on either side during the late War should be forthwith exchanged." Shirley at first resisted this understanding of the matter; in his view, the northeastern Indians had forfeited these rights during King George's War. But even Shirley was prepared to grant the rights of citizen and subject to Indians from southern New England, "born freemen . . . subjects of his Majesty & have always liv'd in the Heart of this Province" whom Canadians "held as Slaves which is contrary to the practice of all Civiliz'd Nations." The Massachusetts General Court accepted this definition as well. A committee resolved to draft a letter to the governor of Quebec in 1749

> informing him that the Indians Captivated from Nova Scotia in the Late War, are the Subjects of the King of Great Brittain having been Born within this Province . . . Subject to the Laws thereof, and equally enjoyed Priviledges with others under his Majesty's Gove[rn]m[en]t, and ought to be treated as such. . . . It is expected and Insisted upon that the French Gov[e]r[nor] forthwith give liberty and Signifie it to any and Every Indian (that may still remain in Canada Captivated as aforesd.) his Leave for them to return to this province. And by no means to detain them against their Wills, which they have Suggested they are, and so injuriously treated as to have been sold for slaves.[40]

In return, British commanders insisted that twenty-six captive Wabanaki within New England would have to be returned rather than kept or sold as servants or slaves. Indians were now formally categorized as "prisoners of war." The King's Council in 1749 and again in 1750 ordered Massachusetts to release "all Abnakis Indian prisoners, and all slaves taken . . . in the late war."[41] King Louis XV agreed and ordered his own officials to exchange first European prisoners, then the "Indian Prisoners" among the French and English, and finally to free captive Indians being held by France's own Indian allies.[42]

The Board of Trade pressured Governor Shirley about nearly two dozen recent captives, and local authorities followed up, forcing Bostonian John Gorham to surrender an Indian girl whom he had placed "with his wife" in his own household and return her to her family near Halifax along with several other captives.[43] Reluctantly, perhaps, the British had now defined the northeastern Indians as subjects and citizens with "privileges" and immunities.[44] This represented a major shift in the Indians' overall place in England's schemes for its North American empire. Just as meaningfully, war had also forced the British and colonists to extend these same privileges to the Indians of southern New England—a decision with legal implications for Indian slavery.

Indians to the South: Carolina and Spanish Indians

The recasting of northeastern Indians as subjects and citizens ended one era of New England Indian slavery. At least officially, Indians in both southern and northern New England could not be enslaved as "lawfull captives in a just war" under the seventeenth-century legal definition. This, however, still left as potential slaves "such strangers as willingly sell themselves, or are solde to us," and that is where colonists sought new labor supplies in the late seventeenth and early eighteenth century. Africans and Indians from outside New England began to appear in advertisements, court records, and inventories in larger numbers, shifting the demography of the New England slave population and also creating new and complex ethnic and racial associations with servitude that would complicate the status of bound New England Indians.

The first slaves from outside the region were Indians from New York, northern New Jersey, and Virginia who trickled into New England in the 1640s and 1650s. At least one of the Virginia Indians actually challenged the legality of his enslavement under the Massachusetts 1646 "just war" rubric. Robert Hilton had sold the Indian James to George Carr, a shipwright and ferry operator in Salisbury, Massachusetts, in 1649 in exchange for a one-fourth share in a ship. Hilton conveyed James to Carr as a slave "to be his servant for ever."[45] But at some point James challenged this disposition, and his case reached the Massachusetts Court of Assistants in 1672. According to the court, James or his patrons questioned "whether a broyle amongst a few Indians" qualified as a "just war" under the Massachusetts statute. Edward Rawson, the Massachusetts clerk, failed to record the court's decision, but James had actually cut to the heart of the problem involving the importation of any slaves from outside the colony: Who was to judge the justness of wars conducted outside New England and therefore the appropriateness of slaves' captivity?

Meanwhile, from the beginnings of settlement in the early 1670s, English settlers in the Carolinas had been enslaving local Indians. The colony expanded aggressively after 1684, and growing English markets for captives spurred Anglo-Indian wars against the Westos in 1680, the Yaddos in 1704, and the Yamasee in 1715 that resulted in mass enslavements of those peoples. In addition, South Carolinians had joined the Yamasee earlier in an invasion of Spanish Florida in 1702–5, carrying away Apalachee and other captives, and the English encouraged subsequent raids on Spanish-allied Indians and missions to the south and French-allied Indians to the west.[46] These conflicts, augmented by chronic English slaving raids on Indian missions in Spanish Florida, fed an exploding regional and international Indian slave trade in Charleston, one that exported captives throughout the British Empire—including to New England.[47] The *Boston News-Letter* covered the Carolina Indian wars almost as avidly as it did the wars on the northeastern frontier. The newspaper published letters from Carolina officials and reports of battles, including accounts of raids on missions and numbers of Indian captives taken at various engagements. As New England merchants' global reach expanded, indigenous people from Dutch Surinam, the Azores, Cape Verde, Central America, and other Atlantic centers entered New England as slaves as well.

The Spanish and Carolina Indians arrived as something of a cohort, appearing in relatively large numbers between 1707 and 1718 and occasionally for about five years thereafter. Advertisements for the sale of Indian slaves in the *Boston News-Letter* provide a window into this boomlet: in an eleven-year period, fifteen different ads (approximately 33 percent of the total number of sale advertisements involving Indians) offering eighteen Carolina Indians appeared.[48] Ten were females, seven were males, and one ad failed to specify the Indian's gender. Six were children under the age of twelve—four sold alone and two as part of likely family groupings. Two other advertisements offered Spanish Indians for sale (one male, one female), and two during this period mentioned Surinam Indians (a mother and child, and a man). Cotton

Mather, Benjamin Colman, William Hutchinson, and several other prominent Bostonians acquired them. Analyzing ethnic information in advertisements probably undercounts the Spanish and Carolina Indians in this sample
because of subsequent prohibitions on their sale. After 1717, sellers generally
left off the southeastern Indians' place of origin and merely referred to them
as "Indians," but hints in the descriptions identify them as Indians from outside New England. John Powell of Boston offered for sale "an Indian woman
. . . well-seasoned to the country" in 1719, which implied that she was from
outside the region. Anthony Blount described a female Indian slave as "in
country about three years, speaks good English."

Carolina and Spanish Indians sometimes arrived with particular skill sets
attractive to New England buyers. Some of the Carolina Indians had worked
for English in the Southeast. Likely a few Spanish Indians had been trained
through their work at the missions in blacksmithing, a trade rare among New
England Indians because of the prohibition on their learning to repair guns.
In a petition, Francis Holmes of Boston attested to the value of his Carolina
Indian man who worked for him as a "brick mason."[49] Newspaper advertisements for female Carolina and Spanish Indians tended to mention specific
work experiences, such as dairying, "household work" needlework, and the
ability to "spin linen." A surprising number spoke English, suggesting they
had already worked in English plantations, and at least one of the men listed
in the *Boston News-Letter* was literate.

Rebels and Runaways

Despite these advantages, however, Spanish and Carolina Indians demonstrated less attractive qualities. They appeared frequently in runaway ads and
engaged in dramatic group escapes that evidenced coordination and collaboration across many households and often with Africans, English, and Indians
from other regions. Spanish Indians pulled off several eye-opening escapes in
the early 1700s by stealing entire ships. In 1701, "a Spanish Indian" named
Phillip and James Pryer, servants of Peter Collamer of Scituate, "absconded
with a Fishing shallop lying at Anchor in said Scituate Harbour and carrying
her out of said harbour with Sundrey Goods in said Shallop."[50] The boat ran
aground, however, and the recaptured men faced tough penalties: the Plymouth court sentenced Pryer, an English servant, to a whipping and seven years
of service, although his master intervened and paid a fine on his behalf in lieu
of corporal punishment. The Indian man received a much harsher sentence.
As "said Indian was the contriver and chief acter in the said theft" in the
court's eyes, he received twenty lashes and was sentenced as a "slave for life"

to make restitution for the lost boat and cargo. In a more successful venture, eight Spanish Indians and "two or three Negroes" took a thirty-three-foot ship from Sandy Hook harbor and were "design[ed] for St. Augustin"; the men managed to evade the pursuit of a specially fitted privateer.[51]

Carolina Indians also staged their fair share of spectacular escapes. In December 1705, a Carolina Indian man enslaved to William Pepperell in Maine joined forces with an African slave to run away; they may also have stolen a boat, because the men made it all the way to South Carolina before they were recaptured.[52] In another collaborative effort that bordered on insurrection because of the sheer number involved, at least five Indians—one Carolina man, two Carolina women, and two Spanish Indian men—organized an escape together in September 1711 from the households of Thomas Savage, the Reverend Samuel Myles, John Stanford, and Daniel Loring. Five years later, in September 1716, one female and two male Carolina Indians carried off a daring escape. One had worked for the maltster Samuel Adams; another, Robin, for a ship carpenter named Nehemiah Yale; and the woman, "America," worked for cordwainer Thomas Salter.[53] As in the case of the men who traveled from Maine to South Carolina, masters increasingly expected that slaves from outside the region would travel equally far as runaways. One advertisement for a runaway girl from New York who spoke "English, Dutch and French, the last best"—probably from Surinam or elsewhere in the Caribbean—included the names of agents in seven different colonies from New Hampshire to Carolina who could receive the girl if she was found elsewhere.[54]

The growing numbers of so-called "eastern," "Spanish," and "Carolina" Indians (all of whom New Englanders perceived as being more warlike and less acculturated than the local Indians) began to worry authorities in the eighteenth century. The reasons for this backlash were complex. Partly it stemmed from a growing uneasiness about the number of African and Indian laborers visible in cities such as Boston, which had about sixty-seven hundred inhabitants. Publication of annual censuses or lists of city deaths became occasions for the printer of the *News-Letter* to complain about the high proportion of people of color. In 1702 "Negroes and Indians, who had a Singular Share in the Mortality," numbered forty-nine deaths, more than 10 percent of the total deaths for the city.[55] Another commentator noted in 1706 that Africans' and Indians' higher death rates reflected their bodily weakness relative to European workers, including their greater susceptibility to smallpox and other contagious diseases that were part of seaport life, which meant that capital invested in slaves was a dead loss when they died. People of color tended to theft and other disorders. Nor could Africans contribute to the town's defense properly because of restrictions pertaining to arms and militia training. In one of the first print references to race rather than national origins, the author noted that as bondsmen Africans "do not people our Country as Whites would do whereby we should be strengthened against an Enemy."[56] The Carolina Indians' reputation for organizing resistance and running away must also have attracted public attention. As with African slaves, rumors of poisoning and other threats to white communities also became associated with the Carolina and Spanish Indians.

Officials in Rhode and Massachusetts responded to these complaints with legislation. As part of a 1709 law titled "An Act to Encourage the Importation of White Servants," the Massachusetts General Court subjected the Indian slave trade to the same taxes as the trade in enslaved Africans. Later that year, authorities added a requirement that importers provide some proof that Indians had been legally enslaved in the plantation that exported them. Rhode Island passed similar laws, but the taxes apparently failed to discourage importers, because both assemblies, joined by Connecticut, eventually mandated the immediate reexportation of any eastern, Spanish, or Carolina Indians brought into the area on pain of a fifty-pound fine. In language very similar to the laws in the Caribbean prohibiting entry of New England Indians after King Philip's War, New England governments warned about the dangers of outsider Indians. By the eighteenth century, Pequot, Mashpee, Wampanoag, and Narragansett Indian servants and slaves had become a known quantity. Some were second- or third-generation bound laborers. Advertisements began to stress the New England origins of some of the Indian slaves for sale, noting that they were "bred in the country" and therefore civilized in the eyes of contemporaries, although not all New England Indian slaves were English speakers in this period. The legislation signaled fear of once again trying to incorporate a captive population, and it reflected the intensity of the warfare that engulfed northern New England from 1689 onward, as some areas of English settlement literally faced an existential military threat at the hands of the Wabanaki and Iroquoians. Its actual language, though, echoed the Black Codes and laws passed in response to slave revolt in more slave-centric islands in the Caribbean, and in Virginia and New York.

In April 1712, a group of slaves, a free man of color and—reportedly—several Native Americans, staged a revolt in New York City. Armed with hatchets, guns, swords, and other weapons, they set fire to a warehouse and then attacked the colonists who arrived to douse it, killing nine and wounding another six. Governor Hunt called in militia from as far as Westchester to battle the rebels, and the event caused consternation throughout English America; it was the first slave revolt in North America involving more than a few participants. Authorities interrogated forty-seven suspects or people with knowledge of the event; eventually, New York officials arrested thirty-three slaves, including two Spanish Indians, and tortured and executed twenty-one of them.

Although in this case the governor of New York, Thomas Hunt, intervened to pardon the Spanish Indians, initial reports of the uprising stressed their participation. The *Boston News-Letter* published its report within days of the revolt, noting that "*Cormentine* Negroes to the number of 25 or 30 and 2 or 3 Spanish Indians, conspiring to murder all the Christians here, and by that means thinking to obtain their freedom . . . put their bloody design into execution."[57] The term "Cormentine" conveyed that the Africans were fairly recent arrivals, Akan speakers from the Gold Coast of Africa, a population considered by some North Americans to be prone to conspiracy and resistance. Two earlier incidents had also pointed to the possibility of Indians and Africans joining together in violence: an Indian man and an African woman together had murdered their master and his family on Long Island in 1708, and in 1709 a group of Africans and Native Americans had attempted a revolt in Norfolk, Virginia.

The latter incidents had excited official commentary, but the New York uprising made a particularly strong impression on New Englanders, judging from the language of laws they passed almost in conjunction with Governor Hunt's crackdown. The Rhode Island law requiring reexport of Spanish Indians cited the "divers conspiracies, insurrections, rapes, thefts and other execrable crimes, [which] have been lately perpetrated . . . by Indian slaves" as a reason for ordering the new restrictions. Both colonies granted numerous exemptions to individual owners permitting them to keep their "Carolina Indians," however, and other importers simply ignored the law.[58] Carolina and Spanish Indians continued to be bought and sold in Boston through the early 1720s, and held as slaves decades thereafter in Connecticut, Rhode Island, and Massachusetts.

The restrictions, duties, and security concerns reduced the desirability of southeastern Indians as a workforce for New England farms and families, but availability also factored in. The southeastern Indian slave trade continued, but English South Carolinians themselves turned increasingly to African slaves, as the latter became less expensive and more accessible as a result of the expanding English and American involvement in the African slave trade. Another complication affected Spanish Indians: there were questions about the legality of their enslavement. The New England restrictions on Spanish Indian slaves did not question the legality of their enslavement, but rather the imprudence of incorporating subversive groups into the enslaved community. Disputes about the status of Spanish Indians as slaves or subjects had occasionally arisen in the seventeenth century, as in the case of the Central American Indians brought to Bermuda. The issue became even more complicated for authorities in the eighteenth century because of the racialization of slavery. The legality of enslaving any of these outsider Indians was in the eye of the beholder, especially since the category of "Spanish Indian" had become a rather loose term. In practice if not law, racial appearance was becoming a major determinant of slave status for many in the English Atlantic world. The wars of the 1690s, 1710s, and 1730s all had Atlantic components as well as continental theaters, with battles fought in Martinique as well as in Maine, and active privateering on all sides.

Individuals taken by English ships in such conflicts often found themselves enslaved despite their claims to European ancestry and citizenship. Azorean, Cape Verdean, and Caribbean Spanish Americans who qualified as European in their own societies' complex racial hierarchies found themselves deemed "swarthy" by English captains and thus susceptible to enslavement. A few such individuals petitioned for their freedom. Connecticut authorities compensated one man ten pounds in 1701, apparently because he had to surrender a Spaniard whom the General Court viewed as illegally enslaved. Bostonians were also aware of the debates over the status of Spanish Indians. In one account of a South Carolina attack on Florida Apalachee Indians who took shelter in a Spanish mission, the *News-Letter* reported that the "Fryers" had refused to surrender the Indians because they were "subjects of the King of Spain and not slaves."[59]

Governor Hunt of New York, who oversaw the prosecution of those slaves involved in the 1712 uprising, protected the two Spanish Indians from execution, much to the anger of many New Yorkers. Hunt concluded that the men were not really Indians; they had been taken by a privateer, enslaved, and then sold in Jamaica because of their relatively dark complexions. Since arriving in New York in 1703, Hunt had received many petitions from people in a similar situation from "these Spanish Indians as they are called here, representing to me that they were free men subjects to the king of Spain."[60] New York had outlawed all forms Indian slavery in 1689, except for Indians "from the Bay of Campeachy [Honduras/Belize]," and although enforcement had been nonexistent, some individuals now used the law as the basis for petitions. Like Nicholson, Vetch, Dartmouth, and other British officials, Hunt was moving toward a definition of citizenship and freedom associated with nationality and subjecthood. It was enough for him that the men were subjects of a European nation. This made them unenslavable.

In 1739, Boston newspapers reported that the governor of Florida had offered freedom to any Negro or Indian slaves who fled to Florida. New England officials, though, were moving in the opposite direction; they interpreted the status of Spanish Indians differently than did the Spanish in Florida or Governor Hunt in New York. In fact, the enslavability of Spanish and Carolina Indians became an important distinction that theoretically separated them from New England native Indians between 1720 and 1750, as second- and third-generation New England Indians illegally held as slaves began to challenge their bondage. In New England, "Spanish Indian" became an accepted category of enslavement in law and custom, even as other forms of Indian slavery drew scrutiny. Association with Spanish Indians figuratively colored their New England kin as slaves. Connecticut specifically included the term "Spanish Indian" along with "Negro" and "Mulatto" in a 1711 bill regulating manumission.[61]

The surge in importation of Africans between 1710 and 1730 had similar important effects. New England Indians desirous of escaping enslavement would have to avoid categorization as Spanish or Carolina Indians or, increasingly, mulatto or Negro, in order to secure their freedom. Indians would have to prove associations with local tribes in order to have any legal basis for petitioning their freedom. Yet local Indians remained the most plentiful, most accessible, most acculturated, most useful and knowledgeable, and the cheapest potential slaves, especially given the new taxes and regulations on imports from the Southeast and British restrictions on taking captives from the northeastern Indians. As a result, English colonists interested in obtaining Indian labor focused on local Indian populations in southeastern New England in the early eighteenth century.

CHAPTER 9

To be sold "in any part of ye kings Dominyons"

Judicial Enslavement of New England Indians

With Indian slavery outlawed or limited by post–King Philip's War legislation, colonists in the eighteenth century looked for other ways to maintain a local supply of bound Native American workers. Court-ordered servitude and other, even more informal claims to Indian labor proved effective substitutes for warfare during the eighteenth century. Trends that had just begun to appear before the 1676 war—the sale of Indians for debt or in restitution for criminal penalties and legal fees, the legal and illegal extension of indentures, and the forcible apprenticeship of children—all became more prevalent in the eighteenth century. Unlike in the seventeenth century, now most of these arrangements that bound Indians into servitude had the sanction of law and, often, formal indentures.

Entry into any kind of servitude had consequences for Indians and their families. Some managed to emerge into freedom and maintain autonomy as adults. But many others found even voluntary servitude extremely difficult to escape for themselves and for their offspring. Once categorized as a servant, even supposedly for a set term with indenture papers, Indians entered restrictive situations where it was easy to fall afoul of the many regulations covering servant behavior—violations of which added additional years of servitude onto the penal sentence. Masters kept indenture paperwork, and many simply ignored their obligations specified in the contracts and also failed to release Indian servants at the end of their terms. Indian women who bore children while servants discovered that they lost ownership of those children; under Rhode Island law masters could charge for Indian children's upkeep, effectively claiming them as servants. Children in turn became bound to the same master or sold to third parties as "apprentices" until age twenty-one, twenty-five, or thirty. Indians in servitude also faced the danger of being claimed—or sold—as slaves by masters despite the latter's lack of legal title.

In this way, English colonists constructed an ad hoc form of slavery no less real for all its legal haziness. In order to reduce native people to involuntary servitude in the face of laws and statutes theoretically designed to halt Indian slavery, colonists mobilized the structures of town governance and county courts, as well as the tacit consent of English neighbors. They also exploited relatively new racial categories in New England society—African, mustee, mulatto, Spanish Indian—and assigned Indians to them. In an age where African slavery became more prevalent and King Philip's War had reduced thousands of Native Americans into involuntary servants, even free Indian workers remained at risk for kidnapping and sale as slaves. Occasionally, Indians managed to challenge enslavement by drawing on the same social capital as their would-be enslavers. English justices, juries, and neighbors sometimes intervened to protect individual Indians, pointing to the existence of powerful networks and relationships that connected Indians and English together.

After King Philip's War

Following King Philip's War, Massachusetts forcibly resettled most of the decimated population of "friend" Indians (except those already bound into labor) into designated enclaves—four towns in the seventeenth century, and four more after Massachusetts annexed Plymouth and Martha's Vineyard, both of which had sizable Indian populations, in 1691.[1] Rhode Island and Connecticut did not conduct a resettlement on this scale, but both colonies drew sharp boundaries between English settlements and the now shrunken Indian town and tribal land claims, essentially creating reservations in the Narragansett country and Sakonnet in Rhode Island and in southeastern and northern Connecticut. Indians residing in the designated towns or reservations enjoyed privileges that might include shared rights to land, lease incomes, and protection from enslavement. Still, the transition was far from peaceful, and suspicions about the Indians smoldered after the war and reignited with the onset of conflict to the northeast.

The brutality of the northeastern border wars incited new levels of violence and backlash against all Indians in New England. In July 1677, Wabanaki Indians had successfully taken many New England fishing and trading vessels off the Maine coast, much to the colonists' anger and dismay at the "Indian Pirates." The crew of one Salem boat, the *William and Sarah*, managed to overpower the Indians, and Captain Watts and his vessel brought the Indians to Marblehead. "We thought if we brought them in alive, we might get something by our losses," either by selling the captives or claiming the bounty, mate Robert Roule reported, but instead an angry and largely female crowd armed with stones and wooden clubs beat the Indian men to death on the pier.[2] Security concerns lay behind the orders to round up Indians and keep them within the designated town boundaries, "it being very difficult to discern between Friends and Foes." The measures exempted only those Indians "abroad"—on military service, or sailors—and "others who are constant dwellers in English Houses," that is, Indian servants. During King William's War, the Indians at Natick and Punkapoag had to appear for a roll call every morning.[3] Benjamin Church reported that in Bristol County tensions were high between the English and Indians in 1694–95. He was "forst to hear thar [the Indians'] Complants daly of injoryes don to them prevatly against which there is no help and that it is a great deal wors for them then formerly." Local residents prevented Indians from cutting wood for their wigwam poles and harassed them in many ways; one old man "that had lived quietly in the woods" miles from an English town went to visit friends only to return to find his house on fire and his corn burned.[4]

Southern New England Indians continued to pursue traditional subsistence economies supplemented by day labor, military service, and longer-term contract work as sailors and fishermen well into the eighteenth century. The Indians' already decimated land resources declined steadily through sale and appropriation, however, and the dwindling land base meant that Indians depended on English markets and storekeepers for a variety of goods that had become necessities: food, clothing, medical care, "shott and powder," tobacco, knives, guns. Some Indians resisted resettlement and continued to live in or near English towns, where they worked as day laborers or servants alongside Indians bound to English during the wars. Such individuals occupied a precarious position, however, since they lacked even the minimal legal and economic protections that tribal membership afforded.

Meanwhile, the continued growth of the English population and the expansion of settlement brought colonists and Indians into frequent contact. As in the period prior to King Philip's War, proximity to English settlers increased the potential for charges of trespass, destruction of property by livestock, damages, assault, contention over the ownership of resources or goods, and other encounters that had first brought Indians into the criminal justice system in the seventeenth century. Increased access to alcohol contributed both to the loss of Indian assets and to drunken assaults and conflicts.[5] Indians began to appear more frequently before colonial courts immediately following King

Philip's War, and this pattern continued throughout the eighteenth century. Many defendants now lacked the resources to pay their fines and debts, or else they shared collectively owned lands that could not be liquidated.

By the late seventeenth century, too, many of the sachem-patrons who had protected earlier generations of Indians in New England courts had died, and few would-be successors could claim similar wealth and power. Indian leadership structures persisted, and sachems continued to advocate for their people in many effective ways, but particularly in Rhode Island and Massachusetts the sachems' economic clout and jurisdiction—and their ability to post bond and pay penalties for large numbers of members—were now severely compromised. Because of enduring alliances with colonial leaders, Connecticut's Indian leadership exercised a bit more influence. Into the 1700s, Uncas's sons Ben and Owaneco and a few other leaders occasionally appeared in court to pay their subjects' fines and fees or to post bond, as did Robin Cassacinamon before his death in 1692.[6] But the Uncases did not step in when a New London court sentenced the Mohegan John Ashpo to a fine of forty-five pounds in June 1703.[7] This inability to act left Indian defendants such as Ashpo vulnerable to long terms of involuntary servitude.

The Turn to Judicial Enslavement

These long-term socioeconomic factors combined with a number of legal changes to create conditions for what I call "judicial enslavement," or court-ordered servitude.[8] All the New England colonies passed legislation between 1670 and 1700 that increased the damages defendants could claim in cases of theft to double or triple the value of the goods stolen, plus restitution. If individuals could not pay fines, they would be assigned to service in order to pay off the penalty. These laws were not specifically aimed at Indians (except in Plymouth, where officials singled out Indians for a harsher, fourfold restitution penalty), but the legislation did reflect fears about theft and sale of stolen goods by servants at a time when thousands of Indian war captives and a trickle of Africans now worked in English households. The high restitution requirements added to existing burdens for Indians accused of crime. Courts charged higher legal fees and costs in the eighteenth century, which could double or triple defendants' total monetary obligations and add years of servitude to their sentences. Martha's Vineyard's 1672 legal code included a provision aimed at protecting the inhabitants from the evils of debtors' prison—but the law provided that, in lieu of prison, the debtor's "Person shall be sold for Satisfaction." This meant that even noncriminal defendants could be sentenced to servitude. To make matters worse, there is evidence that court officials valued Indian labor lower than the prevailing wage rates for European workers. As a result, Indians might have to serve longer terms to pay off the debt.[9]

Samples from several counties in New England—Dukes County on Martha's Vineyard; Bristol County, on the Massachusetts–Rhode Island border near the lower Cape; New London County, a center of slavery in Connecticut; Plymouth County, a region with a high concentration of Indians; and Newport, Rhode Island, whose Superior Court and Court of Trials also heard cases from Providence and Portsmouth, show the prevalence of judicial enslavement. In some areas the shift was dramatic. In Dukes County, comprising Martha's Vineyard, of the twenty-two Indians convicted of trespass, theft, or assault between 1675 and 1687, only two received sentences involving servitude—one for twelve days, one for two years.[10] In January 1688 alone, however, the Dukes County Court convicted thirteen Indians of "killing Cattle and Shepe" and eating stolen mutton. The court ordered the Indians sold into service for periods ranging from three months to seven years if they failed to pay fines and costs. Those who received sentences of over two years could be sold "in any part of ye kings dominyons."[11] In 1689–90 the court bound eight more Indians to terms of six months to thirty years for offenses that included stealing a handkerchief. Some victorious plaintiffs took the Indians as servants, but others chose to receive their restitution in cash, so Martha's Vineyard instituted a regular vendue (or "vandue")—a public auction of Indian convicts. Other towns began to employ similar systems.

Auctioned Indians might easily end up in other colonies. In 1693, Matthew Mayhew sold two Indians named Keiape and James, convicted of stealing about eight pounds in money, to New York merchant Jacob Mayle for seven-year terms.[12] Mayle in turn sold Keiape to another planter-merchant in Southold, Long Island.[13] Mayhew specified the length of the boys' terms in the bills of sale, but many other conveyances lacked this crucial information when it came to Indians. In New York, with its more elaborate slave codes and legislation, Keiape and James might easily be resold as slaves rather than servants. Mayhew signed as clerk of court for this case and processed it, even as he also played the role of plaintiff, a conflict of interest that attended many such trials. Another woman, named Hannah, who was already a servant of Mayhew's, received one of the stiffest penalties of any defendant—thirty years of servitude "in any part of there Ma[je]st[ie]s dominions." A recidivist thief, Hannah stole over one hundred bushels of corn, along with money, linen, personal effects, and other items from Mayhew's home. She reportedly continued to steal while in prison, although Mayhew did not explain how in his affidavit. An Indian man suspected of helping Hannah fence the goods received a sentence of fourteen years' service.[14]

Table 2 Indians presented and sentenced to servitude in County Court

	DUKES COUNTY 1675–1730		BRISTOL COUNTY 1697–1726		NEWPORT COURT 1671–1730		PLYMOUTH 1686–1741		NEW LONDON COUNTY 1669–1732	
	PRESENTED	SENTENCED	PRESENTED	SENTENCED	PRESENTED	SENTENCED	PRESENTED	SENTENCED	PRESENTED	SENTENCED
# Male Indians	99	25	27	12	43	12	36	24	29	10
Percent	77%	76%	77%	92%	88%	75%	69%	67%	83%	83%
# Female Indians	29	8	8	1	6	4	16	12	6	2
Percent	23%	24%	23%	8%	12%	25%	31%	33%	17%	17%
Total # Indians	128	33	35	13	49	16	52	36	35	12

Table does not include those who were acquitted or who were non-defendants (i.e., plaintiffs or witnesses)

Similarly, in Bristol County, Massachusetts, Indian defendants abruptly began to receive terms of servitude from the Court of General Sessions in 1705.[15] Captain Thomas Newton of Bristol paid ten pounds at the Bristol Vandue to purchase a boy named William Wannumpson, or Wannups, in 1706. William was already a servant in the household of Nicholas Porte of Rehoboth when he was convicted of setting fire to his master's barn; a horse also died in the blaze. Servants who committed arson potentially faced the death penalty, but because he was only eleven, the court commuted William's sentence to ten additional years of servitude and thirty lashes. No parent appeared in William's trial proceedings to intercede on his behalf, another factor that disadvantaged young Indian defendants.[16] In nearby Newport, Rhode Island, the Supreme Judicial Court, between 1704 and 1725, condemned at least fifteen Indian men, women, and children to terms of service.[17] In Plymouth, a staggering 69 percent of cases involving Indians presented to the quarterly court for crime or debt ended in sentences of servitude. In Newport, the earliest condemnations included restrictions on where Indians could be sold and required that masters keep the Indians in the colony, and other colonial courts specified sale within British America. Phoebe Crandall was "not to be sold out of ye country" without her consent. But such restrictions became less common over time, which meant that with the proper permissions, owners and purchasers could export Indian servants to global slave markets.

Officers of the Court, Brokers of Indian Labor

These numbers undercount the number of Indians sentenced to involuntary servitude, because many cases never entered the record in county court. As part of the postwar reorganization of Indian communities, all three colonies created a multitiered system of adjudication for cases involving reservation Indians. In Massachusetts and Connecticut, Indian courts had the authority to resolve disputes within Indian communities. In criminal cases, or any case involving an English plaintiff or defendant, however, Indians had to appear before colonial authorities. Colonial governments appointed special justices of the peace—sometimes called "overseers," "guardians," or "trustees"—to supervise legal affairs on the new Indian reservations. These justices held court, took evidence, rendered decisions, and decided whether cases were serious enough to merit hearing in higher courts. This process meant that many civil and criminal cases involving Indians did not receive jury trials.[18] Apart from these provisions affecting Indians alone, justices of the peace throughout New England were authorized to hold court in their homes and decide civil cases worth less than forty shillings and criminal misdemeanor cases. Many cases involving Indians fell into these two categories.

FIGURE 17. Portrait of Benjamin Church engraved by Paul Revere for the frontispiece of *Entertaining History of King Philip's War* (Newport, 1772), a memoir originally published by Church's son Thomas Church in 1722. Courtesy of the John Carter Brown Library at Brown University.

Thus justices of the peace could sentence Indians to servitude without any other due process. Unlike county court records, the justices' court papers were considered the private property of the men who held the office. Very few of these records survive, which makes it difficult to determine exactly how many Indians they sentenced to servitude.

Many justices and Indian guardians had a personal stake in Indian slavery. Some magistrates, such as Benjamin Church of Bristol, were sincere advocates for Native Americans—in their way. Church also personally presided over an Indian labor force enmeshed in various levels of clientage and servitude. Church was a late seventeenth-century heir to the quasi-*encomienda* system that John Winthrop Jr., Lion Gardiner, and other English landowners had established in the wake of the Pequot War. Church already had constructed a web of clientage relationships with Indians near his Sakonnet plantation even before King Philip's War. By the end of the conflict, he added approximately fifteen Indian men and their families to his labor force. At a moment when Plymouth Colony authorities had demanded the exportation of adult male Indian servants, the Sakonnet Indians doubtless saw submission to Church as an alternative to enslavement in the Caribbean. Because of Church's reputation as an Indian fighter and captive taker, Plymouth permitted this special amnesty: "that incase they did carry well they should abide in this Jurisdiction; and not be sold to any fforaigne p[a] rtes; accordingly the Court doth confeirme the said engagement and doth hereby tollarate theire stay as aforsaid; notwithstanding any law of this Collonie to the contrary."[19] The Indians lived on lands formerly belonging to Metacom but now deeded to Church, and worked under an informal tenancy arrangement. Some of them took his surname, and one man adopted his entire name. Church's son and grandson inherited these judicial and economic roles over time.

Beyond labor on his farms, the Indians contributed to Church's status in other important ways. The colonel expected "his" Indians to accompany him during King Philip's War and the northeastern wars, and the ability to supply twenty, fifty, or a hundred Indian soldiers when called upon made Church an extremely valuable figure in the eyes of both colonial and British administrators. In return the Indians enjoyed Church's protection—sometimes at a personal cost to himself—at times when public sentiment became "disaffected to Indians and to aney parson [person] that is imployed aney way for them."[20] Captains of Indian units enjoyed other advantages. Officers could profit handsomely by handling the debentures—pay orders—of their soldiery. If the Indians were servants, then officer-masters received the Indians' pay and bounties, and free Indians often signed over their debentures to

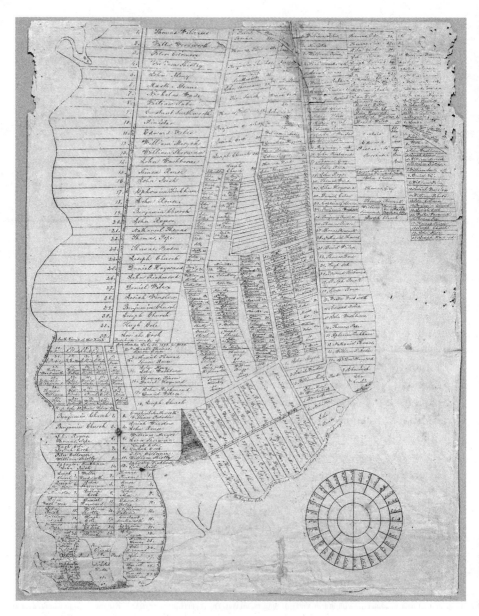

FIGURE 18. 1691 map of Little Compton showing Metacom's former village of Mount Hope subdivided into lots. Benjamin Church acquired many holdings. Courtesy of the John Carter Brown Library at Brown University.

officers because of debt or coercion. Either way, commanding Indian soldiers offered a lucrative supplement to the incomes of Indian guardians such as the Churches, the Wiswalls, the Bournes, the Winthrops, and other colonial dynasties.

Church protected his Indians but also policed them. As justice of the peace, he, and later his heirs, sentenced Indians to servitude and vigorously pursued runaways from their own estate.[21] Other local officials abused their authority to entrap Indians. William Woddell and Thomas Thornton of Rhode Island and Noah Wiswall and Samuel Sturgis of Cape Cod were among several constables and justices who appeared frequently as signatories on Indian indentures and bills of sale. They profited personally from these transactions, sometimes buying Indian contracts themselves for employment or resale, keeping Indian debentures in wartime, or otherwise gaming the system. Thornton's activities became so outrageous that ten English residents of Portsmouth and Providence petitioned the assembly at Newport in 1732 to intervene in a case involving an Indian named Grigory. Thornton and his partner Zechariah Jones had schemed to entrap Grigory, who had done day labor for Jones. Jones "had let ye Indan have neare as much drink as his work come too," and now claimed that Grigory owed him money. Jones hoped if he "Could Catch ye Indian he would sell him for fore or five years," and went to Thorton for an arrest warrant.[22] Thornton (who was the town constable and also served terms as a judge) violently seized Grigory, dragging him and tearing his clothes. Several colonists offered to pay Grigory's fines, but Thornton refused. Instead, he forced Grigory to sign a note for quintuple the original amount of money he owed, and Grigory became bound to Thornton as a servant. The petitioners charged Thornton with breaking the laws designed to protect Indians "from being Defra[u]ded or Cheeted and Especeally that Law which Exspressly says that no Indian shall be made a sarvant but for good Consideration and by the assent and approbation of two Justices."[23] Grigory's defenders may or may not have had the Indian's interests at heart; the men who offered to pay Grigory's fees likely wanted to control Grigory's labor themselves.

This incident showed how officials made free Indians into involuntary servants for their own profit. But it and many other cases also underlined the importance of local communities in permitting enslavement of Indians. The transformation of Indians such as Grigory from autonomous members of the community into involuntary servants or slaves required the active participation of multiple town officials and the tacit assent of many more colonists. Markets in the Atlantic world had declared Indians and Africans to be enslavable, but from a practical standpoint New England colonists could not convert free people—friends, neighbors, veterans, employees—into slaves, nor hold and control them, without help. Given the intentionally sparse statutory law regarding slavery in New England, answers to questions about who could be sold as a slave and where, and whether slavery was an inherited status, often depended on decisions made by neighbors. Constables had to serve writs and arrest the Indians, punish them physically, and sell them at vendue; juries and judges had to condemn them; neighbors had to testify against them, help capture them when they ran away, and otherwise reinforce the claimant's ownership.

Central authorities provided general frameworks, but higher courts intervened only when victims mounted persistent challenges to enslavement, and these were successful only when local communities backed them. In the case of Grigory, controversy exposed a lack of consensus on his enslavability. Prominent supporters defended his autonomy. Still, higher authority—the Newport court—was reluctant to interfere with Thornton's contract. Indians would need more community support to make their case for freedom.

In Connecticut's New London County between 1661 and 1729, the Court of Trials sentenced approximately eighteen Indians to servitude, most in the period 1689–1712. Local justice John Prentiss of New London traded in Indian labor even as he presided over cases involving Indians, as did his neighbor and fellow justice, Joshua Hempstead. Prentiss had fought in the Indian wars, recruited Indian soldiers, and returned with captives for sale. In the aftermath of King Philip's War he acquired a child captive named Rachel, who served in his household for sixty years. Rachel married an African slave named York and became a Christian, a mother, a church member—and, somehow, a slave, despite the set terms provided for Indian captives in Connecticut law.

The Prentiss home included other Africans and Indians who occupied varying points on the spectrum from servitude to slavery, including Sarah Wright, whom court papers listed as a "Negro." Sarah's father was in fact an Indian, William Wright, a member of a radical sect called the Rogerenes (their beliefs anticipated the Seventh-Day Adventists) and a servant in the household of its founder, John Rogers. While other Rogerenes received corporal punishment and fines for their apostasy and disruptive behavior, William received harsher penalties: in 1698 a Connecticut court ordered him to be exported as a slave from the colony.[24] William's African wife, Hagar, traveled to Hartford to visit her husband in jail, but authorities arrested her and her children and shipped them back to New London. There a court charged Hagar transportation costs and forcibly placed the children as servants in English households. Judge Prentiss claimed Sarah.[25]

Prentiss's friend Joshua Hempstead presided over a justices' court in New London. Hempstead was a farmer, craftsman, and occasional merchant. He made coffins, and so he carefully recorded baptisms and deaths in a diary. He also kept a detailed account of the work on his estate, where he relied on the labor of his sons, supplemented with hired neighbors, two African slaves—and the occasional bound Indian servant. Hempstead made periodic voyages to Jamaica with some of his neighbors. The men took items such as pork, shingles, and corn to the islands and brought back rum, sugar, and slaves to sell in New England and New York. Thus the judge was intimately familiar with Atlantic slavery even as he sat in judgment on cases involving Indian and African defendants. In 1713, he noted in his diary that Josiah Topping "came to my house & Signed over an Indian to me as per Indenture I to sell him for wt I can & to pay my self."[26] Hempstead sentenced several Indians to relatively short terms of servitude and then sold their time to his neighbors or bought it himself. Three different Indians worked for Hempstead, including Jo and another whom Hempstead arrested in a debt case and then purchased from the defendant.[27] Jo performed essential tasks, such as cutting shingles, sawing boards for boatbuilding, and mowing hay.

Debt Slavery

Meanwhile, other New England natives, though technically free and not defendants at court, became enmeshed in debt—to merchants, to local landowners, to ships' captains—that could lead to servitude. From the 1730s through the 1770s Connecticut storekeeper, Indian guardian, and future governor Jonathan Trumbull kept running tallies of debits and credits with scores of Indians alongside his "English accounts." Some paid Trumbull in traditional ways that fit their own household economies. John Todson and John Occatowsitt, two Niantic Indians, traded deerskins and furs for the powder, rum, sugar, tobacco, and cash that Trumbull advanced them. But others, including a Colchester Indian named Pyras and his wife, Hannah, paid debts in ways that showed how integrated Native Americans had become in the New England economy. Pyras prepared flax for spinning into linen, chopped wood, ran Trumbull's mill, did "small jobbs," mowed hay, built stone walls, made shoes, ran errands, handled livestock, and butchered cows and hogs for Trumbull at a rate of four to seven shillings a day. Hannah "bottomed chairs" by making cane or rush seats. Pyras worked by the day, the week, and the month; in 1737 he became indentured to Trumbull for an entire year, likely over debt.[28] During the Crown Point expedition of 1746 and again at the outset of the French and Indian War in 1755, Pyras served as a member of the town military unit, probably because he needed the pay.[29] He also owed money to another trader, William Williams. After Pyras's death, Hannah found herself in trouble with debt and accused of theft, and eventually became bound as a servant.[30]

Large landowners throughout New England, such as Fitz-John Winthrop, the Bournes of Cape Cod, and the Champlin family of Westerly, Rhode Island, employed similar tactics to ensure a steady supply of labor. In some cases, these relationships resembled the kinds of relatively benign ongoing book-debt relations that many English New Englanders maintained with neighbors and storekeepers, with constant exchanges and credits for goods and labor. In other cases, however, creditors converted informal tenancies into formal indentures by suing indebted Indians. As Pyras and Hannah discovered, book debt could lead to judicial enslavement when creditors turned to court for judgments. Sixteen Connecticut Indians faced actions for book debt in New London in 1714 to 1718 alone, and at least three became forcibly indentured in lieu of payment. Four other Indians who appeared in court proceedings had already become indentured servants for the same reason. Some English plaintiffs, such as Mercy Raymond of Fisher's Island, sold debt indentures to third parties, so that involuntary debt servants themselves became commodities to be exchanged and litigated over.[31] Service for debt became the norm in the fishing industry. Daniel Vickers notes that whaling vessels operating out of Cape Cod, Martha's Vineyard, and Nantucket relied almost exclusively on Indian labor, and he estimates that nearly three-quarters of the Indian whalemen in Nantucket by the mid-1730s turned over their entire earnings to white masters after every voyage.[32]

Debt peonage could trap entire families in its web. Gideon Hawley, a Congregationalist missionary among the Mashpee Indians at Plymouth, explained that many Indian men became debt peons in the whaling industry and worked until death, injury, or old age left them incapable, with nothing but debt to show for their labor. Then, families bound their own children into servitude to cover ongoing expenses. As a result, "there is scarcely an Indian Boy among us not indented to an English Master . . . the true reason of it is, their [English] neighbours find means to involve the Indians so deeply in debt as they are obliged to make over ye boys, if they have any, for security till payment."[33] Rev. Hawley believed that many creditors intentionally encouraged Indians to pledge their credit for food, liquor, or funeral costs. Once in debt, it was difficult for Native Americans to clear their commitments. In 1703, "Jefrey Indian" of Stonington, Connecticut, mortgaged his five-year-old daughter Ann to serve Daniel Mason for twelve years in order to clear debts incurred during his wife's illness and funeral.[34] Even Indians living in town reservations did not escape debt slavery. The Narragansetts of Charlestown, Rhode Island, complained of the "Sinister" activities of ill-intentioned colonists who "Oblig'd [us] to Bind our Children Servants to the English Credi[itor]s, to keep out of Prison."[35]

One Rhode Island woman named Betty Thompson managed to fend off repeated efforts by Christopher Champlin to bind her into service for debts incurred by her husband. Betty, her husband, and at least two children lived in a wigwam on Champlin's Westerly estate and worked for him and for other nearby planters. The family's debt had increased during the illness and death of Betty's husband, Peter Coyhees. In a case that dragged on for nearly seven years, Betty dodged sale into servitude by successfully challenging the arrest warrants that Champlin had issued against her. Betty cleverly capitalized on the fact that Indian households did not always fit the English norm, and managed to quash the warrants over technicalities. The first warrant called her Peter's wife, but Betty and Peter had not married after the English fashion, so Betty claimed she could not be held responsible for Peter's debts. A subsequent writ tried to hold her liable as Peter's "partner," but Betty noted that she had not entered into a formal business partnership agreement with Peter. Finally, Champlin sued Betty as an individual, but because the warrant gave her the title of "laborer"—a uniquely male designation—Betty convinced the court that as a woman she simply could not be the person named in the suit.[36]

Through all this litigation Betty remained free, but she also drew on the assistance of a nearby patron, George Babcock Jr., for legal advice and representation. His help came at a high cost: Betty had to indenture her two sons to Babcock in exchange for his aid.[37] The Thompson-Coyhees family tried to maintain kin ties despite economic pressure and servitude. The boys' grandmother sought and received Babcock's permission for the children to attend their father's funeral, where they mingled with relatives and English neighbors; but preserving connections to relatives, language, and native culture during more than a decade of service in Babcock's household proved difficult. Adults also faced challenges, especially since indentured servants had no right to marry. Mature householders such as Pyras who entered into debt indentures had to live in their masters' homes apart from their spouses and families. Samuel Gookin gave his married adult Indian servant, Tom, leave to visit "his Squaw" in Providence—but only for two weeks a year. If Tom absented himself longer he might be sold outside of Rhode Island.[38]

Betty Thompson was one of many Indian women who entered the workforce in much larger numbers than they had in the seventeenth century. Indian men were more likely overall to be bound to service by courts, which meant Indian women now headed households in larger numbers than previously. The participation of so many Indian males in military service, whaling, and maritime trades also heightened women's responsibilities. These activities not only took men away from home; they were also extremely dangerous, which meant a higher male death rate and a community in which women outnumbered men. Whereas Nathaniel Sylvester's 1680 Shelter Island account book had featured nine times as many men as women, Native American women composed more than half the accounts in one of Jonathan Trumbull's ledgers sixty years later.[39] Trumbull devoted entire sections of several ledgers to "Indian Accounts" (he began to organize his accounts by race in the late 1730s). Indians, particularly women, were also overrepresented on his list of "bad debts."

Indian women's accounts were smaller than men's. They paid their debts with baskets, brooms, hats, and caned chairs (Trumbull took chairs for caning to "Indian Town" by the dozens), all jobs that reflected traditional Native American skills. A few Indian women engaged in farm and industrial work. Betty Thompson performed agricultural tasks for the Champlins even after the death of her husband, perhaps assuming roles Peter had played on the farm, and her actions blurred gender lines and won her the designation of "laborer." Others worked at the Simsbury copper mines and the New Haven ironworks. One could view this as an extension of the traditional labor roles of Native American women, but it marked a shift from how English households had deployed female Indian workers in the previous century. Female farm, mining, and manufacturing work credits in the ledgers of Trumbull, Champlin, and other employers may have signaled changed expectations about Indian women's labor in which color trumped gender in ways that did not bode well for Indian freedom. Female African slaves worked in the fields like men, and this gendered difference was one of the key factors that distinguished slaves from Euro-American servants and free people. Now, in the eighteenth century, at least some Indian women in servant or clientage relationships did men's work as well.

In another gendered shift that affected judicial enslavement, Native American women entered the criminal justice system with greater frequency by the mid-1700s as they became more integrated into the colonial economy and assumed primary responsibility for family debts. Indian women faced arrest not just for theft and debt, however, but also physical crimes such as alcohol-fueled assault and murder.[40] Together, these trends—native women's entry into labor markets and increased household responsibilities, combined with debt and criminality—made Indian women and their children vulnerable to involuntary servitude. Yet another factor that had nothing to do with race put female-headed households at heightened risk: all the New England colonies passed laws in the eighteenth century that empowered local authorities to bind into service children from families too poor to support themselves.[41] Although these so-called pauper indentures and vagrancy actions captured

Euro-Americans in their nets, households headed by Indian women were disproportionately poor and therefore became frequent targets of forced indentures. Indian women resisted indenturing their children. In 1692 Mary Mecumpas declared in her will that "she hath not nor will not give her young Girle she had by mingoe, Thomas Olmstead's Negroe, to any English man."[42] Instead Mary left the girl to the care of an Indian cousin and bequeathed her a parcel of land in the hope that such assets would protect her daughter from servitude or slavery. But even mothers who tried to find placements for their children discovered that judges could overrule these arrangements.[43]

As involuntary servitude caused havoc in their communities, Indians themselves protested judicial enslavement, using their new protected status as subjects. Simon Popmoney, George Wapuck, and other Mashpee Indian leaders petitioned in the Massachusetts General Court in 1700. They complained that "Thro Ignorance of the Law, weaknes, foolishnes, & Inconsideration some of us that are Elder, & severall of our Children have run in to the English mens Debts, and not being able, nor perhaps careful to pay att the time appointed; our Selfs & our poor Children, are frequently made Servants for an unreasonable time." The petitioners delicately accused English plaintiffs of abusing debt proceedings to control Indian labor.[44] In the end, Massachusetts adopted the Indians' suggestions for amelioration in an "Act for Preventing Abuses to the Indians" passed later that year. The law acknowledged "the Executions [seizure for debt] and oppression which some of the English exercise towards the Indians by drawing them to consent to covenant or bind themselves or Children apprentices or Servants for an unreasonable term on pretence of or to make Satisfaction for some small debt contracted or damage done to them."[45] Again, the law attempted to reform the indenture process. Each indenture would require the approbation of two or more justices of the peace, who were to review the contracts and ensure that they followed the proper form. Contracts were to be finite in term, specific about the master's obligations, and signed by the Indian in question. The law forbade married Indians from entering into indentured servitude. Indians already bound into suspect indentures could petition local justices to review their cases. At least some Indian servants used these provisions to challenge abuse of the indenture process in Massachusetts.[46]

Still, this law and others like it subsequently adopted in Connecticut and Rhode Island seem to have had little impact on the sentencing of Indians to servitude for debt or criminal activity. Individuals continued to try to entrap Indians in debt in order to obtain their labor. Fierce competition for Indian labor led to situations such as the one that Grigory of Providence found himself in, where contending English owners sought to bind his labor by unscrupulous means if necessary, and authorities remained reluctant to break written contracts, even those "unjustly obtained."[47] Encouraging Indians to appeal for review of indentures essentially sent the documents back to the discretion of the very men who had approved them in the first place. The efficacy of the laws depended on the integrity of local judges and whether they had a personal interest in the labor of the Indians in question, which many did. Colonial governments passed more legislation in the 1720s and 1730s; finally legislatures in Massachusetts and Connecticut, and localities in Rhode Island, forbade extending credit to Indians or bringing suits against Indians for any debt above ten shillings. But abuses persisted. Because of the importance of Indian labor in the whaling and fishing industries, the revised laws exempted Martha's Vineyard, and Nantucket, Plymouth, and Barnstable counties—places with some of the largest remaining Indian populations—from the restrictions on credit, peonage, and lengthy indentures.[48]

Once indentured, whether voluntarily or involuntarily, Indians encountered many abuses. They could find themselves bought and sold, separated from families and taken from the region. Running away, stealing from one's master, engaging in a sexual relationship, bearing a child, and a host of other violations could double or triple a servant's time obligations. Since the early seventeenth century, owners of European and African servants throughout British America had employed all these methods to extend periods of service. But by the eighteenth century colonial governments had taken steps to protect first English and eventually other European nationals from the worst abuses.[49] Moreover, whereas for English colonists servitude was a stage in life rather than a lifetime state, Indians (once enmeshed in apprenticeship or servitude) found it difficult to escape the status for long, if at all, because of their ill-defined place in colonial civil society.

Joseph Quasson entered servitude "voluntarily" at first. The Quasson family had been sachems and large landholders in Menamoy on Cape Cod—some even owned Indian indentures—but had lost many of their assets by 1720.[50] Joseph's father died owing money to town clerk Samuel Sturgis, so Joseph's mother bound him out at age six to pay the five-pound debt. Mistress Sturgis energetically and somewhat successfully catechized young Quasson, who worked in the family's Yarmouth warehouse. Proud of his appearance, he attended the English church alongside the Sturgises and felt like a welcome member of the congregation. Quasson expressed feelings both of loyalty and distance concerning the Sturgis family; he did not actively resist servitude but did so passively by allowing other servants and apprentices to steal. At the end of his term, the Sturgises released him from their service well-clothed and with a Bible in his hand, but Joseph floundered in freedom.

He got some work but soon found it difficult to pay his expenses. Having pawned his clothes, Quasson became so ragged he felt embarrassed to attend the English church. Church attendance was mandatory, though, so to avoid the fine he joined the "Indian meeting." But Quasson did not understand the preaching there: fifteen years of service in the Sturgis household had left him fluent in English but ignorant of Wampanoag. He had lost touch with most of his kin. Unsuccessful at finding a place in the English community, and alienated from his Indian family, he began drinking, and finally in 1725 joined an expedition to Maine during Dummer's War. There he encountered other Indians, including kinfolk from Cape Cod, still attached to their villages and serving in their own military company under their English "guardian," Captain Richard Bourne. Quasson could not understand them, and they mocked him for his English ways. One evening he got into a brawl with an Indian soldier named John Peter (who turned out to be his cousin) and ended up killing him.

The murder and his eventual execution made Quasson's story unusual, but the economic, social, and cultural difficulties that attended his transition from the Sturgis household to freedom formed a more typical narrative. Indians raised in English households were no longer wholly Indian in culture, but neither were they full English citizens with opportunities and connections to help them begin an independent life. The leadership roles that former servants such as Robin Cassacinamon had assumed among their own people a century earlier no longer existed in the same form. Nor did the position as cultural intermediary: few English needed intermediaries to deal with Indians anymore, given a century of acculturation and knowledge on both sides. Joseph Quasson had the lineage status to become a leader but lacked cultural capital among his own people. Nor had his long service with the Sturgises created sufficient social and economic capital for him to achieve personal independence in colonial society. Quasson managed to remain free for about a year. Other former servants ended up not on the scaffold but at the public vendue, being auctioned off in restitution for debt or crime. Interestingly, the first Indians sentenced to judicial servitude by civil courts in Bristol County were already servants.

From Servitude to Slavery

Under such conditions, a Native American indentured servant—especially a woman or a child—could easily become a de facto slave. One such case involved "Phebee an Indian Maid or Girle," who petitioned Bristol authorities for her freedom in 1701. Phebee's owner, James Smith, had put her out to service to another master, John Burt. But when she reached her majority, which signaled the end of her obligation to Burt, Smith claimed her as "his slave for life" on the grounds that her parents had been his servants, and demanded that she be returned to him. Again, veiled allusions to sexual abuse and Phebee's express fears about returning to Smith's household further complicated the case in the justices' eyes. In the end the court ordered Phebee to work as Burt's indentured servant for an additional four years, with Smith to receive her yearly wages—this despite the fact that according to her indenture Phebee should already have been freed.[51]

The case of Phebee was by no means unique. Another servant, Sarah Chauqum of Rhode Island, confronted a similar situation in 1733 when her master sold her as a slave to Edward Robinson of New London, Connecticut. Sarah won her freedom by establishing her Indian ancestry to the court's satisfaction because her mother resided in the Narragansett Indian reservation town South Kingstown.[52] Sarah protected her free status, but Indians like her who challenged illegal enslavement publicly in court likely represented a small subset of a much larger group whose status came under attack but who had insufficient money, support, and knowledge to prevent such an assault.

One of the things that distinguished chattel slavery from servitude was its heritability, and evidence suggests that in practice New England colonists began to assert, in custom, the ownership of Indian servants' children. The outright kidnapping or removal of Indian children for sale as slaves in other colonies was prevalent enough to be the target of special legislation. In the case of Indian indentured servants, it is difficult to determine the extent to which children automatically followed in their parents' footsteps, but at least some did. Eighteenth-century probate inventories and advertisements for the sale of servants and slaves sometimes listed Indian women and their children together—indirect evidence that those children were following the status

Table 3   Cases where Indians challenged wrongful enslavement and/or abuse of indentures

	NUMBER OF DISPUTES
Dukes	6
Bristol	12
Newport	2
Plymouth	2
New London	6
Essex	0
Suffolk	1
Total	27

of their mothers. Occasionally, wills revealed the assumption that Indians were slaves for life, as in the case of Daniel Coggeshall of Kingstown, Rhode Island, who left "my Indian woman and her sucking child Jeffery" to his wife and children "during the term of their natural lives." And whereas probate administrators and newspaper advertisements often noted the time remaining on the contracts of white servants, they omitted such information in entries for Indians.[53] Caleb Pendleton of Colchester left "three Indian boy servants" in his estate, but their high valuation, which ranged from fifteen to twenty-two pounds, the lack of reference to terms, and his instructions to sell the boys all implied that the Indians could be sold as slaves.[54] For the sixteen Indians who appear in manuscript Rhode Island wills, none of the wills specified time remaining to be served, which meant that the Indians were willed to heirs as slaves for life. Similarly, only 3 out of the 70 newspaper advertisements offering Indians for sale in Boston 1707–1742 explicitly identified the Indians as term servants with time of service remaining.

Colonial courts also fielded numerous complaints that masters unlawfully sold or extended the contracts of apprenticed Indian children just before the children came of age, or sold young children out of the colony to places where they had no kin to protect them. A woman named Hester complained that in 1710 Daniel Mannering of Newport had taken her six-year-old daughter away from her and sold her "out of the province."[55] In a similar case, a mother was able to protect her child against possible sale as a slave, although she could not protect him from extended servitude. Ruth Coseaway had become bound to William Briggs of Tiverton in a case whose file is lost, although there are suggestions that she struggled with debt. She either brought a child into the household or had her son Tobey while a servant for Briggs. Briggs might have charged her for Tobey's upkeep. In January 1719, Ruth accused Briggs of "abuseing her & selling her for an unreasonable time," and for selling six-year-old Tobey "out of the province."[56] Because Ruth had a written contract specifying her obligations to Briggs, the court perused the document and found that Briggs had indeed exaggerated her term of service.

Then the court took up Tobey's sale. Several other children in Bristol County had suffered a fate similar to Tobey's. Once sold into another colony distant from any advocate or patron, Indian children became vulnerable to enslavement. Ruth was able to prevent this outcome in Tobey's case—the court made Briggs post bond and get him back—but it did not prevent Tobey from experiencing extended servitude. The court bound Tobey to work for Briggs until he was twenty-one. Ruth and Tobey's experience illustrates how even a short sentence of servitude could leave an Indian and her family vulnerable to lengthier service. Their story testifies to the importance of having a parent-advocate present—but also to the limits of what that advocacy could achieve. In response to complaints about cases such as Tobey's, Plymouth colony merely required that colonists interested in purchasing the children of enslaved captives obtain the court's permission first. Massachusetts passed similar laws three times in the eighteenth century, imposing heavy fines on those who sent Indian children "across the sea," but the repeated legislation suggests that the practice continued.[57]

At minimum such children probably served until adulthood, and perhaps for life. "Apprentice" was becoming a misnomer in the case of Indian children, since their indentures differed from those of their English counterparts, as a survey of such contracts in Rhode Island indicates.[58] Indian children's indentures more commonly omitted the masters' obligations for food, clothing, and education and instead focused on the apprentice's duties and limitations. Similarly, whereas apprenticeships involving middling Euro-American children generally specified training in skills they could use after completing their terms, and required masters to give "freedom dues"— awards of cash, clothing, livestock, and/or equipment designed to give the young adult a start in freedom and a new occupation—few Indian apprentice contracts included these provisions. By the eighteenth century fewer Indian parents signed their children's contracts—and parental advocacy could be crucial in securing benefits such as better treatment, freedom at age eighteen, and skills-training for apprentices. Instead, local justices commonly bound out such children. The absence or death of a parent advocate might mean slippage into enslavement for a child. In 1723 David Green of Jamestown, Rhode Island, bound "Hannah being a Girl half Indian and Half Negro" as an indentured servant to another master when her mother, his servant, died. Hannah was one and a half. The indenture refers to her as a "servant or slave," but tellingly, her new master, George Mumford, was to return Hannah to Green upon completion of the indenture twenty years later, which suggests that Green planned to claim her labor for life.[59] The confused wording and elisions in contracts like this one obscured Hannah's status—or, possibly, revealed how unsure even Mumford and Green and the witnesses were about the legality of the agreement.

During this same period, the New England colonies refined the legal parameters of the institution of slavery in ways that hurt Indian servants. Legislatures did not do this completely—they did not adopt clear definitions of slavery—but the laws established a kind of racial frontier in New England. Between 1685 and 1720, colonial governments passed a spate of legislation regarding people of color. This new wave of New England slave laws specifically included Indian slaves and servants in their strictures, which ranged from restrictions on travel and assembly to urban curfews for "Indian, negro, or mulatto servants and slaves." Massachusetts passed a statute prohibiting intermarriage between colonists and people of color. The laws dehumanized Indian and African servants and slaves, and distanced them from their English counterparts in servitude and freedom. Ironically, the English colonists adopted the policing and behavioral controls of other contemporary slave societies without adopting the laws that actually defined slavery.

Almost immediately after King Philip's War, all three New England colonies passed tough fugitive slave laws to punish runaways and to discourage Indians from protecting African or Indian escapees from servitude. Servants experienced increased surveillance and had to carry passes when traveling on public transport such as ferries. Roughly between 1680 and 1725, New England officials also created separate penalties and processes (including summary courts without juries) for "Indians, negroes, mulattoes, slaves or others" who stole or disposed of stolen goods and who struck or defamed Euro-Americans. Blacks and Indians received harsher punishments and more frequent corporal punishment than Euro-Americans for identical crimes in the eighteenth century, and often faced fines *and* corporal punishment rather than one or the other.

Perhaps even more significantly, during the same period Massachusetts shifted the tax status of both Indian and black servants and slaves from that of persons subject to the regular poll tax—a category that included white servants—to that of personal property. Connecticut legislators eventually did the same. These laws represented a conscious departure from a policy that only a few years before had required Indian servants to pay a poll tax just as white servants did.[60] Now, Indians and Africans became possessions to be "rated with horses and Hogs"—a loss of personhood that represented a defining characteristic of slavery.[61] These changes in law had to overcome serious opposition from within both legislatures, however; not all New England colonists felt comfortable viewing Indians in particular as personal property.

At the same time, Indian servants and slaves were becoming embedded in colonial society more than ever. To a much greater degree than in the previous century, free and enslaved people of color in New England joined town churches. Joshua Hempstead recorded the baptisms of Indian and African servants in his New London church. He presided over marriages between Indians and Euro-Americans, such as the one between Samuel Ways and Barbara Ryan (an Irish woman) without a blink (Connecticut did not ban such unions). Servants and sometimes slaves in all three colonies mustered with militias and participated in other institutions of communal life alongside their colonial counterparts. Slaves in New England retained rights that their Virginia counterparts did not; for example, in Connecticut they could own property and testify against whites in court. Still, the adoption of slave codes that otherwise mirrored practices in the Caribbean and Virginia meant a diminution of status for Indians and Africans. More ominously, such laws further blurred the line between servitude and slavery.

As judicial enslavement became more common in cases involving Indians, it became less common for Europeans. In Massachusetts such sentencing of whites all but ended. Rhode Island and Connecticut courts continued to sentence Euro-Americans to servitude after 1730, but they generally only handed such punishments to Europeans if they were Irish, Spanish, or members of other outsider groups.[62] Whites were also more likely to be offered other court-mandated solutions, short of servitude, for working off their debt in ways that recognized their citizenship and permitted them to remain with their families. Judicial enslavement was becoming racialized, part of the move toward the racialization of slavery and servitude in general.

The racialized laws of 1685–1720 had a circular effect, especially as the number of African slaves in New England increased in the eighteenth century. Color became associated with slavery, and slavery with color, and in the process the very "Indianness" of many Indian servants came under attack. Court documents fostered ethnic slippage by designating Indian servants as mixed-race or black, often over their objections.[63] Racial designations had enormous significance, as the case of Sarah Chauqum illustrates. Enslaving Indians in Rhode Island was technically illegal, but her master listed her as a "mollato" in the bill of sale to Edward Robinson. Sarah won her freedom by asserting her Narragansett Indian identity and proving her mother's residence in the Indian town there, but not all Native Americans avoided passing from servitude to slavery.

Moreover, by the 1720s some New England Indians and their offspring *were* of mixed race, and this trend increased during succeeding decades.[64] Wealthy households that could afford African slaves often already employed Indians, and marriages or sexual relationships within or across households were common. William Wright agreed to serve John Rogers for six years in order to help purchase the freedom of his intended wife, Hagar, a slave in the Rogers household. Even though Hagar received manumission papers from Rogers, both she and her "Molata Mongrel Indian & Negro" children with Wright remained at risk for reenslavement.[65] Rogers's own son tried to claim them as part of his father's estate, as did a notorious slaver named Samuel Beebe, and Hagar had to fight off several lawsuits and even kidnappings targeting herself and her children.

Even more frequently, Indian women married African men. The demographic catastrophes wrought by war and enslavement left many tribes facing extremely skewed sex ratios, so Indian women on reservations and in English towns found partners among free, servant, and enslaved African populations whom they worked alongside or socialized with in their free time. Joshua Hempstead mentions five such unions in his diary (two other Indians married Euro-Americans). In the Indian towns these choices brought few consequences, but for Indians who were already servants, choosing an enslaved black partner could have serious ramifications, as in the case of Patience Boston. Bound into "apprenticeship" to an English household by her father at age three, Patience was a self-described "mischievous and rebellious servant." She completed her term of service at age twenty-one, "happy that I had no Body to Command me." But when she married an African servant or slave (the precise status of her husband, a whaleman, is unclear) she became "bound for life" to her husband's master.[66] Some masters, like Patience Boston's owner, required servants who married their bondsmen to sign contracts that effectively enslaved them as well.

The biracial children of such unions in turn risked seizure as slaves by their parents' owners. Rachel Prentiss (she had taken the name of her master's family) married a slave named York in the nearby Pygan household, and this may in part explain why she remained a servant for life. Rachel and York's daughter, Dido, continued in Captain Prentiss's household, first as a slave and then as a servant of indeterminate legal status. Prentiss signaled his intention to manumit her when she reached the age of thirty-two, but in the meantime he bequeathed Dido to his daughter, Irene. In 1732 Dido "bound herself" for four and a half years to John Prentiss's widow, Sarah, yet her wages went to Naboth Graves, Irene's husband.[67] Seemingly, Dido had to buy herself from the Graveses.

The identification of people of color and slavery—and of Indians with servitude—meant that free Indians faced danger even if they steered clear of the courts. In the seventeenth century Indians had experienced terrifying incidents of kidnapping and sale into slavery, but these generally occurred during wartime. In the eighteenth century, however, such kidnappings became more common. Indian mariners in particular faced the constant threat of enslavement by unscrupulous captains. A group of Indian freemen and indentured servants contracted to work as divers and help search for a wreck in the Bahamas in 1705, only to have the captain of the vessel promptly sell them as slaves in Exuma.[68] A Rehoboth Indian named John Frost complained in 1709 that his son Tom had accepted a position on a voyage to Surinam, but that the captain, Nathaniel Jarvis, had sold the boy as a slave in Antigua. Tom had been missing for three years, and Frost begged the Bristol court to punish Jarvis and recover his son.[69] The judges, who included Benjamin Church, agreed to contact the governor and investigate the incident, "so that Justice may be done and the Indians may not be Dyscouraged." But no record tells us whether Tom Frost ever escaped Caribbean slavery.[70]

Judicial enslavement of Indians had important consequences for both the Native American community and for New England society as a whole. By 1774, the first Rhode Island census indicated that over a third of all Indians in the colony lived in white households—and the proportion rose to half in towns like Newport and Providence. Black and Indian workers helped construct the New England economy, but at a terrible cost. Forced servitude undermined Native American fertility rates, mortality, child rearing, kin networks, gender roles, and other aspects of Indian life. Time spent in English homes influenced Indian dress, religion, language acquisition, and a host of other practices. Indian laborers created a hybrid culture with their English neighbors but remained at the margins of colonial civil society in terms of citizenship, economic power, and political influence. The persistence of Indian slavery into the eighteenth century also illustrates the complex relationship among law, behavior, and the creation of racial identity in multiethnic colonial societies. New England was a legalistic society, yet it was slow to create a body of law regarding slavery, and the existing law was unevenly enforced. When Justice Hempstead memorialized "old Rachel formerly a Servt to Capt. John Prenttis" in his diary in 1746—"I Supose She was near 80 years of age. She was a Captive taken in the Narhaganset war in 1675"—did he question why Rachel, a child captive who should have served only a set term under Connecticut law, spent her entire life in service to the Prentiss family?[71]

Despite its weak legal foundations, Indian slavery remained a central part of this "society with slaves." In the 1730s and 1740s a number of second- and third-generation Indians held in involuntary servitude challenged their enslavement in colonial courts. The children and grandchildren of people such as Rachel Prentiss sued for freedom on the grounds that their ancestors had been illegally enslaved. These individuals enjoyed the support of at least some of their communities, both English and Indian, as some colonists came to perceive moral wrong in the enslavement of Indians. These wrongful enslavement suits formed the beginning of an abolitionist movement in New England that had implications for enslaved persons of all races. The intentionally ad hoc nature of slavery in New England also may help explain why it was so hard to abolish there.

EPILOGUE

Indians and the Origins of American Slavery— and Abolitionism

Antislavery and abolitionism have come to be almost exclusively associated with ending African slavery. But this was not always the case. Benjamin Church's grandson published his grandfather's memoir of King Philip's War in 1746; but when historian and abolitionist Henry Martyn Dexter republished the work a century later, he included an extensive critique of his ancestors' enslavement of Indians. Similar mea culpas accompanied histories and fictional accounts of the Indian wars by other nineteenth-century writers.[1] Samuel Drake paused his otherwise celebratory account of King Philip's War to deplore Benjamin Church's enslavement of Indian captives. Church's grandson had described the booty as a just reward for "success from Heaven," but in a caustic footnote Drake wondered "whether Heaven had any thing to do with making slaves of the Indians after they were made prisoners." Drake identified with the "skepticks, on the same principle that every feeling man now doubts the justness of our Southern brethren to make slaves of Negroes."[2] For Dexter and Drake, slavery was slavery, and New England's own history of Indian slavery made them uncomfortable. But they could criticize it at a distance: these writers ignored the North's own heavy involvement in African slavery. Willing to acknowledge Indian slavery in the past, they avoided confronting a present of slow emancipation and inequality for Africans—and Indians—in antebellum New England.

For subsequent generations, the reverse was true. Indian slavery became the forgotten story subsumed in the larger story of racialized slavery in both history and memory. But Indians were the charter generation. Indian slavery was an integral part of New England history—both for Native Americans and for Euro-American colonizers. Indians were the main non-English labor supply, and in that capacity they were crucial to the success of the colonization project and the prosperity enjoyed by English colonists. Indians, not Africans, were the objects of the first laws regarding slavery, and of the masters who competed for bound labor. As the first cohort to experience slavery in New England, Indians shaped the institution of slavery. Within New England households they interacted on intimate terms with the English and with other Indians and eventually Africans. Free and bound Native Americans resisted enslavement and prevented the English from defining all Indians as slaves. As a result, New England colonists created a slave regime that purposely refrained from clearly identifying which populations were susceptible to slavery and the precise conditions that slaves would face.

Indians experienced the first, great costs of slavery in the region, in terms of mortality, loss of family, and cultural pressure, even as they created new relationships and regional identities with English, Indians, and Africans alike. Of course, New England Indians did not rush into hybridity, either; they held English and Indian cultural values in tension in the eighteenth century, and tried to maintain elements that best suited the changing material and strategic circumstances they faced in the eighteenth century.[3] By pushing first for autonomy, and subsequently for rights and liberties within colonial jurisdiction, New England Indians forced the English to consider what citizenship meant in a hybrid society.

African slavery proved transformative for all members of this society. The enslaved Africans who arrived in New England households encountered a system already in place, work roles assigned, and existing multiracial servant communities to join. Africans in turn reshaped colonial understandings of enslavement, however, precipitating a racialization of New England society that undermined its earlier hybrid qualities—and which also undermined the status of Indian servants and slaves. As Indians entered an Atlantic world of slavery, the social capital, kin networks, and claims to nativity and citizenship that helped ameliorate their enslaved condition closer to home failed to protect them. Eventually the global convergence of the law and practice of slavery undermined these protections even within New England. If the legal status of free Indians improved or at least remained steady after 1700, the status of Indian servants and slaves declined.

Samuel Sewall's New England

Many of these threads come together in two sets of documents: the diary of Samuel Sewall, and freedom suits brought by Connecticut Indians. Both show how Indian slavery and African slavery became intertwined, and how the abolition of one became linked to the other. Indians challenged slavery first (and ultimately more successfully) than did Africans, with lasting implications for the abolitionist movement in New England. Sewall left one of the more famous and detailed diaries of any provincial New Englander. The man, seemingly, was everywhere between 1674 when he began the diary and his death in 1729, participating in one significant event after another. He watched the execution of Tom Indian during King Philip's War; he lost papers relating to the case of Plagamore Sachem and Bernard Trott as an assistant in the General Court in 1677; he helped preside over the Salem witchcraft trials as a judge; he courted well-connected Winthrop widows in Boston; he wrote one of the earliest antislavery tracts in New England; and he rode circuit both as a justice and as a commissioner for the New England Company for the Propagation of the Gospel, the body charged with raising money to support the evangelization the Indians.

During King Philip's War and the eastern wars that followed, Sewall reported on the progress of the conflicts, especially the number of Indians killed and taken. He attended an auction where "9 Indians sold for £30" in June 1676, and on June 1690, summoned "by Beat of Drum," joined other Bostonians as they gathered and received an invitation to "the Sale of the Souldiers part of the Plunder taken at Port Royal [Nova Scotia]," to be held the following Wednesday afternoon.[4] The "plunder" included captives. Perhaps intending to go, Sewall carefully noted the time of the auction in his diary. As a captain of militia after 1689, Sewall occasionally patrolled with the town watch, enforcing the rules against night walking and other disturbances involving young people, servants, and slaves. These were mostly uneventful evenings that involved arresting ninepin players and breaking up card games and informal drinking parties. One night, gunfire in Charlestown roused the watch in a general alarm about a feared Indian attack, but it turned out to be a group of escaping Indian servants, not invaders from the northeast.[5] Sewall approved of paying troops for bringing in scalps and captives during the eastern wars. "Skin for Skin" was how he phrased it.[6]

Sewall became equally fascinated by the experiences of English captives among the Indians, and interviewed returnees whenever he could. He entertained them, gave gifts—Hannah Dustin, who killed and scalped the family that held her prisoner, received "Connecticut Flax"—and gathered tidbits of information, including the fact that Dustin's captor "did formerly live with Mr. Rowlandson of Lancaster." In other words, the husband of Mary Rowlandson, perhaps the most famous English captive of all, had formerly held Dustin's Indian master as a servant. How had this experience affected Dustin's Indian captor and shaped his decision to in fight against the English now? The Indian had "pray'd the English way," Dustin reported, "but now he found the French way was better."[7] Sometimes redeemed captives brought news of those still missing. Sewall expressed relief when he discovered the fate of Gershom Hobart, the son of a friend. Wabanaki had kidnapped the boy, but Sewall heard he was now settled in a fort in Maine among Bomazeen's people. "Masters name is Nassacombewit, a good Master, and Mistress," he noted with surprising unconcern, as if he were describing Gershom's placement in a solid English home among people with shared values and similar understandings of what constituted a master-servant relationship.[8] Perhaps he was. If Indians could be "good masters," how did Sewall construct Indian slavery and captivity among the English?

Sewall interacted frequently with Indians—free people, servants, and slaves—in his daily life. The casual way in which he accepted Indians' presence showed the extent to which English and Indians had become embedded in each other's daily lives. Many of his urban contemporaries used Indians as drivers. When he and his wife and son drove in their coach along Dorchester Road, "Brigs's Indian" managed the horses. Daughter Betty, while riding on a horse-drawn sled with some other children, received an accidental blow on her head from the goad wielded by the Indian who drove the sleigh. The sister of Governor Joseph Dudley, Mrs. Hunting, asked Sewall for help in procuring an "Indian youth of 10 or 12 years of Age, to live in Service till he be 21 years. . . . They keep a Calash [buggy], and want a Lad to drive it." Sewall passed the request along to a company associate in Mashpee country, along with a guarantee that "by means of her Inspection" the boy "would be well educated."[9]

Other acquaintances employed Indians as household servants, and relied on them for nursing and other intimate help. When Isaac Addington, secretary of the governor's council, experienced a hemorrhage on the floor of the assembly and ran to the latrine, he "call'd for his Indian Girl" to care for him. For a period of time, Sewall unsuccessfully courted the widow of his old friend Wait Still Winthrop, grandson of the founder. The Winthrops had acquired two Indian captive girls who cared for the Winthrop children. One of the captives died in adolescence, but Madam Winthrop retained least one Indian servant, Juno, who fetched wood, cooked, and performed other duties around the home. Sewall viewed Juno's services as a barometer of the widow's regard for him: when he was in favor, Madam Winthrop sent the girl to "walk him home with a lantern" after late-night visits, but as the romance soured she refused, claiming that Juno "was weary and gon to bed."[10] Sewall liked to give Juno and other servants small tips when he visited friends and family—five-shilling notes, sweets—and nearly every visit to a friend or associate involved such a transaction with an Indian. His friend Nathanial Sparhawk, who entertained Sewall in Bristol when the judge traveled to properties in Rhode Island or to court session, owned an Indian boy; so did Sewall's own son, Sam. Sewall also delivered Bibles to Indian servants enrolled with the army in the northeast.[11]

Along with these quotidian encounters with Indian slavery, Sewall recorded glimpses of the violence, vulnerability, and alienation that attended the lives of Indian servants and slaves. The local Suffolk County inferior courts—the district that included Boston—sentenced eight Indians to be sold "in the plantations" between 1683 and 1691, whipped and/or mutilated these and seven others in public, and added to the terms of four Indians already bound as servants to English masters. Sewall described some of the cases. One attracted extra attention—perhaps because the punishment seemed so extreme, or perhaps it might have involved an Indian he knew from his frequent trips to Martha's Vineyard to observe the Christian Indian communities there. In response to a burglary charge from Martha Parke, the court had ordered Sam Indian publicly branded with a "B" on his forehead, cropped of one ear, and banished—sold—for life.[12] When Thomas, an Indian belonging to his friend Daniel Oliver "and a very useful Servant hang'd himself in the Brewhouse," Sewall noted the man's death with surprise and reported the inquest results.[13]

As a justice on the Supreme Court of Judicature, which heard capital crimes, Sewall adjudicated cases in which the infant children of young Indian servants died and the mothers stood accused of infanticide. In one such case, the jury found his friend Edward Hutchinson's Indian woman Maria innocent of killing her child in an outhouse. In another case, the guilty mother faced execution. Yet another case involved a girl named Hittee who set fire to her master's residence. Infanticide—the murder of one's own children and of English children under Indians' care—and arson were classic acts of slave resistance but also open to different interpretations. In these instances, Sewall sought to avoid the death penalty for the accused servants. He pushed to overturn the guilty jury verdict in Hittee's case because the convicted Indian arsonist might have been a minor when she committed the act and therefore not subject to the capital law.[14]

Sewall also had more uplifting interactions outside the courtroom as he toured Indian congregations in Mashpee, Point Judith, and Martha's Vineyard, marveling at the economic activity, religiosity, and learning he observed among the free Indian Christian population. The Indians served him milk and showed off their spinning wheels and wheat fields, their plow agriculture and their English houses. In his deliberations on the General Court, where he served as an assistant regularly after 1688, Sewall tried to consult with Indians when relevant legislation came before that body. During the discussion about proposals to segregate Indians into reservation towns in 1689, he set up meetings "with a discreet person or two of Punquapoag Indians," including William Ahaton and other Indian leaders from the praying communities, to see if they believed this would be advantageous for them in the long run.[15] For several years he housed an Indian boy from Taunton named Benjamin Larnell so the child could attend Boston Latin School and eventually Harvard. He had to write certificates for Indian students and preachers such as John Neesnummin who wished to pass from Indian towns to English towns during the war years; such written passes were essential, lest the traveler be killed or captured and sold.

These issues loomed larger as Sewall aged and continued to think about the place of Indians in New England society. He adhered to a not-uncommon contemporary ethnographic view of Indians that saw them as a lost tribe of Israel whose conversion would help bring about the Second Coming of Christ, an event he devoutly anticipated. He read Bartolomé de Las Casas and other Spanish commentators on the question of Indian origins and the morality of enslaving them. He dreamed of converting Wabanaki—and, indeed, all Indians in the Western Hemisphere—to Christianity. But Sewall wondered if that goal might require temporary segregation of the population in New England in order to protect the Indians' rights, land, and persons.

One factor that apparently soured his courtship with Madam Winthrop was Sewall's growing reputation as an opponent of slavery, particularly Indian slavery, and his advocacy of Indian rights. After a conversation in her parlor about an Indian slave who had recently won her freedom in a legal case, Winthrop suddenly turned on Sewall and "charg'd me with saying, that she must put away Juno, if she [Winthrop] came to [wed] me."[16] Sewall denied the accusation vehemently, and in truth he was far from an abolitionist. He owned a slave named Scipio who lived in his attic, and many of his close friends and associates owned African as well as Indian slaves. "Having been long and much dissatisfied with the Trade of fetching Negros from Guinea," he began portentously in one entry, "I had a strong Inclination to Write something about it; but it wore off."[17] Sewall finally became sufficiently agitated to take action not by freeing Scipio but rather by publicizing the plight of a slave belonging to Joseph Saffin. The man, named Adam, had sued for his freedom because Saffin had violated an agreement to manumit him if Adam worked diligently for a third party for an agreed-upon term. When Saffin reneged, Adam ran away, and Saffin filed a suit to re-enslave him.

Sewall ridiculed Saffin in a poem that captured the asymmetries of power involved when enslaved persons tried to challenge their status through English-dominated institutions:

> Superannuated Squier, wigg'd and pow'd[ered] with pretence,
> Much beguiles the Assembly with his lying Impudence.
> None being by, his bold Attorneys push it on with might and main,
> By which means poor simple Adam sinks to slavery again.[18]

Adam's case touched upon one of Sewall's other obsessions: the right of servants and enslaved persons to marry. Adam wanted his freedom in part so he could earn money to purchase the freedom of his wife, also Saffin's slave. A flurry of activity ensued, as Adam marshaled some important friends. Sewall thought the time was ripe for some move on the slavery issue because key opinion makers had become involved—Joseph Belknap began circulating a petition on Adam's behalf, Cotton Mather planned a treatise on masters' responsibility toward slaves, and the Boston town meeting had made a motion to tax the slave trade "to discourge the bringing of them." Inspired by reading scripture—and Bartolomé de Las Casas's epic critique of Spanish abuse and enslavement of Indians—in 1700 Sewall penned a roman à clef of the Saffin case and called it *The Selling of Joseph*.

Although this publication made him an important footnote in the history of antislavery in colonial America, Sewall cared more about protecting Indians than Africans from the worst of slavery. Familiarity, history, and eschatology all favored Indians in his eyes. Madam Winthrop correctly sensed the connection between Indian slavery and African slavery, however, as much as Sewall latter denied it when confronted in her parlor. The judge understood that worsening conditions for Africans would affect Indians as well. Sewall's diary illustrates the process of racialization that attended the period 1680–1730, how contemporaries understood it, and the ways it undermined the position of all people of color in New England society.

Sewall's insider commentary on the sharp debates about race and slavery revealed the deep divisions that roiled government and by extension the entire society over these issues. As the General Court adopted codes to limit Indian and African servants' and slaves' freedom of movement and legal standing in the 1690s and early 1700s, Sewall went along—except for three issues. The Deputies—the lower house of the legislature—proposed an antimiscegenation bill in December 1705 for the Assistants' consideration. Sewall adamantly opposed such a measure. He favored solemnizing slave marriages as a way of enhancing monogamy and out of a basic recognition of slaves' humanity. He also thought that blocking consensual relationships might lead to sexual violence on the part of enslaved persons. Sewall was not an advocate of relations between Africans and English, but he did accept Indian-English marriage. In Martha's Vineyard and some of the other communities that Sewall visited where Indians outnumbered English in some cases, intermarriage between Indians and English had been more the norm. He certainly presided over fornication cases involving Indians and English, and noted the negative public reaction when a soldier brashly strolled through the Boston Common in broad daylight with "an Indian Sqaw" on his arm. In the end, the bill, called "An Act for the Better Preventing of Spurious and Mixt Issue," passed on December 5. But in a partial victory Sewall "got the Indians out of the bill, and some mitigation for [Negroes] left in it, and the clause about their masters not denying their Marriage."

The next issue regarding Indians that caught Sewall's attention was a petition brought by Samuel Penhallow regarding the prohibition on importation of Spanish and Carolina Indians. Penhallow had sought exemption for a Carolina woman and her three children he had imported aboard the *Neptune* in April 1713 and sold to customers in Plymouth. Governor Gurdon Saltonstall called upon the Assistants who formed his handpicked council, which included Sewall, to review Penhallow's claim. The councilors rejected Penhallow's request, although the Plymouth residents who purchased the slaves from him successfully petitioned to keep them. Race entered into the last major legislative debate when, in 1716, Sewall "essay'd . . . to prevent Indians and Negros being rated with Horses and Hogs." This bill changed the tax valuation of servants and slaves of color from that of people—a poll tax generally applied to English servants—to that of possessions, livestock, and other property. Connecticut legislators debated a similar law much earlier, in 1679–80.[19] Such bills raised fundamental questions about the status of Indian captives and other servants. They were "servants *pro tempore*"—literally "servants for the time being"—in Connecticut; did that make them chattel slaves? The Connecticut Assembly was so divided over this issue that a special committee had to reconcile contradictory votes from each house of the legislature.[20]

This time, Sewall recognized that the fate of Indians and Africans in slavery could not be separated. He did not simply try to keep Indians out of the bill but rather fought to scotch the law completely. Sewall's main opponent, Deputy John Thaxter, had taken Indian captives in the war and owned them in his household. Sewall tried to make an economic argument rather than a justice argument, saying the move would reduce revenue. But Thaxter also couched his proposal in similar "valuation" terms rather than acknowledging the bill for what it was: a conscious move that brought Massachusetts slave law more in line with that of other slaveholding colonies, one that advantaged slaveholders by redefining people of color as forms of property and implicating indentured servants as well as slaves. The conflation of these two categories of service meant a serious de jure, not just de facto, deterioration of Indian status.

Like his contemporaries, Sewall thought about race often in the eighteenth century and in ways he had not previously. He "Spake much of Negroes" with Paul Dudley one evening during a convivial meal of "Pippins, Anchovas, Olives, Nuts," Madeira, and other comestibles available to upper-class merchants. Africans still represented an unknown to Sewall and to many of his contemporaries in ways that Indians did not. The two friends debated whether during final judgment the saved became white or whether color persisted in the afterlife (Sewall thought color persisted, but his friend Dudley thought spirits were colorless). Sewall and his fellow justices confronted a system of Atlantic slavery that had changed in their lifetimes. Before, slavery had been about warfare, nationality, and religion; now race increasingly defined it. The Massachusetts Council received a petition in 1708 from "a Spaniard"—possibly an Indian, a biracial individual, or a person from the Atlantic Islands—who begged to be freed from slavery. The mariner who had sold him claimed that he had bought him as a slave and that "all of that Color were Slaves."[21] If color became a definition of slavery, then free Indians were at risk.

This had already happened to numerous New England Indians, free people whom unscrupulous employers entrapped or sold into Atlantic servitude. Sewall attended a meeting in 1708 to hear complaints from Indians at Woodstock—a region close to the conflict zone during Queen Anne's War—who claimed that so many of their number had been kidnapped that it seemed to be an official policy "to send us to Salt Water."[22] Indians considered the implications of race as well. Many began questioning earlier colorblind attitudes toward marriage and incorporation of others, largely because they perceived that race mattered in new ways to colonial authorities. Samson Occam and other Mohegans wrote to the Connecticut Assembly with a predicament:

> In Overhalling the list of our Tribe we have found one Name, that We Cannot find out where it Came from, We find the Families of Mohegan and the Number of the Families, and their Christian or given Names and Sir Names, but there is one of Moses Muzzeens Family,

is calld Ben, but What Ben, no Body can Tell it is Moses Mazzeens Daughter Hannah's Son, and he is Blacker than our Indians, and we think he is from Guinny partly. and the whole Tribe objects against him and We Cannot tell how his Name was put down amongst the names of the Mohegan Tribe it must be thro the inattention of the Tribe, and now We object against his having Right amonst us more over if he takes rite amongst us not only guinney Children, but European Children and some other Children Will take also, and it Will also give Libertes to our Daughters to borrow children from all Quarters. And therefore We beg your Honr wou'd positively join . . . in our Objection.[23]

If Ben met with resistance in a Mohegan society, outside of "Indian Town" his fate might be much worse: as a mulatto or mustee he might be a likely candidate for enslavement if he ever became enmeshed in servitude or convicted of a crime. Connecticut had targeted free mulatto and Negro children for forced apprenticeship in 1724, and similar laws in Massachusetts and Rhode Island pulled many into servitude.[24]

Indians, Colonists, and Africans in Freedom and Slavery

Various groups pushed back against the construction both of a slave regime and a racial frontier in New England in the eighteenth century. Most notably, second- and third-generation Indian and biracial slaves began to contest their enslavement in courts throughout New England after 1700, and with even greater frequency after 1720. Drawing on a natural rights argument, they asserted New England—and British—citizenship, and declared that freedom was a possession they had all along. These suits exposed many of the holes in New England's law of slavery, which relied so heavily on custom and local enforcement of masters' demands. The plaintiffs also relied on social capital and support to bring the suits. Often, wrongfully enslaved people had to pass through justices' courts, then a jury trial. If owners continued to appeal, the case eventually came before the General Assembly, which served as both a legislature and a supreme or final court of appeals. If Indians wished to avoid incarceration or re-enslavement during the period of appeal, which typically dragged on for years, plaintiffs needed to post significant sums as bond, which meant they needed patrons willing to assume such costs.

Lower courts and juries had tended to be hostile toward Indians in the seventeenth century. But in Connecticut during the eighteenth century, the situation began to tilt slightly. Indians were no longer the enemy but rather the soldiers in the colony's own forces. They were friends and neighbors. People testified on their behalf. Literacy and clientage, which could have potentially negative effects, also brought tools with which to challenge enslavement. And a group of attorneys began pleading wrongful-enslavement cases in a prelude to formal antislavery movements of the Revolutionary era. They represented Indian and African clients before the Inferior and General Courts and wrote elaborate briefs to justify new positions. In this way, the goal of ending Indian slavery laid the groundwork for more widespread eventual abolition. Such actions may have contributed to the linking of Indian and African slavery among English abolitionists, since Granville Sharp and other early antislavery advocates included Indian victims in their indictment of the slave system.[25] Indeed the progress of some of the cases—including the reluctance of courts and legislators to rule—resembled the pivotal Mansfield case and other crucial landmarks in English antislavery.

Peter Pratt, the Connecticut king's attorney from 1719 to 1727, was one such lawyer. Perhaps his former association with the Rogerenes, a religious group that had included bound Indians and Africans as members, predisposed Pratt to take up the case of Indian slaves. Pratt prepared a detailed memorandum for the General Assembly in 1722 that laid bare the contradictions inherent in holding children and grandchildren of Indian captives from King Philip's War. He first offered some history: "That Divers Children of Both Sexes of ye Indian natives of Mount-hope, had bin taken Captives by the English in their warr with yt People and ye same Dispersed into Servitude," and "have borne Children in ye Service of their Respective masters." Pratt focused on female Indians, since masters often made heritability arguments by invoking the practices in "other of ye Majesties plantations" as guidelines. But Pratt contended that "whether these Children so born are holden as proper Slaves there is no Law or usage of this Colony Sufficient to Determine." The lack of a positive law of slavery in Connecticut, as in Massachusetts, meant that no clear definition existed. Pratt called upon the court to consider "whither the sd Children so Born . . . ought to be deemed Slaves as ye Negroes or as ye Spanish or other Indians of ye foreign nations, imported here from beyond ye Seas, or whither they ought to be deemed free." At the very least the court should impose time limits on the servitude of such children rather than allow slippage into slavery. Colonial governments had abdicated their responsibility to act, instead leaving it up to individuals to assert identities and status in an unequal environment. Indians, Pratt concluded, "ought not to be Slaves at their masters pleasure, nor free at their own, but yt a Rule of Righteousness by the Wisdom of a protestant Christian Common-Wealth ought to be ye Standard of ye Duty and Privilege of Both."[26] But no such legislative clarity was forthcoming.

Instead, in the following year's session magistrates focused on social control and preventing interracial socializing.[27]

A narrow focus on New England–born Indians meant that the kinds of interventions Pratt requested would not dismantle the entire slave regime. Other cases challenged African enslavement and its heritability. Abda, the biracial child of an African or Afro-Indian woman and English man, won his case at justices' court and at the Inferior Court of Common Pleas, where the jury "judg'd him to be a Freeman," much to the ire of his former master Thomas Richards. Abda obtained a "hue and cry," a call to fellow townsmen for help; as a result the community watch literally broke him out of Richards's house. Richards noted that Abda had been listed as slave property on his father's probate inventory, and thus the government had previously declared him to be "Chattells" belonging to the Richards estate. Richards believed that he had precedent, common usage, and the law of slavery as practiced in other English colonies on his side. No jury had the right to "take Commission according to law to as the Plea of Liberty pretended," because no express Connecticut law empowered the courts to go around freeing slaves. But even when the General Assembly ruled in Richards's favor on appeal, Richards felt he had lost. The "orders given by the Government, thereon, for returning the sd Abda," he complained incredulously, "have hitherto been so wholly ineffectuall, that the sd Abda, notwithstanding He doth reside within the sd Town of Hartford, doth still refuse to return."[28] Abda refused to turn himself in, and local authorities refused to compel him to do so. The same informal networks of enforcement that had permitted individual masters such as Richards to turn servants into slaves now permitted Abda to go about his business with impunity.[29]

Caesar, the Indian man whose suit Joshua Hempstead heard in 1739 in New London, also made an argument based upon natural rights, subjecthood, and citizenship. Two important New London lawyers, John Lee and John Curtiss, helped argue Caesar's case.[30] Their brief to the General Assembly, written by Curtiss, borrowed from Pratt's earlier reasoning. Caesar "was one of [the] Subjects of our Sovereign Lord the King . . . not to be subjectd to Bondage & Slavery." In the absence of other statutory law about slavery, Caesar's claim went back to the only law that Connecticut had: the statutes regarding the treatment of Indian captives and "surrenderers" from King Philip's War in 1676. Curtiss stressed Caesar's relationship to a captive who had completed her term of service as specified in wartime legislation. His mother, Betty, had "surrendred her Self or was given to the mercy of the Government of [Connecticut] in or before ye year 1676 among many others [of the] Indian nation & . . . become the property of ye Government aforsd."

The October 12, 1676, session law had stated those Indians "as Cannot be prov'd muertherer [murderer] . . . their Lives & shall not be sold out of the country for slaves . . . [but] be well used in Service wth the English." Since Caesar's mother had been illegally held as a slave, his natal status could not be assumed to indicate slavery. After ten years Betty and subsequently Caesar should have had "their Liberty as Sojourners or to dwell in our Respective [towns]" and to "work for themselves." The law had included a procedure for Indians to apply for a certificate of freedom if the master failed to provide one, and that is exactly what Caesar was doing. Even so, Caesar and Curtiss were careful to argue that Betty had already served ten years and had been legally free when Caesar was born, so that "her posterity in their Generations [should be] Manumitted & sett at Libertie." The argument that a child born to a person in a condition of involuntary servitude would take on that status even if the parent subsequently became free had been made by several owners in the previous decades, and clearly Caesar and Curtiss assumed it carried some weight with the magistrates.[31]

A thirty-four-year-old Indian named Elisha challenged the enslavement even of non–New England Indians in 1749.[32] His suit began as many did, with his running away. When brought before the Justice's Court at Windham, Connecticut, Elisha announced that "he was freeborn and no Slave" and refused to return to his purported owner. The justice allowed him to remain free on bail while the case continued. Elisha won his case at the lower court, but the would-be owner, William Marsh of Plainfield, appealed to the General Assembly. Marsh claimed that Elisha was his "Spanish Indian man servant." Many revisions decorated the former's petition to the magistrates. Next to "servant" someone inserted "slave"; next to "Indian," an addition read "Negro Mulatto." Marsh was relying on racialization to buttress his claim to Elisha. At the lower court, Elisha mustered enough depositions to convince a jury that his mother Betty was from the Carolinas and had been unjustly enslaved there, rendering her, and by extension himself, free. In Rhode Island, freedom plaintiffs generally had to prove that they were New England Indians and not persons of color to gain release from slavery if not servitude, as in the case of Sarah Chauqum.

Masters wishing to retain their slaves often mustered testimony that the Indian or his or her ancestors were Spanish, Caribbean, or Carolina Indians, or Africans. In both Rhode Island and Massachusetts, such an argument could defeat a freedom suit, and Peter Pratt had made his support of Indian freedom conditional on New England origins as well. This is exactly what Elisha's master, Marsh, tried to do, as the Assembly ordered a retrial. By the 1740s in Connecticut, however, the racial and ethnic qualifications for freedom had become more complex and fluid. Elisha did not even try to establish New England roots for Betty, but he did try to establish English citizenship for her. Deponent William Dunlap claimed that Betty had told him her son Elisha was "freeborn" and ought not to be a slave because she was "born in ye Kings Dominion" and had been "deluded and perswaded to Come from Carolina and kept as a slave since." Since Betty was a freeborn English subject, so was Elisha, who clearly had been born in New England. These arguments convinced a local jury, much to Marsh's chagrin.

Marsh mobilized new evidence for his appeal, which he crafted to cast her as a Spanish Indian, one not born in "ye King's Dominions." He had depositions from Thomas Power, who had owned Betty, and from Edward Lillybridge of Rhode Island, who had purchased her from William Crawford, the Newport trader who allegedly brought her from Carolina. Elisha had been born while Betty lived in Rhode Island as "a slave." The father's identity seemed irrelevant to the case, suggesting that the Native American—or slave regime—precedent of children's status following the mother had become ingrained in practice if not in law in Connecticut. Several locals offered reminiscences about their interactions with Betty over nearly forty years of service. Jurors learned that Betty was about seventy years old when she died, and she had six toes on each foot.

Thomas Williams, for one, often dropped by the Power household to chat with her. Betty had told him she came via ship from Carolina as a child but was in fact a Spanish Indian. His testimony shifted from third person to first person while recounting her tale, and he seemed enthralled with her gripping story. Betty and her mother had retired to a Spanish fort while her father was away hunting, but it came under attack by Carolina Indians, whose guns soon overpowered the arrows of Betty's group. Her mother had strapped her to her back and attempted to swim to safety, but the attackers pursued and "shot her Mother through the body" and killed her. Betty kept swimming, but the Carolina group soon seized her. At the first stop on the way back to Carolina, her captors chopped off the heads of the older adults in the party and "saved the young alive." After ten days travel the Indians "came to a White people's settlement, being very much pinched with famine." There the Indians sold Betty to "a white man," who in turn sold her to a New England vessel, whose captain in turn sold her to Lillybridge, the first of three English masters she served before Power.[55] Elisha had his passionate advocates—an antislavery cadre within the Connecticut elite in Hartford and even New London, and the local friends and associates who testified for him and helped him win his local case. But Marsh had strong supporters as well who worried that ruling in Elisha's favor might make the existing opaque system of slavery collapse and undermine citizens' holdings in African slaves.

Slave owners fought such rulings—and the community involvement that undermined slavery—hard. Caesar's and Elisha's successes inspired other enslaved persons to claim their freedom more directly. In 1757, Lyme resident James Ely helped a slave named Zaccheus to escape from his master, Richard Lord. Unable to find Zaccheus, Lord (himself a justice of the peace) successfully sued Ely for a male slave's market value of 55 pounds. Ely did not dispute the charge, but he argued that Lord had no claim on Zaccheus, who was not a slave but rather a free person. Why Ely interfered remains a mystery. His family seems to have had a personal connection with Zaccheus—and with antislavery—although they kept other slaves.[34]

Like Caesar and Elisha, Zaccheus had a connection to a former captive— his grandmother Jane. At trial Ely produced a deposition from an "aged" Southampton resident, Thomas Halsey, who recalled that a Narragansett woman, Jene or Jane, had lived in his household. It was "allwais understood [she] was taken Captive in the Narragansett Indian war." Jane had attained her freedom before leaving to serve in another household, and "Shee was a free woman before Shee had any Children."[35] This meant that Zaccheus's mother, Temperance, was also free. Despite this evidence, the County Court ignored the basis for Zaccheus's claims and found Ely guilty of more narrow damages based on his own admission of involvement in the incident, but Ely appealed to the Superior Court and then the General Assembly.

Justice Lord sought to undercut Ely's argument by questioning whether Indian captives from King Philip's War could ever become free. His brief cited the 1677 Connecticut law that allowed Indians taken in combat to be enslaved as "prizes" of the war. The Superior Court jury "studied" the law and endorsed Lord's position. In his appeal, however, Ely asked the court to delve more deeply into the law's intentions and application. Echoing Peter Pratt's criticisms from thirty years earlier, Ely noted that Zaccheus's grandmother, Jane, had entered Halsey's household at age two. He respectfully pointed out that the General Court had provided limited terms for most captives and enslavement only of known, violent participants in conflict, or runaways—a description that hardly applied to a toddler.[36] Jane had "lived and died as a free woman," therefore Temperance and Zaccheus had been born free. The Connecticut General Assembly debated the case and issued a ruling "in abatement," which effectively meant that they agreed to permit Ely's new argument. Meanwhile, Zaccheus remained at large, presumably protected by a community that no longer regarded him as enslavable.

The drumbeat of cases presented a real challenge to colonial authorities, according to representative William Williams. Williams was a Lebanon storekeeper turned elected official who would later sign the Declaration of Independence. He knew scores of Indians personally as clients and workers. Like Samuel Sewall, Williams kept a private journal of the backroom proceedings in the Connecticut Assembly, which served as the final court of appeals in the colony. Colonial legislatures left no formal record of debates, in order to protect their members from voters' retribution at election time and to preserve an image of consensus. But Williams's diary reveals just how reluctant the magistrates were to rule on cases like Elisha's, and how divided they became when confronted with issues of slavery. The magistrates simply did not want to rule on litigation involving claims of English citizenship or wrongful enslavement of Indians.

Williams kept his diary during May 1757, a time when several controversial freedom suits came before the General Assembly on appeal.[37] One involved Cephas, a young boy who served in the household of Simon Brewster as an indentured servant, having been bound out by his mother.[38] But one day local landowner Samuel Huntington simply "took him," claiming Cephas was the child of two slaves Huntington owned and therefore his property. Brewster sued for possession of Cephas. He admitted that Huntington owned Cephas's father, Prince, an African slave, but not the boy's mother, Patience, a free "Indian woman lawfully married and in the service" of Huntington. Marriage to a slave did not change her free status, Brewster reasoned. If his neighbors wanted to assert informal ownership over slaves' and servants' children by citing the custom of "Virginia & Barbados" that children inherited the condition of their mothers, then that same logic made Cephas free.

According to Williams, his colleagues dreaded such cases because they created conflict in a body that sought consensus. The legislators tried to dodge hearing wrongful-enslavement cases, tabled them, and often held inconclusive debates over several months. In ruling, they would either have to define slavery and its inheritability clearly and adopt fully the kind of legal code that prevailed in slave societies—anathema to magistrates uncomfortable with such an endorsement of slavery, particularly Indian slavery—or open the door to eventual abolition, which a majority of delegates simply did not wish to do. "Many seemed willing to grant" Brewster's petition, Williams noted, "most of 'em fr[om] a suspicion yt. ye Deciding it otherwise will settle ye point for ye Slavery of ye children." Others hoped to slide by and uphold the lower court's decision on a narrower grounds, granting Huntington possession of Cephas "at present age" in compensation for having supported the child as an infant: a temporary solution that fit past practices. With the upper house inclining to Huntington's position, the lower house supporting Brewster, and other difficult cases of wrongful enslavement pending, the assembly referred the petition to a reconciliation committee and did not rule.[39]

These early freedom suits did not end Indian slavery in New England. In fact, the process of abolition in the North proved tortuous—an outcome that the Connecticut Assembly's indecision predicted. Even the American Revolution did not quickly transform the system. Connecticut adopted a gradual emancipation law in 1784 but did not formally outlaw slavery until 1848. Rhode Island's 1784 statue also only applied to children born after the law. Except for Vermont, new republican state governments in New England resisted abolishing slavery, despite pressure from African American, Indian, and Euro-American petitioners and advocates. In part this lag resulted from the ways in which Indian servitude had shaped colonial law in the first place. The opacity of the law of slavery and its customary basis in New England made it difficult—though certainly not impossible—to achieve abolition in statutory form. The unwillingness of legislators to prioritize antislavery over property rights, signaled earlier in the cases of Caesar and Elisha, also contributed to the delay. Instead, these states forced individual Indians and African Americans to free themselves one by one through lawsuits—or, with the support of neighbors, by simply walking away from masters.

This made suits such as those brought by Caesar and Elisha crucial, in that each one established new parameters and arguments that other individuals could follow, until an accretion of victories convinced putative masters that it was no longer worth fighting. New state constitutions that incorporated declarations of universal rights and natural-law language helped. But advertisements for "mulatto" slaves with Indian names appeared through the 1780s in Connecticut, and deeds continued to transfer ownership of Indians through the Revolution in all the New England colonies. The so-called black regiment in Revolutionary-era Rhode Island included a significant number of Indian slaves and servants, and no doubt numerous mixed-race soldiers as well. Founders of the earliest formal antislavery societies in New England understood this history. All included Indian as well as African slaves as their constituency.

After 1800, incarceration rather than servitude became the punishment of choice for civil and criminal offenders, and servitude as an institution declined dramatically after the Revolution. Fewer Indians entered unfree status to begin with. Pauper indentures still entrapped families, but other forms of judicial enslavement effectively ended. Yet informal modes of controlling

Indian labor persisted, backed by states' police power. Narragansett ethno-historian Ella Sekatau recalls that wealthy white households expected Narragansett Indian parents to hire their children out to labor into the 1930s.[40] If the Indians refused, then local sheriffs intervened. It was the custom of the country. Changing the inequalities of New England society would take more than abolition.

ABBREVIATIONS

BCC   Bristol County, Massachusetts, Court of General Sessions of the Peace record book, 1697–1727. Massachusetts State Archives, Columbia Point, Boston.

Conn. Recs.   J. Hammond Trumbull, ed. *The Public Records of the Colony of Connecticut.* 6 vols. Hartford, 1850. AMS Press repr., New York, 1968.

CRW   *Correspondence of Roger Williams.* Edited by Glenn LaFantasie. 2 vols. (Providence: Brown University Press/University Press of New England, 1988)

CSA Misc.   Connecticut State Archives Miscellaneous Files. Connecticut State Library, Hartford.

CSP Col.   W. Noel Sainsbury, ed. *Calendar of State Papers, Colonial Series, 1574–1660.* London, 1860.

DCC   Dukes County Court Records, Edgartown, Martha's Vineyard, MA.

ECC   George F. Dow, ed. *Records and Files of the Quarter Courts of Essex County Massachusetts.* 8 vols. Salem, MA: Essex Institute, 1911–21.

EHTR   Henry Parsons Hedges, ed. *Records of the Town of East Hampton.* 5 vols. Sag Harbor, NY, 1887–1905.

Hempstead Diary Joshua Hempstead. "The Diary of Joshua Hempstead, 1711–1758." In *New London County Historical Society, Collections.* Vol. 1. Providence: Published by the Society, 1901.

JAH *Journal of American History.* Published by the Organization of American Historians, Bloomington, IN.

Key Roger Williams. *A Key in to the Language of America.* Edited by John J. Teunissen and Evelyn J. Hinz. Detroit: Wayne State University Press, 1973.

MA Massachusetts Archives Collection. Massachusetts State Archives, Columbia Point, Boston.

Mass. Acts *The Acts and Resolves, Public and Private, of the Province of the Massachusetts-Bay.* 21 vols. Boston: Wright and Potter, 1869–1922.

Mass. Assistants John Noble, ed. *Records of the Court of Assistants of the Colony of the Massachusetts Bay, 1630–1692.* 3 vols. Boston, 1901, published by the County of Suffolk.

Mass. Recs. Nathaniel B. Shurtleff, ed. *Records of the Governor and Company of the Massachusetts Bay in New England.* 6 vols. Boston, 1854.

NEQ *New England Quarterly.* Published by Northeastern University, Boston.

Newport SCR Supreme Court Records for Newport, Book A (1671–1724) and Book B (1725–41). Rhode Island Judicial Records Center, Pawtucket.

NLCC New London County, County Court Files. Archives, Connecticut State Library, Hartford.

PCT *Records of the Court of Trials of the Colony of Providence Plantations, 1647–1670.* 2 vols. Providence: Providence Historical Society, 1920–22.

PRO/NAUK Public Records Office / National Archives of the United Kingdom, Kew, England.

PTP Providence Record Commissioners. *Early Records of the Town of Providence.* Vol. 15, Providence Town Papers. Providence, 1899.

PTP mss. Providence Town Papers, manuscript. Rhode Island Historical Society, Providence.

RCNP Nathaniel B. Shurtleff, ed. *The Records of the Colony of New Plymouth.* 12 vols. Boston, 1856–61.

RI Recs.	John Russell Bartlett, ed. *Records of the Colony of Rhode Island and Providence Plantations in New England.* 10 vols. Providence, 1857–65.
WCC	Washington County Court Records. Rhode Island Judicial Records Center, Pawtucket.
WJ (Dunn)	Richard S. Dunn, James Savage, and Laetitia Yeandle, eds. *The Journal of John Winthrop, 1630–1649.* Cambridge, MA: Belknap Press of Harvard University Press, 1996.
WMQ	*William and Mary Quarterly.* Published by the Omohundro Institute of Early American History and Culture, Williamsburg, VA.
WP	*The Winthrop Papers.* 6 vols. Boston: Massachusetts Historical Society, 1931–92.

Notes

Introduction

1. Justices Courts, New London, 1739–79, Joshua Hempstead and John Hempstead, Court Records, box 565, Connecticut State Archives, Hartford.

2. Ibid.

3. *Richard v. Cesar*, June Term 1739, NLCC, Native Americans, box 1, folder 39 (Cezar file).

4. William D. Pierson, *Black Yankees: The Development of an Afro-American Subculture in Eighteenth-Century New England* (Amherst: University of Massachusetts Press, 1988), 14–16.

5. *Hempstead Diary*, 18, 27, 40, 55, 57, 189, 290.

6. William Williams, *Journal Kept by William Williams of the Proceedings of the Lower House of the Connecticut General Assembly, May 1757 Assembly*, ed. Sylvia J. Turner (Hartford: Connecticut Historical Society, 1975), 46–47.

7. Ira Berlin distinguishes between "slave societies," where slavery was a dominant form of labor, and "societies with slaves," where slavery shared the stage with other labor arrangements and where slave owners did not dominate the political system. Interestingly, although New England met Berlin's definition of the latter on economic grounds, one could argue that since slave ownership was concentrated among the elite who dominated political office, the political system even in such "societies with slaves" served and protected slaveholders' interests. Ira Berlin, *Many Thousands Gone: The First Two Centuries of Slavery in North America* (Cambridge, MA: Harvard University Press, 1998), 8–9.

8. Pavilion Theater, mixed playbill for *Magawisca! or, The Indian chief's revenge; The four Mowbrays; Damon and Pythias!; Rough Rob* (London, 1851), Theater Collections, Victoria and Albert Museum, London. Cataloged as part of the JISL East London Theater Project.

9. For Euro-American captives see James Axtell, *The Invasion Within: The Context of Cultures in Colonial North America* (New York: Oxford University Press, 1985), esp. chap. 13, and John Demos, *The Unredeemed Captive: A Family Story of Early New England* (New York: Alfred A. Knopf, 1994). Almon Lauber published a volume on Indian slavery in the Americas in 1913 that included a discussion of Indian slavery in New England. Almon Wheeler Lauber, *Indian Slavery in Colonial Times within the Present Limits of the United States* (New York, 1913; repr., 1979). Jill Lepore, *The Name of War: King Philip's War and the Origins of American Identity* (New York: Alfred A. Knopf, 1998), discusses Indian slavery but only in the aftermath of King Philip's War. Scholars who have examined Indian servitude and slavery in a broader context include David J. Silverman, "The Impact of Indentured Servitude on Southern New

England Indian Society and Culture, 1680–1810," *NEQ* 74 (2001): 622–666, and *Faith and Boundaries: Colonists, Christianity, and Community among the Wampanoag Indians of Martha's Vineyard, 1600–1871* (New York: Cambridge University Press, 2005); Ann Marie Plane, *Colonial Intimacies: Indian Marriage in Early New England* (Ithaca, NY: Cornell University Press, 2000); Yasuhide Kawashima, "Indian Servitude in the Northeast," in *Handbook of North American Indians*, vol. 4, *History of Indian-White Relations*, ed. Wilcomb E. Washburn (Washington, DC: Smithsonian Institution, 1988); John Sainsbury, "Indian Labor in Early Rhode Island," *NEQ* 47 (1974): 378–93; Joshua Micah Marshall, "'A Melancholy People': Anglo-Indian Relations in Early Warwick, Rhode Island, 1642–1675," *NEQ* 68 (1995): 402–28; Kathleen Bragdon, *Native People of Southern New England* (Norman: University of Oklahoma Press, 1996); Colin Calloway, ed., *After King Philip's War: Presence and Persistence in Indian New England* (Hanover, NH: Dartmouth College Press, 1997).

10. For the Spanish southwest see James F. Brooks, *Captives and Cousins: Slavery, Kinship, and Community in the Southwest Borderlands* (Chapel Hill: University of North Carolina Press, for the Omohundro Institute of Early American History and Culture, 2002), and Juliana Barr, "From Captives to Slaves: Commodifying Indian Women in the Borderlands," *JAH* 92 (2005): 19–46; for New France see Daniel Usner, *Indians, Settlers, and Slaves in a Frontier Exchange Economy: The Lower Mississippi* (Chapel Hill: University of North Carolina Press, 1992), who examines the New Orleans colony, and Brett Rushforth, *Bonds of Alliance: Indigenous and Atlantic Slaveries in New France* (Chapel Hill: University of North Carolina Press, for the Omohundro Institute of Early American History and Culture, 2013), who focuses on the Great Lakes region. For the Southeast see Alan Gallay, *The Indian Slave Trade: The Rise of the English Empire in the South, 1670–1716* (New Haven, CT: Yale University Press, 2002).

11. Works that stress the household model of labor include Daniel Vickers, *Farmers and Fishermen: Two Centuries of Work in Essex County, Massachusetts, 1630–1850* (Chapel Hill: University of North Carolina Press, for the Omohundro Institute of Early American History and Culture, 1994); John Demos, *A Little Commonwealth: Family Life in Plymouth Colony* (New York: Oxford University Press, 1970); James Henretta, "Families and Farms: *Mentalité* in Pre-Industrial America," *WMQ* 35 (January 1978): 3–32; Christopher Clark, *The Roots of Rural Capitalism: Western Massachusetts, 1780–1860* (Ithaca, NY: Cornell University Press, 1992); and the essays in Stephen Innes, ed., *Work and Labor in Colonial America* (Chapel Hill: University of North Carolina Press, 1988). Christopher Tomlins, *Freedom Bound: Law, Labor and Civic Identity in Colonizing English America, 1580–1865* (New York: Cambridge University Press, 2011), and Barry Levy, *Town Born: The Political Economy of New England from Its Founding to the Revolution* (Philadelphia: University of Pennsylvania Press, 2009), describe state interventions in monitoring household labor regimes. Both focus on European and Euro-American labor, however, especially in New England, although Tomlins discusses the emergence of "societies with slavery" in the North. For the argument that African slavery was essentially a symbolic rather than material choice for New England practitioners see Jackson T. Main, *Society and Economy in Colonial Connecticut* (Princeton, NJ: Princeton University Press, 1985). An eloquent exploration of this link between ownership of slaves and honor in societies across time—particularly in precapitalist societies, where he argues that honor and symbol

represented the main purpose of enslavement—appears in Orlando Paterson, *Slavery and Social Death: A Comparative Study* (Cambridge, MA: Harvard University Press, 1982), 10–12, 79, 99. For a rebuttal of the "honor" or symbolic argument regarding New England slavery see Joanne Pope Melish, *Disowning Slavery: Gradual Emancipation and "Race" in New England, 1780–1860* (Ithaca, NY: Cornell University Press, 1998), esp. 16–17. Melish also has a thoughtful discussion of the experiences of Hempstead's African slave, Adam, as does Allegra Di Bonaventura in *For Adam's Sake: A Family Saga in Colonial New England* (New York: Liveright / W. W. Norton, 2013).

12. For the "myth of the disappearing Indian" see Lepore, *Name of War*, 223–26, and Jean M. O'Brien, *Firsting and Lasting: Writing Indians out of Existence in New England* (Minneapolis: University of Minnesota Press, 2010), esp. chap. 3.

13. Margaret Ellen Newell, *From Dependency to Independence: Economic Revolution in Colonial New England* (Ithaca, NY: Cornell University Press, 1998), 99–101. See also James McWilliams, "Butter, Milk, and a 'Spare Ribb': Women's Work and the Transatlantic Economic Transformation in Seventeenth-Century Massachusetts," *NEQ* 82 (March 2009): 5–24, and Melish, *Disowning Slavery*, 8, 18–22, on the economic value of women's domestic work.

14. Diary of Peter Thacher, May 7, 1679, vol. 1, Massachusetts Historical Society, Boston.

15. Berlin, *Many Thousands Gone*, 8–9.

16. [Henry Dunster?], *New England's First Fruits; in Respect, First of the Conversion of some, the Conviction of divers, and the Preparation of sundry of the Indians. . . .* (London, 1643), 6.

17. Ann Marie Plane is one of the few historians to analyze the household—both English and Indian—as a nexus of Indian-English interaction. See Plane, *Colonial Intimacies*, 99–100.

18. David Eltis, *The Rise of African Slavery in the Americas* (Cambridge: Cambridge University Press, 1998).

19. Winthrop Jordan, in *White over Black: American Attitudes toward the Negro, 1550–1812* (Chapel Hill: University of North Carolina Press, 1966), 20–25, contended that Europeans arrived with negative associations toward Africans and viewed African skin color and "heathenism" as unchangeable. Indians, by contrast, displayed "savage" behavior, but their differences from Europeans appeared less insurmountable. More recent inquiries into the antecedents of racism in Renaissance Europe include essays by James H. Sweet and Robin Blackburn in the "Constructing Race" symposium, *WMQ* 54 (1997): 143–66, 65–102. Joyce E. Chaplin, *Subject Matter: Technology, the Body, and Science on the Anglo-American Frontier, 1500–1676* (Cambridge, MA: Harvard University Press, 2001), argues that Europeans did not arrive in the Americas with preconceived notions of Indian biological inferiority but had developed such views by the late seventeenth century. For a nuanced discussion of the emergence of racial categories that includes the Caribbean see Roxann Wheeler, *The Complexion of Race: Categories of Difference in Eighteenth-Century British Culture* (Philadelphia: University of Pennsylvania Press, 2000).

20. *Key*, 133.

21. See the "Response of the Royal Commissioners," May 1665, *Mass. Recs.*, 4:213.

22. Roger Williams to John Winthrop, June 30, 1637, in *CRW*, 1:88.

23. Rolena Adorno, "Discourses on Colonialism: Bernal Díaz, Las Casas, and the Twentieth-Century Reader," *Modern Language Notes* 103 (March 1988): 239–40, 242.

24. Juan Ginés de Sepúlveda, *Democrates segundo: O, de las justas causas de la guerra contra los indios, 1547* (Madrid: Consejo Superior de Investigaciones Científicas, Instituto Francisco de Vitoria, 1951); Anthony Pagden, *The Fall of Natural Man: The American Indian and the Origins of Comparative Ethnology* (New York: Cambridge University Press, 1982), 116–18.

25. Patricia Seed, "Taking Possession and Reading Texts: Establishing the Authority of Overseas Empires," *WMQ* 49 (1992): 205–7, contrasts the Spanish imperial authorities' focus on controlling the peoples of the Americas—and their labor—with the English focus on land, although I would argue that the English became equally interested in subjecting Indian peoples.

26. John Winthrop, "General Observations [Higginson Copy]," *WP*, 2:120.

27. Wesley Frank Craven, "Indian Policy in Early Virginia," *WMQ* 1 (January 1944): 65; quote is from Gray's sermon in praise of the Virginia Company's settlement at Jamestown.

28. James Muldoon argues that the Virginia and Massachusetts charters echoed Alexander VI's *Inter caetera* grant to Isabel and Ferdinand, suggesting the persistence of canon law in shaping international law and custom in post-Reformation Europe. See Muldoon, "Discovery, Grant, Charter, Conquest, Purchase," in *The Many Legalities of Early America*, ed. Christopher L. Tomlins and Bruce H. Mann (Chapel Hill: University of North Carolina Press, 1991).

29. *Mass. Recs.*, 1:393–94; John Winthrop to John Endecott, Jan. 3, 1633, *WP*, 3:149.

30. Alfred Cave, *The Pequot War* (Amherst: University of Massachusetts Press, 1996), esp. 169–174.

31. Katherine Hermes, "'Justice Will Be Done Us': Algonquian Demands for Reciprocity in the Courts of European Settlers," in Tomlins and Mann, *Many Legalities*, 128.

32. Nicholas P. Canny, "The Ideology of English Colonization: From Ireland to America," *WMQ* 30 (October 1973): 575–98; David Armitage, *The Ideological Origins of the British Empire* (Cambridge: Cambridge University Press, 2000), chap. 2, 54–58; David Beers Quinn, "Sir Thomas Smith and the Beginnings of English Colonial Theory," *Proceedings of the American Philosophical Society* 89 (1945): 543–60, and "Renaissance Influences in English Colonization," *Transactions of the Royal Historical Society* 26 (1976): 73–92.

33. Stephen Saunders Webb, *1676: The End of American Independence* (Syracuse, NY: Syracuse University Press, 1995).

34. Rachel Foxley, "John Lilburne and the Citizenship of 'Free-Born Englishmen,'" *Historical Journal* 47, no. 4 (December 2004): 852–53.

35. Among the best works on the question of Indian citizenship in colonial New England is Jennifer Hale Pulsipher, *Subjects unto the Same King: Indians and the Contest for Authority in Colonial New England* (Philadelphia: University of Pennsylvania Press, 2006). Pulsipher focuses on the shift from Indian autonomy to a search for equality vis-à-vis colonial governments within the English empire. In the case of Indian slavery, however, English authority failed to restrain colonial law and local practice. Patrick Griffin also discusses Indian citizenship (although he sees it as a nonstarter for

British and colonial authorities by the 1760s) in *American Leviathan: Empire, Nation, and the Revolutionary Frontier* (New York: Hill & Wang, 2007).

36. April Lee Hatfield argues for an Atlantic/Caribbean influence on evolving slave codes rather than finding antecedents in European law and experience: Hatfield, *Atlantic Virginia: Intercolonial Relations in the Seventeenth Century* (Philadelphia: University of Pennsylvania Press, 2004), 154.

37. Warren M. Billings, "The Law of Servants and Slaves in Seventeenth-Century Virginia," *Virginia Magazine of History and Biography* 99 (1991): 46; David Konig, "'Dale's Laws' and the Non-Common Law Origins of Criminal Justice in Virginia," *American Journal of Legal History* 26, no. 4 (1982): 357.

38. Mary Hershberger writes that some proto-abolitionist New Englanders supported Indian interests and opposed removal in the 1830s. Still, the marriage of Cherokee student John Ridge to a white woman, Sarah Bird Northrup, prompted threats of mob violence in Cornwall, Connecticut, in 1824. See Hershberger, "Anticipating Abolition: The Struggle against Indian Removal in the 1830s," *JAH* 86 (1999): 15–40.

Chapter 1

1. John McDermott, *Martin Frobisher: Elizabethan Privateer* (New Haven, CT: Yale University Press, 2001), 187–89; William C. Sturtevant and David Beers Quinn, "This New Prey: Eskimos in Europe in 1567, 1576, and 1577," in *Indians and Eskimos in Europe: An Interdisciplinary Collection of Essays*, ed. Christian F. Feest (Aachen: Edition Herodt with Rader-Verlag, 1987), 76–112, esp. 85–86.

2. Ronald T. Takaki speculates that Epenow inspired the character of Caliban in William Shakespeare's *The Tempest*: Takaki, "*The Tempest* in the Wilderness: The Racialization of Savagery," *JAH* 79 (December 1992): 892–95. For Epenow and other Indians in England see Alden Vaughan, *Transatlantic Encounters: American Indians in Britain, 1500–1776* (New York: Cambridge University Press, 2006), 63–68.

3. Gorges recalled that a group of Malagan "Friers" rescued at least some of the New England Indians from slavery "and kept them to be instructed in the Christian faith." Quoted in Neal Salisbury, *Manitou and Providence: Indians, Europeans, and the Making of New England, 1500–1643* (New York: Oxford University Press, 1982), 107, and Salisbury, "Squanto: Last of the Patuxets," in *Struggle and Survival in Colonial America*, ed. David G. Sweet and Gary B. Nash (Berkeley: University of California Press, 1981).

4. Smith criticized the "savage-like" "trechery" of Hunt's actions. Philip L. Barbour, ed., *The Complete Works of Captain John Smith*, 3 vols. (Chapel Hill: University of North Carolina Press, 1986), 2:401. Alden Vaughan notes the possibility that Squanto had traveled to England on an earlier voyage and returned to New England to aid Smith a year prior to his capture by Hunt; Vaughan, *Transatlantic Encounters*, 70.

5. Salisbury, *Manitou*, 90–96.

6. Ibid., 29–30.

7. Lisa Brooks, *The Common Pot: The Recovery of Native Space in the Northeast* (Minneapolis: University of Minnesota Press, 2008), 16–21, 54–57; Salisbury, *Manitou*, 147–50, 205–11.

8. Mark Meuwese, "The Dutch Connection: New Netherland, the Pequots, and the Puritans in Southern New England, 1620–1638," *Early American Studies: An*

Interdisciplinary Journal 9 (Spring 2011): 295–323, 303–6; Michael Oberg, *Dominion and Civility: English Imperialism and Native America, 1585–1685* (Ithaca, NY: Cornell University Press, 2003). Donna Merwick argues that the Dutch initially acknowledged Indian governance in the region and viewed Indians with a "measured inclusiveness." This changed when Willem Kieft and others who wished to emulate the growing militarism of the global Dutch empire began to target Indians. Merwick, *The Shame and the Sorrow: Dutch-Amerindian Encounters in New Netherland* (Philadelphia: University of Pennsylvania Press, 2006), 68–76, 104, 108, 118, 125–28.

9. Kevin McBride, "Historical Archaeology of the Mashantucket Pequots in the Early Seventeenth Century," in *Pequots in Southern New England*, ed. Laurence M. Hauptmann and James D. Wherry (Norman: University of Oklahoma Press, 1990), 99; William Starna, "The Pequots in the Early Seventeenth Century," ibid., 33–47.

10. Salisbury, *Manitou*, 147.

11. Michael Leroy Oberg, *Uncas: First of the Mohicans* (Ithaca, NY: Cornell University Press, 2003); Eric Johnson, "Uncas and the Politics of Contact," in *Northeastern Indian Lives, 1631–1816*, ed. Robert S. Grumet (Amherst: University of Massachusetts Press, 1996), 30–33, 35–36.

12. Alfred A. Cave, *The Pequot War* (Amherst: University of Massachusetts Press, 1996), 57–61; Edmund B. O'Callaghan, *History of New Netherland* (New York, 1845), 1:145–150; Charles Orr, ed., *History of the Pequot War: The Contemporary Accounts of Mason, Underhill, Vincent, and Gardiner* (Cleveland, 1897), 56–57.

13. Alden T. Vaughan, "Pequots and Puritans: The Causes of the War of 1637," *WMQ* (April 1964): 256–69; Vaughan, *New England Frontier: Puritans and Indians, 1620–1675* (Boston: Little, Brown, 1965), 93–154; Francis Jennings, *The Invasion of America: Indians, Colonialism, and the Cant of Conquest* (Chapel Hill: University of North Carolina Press, 1975), 177–227; Salisbury, *Manitou*, 203–24. Contemporary English accounts did stress horror at Indians' ritual torture of captives; eyewitness accounts of torture, and condemnation of Indian cruelty, appeared in three of the four published Puritan accounts of the war.

14. Cave, *Pequot War*, 64. Katherine A. Grandjean suggests that climate change and regional food shortages helped spark the conflict; she finds significance in the deaths of Oldham and Stone, but the model does not explain the unique targeting of the Pequots or the enslavement of captives during the war. See Grandjean, "New World Tempests: Environment, Scarcity, and the Coming of the Pequot War," *WMQ* 68 (May 2011): 75–100.

15. *WJ* (Dunn), 108, n.46 (January 21, 1634), 133–34 (November 6, 1634).

16. John Mason, *A Brief History of the Pequot War* (London, 1736; Ann Arbor: University Microfilms, 1966); John Underhill, *Newes from America* (London, 1638; Amsterdam: Theatrum Orbis Terrarum, and New York: Da Capo Press, 1971), 10–12; Alden T. Vaughan, *New England Frontier: Puritans and Indians, 1620–1675*, rev. ed. (Norman: University of Oklahoma Press, 1995), xxiii–lxv, 122–54; Jennings, *Invasion*, 186–227; Salisbury, *Manitou*, 215–25; Lion Gardiner, *Relation of the Pequot Warres (1660)*, ed. W. N. Chattin Carlton (Hartford, CT: Acorn Club, 1901), 6. Gardiner was particularly agitated about the aggressive stance emanating from Massachusetts Bay.

17. Gardiner, *Relation*, 6.

18. Underhill, *Newes*, 8.

19. *WJ* (Dunn), 183.

20. *Mass. Recs.*, 3:181.

21. For Iroquois violence see Kathryn Magee Labelle, *Dispersed but Not Destroyed: A History of the Seventeenth-Century Wendat People* (Vancouver: University of British Columbia Press, 2013); Richard White, *The Middle Ground: Indians, Empires, and Republics in the Great Lakes Region, 1650–1815* (New York: Cambridge University Press, 1991); and Daniel K. Richter, "War and Culture: The Iroquois Experience," *WMQ* 40 (1983): 528–59.

22. R. Todd Romero notes some similarities in the two groups' war cultures and notions of martial masculinity in the Pequot era. Romero, *Making War and Minting Christians: Masculinity, Religion, and Colonialism in Early New England* (Amherst: University of Massachusetts Press, 2011), esp. pt. 3.

23. Gardiner, *Relation*, 8.

24. Ibid., 15.

25. Underhill, *Newes*, 35–39 (quotes on 39).

26. Ibid., 35.

27. Williams to Winthrop, June 30, 1737, *WP*, 3:437.

28. For Puritan frustration with the Indian way of war see Adam J. Hirsch, "The Collision of Military Cultures in Seventeenth-Century New England," *JAH* 74 (March 1988): 1187–1212, esp. 1190, and also Patrick M. Malone, *The Skulking Way of War: Technology and Tactics among the New England Indians* (Baltimore: Johns Hopkins University Press, 1991), 28–32. For failures of diplomacy and rule setting see Ronald Dale Karr, "'Why Should You Be So Furious?': The Violence of the Pequot War," *JAH* 85 (December 1998): 876–909.

29. Gardiner, *Relation*, 14–15.

30. Barbara Donagan, "Codes and Conduct in the English Civil War," *Past and Present* 118 (1988): 67–8; [P.] Vincent, *The Lamentations of Germany* (London, 1638).

31. Roger Williams to the General Court of Massachusetts Bay, October 5, 1654, *CRW*, 2:409.

32. Ibid.

33. Jennifer Hale Pulsipher, *Subjects unto the Same King: Indians and the Contest for Authority in Colonial New England* (Philadelphia: University of Pennsylvania Press, 2006).

34. Williams to Winthrop, [October–November 1637?], *WP*, 3:12.

35. Charles J. Hoadly, ed., *Records of the Colony and Plantation of New Haven, 1638–1649* (Hartford, CT: Case, Lockwood, 1857), 22–24; John Menta, "The Strange Case of Nepaupuck: Warrior or War Criminal?" *Journal of the New Haven Historical Society* 33 (Spring 1987): 3–17.

36. On Scots prisoners of war in New England see Stephen Innes, *Labor in a New Land: Economy and Society in Seventeenth-Century Springfield* (Princeton, NJ: Princeton University Press, 1983), 9–10, 58, 86, 109.

37. Roger Williams to John Winthrop, July 31, 1637, *WP*, 3:458–59.

38. Hugh Peter to John Winthrop, July 15, 1637, *WP*, 3:450.

39. Williams to John Winthrop, July 10, 1637, *WP*, 3:446–48; Roger Williams to John Winthrop, June 30, 1637, *WP*, 3:436–37; see also Israel Stoughton to John Winthrop, [ca. July 6, 1637], *WP*, 3:458.

40. See *WP*, 3:480–81.

41. John Winthrop, *Winthrop's Journal: "History of New England,"* ed. James K. Hosmer, 2 vols. (New York: Charles Scribner's Sons, 1908), 1:225, n.16; 226.

42. Richard Davenport to Hugh Peter, *WP*, 3:452–54.

43. Israel Stoughton to John Winthrop, [ca. June 28, 1637], *WP*, 3:435–36.

44. John Winthrop to William Bradford, July 28, 1637, *WP*, 3:456–58.

45. James F. Brooks, *Captives and Cousins: Slavery, Kinship, and Community in the Southwest Borderlands* (Chapel Hill: University of North Carolina Press, for the Omohundro Institute of Early American History and Culture, 2002); Juliana Barr, "From Captives to Slaves: Commodifying Indian Women in the Borderlands," *JAH* 92 (2005): 19–46.

46. Roger Williams to John Winthrop, July 15, 1637, *WP*, 3:451.

47. Roger Williams to John Winthrop, July 31, 1637, *WP*, 3:459.

48. Sacvan Bercovitch, "Typology in Puritan New England: The Williams-Cotton Controversy Re-assessed," *American Quarterly* 19 (1967): 166–91, esp. 175–76.

49. Underhill, *Newes*, 36–37.

50. Roger Williams to John Winthrop, July 15, 1637, *WP*, 3:451, 459; Williams to Winthrop, July 31, 1637, *WP*, 4:17.

51. Williams to Winthrop, February 28, 1637/38, *Old South Leaflets*, no. 54, ed. Edwin D. Mead (Boston: Old South Association, 1917), 15.

52. Williams to Winthrop, June 30, 1637, *WP*, 3:436.

53. Williams to John Winthrop, [May 1637], *Old South Leaflets*, 7–8; also *CRW*, 1:73.

54. "Articles of agreement between the English of Connecticutt and the Indian Sachems," 1748 copy of the original signed September 21, 1638, Connecticut Historical Society. Roger Ludlow, Edward Hopkins, and John Haynes were the English signatories.

55. In the Tripartite Treaty of 1638, the United Colonies assigned approximately eighty captives to the Narragansetts, twenty to Ayanemo (Ninigret), the Niantic sachem, and one hundred to the Mohegans—a post-contact client tribe of Connecticut that had numbered approximately fifty before the Pequot War. Harry M. Ward, *The United Colonies of New England* (New York: Vantage Press, 1961), 29–38.

56. According to Francis Jennings, the Narragansetts also deplored the English practice of killing noncombatants in battle. See Jennings, *Invasion*, 223, and Malone, *Skulking Way of War*, 29–30, 102–3.

57. Williams to Winthrop, [ca. June 21, 1637], *WP*, 3:433–34.

58. Uncas's Mohegans increased their numbers from at most six hundred in 1636 to twenty-five hundred in 1643.

59. Kathleen J. Bragdon, *Native People of Southern New England, 1500–1650* (Norman: University of Oklahoma Press, 1996), 99–100. For Indian traditions of slavery and the experiences of Indian, Euro-American, and African captives among native communities see Christina Snyder, *Slavery in Indian Country: The Changing Face of Captivity in Early America* (Cambridge, MA: Harvard University Press, 2010); also Richter, "War and Culture," 528–99; Leland Donald, "Slavery in Indigenous North America," in *The Cambridge World History of Slavery*, vol. 3, *AD 1420–AD 1804*, ed. David Eltis and Stanley L. Engerman (Cambridge: Cambridge University Press, 2011); Catherine Cameron, ed., *Invisible Citizens: Captives and Their Consequences* (Salt

Lake City: University of Utah Press, 2009); Brett Rushforth, *Bonds of Alliance: Indigenous and Atlantic Slaveries in New France* (Chapel Hill: University of North Carolina Press, for the Omohundro Institute for Early American History and Culture, 2013); Pauline Turner Strong, "Transforming Outsiders: Captivity, Adoption, and Slavery Reconsidered," in *A Companion to American Indian History*, ed. Philip J. Deloria and Neal Salisbury (Oxford: Blackwell Publishers, 2002), 339–56; Joyce E. Chaplin, "Enslavement of Indians in Early America: Captivity without the Narrative," in *The Creation of the British Atlantic World*, ed. Elizabeth Mancke and Carole Shammas (Baltimore: Johns Hopkins University Press, 2005), 45–70.

60. *Key*, 96.

61. Kevin McBride, "The Legacy of Robin Cassacinamon: Mashantucket Pequot Leadership in the Historical Period," in Grumet, *Northeastern Indian Lives*, 76–77.

62. John Winthrop to William Bradford, [July 1637], *WP*, 3:457.

63. Gardiner, in *Relation*, 8, recalled her encounter with Thomas Stanton, who had blundered into one of the Indian dwellings: "Wincumbone his Mothers sister was then the Great Pequit Sachems wife who made signes to him yt he should be gone or they would cut off his hed."

64. Roger Williams to John Winthrop, August 1639, *CRW*, 1:200.

Chapter 2

1. Emanuel Downing to John Winthrop, ca. August 1645, *WP*, 4:38.

2. *Mass. Assistants*, 2:11; *RCNP*, 1:50, 54.

3. Hugh Peter to John Winthrop, July 15, 1637, *WP*, 3:450.

4. *RCNP*, 11:14, 17.

5. For Dutch and English enslavement and export of Indians in the 1640s see Edmund B. O'Callahan, *History of New Netherland; or, New York under the Dutch* (New York, 1846), 1:274, 2:420; O'Callaghan, *Calendar of Historical Manuscripts in the Office of the Secretary of State, Albany*, pt. 1, 396; H. R. McIlwaine, ed., *Minutes of the Council and General Court of Virginia* (Richmond: Virginia State Library, 1924), 477–78, 483, 501, 564–65; "Mr. Streeter's Extracts from the Minutes of the Council and General Court, 1642–45," *WMQ* 20 (1940): 69.

6. Jerome Handler, "The Amerindian Slave Population of Barbados in the Seventeenth and Early Eighteenth Centuries," *Journal of Caribbean Studies* 8 (1969): 38–64, esp. 44–47; "An Account of His majesty's Island of Barbados and the G'overnmt Thereof Prepared by Gov'r Sir Richard Dutton, 1684," *Journal of the Barbados Museum Historical Society* 3 (November 1935): 44 [Sloan mss. 2441, British Museum].

7. Handler, "Amerindian Slave," 46; Betty Wood, "The Origins of Slavery in the Americas, 1500–1700," in *The Routledge History of Slavery*, ed. Gad Heuman and Trevor G. Burnard (New York: Routledge, 2010), 72–73. Wood emphasizes the significance of Hawley's declaration in the shift toward enslavement in other colonies. For a broader discussion of slavery in Barbados see Hilary McD. Beckles, *White Servitude and Black Slavery in Barbados, 1627–1715* (Knoxville: University of Tennessee Press, 1989); Simon Newman, *A New World of Labor: The Development of Plantation Slavery in the British Atlantic* (Philadelphia: University of Pennsylvania Press, 2014); Larry Gragg, *Englishmen Transplanted: The English Colonization of Barbados, 1627–1660* (New York: Oxford University Press, 2003). See also Richard S. Dunn, *Sugar and*

Slaves: The Rise of the Planter Class in the English West Indies, 1624–1713 (Chapel Hill: University of North Carolina Press, 1972).

8. Virginia Bernhard, *Slaves and Slaveholders in Bermuda, 1616–1782* (Columbia: University of Missouri Press, 1999), 65; Michael Jarvis, *In the Eye of All Trade: Bermuda, Bermudians, and the Maritime Atlantic World, 1680–1783* (Chapel Hill: University of North Carolina Press, for the Omohundro Institute of Early American History and Culture, 2011). For the Indian slave trade in the western Caribbean Rim see Michael D. Ollen, "After the Indian Slave Trade: Cross-Cultural Trade in the Western Caribbean Rimland, 1816–1820," *Journal of Anthropological Research* 44 (Spring 1988): 41–66, and Mary W. Helms, "Miskito Slaving and Culture Contact: Ethnicity and Opportunity in Expanding Population," *Journal of Anthropological Research* 39 (1983): 179–97.

9. Karen Ordahl Kupperman, *Indians and English: Facing Off in Early America* (Ithaca, NY: Cornell University Press, 2000), 200.

10. Owen Stanwood, "Captives and Slaves: Indian Labor, Cultural Conversion, and the Plantation Revolution in Virginia," *Virginia Magazine of History and Biography* 114 (2004): 434–63, and C. S. Everett, "'They Shalbe Slaves for their Lives': Indian Slavery in Colonial Virginia," in *Indian Slavery in Colonial America*, ed. Alan Gallay (Athens: University of Georgia Press, 2009), 67–108.

11. For an overview of the New Spain Indian slave trade see Nancy Van Deusen, "Seeing Indios in Sixteenth-Century Castile," *WMQ* 69 (October 2012): 885–89.

12. John Henry Lefroy, *Memorials of the Discovery and Early Settlement of Bermuda, 1515–1685 [1511–1687]*, 2 vols. (London, 1879), 2:219–20.

13. Hollis Hallett, ed., *Bermuda under the Sommer Islands Company, 1612–1684: Civil Records*, 3 vols. (Bermuda Maritime Museum Press & Juniperhill Press, 2004/5), "William Jackson, Bills of Sale," January 1644/45, 3:265; Bill of Sale from William Jackson of "three Nigroes" and "one nigro boy" to William Sayle, January 1644/45, Bermuda Colonial Records, vol. 2, Indentures and Deeds, reel 496, 102. See also Bernhard, *Slaves*, 65.

14. For a sample of Wentworth's activities see Bermuda Colonial Records, vol. 2, Indentures and Deeds, reel 496, December 1637.

15. "Marriage Contract of James and Frances, both Indians," August 1651, in Hallett, *Bermuda*, 3:273.

16. "The 5 May 1652 it is [agreed as] followeth [agreement with Frank Fernandes]," Bermuda Colonial Records, 3:62A, Hallett, *Bermuda*, 1:321.

17. "Petition of Katherine Wilson, Snr," December 1653, Bermuda Colonial Records, 3:91B–99B, in Hallett, *Bermuda*, 1:357. Kristen Block and Heather Miyano Kopelson both examine the shift from religion to race as a defining characteristic of identity in the Atlantic world. Block finds that although religion could be a weapon for individual members of the Caribbean laboring classes, it failed to halt the rise of slavery in either Catholic or Protestant labor regimes. Kopelson traces similar outcomes in Virginia but argues that in Bermuda, religion remained an area of social interaction and identity across racial lines. Block, *Ordinary Lives in the Early Caribbean: Religion, Colonial Competition, and the Politics of Profit* (Athens: University of Georgia Press, 2012), and Kopelson, *Faithful Bodies: Performing Race and Religion in the Puritan Atlantic* (New York: NYU Press, 2014).

18. Company General Letter to Governor Sayle, Bermuda Company Records, August 30, 1661, Hallett, *Bermuda*, 1:508.

19. Records of Barbados, RB 3/1 (Deeds), 9, Barbados Archives.

20. Company General Letter to Josias Foster, Feb. 1654/55, Hallett, *Bermuda*, 1:369, 508.

21. Karen Ordahl Kupperman, *Providence Island, 1630–1641: The Other Puritan Colony* (New York: Cambridge University Press, 1995), 172. One colonist received permission to leave Providence Island with "two negroes and an Indian" in 1638.

22. Letter from the Company of Providence Island to the Governor and Council, April 28, 1638, *CSP Col.*, 9:271.

23. *CSP Col.*, 277–78 (from Colonial Entry Book, 4:124, PRO/NAUK); see also George H. Moore, *Notes on the History of Slavery in Massachusetts* (New York, 1866), 17, and n.2. For an argument that the Providence Island "cannibal Negroes" were actually Angolan slaves and not New England Indians see Linda M. Heywood and John K. Thornton, "'Canniball Negroes,' Atlantic Creoles, and the Identity of New England's Charter Generation," *African Diaspora* 4 (2011): 76–94.

24. *WP*, 1:361–62, 2:69.

25. *WJ* (Dunn), April 1645, 573.

26. Ibid.

27. Johnson, 247; *WJ* (Dunn), 602–4, and nn.70, 71; *Mass. Recs.*, 3:50, 58; Larry Gragg, "The Troubled Voyage of the Rainbow," *History Today* 39 (August 1989): 36–41.

28. Patrick Copeland to John Winthrop, December 4, 1639, *WP*, 4:157–59; William Berkeley to John Winthrop Jr., June 25, 1648, *WP*, 5:232.

29. For a request that Winthrop send some Indians to labor in Bermuda's nascent "Shuger workes" see William Berkeley to John Winthrop, June 12 and 25, 1648, both in *WP*, 5:229, 232.

30. Emanuel Downing to John Winthrop, ca. August 1645, *WP*, 5:38–39.

31. MA, 2:293a.

32. For Maverick's Virginia and Barbados connections see *WJ* (Dunn), entries for March 1632 and July 1636, 64, 182; for William Peirce's voyage there see entries for October–November 1632, 81–82, 89.

33. Nathaniel Sylvester Account Book, East Hampton Town Library, East Hampton, NY; Lion Gardiner probate inventory, Katherine Howlett Hayes, "Field Excavations at Sylvester Manor," *Northeast Historical Archaeology* 36 (2007): 34–50. Sylvester made direct trips to Barbados for trade, including slaves; in 1680 his estate included twenty-three slaves. Nathaniel Sylvester Will, March 1679/1680, Sylvester Manor Archives and Shelter Island Historical Society, New York.

34. The Massachusetts Body of Liberties (1641), *Old South Leaflets* (Boston: Directors of the Old South Work), 7:261–67.

35. *Mass. Recs.*, 3:49, 58, 84. Examinations of slavery and law include April Lee Hatfield, *Atlantic Virginia: Intercolonial Relations in the Seventeenth Century* (Philadelphia: University of Pennsylvania Press, 2004); Kathleen Brown, *Good Wives, Nasty Wenches, and Anxious Patriarchs: Gender, Race, and Power in Colonial Virginia* (Chapel Hill: Published for the Omohundro Institute of Early American History and Culture, 1996), esp. 108–36; Jonathan Bush, "Free to Enslave: The Foundations of Colonial American Slave Law," *Yale Journal of Law and the Humanities* 5 (1993): 417–70; William M. Wiecek, "The Origins of the Law of Slavery in British North America," *Cardozo Law Review* 17 (1996): 1711–92, and "The Statutory Law of Slavery and Race in the Thirteen Mainland Colonies of British America," *WMQ* 34 (1977): 258–80.

36. Hatfield, *Atlantic Virginia*.

37. Edmund B. O'Callahan, *History of New Netherland; or, New York under the Dutch* (New York, 1846), 274, n.1; Donna Merwick, *The Shame and the Sorrow: Dutch-Amerindian Encounters in New Netherland* (Philadelphia: University of Pennsylvania Press, 2006), 146–50.

38. Barry Levy, *Town Born: The Political Economy of New England from Its Founding to the Revolution* (Philadelphia: University of Pennsylvania Press, 2009), esp. 61–66; Christopher Tomlins, *Freedom Bound: Law, Labor, and Civic Identity in Colonizing English America, 1580–1865* (New York: Cambridge University Press, 2011), 246–66.

39. Salem Quarterly Court Records and Files, *Essex Antiquarian* 3, no. 6 (1899): 82–85.

40. "Will of John Winthrop," *WP*, 4:146–47.

41. *Mass. Assistants*, 2:40, 51, 50–60, 78–79, 91, 94, 97, 100.

42. *Mass. Recs.*, 1:201.

43. Daniel Vickers, *Farmers and Fishermen: Two Centuries of Work in Essex County, Massachusetts, 1630–1850* (Chapel Hill: University of North Carolina Press, for the Omohundro Institute of Early American History and Culture, 1994), 37–38, n.11, estimates that 17 percent of the immigrant stream consisted of servants, though others put the number slightly lower; see Virginia Anderson, *New England's Generation: The Great Migration and Formation of Society and Culture in the Seventeenth Century* (New York: Cambridge University Press, 1991), 24. Male workers and servants outnumbered females by 3:1; Tomlins, *Freedom Bound*, 33.

44. Levy, *Town Born*, 57.

45. *WJ* (Dunn), April 1645, 573.

46. Michael L. Fickes, "'They Could Not Endure that Yoke': The Captivity of Pequot Women and Children after the War of 1637," *NEQ* 73 (March 2000): 58–81. Fickes largely accepts contemporaries' assertions that most Indians ran away and that Indian captivity was a brief experiment.

47. Simon Newman contends that in Barbados the mechanisms for exploitation of labor developed before the enslavement of Africans, when European indentured servants formed the workforce, in *A New World of Labor*, esp. chap. 2; Hilary Beckles made a similar case in *White Servitude and Black Slavery*. Both scholars emphasize the role of class, not race, in defining Atlantic slavery. In contrast, Susan D. Amussen identifies gender rather than class as the underpinning of an English work order that racialized slavery gradually replaced. See Amussen, *Caribbean Exchanges: Slavery and the Transformation of English Society, 1640–1700* (Chapel Hill: University of North Carolina Press, 2007). On treatment of indentured servants in Virginia see Edmund Morgan, *American Slavery, American Freedom* (New York: W. W. Norton, 1975), and Henry Wiencek, *George Washington, His Slaves, and the Creation of America* (Boston: Farrar, Straus and Giroux, 2004), 51–56.

48. For a discussion of how local social practices could facilitate slaves' claims to various types of citizenship and identity see María Elena Díaz, "Conjuring Identities: Race, Nativeness, Local Citizenship, and Royal Slavery on an Imperial Frontier (Revisiting El Cobre, Cuba)," in *Imperial Subjects: Race and Identity in Colonial Latin America*, ed. Andrew Fisher and Matthew D. O'Hara (Durham, NC: Duke University Press, 2009), 197–224, esp. 200–203.

49. "Bill of Sale" [January 1648], *WP*, 5:196–97; Richard Vines to John Winthrop, [June 1637], *WP*, 5:171–72.

50. See Council Notes, May 7, 1640, regarding the crippling torture of English servant John Thomas, who was hung up and burned with lit matches between his fingers by Francis Leaven and Ensign Samuel Hodgkins. Barbados Records RB 3/1 Deeds, 17, Barbados Archives.

Chapter 3

1. [Henry Dunster?], *New England's First Fruits; in Respect, First of the Conversion of some, the Conviction of divers, and the Preparation of sundry of the Indians. . . .* (London, 1643), 6.

2. John Demos, *A Little Commonwealth: Family Life in Plymouth Colony* (New York: Oxford University Press, 1970); Edmund S. Morgan, *The Puritan Family*, rev. ed. (1944; New York: Harper Collins, 1966); Charles E. Hambrick-Stowe, *The Practice of Piety: Puritan Devotional Disciplines in Seventeenth-Century New England* (Chapel Hill: University of North Carolina Press, 1986); M. Michelle Jarrett Morris, *Under Household Government: Sex and Family in Puritan Massachusetts* (Cambridge, MA: Harvard University Press, 2013).

3. *Mass. Assistants*, 2:11.

4. *Conn. Recs.*, 1:46–47. Neal Salisbury sees the assaults on Wessagusset and Ma-re Mount (Merrymount) as a reflection, respectively, of Plymouth's and Salem's desire to maintain hegemony over potential rival English settlements, as well as their preference for a more militarized stance vis-à-vis the Indians. It does seem that English officials consciously strove to prevent a "frontier exchange economy" from developing that would have fostered exchange relations among Indians and Europeans to the detriment of other economic plans and more coercive labor arrangements. See Neal Salisbury, *Manitou and Providence: Indians, Europeans, and the Making of New England, 1500–1643* (New York: Oxford University Press, 1982), 129–30; for a counterargument see Michael Oberg, *Dominion and Civility: English Imperialism and Native America, 1585–1685* (Ithaca, NY: Cornell University Press, 2003). See also Daniel Usner, *Indians, Settlers, and Slaves in a Frontier Exchange Economy* (Chapel Hill: University of North Carolina Press, for the Omohundro Institute of Early American History and Culture, 1992).

5. Deed of Cushnamekin to Richard Callicott, October 8, 1636, "Dorchester Town Records [1631–1686]," *Fourth Report of the Record Commissions of the City of Boston, 1880* (Boston, 1883), 142; Charles Henry Pope, *The Pioneers of Massachusetts: A Descriptive List Drawn from Records of the Colonies, Towns and Churches* (Boston, 1900), 111–12; for Weld see *Mass. Recs.*, 2:240.

6. *Mass. Recs.*, 2:229.

7. "Dorchester Town Records," ibid., 5, 16; Boston, MA, Registry Department, *Records Relating to the Early History of Boston,* vol. 2, *Boston Town Records, 1634–1661* (Boston: Rockwell and Church, 1876), 80.

8. Roger Williams to John Winthrop, April 16, 1638, *CRW*, 1:149–52, quote on 150.

9. *Mass Recs.*, 1:127.

10. *WJ* (Dunn), 190–91; Samuel Drake, *Old Boston Taverns and Tavern Clubs* (Boston: W. A. Butterfield, 1917), 108, 73–74. For criminal activity and disorder at the inn see *Mass. Recs.*, 1:208, and *WJ* (Dunn), appendix B, 754.

11. Margaret Cornell Szasz, *Indian Education in the American Colonies, 1607–1783* (Albuquerque: University of New Mexico Press, 1988), 113–14; William Wallace Tooker, *John Eliot's First Teacher and Interpreter: Cockenoe-de-Long Island and the Story of His Career from the Early Records* (New York: Francis P. Harper, 1896), 16; Edward Winslow, *The Glorious Progress of the Gospel, Amongst the Indians in New England, manifested By three Letters, under the Hand of that famous Instrument of the Lord Mr. John Eliot* (London, 1649).

12. Roger Williams to Richard Collicut [*sic*], September 12, 1637, in *CRW*, 1:121.

13. "Will of John Winthrop," *WP*, 4:146–47.

14. Francis J. Bremer, *John Winthrop: America's Forgotten Founding Father* (New York: Oxford University Press, 2003), 323.

15. John Josselyn received a gift of ten "very fine Pippins" from Winthrop's farm; the giver, Captain Luxon, told him they were the only fruit trees in the area in 1639. Josselyn, *Two Voyages to New England: Made during the years 1638 and 1663* (London, 1638), 29.

16. "Conclusions and orders agreed upon by divers Sachems and other principal men amongst the Indians at Concord" (January 1646/47), in Lemuel Shattuck, *A History of the Town of Concord, Middlesex County, Massachusetts* (Acton, MA: Russell, Odiorne, & Co., 1835), 22–23, quote on 23; *Key*, 117.

17. Kathleen Bragdon, "Gender as a Social Category in Native Southern New England," *Ethnohistory* 43 (1996): 573–92, esp. 576; the quote is from Thomas Shepard, *The Clear Sun-shine of the Gospel, Breaking forth upon the Indians in New-England* (London, 1646), 7; Ann Marie Plane, "Childbirth Practices among Native American Women, 1600–1800," in, *Women and Health in America: Historical Readings*, ed. Judith Walzer Leavitt (Madison: University of Wisconsin Press, 1999), 37–47; for English observations of menstrual seclusion among New England Indians see Glenn W. LaFantasie in *Key*, introduction, and Karen Ordahl Kupperman, *Indians and English: Facing Off in Early America* (Ithaca, NY: Cornell University Press, 2000), 119, 147.

18. Patrick died at the hand of a Dutch captain at Underhill's home near Stamford, Connecticut, in 1644. *WJ* (Dunn), 491–92.

19. Orlando Patterson, *Slavery and Social Death: A Comparative Study* (Cambridge, MA: Harvard University Press, 1982).

20. Saidiya Hartman, *Lose Your Mother: A Journey along the Atlantic Slave Route* (New York: Farrar, Straus and Giroux, 2007), 5–6; David Brion Davis, *Inhuman Bondage: The Rise and Fall of Slavery in the New World* (New York: Oxford University Press, 2008), and Davis, *The Problem of Slavery in Western Culture* (Ithaca, NY: Cornell University Press, 1966). As Christina Snyder eloquently puts it, for Indians "the opposite of slavery was not freedom; the opposite of slavery was kinship." Snyder, *Slavery in Indian Country: The Changing Face of Captivity in Early America* (Cambridge, MA: Harvard University Press, 2010), 5.

21. Roger Williams to John Winthrop, July 31, 1637, *CRW*, 1:108–10, also n.5, 110; quotation appears on 109.

22. Mary C. Beaudry and Douglas C. George, "Old Data, New Findings: 1940s Archeology at Plymouth Reexamined," *American Archeology* 6 (1987): 20–30.

23. *RI Recs.*, 1:72 (Portsmouth), 1:103 (Newport).

24. *Key*, 127.

25. Winslow, *Glorious Progress*, 8.

26. *Key*, 230–31; *CRW*, 2:111–12, n.4; Lisa Brooks, *The Common Pot: The Recovery of Native Space in the Northeast* (Minneapolis: University of Minnesota Press, 2008), 51–53.

27. For laws against celebrating Christmas see *Mass. Recs.*, 4, pt. 1:366; William Bradford halted a 1622 Christmas celebration that included ball playing and other games: see *Of Plymouth Plantations*, ed. Samuel Eliot Morison (New Brunswick, NJ: Rutgers University Press, 1955), 97.

28. David E. Stannard, *The Puritan Way of Death: A Study in Religion, Culture, and Social Change* (New York: Oxford University Press, 1979), 101–9; Heather Miyano Kopelson, *Faithful Bodies: Performing Race and Religion in the Puritan Atlantic* (New York: NYU Press, 2014), esp. chap. 3.

29. *Key*, 193–94, 247–49 (quote on 194); Brenda J. Baker, "Pilgrim's Progress and Praying Indians: The Biocultural Consequences of Contact in Southern New England," in *In the Wake of Contact: Biological Responses to Conquest*, ed. Clark Spenser Larsen and George R. Milner (New York: Wiley-Liss, 1994), 35–46; William S. Simmons, *Cauntantouwit's House* (Providence: Brown University Press, 1970).

30. Stannard, *Puritan Way of Death*, 109.

31. Kathleen Bragdon, "The Material Culture of Christian Indians, 1650–1775," in *Documentary Archaeology in the New World*, ed. Mary C. Beaudry (Cambridge, MA: Harvard University Press, 1988), 129; Bragdon, *Native People of Southern New England* (Norman, OK: University of Oklahoma Press, 1996), 239; Michael S. Nassaney, "An Epistemological Enquiry into Some Archeological and Historical Interpretations of 17th Century Native American-European Relations," in *Archeological Approaches to Cultural Identity*, ed. S. J. Shennan (London: Unwin Hyman, 1989), 76–93.

32. *Champlin v. Thompson,* June 1733–, (also case files), WCC.

33. *RI Recs.*, Acts of the General Assembly, June 1729, 4:425–26; *Conn. Recs.*, 3:23–24.

34. *Key*, 117–29.

35. For a general argument about Indian political economy in this regard that also stresses similarities between European and Native American goals see Daniel Richter, *Trade, Land, Power: The Struggle for Eastern North America* (Philadelphia: University of Pennsylvania Press, 2013).

36. Lion Gardiner, *Relation of the Pequot Warres (1660)*, ed. W. N. Chattin Carlton (Hartford, CT: Acorn Club, 1901), 16.

37. Peter Laslett, *The World We Have Lost* (London: Methuen, 1971); David Galenson, "Indentured Servitude in the Americas," *Journal of Economic History* 44 (March 1984): 1–26.

38. Barry Levy argues that adoption among the English often took the form of uncompensated servitude. See Levy, "Girls and Boys: Poor Children and the Labor Market in Colonial Massachusetts," *Pennsylvania History* 64 (Summer 1997): 187–207.

39. The Iroquois tradition of the "mourning war" is the most familiar example of warfare as a search for captives to replace the dead, but many other groups in the Northeast engaged in some captive taking for ritual torture and/or adoption. See Daniel Richter, *The Ordeal of the Longhouse: The Peoples of the Iroquois League in the Era of European Colonization* (Chapel Hill: University of North Carolina Press, for the Omohundro Institute of Early American History and Culture, 1992), esp. 61–77, and Daniel K. Richter, "War and Culture: The Iroquois Experience," *WMQ* 40 (1983): 528–59.

40. *WJ* (Dunn), 192–93, and 192 n.16.

41. Gardiner, *Relation*, 11, 18–19.

42. Winslow, *Glorious Progress*, 23.

43. Virginia DeJohn Anderson, "King Phillip's Herds: Indians, Colonists, and the Problem of Livestock in Early New England," *WMQ* 51 (October 1994): 601–24.

44. Samuel G. Drake, *The History of the Great Indian War of 1675 and 1676, Commonly Called Philip's War; Also, the Old French and Indian Wars, from 1689 to 1704; By Thomas Church, Esq. with Numerous Notes and an Appendix* (New York: H. Dayton, 1860), 139–40.

45. Keith Stavely and Kathleen Fitzgerald, *America's Founding Food: The Story of New England Cooking* (Chapel Hill: University of North Carolina Press, 2004), 12, 278. Stavely and Fitzgerald highlight the colonists' efforts to distance themselves from Indian foodways, but English food dependency upon the Indians, mutual adaptations, and shared histories with common meats and fish made for many similarities. Rayna Green, "Public Histories of Food," in *The Oxford Handbook of Food History*, ed. Jeffrey M. Pilcher (New York, 2012), 82–96, esp. 84–85, 91–92.

46. Josselyn, *Two Voyages*, 91, noted techniques of pest removal that "the English have learnt of the Indians."

47. Ibid., 111–12.

48. *Key*, 117–18.

49. *Boston News-Letter*, November 9–16, 1732; see also November 15–22, 1708; September 22–29, 1712.

50. *Key*, 115–16.

51. [Samuel Moody], *Faithful Narrative of the Wicked Life and Remarkable Conversion of Patience Boston alias Samson* (Boston, 1728).

52. *Mass. Recs.*, 1:224.

53. Paul Robinson, "Miantonomi and the English," in *Northeastern Indian Lives, 1632–1816*, ed. Robert S. Grunet (Amherst: University of Massachusetts Press, 1996), 26; *WJ* (Dunn), 337.

54. William R. Carlton and John Winthrop Jr., "Overland to Connecticut in 1645: A Travel Diary of John Winthrop, Jr.," *NEQ* 13 (September 1940): 505; Roger Williams to John Winthrop, August 1639, *CRW*, 1:199–200, quote on 200.

55. *Key*, 185; Bragdon, *Native People*, 171.

56. *Tears of Repentance: Or, a further Narrative of the Progress of the Gospel Amongst the Indians in New-England* (London, 1653), 19.

57. Roger Williams to John Winthrop, June 7, 1738, *CRW*, 1:161.

58. Hugh Peter to John Winthrop, September 4 [1639], *WP*, 4:139.

59. *ECC*, 1:11; *Mass. Assistants*, 2:95.

60. Ibid., 2:95.

61. *EHTR*, 1:136.

62. MA, 2:290, 291–98.

63. *RCNP*, 9:61, 64, 75–78, 181; see Arnold J. F. Van Laer, trans., *New York Historical Manuscripts: Dutch*, vol. 4, *Council Minutes, 1638–1649*, New Netherland Research Center (Baltimore: Genealogical Publishers, 1974), 66–67, 365; Petrus Stuyvesant, "Correpondence, 1647–1653," trans. and ed. Charles T. Gering, New Netherland Society Electronic Publication, 2011, 11:3d–g, 11:4a–c, http://www.newnetherlandinstitute.org/files/5913/8016/5529/Correspondence_1647–1653.pdf.

64. Newport Court Session, March 1725, "Indictment of Indian Dick" and depositions of Boston, Tom, Dick, Toney, in *Gleanings from New Port Court Files, 1659–1783*, ed. Jane Fletcher Fiske (Boxford, MA: self-published, 1998).

65. *RI Recs.*, 1:219; for one example of how these informal ordinaries worked, and the socializing among Indians and English that occurred, see the June 1672 "presentment of John Hathorne and Robert Potter for Breech of Peace," *ECC*, 5:58–64.

66. Roger Williams to John Winthrop, November 10, 1637, *WP*, 3:509; the letter also appears in *CRW*, 1:131–33, and 134 nn.7, 10.

67. Josselyn, *Two Voyages*, 26. For a gripping account of this incident that tries to capture the experience of the enslaved woman see Wendy Anne Warren, "'The Cause of Her Grief': The Rape of a Slave in Early New England," *JAH* 93 (March 2007): 1031–49.

68. July 14, 1636, entry, "MBC administrative minutes, May 1636–August 1638," in *WJ* (Dunn), appendix B, 749.

69. *RCNP*, 1:4.

Chapter 4

1. Christina Snyder, *Slavery in Indian Country: The Changing Face of Captivity in Early America* (Cambridge, MA: Harvard University Press, 2010), 6; Ira Berlin, *Many Thousands Gone: The First Two Centuries of Slavery in North America* (Cambridge, MA: Harvard University Press, 1998), esp. chap. 1; María Elena Díaz, "Conjuring Identities: Race, Nativeness, Local Citizenship, and Royal Slavery on an Imperial Frontier (Revisiting El Cobre, Cuba)," in *Imperial Subjects: Race and Identity in Colonial Latin America*, ed. Andrew Fisher and Matthew D. O'Hara (Durham, NC: Duke University Press, 2009)," 205–6; David Brion Davis, *The Problem of Slavery in Western Culture* (Ithaca, NY: Cornell University Press, 1966), 229–30.

2. *Boston News-Letter*, September 23–30, October 7–14, October 14–21, 1725.

3. [Henry Dunster?], *New England's First Fruits; in Respect, First of the Conversion of some, the Conviction of divers, and the Preparation of sundry of the Indians. . . .* (London, 1643), 6.

4. Neal Salisbury, *Manitou and Providence: Indians, Europeans, and the Making of New England, 1500 1643* (New York: Oxford University Press, 1982), 134–38; Edward Winslow, *Good Newes From New England* (London, 1624). The literature on evangelization is extensive, and many scholars have examined Puritan motives, and to a lesser extent those of Indian converts. Kristina Bross links evangelization with the English Civil Wars, as Puritans strove to fend off criticism in England in the early 1640s concerning the Bay Company's treatment of Indians. Neal Salisbury sees little interest in evangelization because of the militarization of the Euro-Indian relationship in New England in the early 1620s, and ascribes post-1640 religious efforts to the English desire for Indian land. James P. Ronda and David Silverman find more sincere—yet still mixed—motives for evangelization on the part of the Mayhew family in Martha's Vineyard, as well as complicated reasons for some Indians' acceptance of Christianity, including personal advancement, opportunities for Indian cultural persistence within Christianity, and the search for tools to battle new challenges that accompanied the Europeans, such as alcohol. My contribution lies more in explaining the timing of evangelization and its link to the Pequot captive presence. See Kristina Bross, *Dry*

Bones and Indian Sermons: Praying Indians and American Identity (Ithaca, NY: Cornell University Press, 2004), 6–7; Salisbury, "Red Puritans: The 'Praying Indians' of Massachusetts Bay and John Eliot," *WMQ* 31 (1974): 27–54; James P. Ronda, "Generations of Faith: The Praying Indians of Martha's Vineyard," *WMQ* 38 (1981): 369–94; David J. Silverman, *Faith and Boundaries: Colonists, Christianity, and Community among the Wampanoag Indians of Martha's Vineyard, 1600–1871* (New York: Cambridge University Press, 2005).

5. *WJ* (Dunn), February 1638, 246.

6. Roger Williams to John Winthrop, November 10, 1637, *WP*, 3:509.

7. Edward Howes to John Winthrop Jr., March 26 and April 20, 1632, *WP*, 3:74, 77.

8. Patrick Copeland to John Winthrop, December 4, 1639, *WP*, 4:157–59.

9. *Conn. Recs.*, 1:531–55.

10. David D. Hall, *Worlds of Wonder, Days of Judgment: Popular Religious Belief in Early New England* (Cambridge, MA: Harvard University Press, 1990), 18, 35–47.

11. Margaret Cornell Szasz, *Indian Education in the American Colonies, 1607–1783* (Albuquerque: University of New Mexico Press, 1988), 122–26; Daniel Dorchester, *Christianity in the United States: From the First Settlement Down to the Present Time*, 2 vols. (Boston: Hunt and Eaton, 1895), 1:232–34; Kathleen Bragdon, *Native People of Southern New England* (Norman: University of Oklahoma Press, 1996), and Bragdon and Ives Goddard, *Native Writings in Massachusett*, 2 vols. (Philadelphia: American Philosophical Society, 1988), introduction. In Kristina Bross and Hilary E. Wyss, eds., *Early Native Literacies in New England: A Documentary and Critical Anthology* (Amherst: University of Massachusetts Press, 2008), 5–6, the editors note that European alphabetic literacy simultaneously undermined Indian identity and provided a new means of expressing indigenous cultural identity.

12. [Samuel Moody], *Faithful Narrative of the Wicked Life and Remarkable Conversion of Patience Boston Alias Samson* (Boston, 1728), 2–3. Patience Boston was unmoved, but Joseph Quasson stressed the effectiveness of family evangelism. See Samuel Moody, *Account of the Life and Death of Joseph Quasson, Indian* (Boston, 1726).

13. *New England's First Fruits*, 5–6.

14. *WJ* (Dunn), 246.

15. Salisbury, *Manitou*, 43; Catherine Albanese, *A Republic of Mind and Spirit: A Cultural History of American Metaphysical Religion* (New Haven, CT: Yale University Press, 2006), 103–4; William S. Simmons, *Spirit of the New England Tribes: Indian History and Folklore, 1620–1984* (Hanover, NH: University Press of New England, 1986), 38–40.

16. Boston, Massachusetts, *Documents of the City of Boston for the Year 1880*, 3 vols. (Boston, 1881), 3:173. Registry Department, *Records Relating to the Early History of Boston*, 39 vols. (1876–1919), vol. 6, *Roxbury Church and Land Records* (Boston, 1884), 173.

17. *New England's First Fruits*, 6.

18. Ibid., 7–8.

19. Ibid., 11.

20. George H. Ellis, *Records of the First Church at Dorchester, in New England, 1636–1734* (Boston, 1891), 7.

21. William Wallace Tooker, *John Eliot's First Teacher and Interpreter: Cockenoe-de-Long Island and the Story of His Career from the Early Records* (New York: Francis P. Harper, 1896), 9–12.

22. Edward Winslow, *The Glorious Progress of the Gospel, Amongst the Indians in New England, manifested By three Letters, under the Hand of that famous Instrument of the Lord Mr. John Eliot* (London, 1649), 19.

23. John A. Strong, *The Montaukett Indians of Eastern Long Island* (Syracuse, NY: Syracuse University Press, 2001), 23.

24. Francis J. Bremer, "John Sassamon," in *First Founders: American Puritanism and Puritans in an Atlantic World* (Hanover, NH: University of New Hampshire Press, 2012), 195–212, esp. 196–97. See also Jill Lepore, "Dead Men Tell No Tales: John Sassamon and the Fatal Consequences of Literacy," *American Quarterly* 46 (December 1994): 479–512, 489, n.50; Szasz, *Indian Education*, 115.

25. Eric S. Johnson, "Uncas and the Politics of Contact," in *Northeastern Indian Lives, 1631–1816*, ed. Robert S. Grumet (Amherst: University of Massachusetts Press, 1996), 40; Roger Williams to John Winthrop, July 23, 1628, *CRW*, 1:168; Kevin McBride, "The Legacy of Robin Cassacinamon," in Grumet, *Northeastern Indian Lives*, 81. McBride places the Indian women and Cassacinamon in John Winthrop Jr.'s home in Nameaug in 1638, but evidence from Roger Williams and John Winthrop Sr. locates them in Boston, not Connecticut, and identifies Cassacinamon as the servant of Winthrop Sr. in 1638.

26. Roger Williams to John Winthrop, July 23, 1628, *CRW*, 1:168, and 169 n.5.

27. Walter William Woodward, *Prospero's America: John Winthrop Jr., Alchemy, and the Creation of New England Culture, 1606–1676* (Chapel Hill: University of North Carolina Press, for the Omohundro Institute of Early American History and Culture, 2010), 105, 108–9.

28. See "Deed of Webucksham and Washcomo to John Winthrop, Jr.," January 20, 1645, in *WP*, 5:4–5, which conveyed lands around present day Sturbridge, Massachusetts, where Winthrop and other investors planned a blacklead (graphite) mining operation. For more on the blacklead mine see Margaret Ellen Newell, "Robert Child and the Entrepreneurial Vision: Economy and Ideology in Early New England," *NEQ* 58 (1995): 223–56, and Woodard, *Prospero's America*, 72, 80–82.

29. John Winthrop Jr. to Thomas Peters, September 3, 1646, in *WP*, 5:100; see also the "Petition of the Inhabitants of New London to the Commissioners of the United Colonies," ca. September 15, 1646, *WP*, 5:111; "Protest of the Inhabitants of New London Against Uncas," ca. 1647, *WP*, 5:124; Roger Williams to John Winthrop Jr., January 24, 1648/49, *CRW*, 1:268–69.

30. "Records of the United Colonies of New-England," in *Historical Collections, Consisting of State Papers and Other Documents; Intended as Materials for an History of the United States of America*, 2 vols., ed. Ebenezer Hazard (Philadelphia, 1794), 2:89.

31. McBride, "Legacy," 86–88.

32. MA, 31:505a; Francis Nicholson and Samuel Vetch to the Lords of Trade, "Journal, March-June, 1709," CO 5, box 9, Canada Expedition, Public Records Office / UK National Archives, England.

33. Hazard, "Records of the United Colonies," 2:93–94; McBride, "Legacy," 85–86.

34. *CRW*, 1:129, n.14.

35. Roger Williams to John Winthrop, [ca. October 26, 1637], *WP*, 3:502.

36. Roger Williams to John Winthrop, July 23, 1638, in *CRW*, 1:168–69, and 169 nn.4–5.

37. Williams to Winthrop, July 23, 1638, ibid., 168.

38. Karen Ordahl Kupperman argues that in general Indians resisted putting their children even in elite households, although she does note extensive exchange of child and teen hostages in Virginia in the early decades of settlement. See Kupperman, *Indians and English: Facing Off in Early America* (Ithaca, NY: Cornell University Press, 2000), 153–55, 206, 234.

39. Roger Williams to John Winthrop, September 9, 1637, *CRW*, 1:119; Williams to Richard Callicott, September 12, 1637, *CRW*, 1:121.

40. Roger Williams to John Winthrop, August 12, 1637, in *WP*, 3:479–80, quote on 480.

41. Roger Williams to John Winthrop, July 23, 1638, *CRW*, 1:168.

42. *RCNP*, 9:76, 64.

43. Roger Williams to John Winthrop, July 11, 1637, *CRW*, 1:106–7 and 107–8 n.7; see also *WJ* (Dunn), 468, 471, 716–17; "Acts of the Commissioners of the United Colonies," September 1650, *RCNP*, 9:169, 70. At Connecticut's behest, Uncas took Sonquassen into custody and thence to prison in Hartford for several weeks in September and October of 1646 because of a rumor that he planned to kidnap several magistrates. Negotiations with the Narragansetts and Niantics may have brought Sonquassen to Rhode Island. It is possible that the girl's marriage was linked to alliance maneuverings, but no direct evidence exists.

44. Richard Morris to John Coggeshall, [ca. May 22, 1647], *WP*, 5:164; William Baulston to John Winthrop Jr., May 22, 1647, *WP*, 5:165; John Coggeshall to John Winthrop Jr., *WP*, 5:165–66.

Chapter 5

1. "Articles of Agreement between the English in Connecticut and the Indian Sachems Dated 1638," copy in the Connecticut State Library, Hartford.

2. *WJ* (Dunn), 462.

3. Lisa Brooks offers a terrific discussion of the Mohegan-Narragansett conflict and missed opportunities in *The Common Pot: The Recovery of Native Space in the Northeast* (Minneapolis: University of Minnesota Press, 2008), chap. 2, esp. 62; also Neal Salisbury, *Manitou and Providence: Indians, Europeans, and the Making of New England, 1500–1643* (New York: Oxford University Press, 1982), 232, and "Indians and Colonists in Southern New England after the Pequot War: An Uneasy Balance," in *The Pequots in Southern New England*, ed. Lawrence M. Hauptman and James D. Wherry (Norman: University of Oklahoma Press, 1990), 88–89. On the United Colonies see Harry M. Ward, *The United Colonies of New England, 1643–90* (New York: Vantage Press, 1961).

4. *Conn. Recs.*, 1:73.

5. *RCNP*, 9:28–29.

6. *WJ* (Dunn), 472.

7. *WJ* (Dunn), 473 and n.7.

8. Letter from Pessicus and Canonicus to Massachusetts Bay, May 24, 1644, MA, 30:2. In *Subjects unto the Same King*, Jennifer Pulsipher argues that this Narragansett

strategy of making the imperial center in London the arbiter of Indian-colonial disputes set a precedent. I agree that this represented a significant strategy, but in the end the crown did not intervene much to protect Indian rights or to stop enslavement until the northeastern wars of 1689–1750 cemented Indians' subjecthood in the eyes of imperial authorities.

9. Emanuel Downing to Winthrop, ca. August 1645, *WP*, 5:38–39.

10. For Uncas's attacks on and takings of Nipmuc Indians in July 1661 see MA, 30:85a.

11. *RCNP*, 1:45. Two Narragansett boys were still in the hands of Herbert Pelham, one of the Massachusetts commissioners to the United Colonies, in October 1646; MA, 30:9.

12. *RCNP*, 9:70.

13. Emanuel Downing to Winthrop, ca. August 1645, *WP*, 5:38–39.

14. *Conn. Recs.*, April 11, 1639, 1:27.

15. *CRW*, 1:176–77 and n.4, 194, 223, 311; 2:404, 406; 426.

16. *Mass. Recs.*, June 10, 1644, 3:6.

17. *RI Recs.*, 1:82.

18. *ECC*, June 1674, 5:270–72; June 1677, 6:295.

19. *Mass. Recs.*, 3:73.

20. For the environmental impact of English agriculture and animal husbandry on Indians see William Cronon, *Changes in the Land: Indians, Colonists, and the Ecology of New England* (New York: Hill & Wang, 1983), esp. chaps. 4 and 7; Virginia Anderson, *Creatures of Empire: How Domestic Animals Transformed Early America* (New York: Oxford, 2004); and Richard White, *The Roots of Dependency: Subsistence, Environment, and Social Change among the Choctaws, Pawnees, and Navajos* (Lincoln: University of Nebraska Press, 1988). For English efforts to regulate Indian field burnings see *RI Recs.*, 1:107.

21. *Conn. Recs.*, 1:33.

22. *Mass. Recs.*, "Indian Lands," October 19, 1652, 3:281.

23. For Concord see *Mass. Recs.*, 3:301, 4, pt. 1: 283, and MA, 30:186; for East Hampton see "Copy of Indenture made July 25, 1687 between Wyandance and Sasakotoko with Lt. John Wheeler, Samuel Mulford, Thomas Osborne, Stephen Hand, Stephen Hedges, Samuel Parsons, John Mulford, Trustees of the Town of East Hampton. Also the interpretation of these agreements." Indians, Montauk 13878, Indentures, X(WB), 141, and "Thomas Tallmadge copy of 1670 Indian Deed," Documents Book 1, both in Long Island Collection, East Hampton Town Library.

24. *Conn. Recs.*, April 1640, 1:46–47; see *RI Recs.*, 1:107, for similar language in a 1640 treaty with Miantonomo.

25. *Conn. Recs.*, 1:529–35.

26. New London Town Grants to John Winthrop Jr., [September 1, 1650], *WP*, 5:61–64, quote on 63.

27. *Conn. Recs.*, 1:226, 576.

28. See *Conn. Recs.*, 1:576–77; "Documents Relating to a jurisdiction in the Narragansett Country. At a meeting of the Commissioners for the United Collonies of New England, held at Boston, September 4, 1662," 1:498.

29. "A Declaration of the dealings of Uncas and the Mohegin Indians, to certain Indians, the inhabitants of Quabacouk 21–3–61," in MA, 30:85a.

30. *Mass. Recs.*, May 1647, 3:105.

31. This is Yasuhide Kawashima's argument in *Puritan Justice and the Indian: White Man's Law and the Indian in Massachusetts* (Middletown, CT: Wesleyan University Press, 1986); see also James P. Ronda, "Red and White at the Bench: Indians and the Law in Plymouth Colony, 1620–1691," *Essex Institute Historical Collections* 110 (1974): 214; Kawashima, "Jurisdiction of the Colonial Courts over the Indians in Massachusetts, 1689–1763," *NEQ* 42 (1969): esp. 542–44.

32. For more on the effects of alcohol consumption on New England's Native Americans see Peter Mancall, *Deadly Medicine: Indians and Alcohol in Early America* (Ithaca, NY: Cornell University Press, 1995).

33. *Mass. Recs.*, 4, pt. 2:282.

34. *RI Recs.*, 1:117.

35. *RI Recs.*, 1:477.

36. Joshua Micah Marshall, "'A Melancholy People': Anglo-Indian Relations in Early Warwick, Rhode Island, 1642–1675," *NEQ* 68 (1995): 402–28; John Sainsbury, "Indian Labor in Early Rhode Island," *NEQ* 47 (1974): 379–93. Marshall, Sainsbury, and to a certain extent Cronon link Indians' losses to their economic and ecological marginalization and the collapse of Indian political arrangements, rather than to enslavement and the colonial labor systems. For a similar model of proletarianization in a slightly later period see John Wood Sweet's *Bodies Politic: Negotiating Race in the American North, 1730–1830* (Philadelphia: University of Pennsylvania Press, 2007).

37. Cronon, *Changes in the Land*; Laura Brace, *The Idea of Property in Seventeenth-Century England: Tithes and the Individual* (Manchester: Manchester University Press, 1998); David Grayson Allen, *In English Ways: The Movement of Societies and the Transferal of English Local Law and Custom to Massachusetts in the Seventeenth Century* (Chapel Hill: University of North Carolina Press, 1981).

38. John Frederick Martin, *Profits in the Wilderness: Entrepreneurship and the Founding of New England Towns in the Seventeenth Century* (Chapel Hill: University of North Carolina Press, for the Omohundro Institute of Early American History and Culture, 1991), 122–23, 131–35, 139, 150–52, 185–216; Stephen Innes, *Creating the Commonwealth: The Economic Culture of Puritan New England* (New York: W. W. Norton, 1995).

39. Patrick Conforti, *Saints and Strangers: New England in British North America* (Baltimore: Johns Hopkins University Press, 2006), 6.

40. Patrick Wolfe, *Settler Colonialism and the Transformation of Anthropology: The Politics and Poetics of an Ethnographic Event* (London: Cassell Press, 1999); see also Daniel Usner, *Indians, Settlers, and Slaves in a Frontier Exchange Economy* (Chapel Hill: University of North Carolina Press, for the Omohundro Institute of Early American History and Culture, 1992), and his "American Indians on the Cotton Frontier: Changing Economic Relations with Citizens and Slaves in the Mississippi Territory," *Journal of American History* 72 (September 1985): 297–317.

41. Josiah Stanborough to John Winthrop Jr., April 4, 1650, *WP*, 6:32.

42. *Mass. Recs.*, May 1646, 3:64.

43. Petition from John Winthrop Jr. to the Commissioners of the United Colonies, MA, 30:13; Petition from John Mason to United Colonies Commissioners, June(?) 1649, MA, 30:14.

44. Richard Blinman to John Winthrop Jr., August 6, 1650, *WP*, 6:53–54.

45. *EHTR*, 1:270–71; East Hampton Town Book 2, 107, East Hampton Town Library.

46. Marshall, "'Melancholy People,'" 402–28; Sainsbury, "Indian Labor," 379–93.

47. Daniel Gookin, *Historical Collections of the Indians in New England* [1674], reprinted in *Massachusetts Historical Collections* 1 (Boston, 1792), 210; *ECC*, 6:426.

48. *EHTR*, 1:407–8; Loose Leaf 2–34, East Hampton Town Library. The men were already in debt, and were to go out annually until the debts were paid—a peonage relationship that they never satisfied.

49. Daniel Gookin, *Historical Account of the Doings and Sufferings of the Christian Indians in New England in the Years 1675–1677* (New York: Kessinger Publishing, 2003, repr. of 1836 ed.), 434.

50. Sylvester Account Book, XFE 14, East Hampton Town Library.

51. Margaret Newell, *From Dependency to Independence: Economic Revolution in Colonial New England* (Ithaca, NY: Cornell University Press, 1998), esp. chap. 2.

52. June 1672 "presentment of John Hathorne and Robert Potter for Breech of Peace," *ECC*, 5:58–64; quote on 61.

53. *PTP*, 15:23–25.

54. Ibid.; also verdict and examination of witnesses in the Nanhegin case in PTP mss., ser. 2, vol. 5 (undated), 13, 15, 23, (MS 01106, 01112, 01142); Sainsbury, "Indian Labor," 381–82.

55. *ECC*, 5:400, 6:60, 214.

56. *Conn. Recs.*, 1:532–33.

57. *RI Recs.*, 1:414–15.

58. *PCT*, 1:544, 52–55, 57, 64, 71–72, 72–73 2:45, 64, 89; Marshall, "'Melancholy People,'" 405–6, 410–11.

59. *RCNP*, 3:74, March 1655.

60. Ipswich Quarterly Court, September 1660, *ECC*, 2:240, and 240n–243n.

61. Thomas Doughton, presentation as part of a National Endowment for the Humanities program on slavery in New England, Harriet Beecher Stowe Center / University of Hartford, Hartford, CT, July 2007.

62. *EHTR*, 1:35; the boy was to receive forty acres, but that appears to be a typographical error in the printed version of the Southampton Town Records. See Strong, *The Unkechaug Indians of Eastern Long Island: A History* (Norman: University of Oklahoma Press, 2013).

63. See MA, 30:18, 82a, 85.

64. *EHTR*, 1:104–5.

65. *PCT*, 1:76; for estimates of artisan wages in 1670 see Terry L. Andersen, *The Economic Growth of Seventeenth Century New England: A Measurement of Regional Income*, Dissertations in American Economic History (New York, 1975), 76, and Richard B. Morris, *Government and Labor in Early America* (New York: Harper & Row, 1965), 65–68.

66. General Court of Trials held at Newport, October 21, 1688, *PCT*, 1:88.

67. *Records of the Suffolk County Court, 1671–1680*, ed. Samuel Eliot Morison, 2 vols. (Boston: Colonial Society of Massachusetts, 1933), 1:548–49.

68. *RCNP*, 11:234.

69. Newport Court Book A, Special Court of Trials, June 15, 1671, *Rhode Island General Court of Trials, 1671–1730*, 7, 14.

70. *RCNP*, 5:151–52; Ronda, "Red and White at the Bench," 200–215, 211.

71. "Petition of Edward Bendall and Samuel Scarlet, to Thomas Dudley and the rest of the Commissioners, July 14, 1649," MA, 60:292.

Chapter 6

1. See Jill Lepore, *The Name of War: King Philip's War and the Origins of American Identity* (New York: Alfred A. Knopf, 1998), and James David Drake, *King Philip's War: Civil War in New England, 1675–1676* (Amherst: University of Massachusetts Press, 1999). Lepore has two chapters on captivity and enslavement during King Philip's War, including the experience of English captive Mary Rowlandson. She presents a compelling argument that King Philip's War was "culture war" in which Indians consciously attacked symbols of English civility and culture. Drake also thinks the war spelled the end of a common Anglo-Indian culture. Francis Jennings sees the war as a genocidal one, and argues that colonists targeted the Narragansetts— not the Wampanoags—in order to take their lands in Rhode Island, Plymouth, and eastern Connecticut; Francis Jennings, *The Invasion of America: Indians, Colonialism, and the Cant of Conquest* (Chapel Hill: University of North Carolina Press, 1975), chap. 17. For other takes on the war as a turning point in imperial structures and relations see Michael Oberg, *Dominion and Civility: English Imperialism and Native America, 1585–1685* (Ithaca, NY: Cornell University Press, 2003), and Jennifer Hale Pulsipher, *Subjects unto the Same King: Indians and the Contest for Authority in Colonial New England* (Philadelphia: University of Pennsylvania Press, 2006), although Oberg sees colonists themselves divided between pro- and anti-imperial or "frontier" factions, and implies that similar divisions split the Indians. Pulsipher tends to emphasize Indian agency more before the war and less after the war than does my account. For the connection between the experience of Indian war on the northeastern frontier and witchcraft accusations see Mary Beth Norton, *In the Devil's Snare: The Salem Witchcraft Crisis of 1692* (New York: Alfred A. Knopf, 2002).

2. November 3, 1675, *Mass. Recs.*, 6:59.

3. James D. Drake, "Restraining Atrocity: The Conduct of King Philip's War," *NEQ* 70 (March 1997): 33–56. I am extremely sympathetic to Drake's overall arguments about the cultural hybridity of Indian and New England societies, although he overstates the restraint of English forces and downplays captivity. For Drake the war brings an era of "covalent" society to an end, while I argue that Indians continued to shape a common culture in important ways, both as slaves and as free individuals. For another persistence narrative see Jean O'Brien, *Dispossession by Degrees: Indian Land and Identity in Natick, Massachusetts, 1650–1790* (New York: Cambridge University Press, 1997).

4. Neal Salisbury, *Manitou and Providence: Indians, Europeans, and the Making of New England, 1500–1643* (New York: Oxford University Press, 1982); Kathleen J. Bragdon, *Native People of Southern New England, 1500–1650* (Norman: University of Oklahoma Press, 1996), 28.

5. Pulsipher, *Subjects*, 99–100.

6. Robert Mason to the Lords of Trade, in "Minutes of the Committee for Trade and Plantations respecting the case of Mason and Gorges, wherein was read 'A narrative of the settlement of the Corporation of Massachusetts Bay and Capt. Wyborne's

account of things in 1673,' with the present posture of that country," December 1, 1675. Colonial Papers, vol. 35, no. 50, PRO/NAUK. Connecticut had instituted the same policy in the early 1670s, requiring ten days to three months of public labor as punishment for Indian drunkenness.

7. John Easton, "A Relation of the Indian War," in *A Narrative of the Causes Which Led to Philip's Indian War* (Albany: J. Munsell, 1858), 5–15.

8. Pulsipher, *Subjects*, 57–59; "Documents Related to the Disputed Jurisdiction in the Narragansett Country," *RI Recs.*, 2:225–31, 369–420; *Mass. Recs.*, 4, pt. 2: 175; John Frederick Martin, *Profits in the Wilderness: Entrepreneurship and the Founding of New England Towns in the Seventeenth Century* (Chapel Hill: University of North Carolina Press, for the Omohundro Institute of Early American History and Culture, 1991), 54–55, 62–64; Elisha R. Potter, *The Early History of Narragansett*, Rhode Island Historical Society, *Collections*, vol. 3 (Providence, 1835), 60–63.

9. Daniel Mandell, *King Philip's War: Colonial Expansion, Native Resistance, and the End of Indian Sovereignty* (Baltimore: Johns Hopkins University Press, 2010), 64–68.

10. *RCNP*, 5:70–72; 73; 76.

11. *Conn. Recs.*, 2: 334–35, 338–45.

12. Mandell, *King Philip's War*, 45–46. According to rumors that reached Rhode Island's John Easton, Metacom fired Sassamon for forging bequests to himself in Metacom's will. Jill Lepore, "Dead Men Tell No Tales: John Sassamon and the Fatal Consequences of Literacy," *American Quarterly* 46 (December 1994): 479–512; Jennings, *Invasion*, 295.

13. Drake, *King Philip's War*, 14–15; Lepore, *Name of War*, esp. chap. 7.

14. Jennings, *Invasion*, 297; Easton, "Relation," 8; Mandell, *King Philip's War*, 49–51. Roger Williams attributed the outbreak of hostilities in part to the Sassamon affair. See Williams to John Winthrop Jr., *CRW*, 2: 698–99.

15. "Examination of the Messenger of Pessicus," April 29, 1676, *The Wyllys Papers, 1590–1796*, Connecticut Historical Society *Collections*, vol. 21 (Hartford: published by the Society, 1924), 241–42.

16. On Moseley see Daniel Gookin, *Historical Account of the Doings and Sufferings of the Christian Indians in New England in the Years 1675–1677* (New York: Kessinger Publishing, 2003, repr. of 1836 ed.), 455–56; Roger Williams to Wait Winthrop, July 7, 1675, in n.1, 27–29, and Wait Winthrop to John Winthrop, July 1675, in *A Letter from Wait Winthrop at Mr. Smiths of Narragansett to Governor John Winthrop in Connecticut* (Providence: Society of Colonial Wars in the State of Rhode Island and Providence, 1915), 21–23.

17. For Moseley's May 1676 agreement see *Mass. Recs.*, 5:94–95.

18. John Hull's Daybook, Treasury Records, vol. 4, 20, Massachusetts Historical Society, Boston.

19. Order in Council, September 29, 1675, MA, 30:177a.

20. Samuel Moseley to Governor Leverett, October 5 and 16, 1675, reprinted in George Madison Bodge, *Soldiers in King Philip's War* (Boston: printed for the author, 1891), 26–27; Bodge offers an extensive biography of Moseley and a list of many of the other men in the unit, 18–35.

21. "Petition of Mary Pray to Captain James Oliver, Providence, February 1675/76," MA, 69:91–92; also Pray to Oliver, October 25, 1675, Massachusetts Historical Society *Collections*, ser. 1, vol. 5 (1897), 105–10; Gookin, *Historical Account*, 11.

22. *RCNP*, 5:173; Governor Leverett's Certificate, September 12, 1676, Photo-stats, Massachusetts Historical Society, Boston. Lepore also points out this contradic-tion and its meaning for colonists, especially their construction of Philip's political legitimacy and agency. *Name of War*, 150–53.

23. *RCNP*, 5:174.

24. Ibid.

25. For a similar argument see Drake, *King Philip's War*, 112–14.

26. Samuel Moseley to John Leverett, October 16, 1675, in Bodge, *Soldiers*, 27; William Hubbard, *The Present State of New England* (Boston, 1677), in *Narratives of the Indian Wars, 1675–1699*, ed. George H. Lincoln (New York: Charles Scribner's Sons, 1913), 39.

27. Gookin, *Historical Account*, 474.

28. Leverett Certificate, October 20, 1675, Book of Possessions, Document 46, part 2, *Documents of the City of Boston for the Year 1881*, 3 vols. (Boston, 1882), 1:48; MA, 30:184.

29. Gookin, *Historical Account*, 458–61, 466–67; see also Bodge, *Soldiers*, 52–54.

30. Hubbard, *Present State of New England*, 40–41.

31. MA, 30:184.

32. MA, 30:184a. Contemporary accounts as well as subsequent historical analy-ses of this case are somewhat contradictory. Most mention the Indians' arrest by Moseley, but what happened after remains less clear. Daniel Gookin recorded that all but two were freed. Drake, Bodge, and Mandell have the Indians freed after the trial, but Great David's name appears on the list of Indians sold. See Mandell, *King Philip's War*, 82, and Drake, *King Philip's War*, 102–3.

33. "Petition of William Ahaton," September 12, 1675, MA, 30:176 and 176a.

34. Ibid.; see also certificate "To the Prison house in Boston," signed by Daniel Gookin, MA, 30:176a, September 22, 1675.

35. Benjamin Batten to Sir Thomas Allin, June 21, 1675, Colonial Papers, CO 1/34, no. 108, PRO/NAUK; see also Douglas E. Leach, "Benjamin Batten and the *London Gazette* Report on King Philip's War," *NEQ* 36 (December 1963): 502–17.

36. William Harris to [Sir Joseph Williamson], August 12, 1675, *CSP Col.*, 442.

37. Journal of the Assembly of Barbados, June 13–14, 1676, *CSP Col.*, 403.

38. For the controversy see Surinam, 9/19 August 1675, 675i–675vii, Colonial Papers, vol. 35, nos. 22–22, 50–56; also Col. Entry Bk., vol. 78, 106–18, PRO/NAUK.

39. Atkins to Sir Joseph Williamson, April 1676, Colonial Papers, 3/13, vol. 36; Lepore, *Name of War*, 170–71; Jerome Handler, "The Amerindian Slave Population of Barbados in the Seventeenth and Early Eighteenth Centuries," *Journal of Caribbean Studies* 8 (1969): 44–47; for an analysis of the Barbados statute see Linford D. Fisher, "'Dangerous Designes': The 1676 Barbados Statute to Prohibit New England Indian Slave Importation," *WMQ* 71 (2014): 99–124.

40. *Mass. Recs.*, 5:59–63.

41. Sylvanus Warro had incurred a hefty judgment of twenty pounds related to his paternity of a son with Elizabeth Parker, a servant in the William Parke household. Warro resided in the household of Thomas Wade. His status was murky; Gookin tes-tified that he made an agreement with Warro that if the latter served Wade for eight years then Gookin would free him. After the bastardy judgment, Gookin first offered to help Parke sell Warro as a slave to Virginia to pay the monetary judgment, and

then persuaded Warro to sign a contract making himself a slave for life—to Gookin. Gookin did not recompense Wade, however, and the case ended up in court. Gookin based his right to Warro's labor on the fact that he had "bred him from a child and his parents were my vassals and his Brother is now my servant." Papers from the case *Gookin v. Wade*, Middlesex Court Records, December 1682, appear in Folio 106–3, Middlesex File Papers, Folio Collection, Massachusetts State Archives, Boston; Frederick William Gookin, *Daniel Gookin, 1612–1687: Assistant and Major General of the Massachusetts Bay Colony* (Chicago, 1912), 194–97. For more on the Gookin family and their issues with servants of all races see M. Michelle Jarrett Morris, *Under Household Government: Sex and Family in Puritan Massachusetts* (Cambridge, MA: Harvard University Press, 2013), chap. 1.

42. Gookin, *Historical Account*, 468–70, 476–77.

43. "To the Honorable the Governo: & Council Siting at Boston . . . the humble petition of John Eliot," August 13, 1675, MA, 30:173.

44. Governor Leverett's Certificate, September 12, 1676, Photostats, Massachusetts Historical Society, Boston.

45. "Deposition of Elizabeth Belcher and Martha Remington and Mary Mitchell," MA, 30:192.

46. Samuel Arnold to John Cotton, September 9, 1676, Massachusetts Historical Society, Boston.

47. Governor Leverett's Certificate, September 12, 1676, Photostats, Massachusetts Historical Society, Boston.

48. Petition of Jonathan Fairbanks, April 19, 1676, MA, 30:200. The girl ended up on Deer Island, and Fairbanks offered to pay her expenses if he could have her back.

49. Petition of John Thaxter of Hingham, January 11, 1676/77, MA, 30:234.

50. William Jones to Deputy Governor William Leete, May 2, 1676, *The Wyllys Papers*, 242–44.

51. *Mass. Recs.*, 5:57.

52. MA, 30:185a.

53. Petition of Awaukun son of Cahupnacunumig, MA, 30:191a.

54. *RCNP*, 10:366. For a discussion of this incident in the context of Indian marital relations see Ann Marie Plane, *Colonial Intimacies: Indian Marriage in Early New England* (Ithaca, NY: Cornell University Press, 2000).

55. "James Oliver's Account of the Campaign," January 26, 1675/76, from Thomas Hutchinson's "History of Massachusetts," reprinted in Bodge, *Soldiers*, 126–27.

56. See Patrick M. Malone, *The Skulking Way of War: Technology and Tactics among the New England Indians* (Baltimore: Johns Hopkins University Press, 1991), 110, and Drake, *King Philip's War*, 135. Some of this is a matter of emphasis; Mandell, *King Philip's War*, 67–69, notes the importance of Indian allies for Massachusetts and Plymouth.

57. MA, 30:236.

58. *Conn. Recs.*, 2:290.

59. *CSP Col.*, 18:182.

60. War Council minutes, March 16, 1676, *Conn. Recs.*, 2:418.

61. "Petition of Thos. Danforth asking permission to keep two children that were given him," MA, 30:220.

62. *Mass. Recs.*, 5:72.

63. Deed, "Auwonecoo, Mohegan sachem, Jan. 9, 1675/76," Indian Deeds/ Indians Microfilm 80010, Fr. 0010, Connecticut Historical Society, Hartford.

64. *Conn. Recs.*, 2:297–98.

65. *Conn. Recs.*, 2:482.

66. General Court, May 1677 session, *Conn. Recs.*, 2:308.

67. *Conn. Recs.*, 2:494–95.

Chapter 7

1. "Petition of Ben Indian to the Worshipfull Justices now sitting att Philadelphia," September 1693, Mss. 221, box 1, Rhode Island Historical Society, Providence.

2. "The Humble Request of ye Committee of Militia, and the selectmen of ye town of Dorchester humbly sheweth," March 23, 1676, MA, 30:198b.

3. "Petition of Mary Pray to Captain James Oliver, Providence, February 1675/76" MA, 69: 91–92; also Pray to Oliver, October 25, 1675, Massachusetts Historical Society *Collections*, ser. 1, vol. 5 (1897), 105–10; the quotation appears on 107.

4. *The Early Records of the Town of Portsmouth*, ed. Clarence S. Brigham (Providence: E. L. Freeman & Sons, 1901) [hereafter *Portsmouth Town Records*], 188.

5. *RI Recs.*, 2:534.

6. July 22, 1676, *RCNP*, 5:210.

7. William Harris to Sir Joseph Williamson, August 12, 1676, *CSP Col.*, 442–43.

8. Council of Connecticut to Major John Talcott, July 15, 1676, *The Wyllys Papers, 1590–1796*, Connecticut Historical Society *Collections*, vol. 21 (Hartford: Published by the Society, 1924), 247–49.

9. Richard Dunn, *Puritans and Yankees: The Winthrop Dynasty of New England, 1630–1717* (Princeton, NJ: Princeton University Press, 1962), 209; *Conn. Recs.*, 2:345, 350, 363, 379; Fitz-John Winthrop to Nathaniel Eldred, December 15, 1676, Massachusetts Historical Society *Collections*, ser. 5, vol. 8 (Boston, 1882), 282–83.

10. "To all committees of Militia, Selectmen commissioners & Constables in the Jurisdiction of the Massachusetts," July 28, 1675, MA, 67:210a.

11. Samuel Lynde Petition, April 1677, MA, 30:236b.

12. Writ against Nathaniel Baker, December 18, 1676, Photostats, Massachusetts Historical Society, Boston.

13. "Petition from some Inhabitants of Hingham to the Council," December 21, 1676, Photostats, Massachusetts Historical Society, Boston.

14. March 6, 1677, *RCNP*, 5:223.

15. Connecticut General Court, October 1676 Session, *Conn. Recs.*, 2:297–98.

16. Ibid., 2:298.

17. Ibid., 2:297–98.

18. Ibid., 298.

19. Ibid.

20. See Joel Williamson's suggestive model for the rise of Jim Crow in *The Crucible of Race: Black/White Relations in the American South since Emancipation* (New York: Oxford University Press, 1984).

21. Order in Council, MA, 30:261; "Petition from the Select men of Dedham," October 12, 1681, MA, 30: 261a.

22. Daniel Gookin, "Indian Children Put to Service, August 10, 1676," *New England Historical and Genealogical Register* 8 (1854): 270–73.

23. *RI Recs.*, 2:534–35. See also Glenn W. LaFantasie and Paul R. Campbell, "Scattered to the Winds of Heaven: Narragansett Indians, 1676–1880," *Rhode Island History* 37 (August 1978); Ruth W. Herndon and Ella Sekatau challenge LaFantasie and Campbell on the extent of Narragansett displacement and decline in "The Right to a Name: The Narragansett People and Rhode Island Officials in the Revolutionary Era," *Ethnohistory* 44 (1997): 433–36.

24. LaFantasie and Campbell, "Scattered," 70.

25. *RI Recs.*, 2:549.

26. *RI Recs.*, 2:553.

27. *RI Recs.*, 2:553.

28. *Mass. Recs.*, 4, pt. 2:453, 467.

29. George Henry Moore, *Notes on the History of Slavery in Massachusetts* (New York: D. Appleton, 1866), 15–18; Lorenzo Greene, *The Negro in Colonial New England* (Baltimore: Johns Hopkins University Press, 1948); James O. Horton and Lois E. Horton, *Hope of Liberty: Culture, Community and Protest among Northern Free Blacks* (New York: Oxford University Press, 2004), 10; Junius P. Rodriguez, *Slavery in the United States: A Social, Political, and Historical Encyclopedia,* 2 vols. (Santa Barbara, CA: ABC-CLIO, 2007), 1:6; and M. Michelle Jarrett Morris, *Under Household Government: Sex and Family in Puritan Massachusetts* (Cambridge, MA: Harvard University Press, 2013), 15 and 255 n.6.

30. Account Books of John Hull, 2:398, August 23, 1676, 2:446, September 13, 1676, New England Historic Genealogical Society, Boston.

31. Joanne Pope Melish, *Disowning Slavery: Gradual Emancipation and "Race" in New England, 1780–1860* (Ithaca, NY: Cornell University Press, 1998), 16–17; Lorenzo Greene, *The Negro in Colonial New England* (Baltimore: Johns Hopkins University Press, 1948), 101; Bernard C. Steiner, "History of Slavery in Connecticut," *Johns Hopkins University Studies in Historical and Political Science* 9–10 (1893): 6–83, 382; "Answer to Queries," *Conn. Recs.*, 3:349; Robert E. Desrochers Jr., "Slave-for-Sale Advertisements and Slavery in Massachusetts, *WMQ* 59 (2002): 623–64, 651, 654–55. Jackson Turner Main estimated that by 1700 nearly one in ten Connecticut households wealthy enough to rate a full inventory of their estates listed a slave among the property. See Main, *Society and Economy in Colonial Connecticut* (Princeton, NJ: Princeton University Press, 1985), 177.

32. "Answer to Queries," *Conn. Recs.*, 3:349.

33. *PTP*, 15:156–58, 161.

34. *PTP*, 15:151–55, quotations on 152.

35. James Noyes to John Allyn, October 1676, *Wyllys Papers*, 255–57.

36. Depositions of Richard Arnold, Sam Indian, and two Indian Squaws, April 1682, *PTP*, 15:239–40. Margaret reportedly drowned while demonstrating the use of a canoe to Arnold.

37. Numerous historians have argued that slavery was more of an ornamental or status institution in the North rather than an economic investment, but others have marshaled persuasive evidence to the contrary. See Desrochers, "Slave-for Sale"; Greene, *Negro*, 123; Melish, *Disowning Slavery*, 18–20; also Rachel Chernos-Lin, "The Rhode Island Slave-Traders: Butchers, Bakers and Candlestick Makers," *Slavery and Abolition* 23 (September 2002): 21–38.

38. *RI Recs.*, 2:550–51.

39. Hannah/Woddell Indenture, record 353, January 1677/78, in *Portsmouth Town Records*, 433–34.

40. Inventory of William Almy, April 23, 1677, in *Job Almy v. Mary Townsend and Job Almy*, Newport SCR Record Book A, 248; inventory of Job Almy, 1684, in John Osborne Austin, *Genealogical Dictionary of Rhode Island* (Albany, 1887), 238.

41. Petition of Ben Indian, September 1693, "Copies of Records of Warwick," Mss. 221, box 1, Rhode Island Historical Society, Providence.

42. Deed of Samuel Rodgers to James Loper, March 17, 1677/78, *EHTR*, 1:312.

43. Deed of James Loper to Arthur Howell and Elizabeth Loper, March 26, 1678, ibid.

44. Fitz-John Winthrop to Nathaniel Eldred, December 15, 1676, Massachusetts Historical Society *Collections*, ser. 5, vol. 8 (Boston, 1883), 282–83.

45. Samuel Shrimpton to Elizabeth Shrimpton, July 8, 1676, Photostats, Massachusetts Historical Society, Boston.

46. Captain Thomas Hamilton to the Admiralty Board, December 16, 1675, Admiralty Records ref. ADM 106/31, also ADM 3/276, 50, PRO/NAUK (my thanks to John Wood at the PRO for bringing this document to my attention); Stephen Saunders Webb, *1676: The End of American Independence* (Syracuse, NY: Syracuse University Press, 1995), 228.

47. Nancy Van Deusen, "Seeing *Indios* in Sixteenth-Century Castile," *WMQ* 69 (October 2012): 224–25; Nuala Zahedieh, "The Merchants of Port Royal, Jamaica, and the Spanish Contraband Trade, 1655–1692," *WMQ* 43 (1986): 570–93; A. J. R. Russell-Wood, "Iberian Expansion and the Issue of Black Slavery: Changing Portuguese Attitudes, 1440–1770," *American Historical Review* 83 (1978): 16–42; "The names of such Ships and Masters that have come in and gone out of our Harbours & given Bond for His Majesty's Customs, August 16, 1661 to February 25, 1662," Massachusetts Historical Society, Boston; Paloma Fernández Pérez, "Cádiz," in *The Historical Encyclopedia of World Slavery*, 2 vols., ed. Junius P. Rodriguez (Santa Barbara, CA: ABC-Clio Press, 1997), 1:119.

48. Four New England ships were taken "by the Turks" in the 1670s alone, and over a hundred mariners from the region were enslaved between 1676 and 1686, including Joshua Gee of Charlestown and William Harris. Algeria held four hundred English captives from all parts of the empire in 1669, and their experience echoed that of other enslaved persons, Indian and African. Captivity in the Mediterranean was such a trope for New Englanders that it became the subject of one of the first American novels—Royall Tyler's *The Algerine Captive: Or the Life and Adventures of Doctor Updike Underhill: Six Years a Prisoner among the Algerines* (Boston, 1787)—as well as a play by Susanna Rowson. See Daniel J Vitkus and Nabil I. Matar, eds., *Piracy, Slavery, and Redemption: Barbary Captivity Narratives from Early Modern England* (New York: Columbia University Press, 2001), introduction, 37–38; Frank Lambert, *The Barbary Wars: American Independence in the Atlantic World* (New York: Hill & Wang, 2007); Beth A. Bower, "Captivity with ye Barbarous Turks": Seventeenth-Century New Englanders Held Hostage," *American Ancestors* 13 (2012): 18–24, esp. 19; *A List of Ships Taken since July 1677, from his Majesties subjects, by the corsairs of Algier; with their names, masters names, and places where they belong'd, and time of their taking; with a modest estimate of the loss* (London, 1682); Joshua Gee, *Narrative of Joshua Gee of Boston,*

Mass., while he was captive in Algeria of the Barbary Pirates, 1680–1687 (Hartford, CT: Wadsworth Atheneum, 1943).

49. G. E. Aylmer, "Slavery under Charles II: The Mediterranean and Tangier," *English Historical Review* 114 (April 1999): 378–88. For European slavery in the Mediterranean more generally see Robert Davis, *Christian Slaves, Muslim Masters: White Slavery in the Mediterranean, the Barbary Coast, and Italy, 1500–1800* (New York: Palgrave Macmillan, 2003).

50. Captain Thomas Hamilton to the Admiralty Board, December 16, 1675, ADM, 106/31, PRO/NAUK. The French and Spanish both armed galleys around the same time, and in 1684 Louis XIV ordered his government in New France to send Indian captives to man French oars. Somewhere between thirty-seven and eighty Iroquois served time in the French galleys during the French-Iroquois wars of the 1680s, including Mohawks from Cataraqui. The issue became a central one for the Iroquois in widening the war. On Iroquois galley slavery see Louis XIV to M. de la Barre, July 31, 1684, in *The Documentary History of the State of New York*, 11 vols., ed. Edmund B. O'Callaghan (Albany, 1855), 9:266; Brett Rushforth, *Bonds of Alliance: Indigenous and Atlantic Slaveries in New France* (Chapel Hill: University of North Carolina Press, for the Omohundro Institute of Early American History and Culture, 2013), 145–47; Bruce Trigger, *Natives and Newcomers: Canada's "Heroic Age" Reconsidered* (Montreal: McGill–Queen's University Press, 1986), 287–88.

51. Sheere estimated the mole's dimensions at 18 feet high, 1,500 feet long, and 140 feet wide. Pepys ordered it destroyed when the English abandoned Tangier in 1783, and Sheere thought it would take one thousand men working around the clock nearly a year to pull the mole down. See Sheere to Lord Dartmouth, December 6, 1683, in William Legge Dartmouth, *The Manuscripts of the Earl of Dartmouth*, 3 vols. (London, 1887–96; repr., New York: Gregg Press, 1992), 1:102.

52. Henry Sheere, "A List of Slaves belonging to His Majsts. Bagnio at Tangiers," February 20, 1676, CO 27029, PRO/NAUK.

53. See MA, 30:215–16; the names of some of these men match those on Sheere's list, but they were common names.

54. Aylmer, "Slavery," 384.

55. John Eliot to Robert Boyle, November 27, 1683, reprinted in Martin Moore, *Memoirs of the Life and Character of the Reverend John Eliot, Apostle to the N.A. Indians* (Boston, 1822), 136–37.

56. James C. Armstrong, "Madagascar and the Slave Trade in the Seventeenth Century," *Omaly Sy Anio: Hier et Aujourd'hui* 17–20 (1984): 211–33; Piet Westra and James C. Armstrong, eds., *Slave Trade with Madagascar: The Journals of Cape Slaver Leijdsman, 1715* (Cape Town: Africana Publishers, 2008); Kevin P. McDonald, "Pirates, Merchants, Settlers and Slaves: Making an Indo-Atlantic Trade World, 1640–1730" (PhD diss., University of California, Santa Cruz, 2008), appendix 2; Mary Caroline Cravens, "Manumission and the Life Cycle of a Contained Population: The VOC Lodge Slaves at the Cape of Good Hope, 1680–1730," in *Paths to Freedom: Manumission in the Atlantic World*, ed. Rosemary Brana-Shute and Randy J. Parks (Columbia: University of South Carolina Press, 2008).

57. McDonald, "Pirates," appendix 2; Armstrong, "Madagascar," 220–23.

58. Bernard Bailyn, *The New England Merchants in the Seventeenth Century* (Cambridge, MA: Harvard University Press, 1953), 78, 83, 127; Margaret Ellen Newell,

From Dependency to Independence: Economic Revolution in Colonial New England (Ithaca, NY: Cornell University Press, 1998), 79; for the Madeira trade's importance in the eighteenth century see David Hancock, *Oceans of Wine: Madeira and the Emergence of American Trade and Taste* (New Haven, CT: Yale University Press, 2009).

59. Larry D. Gragg, "A Puritan in the West Indies: The Career of Stephen Winthrop," *WMQ* 50 (1993): 768; A. J. R. Russell-Wood, "The Portuguese Atlantic," in *Atlantic History: A Critical Appraisal*, ed. Jack P. Greene and Philip Morgan (New York: Oxford University Press, 2008): 83–89.

60. T. Bentley Duncan, *Atlantic Islands: Madeira, the Azores, and the Cape Verdes in Seventeenth-Century Commerce and Navigation* (Chicago: University of Chicago Press, 1972).

61. *Mass. Recs.*, 5:64.

62. Geoffrey Plank, *An Unsettled Conquest: The British Campaign against the Peoples of Acadia* (Philadelphia: University of Pennsylvania Press, 2000); Jennifer Hale Pulsipher, *Subjects unto the Same King: Indians and the Contest for Authority in Colonial New England* (Philadelphia: University of Pennsylvania Press, 2006), 223–24.

63. Thomas Gardner to the Council, August 21, 1676, MA, 69:51, and note on abduction of thirty Indians by "Henry Lauton and Maj. William Waldren," MA, 69:52a.

64. "Petition of Bernard Trott," August 3, 1677, *Documentary History of the State of Maine*, 23:2; the original is in MA, 30:492. The council voted to recompense Trott but apparently did not pay him the 55 pounds—the equivalent of the "one hundred Mil Res" he claimed to have disbursed—because he petitioned the council again in 1704. See MA, 31:1–3.

65. A pipe of Canary wine typically sold for 30 pounds in English markets in the 1670s and 1680s; see introduction to *The Letters of John Paige, London Merchant, 1648–58*, London Record Society 21 (1984), 9–39. Depositions of John Sherburne, Thomas Miller, and William Rackliffe before Commissioner Elias Stileman at Portsmouth, New Hampshire, November 13, 1676, quoted in William Hubbard, *History of the Indian Wars in New England*, ed. Samuel G. Drake (New York: Burt Franklin, 1865; originally pub. Boston, 1677), 94. It is not clear that any of the men saw the Prudence Island Indians. The depositions both invoke Lynde's name, but they identify two different dates for the arrival of New England Indians in Fayal, which is the basis for my guess.

66. Other testimony indicated that Paine lacked a certificate from Rhode Island and had hastily procured one after the kidnapping; see depositions of "Jeames Sweet, Phillip Sweet jeames Sweet Jr., David Shippy, John Snook, William Allin," October 1675, MA, 30:180.

67. "Letter to Gov. Winthrop, Gov. Winslow, Gov. Leverett and the Commissioners of the United Colonies from John Payne, Concerning Indians on Prudence Island who were unexpectedly taken captive by Capt. Gorham and Capt. Matthew Fuller," October 1675, MA, 30:181; see also original version in Photostats Collection, Massachusetts Historical Society, Boston; "Indictment for kidnapping Indians and selling them as slaves at Fyal," November 2, 1675, Photostats, Massachusetts Historical Society; *Mass. Recs.*, 5:64.

68. "Depositions of "Jeames Sweet, Phillip Sweet jeames Sweet Jr., David Shippy, John Snook, William Allin," October 1675, MA, 30:180.

69. Ibid., 30:181.

70. Petition of William Waldron to the Council, August 24, 1676, MA, 213a; trial records for William Waldron and John Haughton, September 10, 1676–April 17, 1677, *Mass. Assistants*, 1:86–88; *Mass. Recs.*, 5:72; Jeremy Belknap, *History of New Hampshire* (Dover, NH, 1812), 76; Herbert Milton Sylvester, *Indian Wars of New England*, 3 vols. (Boston, 1910), 2:339.

71. Pulsipher, *Subjects*, 232; Colin G. Calloway, *The Western Abenakis of Vermont, 1600–1800: War, Migration, and the Survival of an Indian People* (Norman: University of Oklahoma Press, 1990), 81.

72. In his *History of New Hampshire*, Jeremy Belknap referred to this incident as "Waldron's Ruse" and noted that all but eight of the captives "were sold into slavery in foreign parts." Belknap, *History*, 76.

73. Mashpee Indians' submission to the Plymouth General Court, July 1671, *RCNP*, 5:71.

74. Governor Leete to Major Robert Thomson, October 23, 1678, *Conn. Recs.*, 3:262.

75. "Address to the King, October 1678"; Leete to Thomson, *Conn. Recs.*, 3:260–61, 261–63.

Chapter 8

1. Jennifer Hale Pulsipher, *Subjects unto the Same King: Indians and the Contest for Authority in Colonial New England* (Philadelphia: University of Pennsylvania Press, 2006), 236–37.

2. Memorial of Jeremy Dummer Jr. to Lord Dartmouth, January 1710/11, CO 5, box 9, "Canada Expedition," PRO/NAUK.

3. Peter E. Pope, *Fish into Wine: The Newfoundland Plantation in the Seventeenth Century* (Chapel Hill: University of North Carolina Press, for the Omohundro Institute of Early American History and Culture, 2003).

4. W. J. Eccles, "The Fur Trade and Eighteenth-Century Imperialism," *WMQ* 40 (1983): 341–62.

5. Memorial of Jeremy Dummer Jr. to Lord Dartmouth, January 1710/11.

6. For more on the crises of 1688–90 see Owen Stanwood, *Empire Reformed: English America in the Age of the Glorious Revolution* (Philadelphia: University of Pennsylvania Press, 2011), and David S. Lovejoy, *The Glorious Revolution in America* (Middletown, CT: Wesleyan University Press, 1987). For the importance of the northeast as an imperial battleground see Stanwood, "The Unlikely Imperialist: The Baron of Saint-Castin and the Transformation of the Northeastern Borderlands," *French Colonial History* 5 (2004): 43–62. For Indian power in the region see John G. Reid and Emerson W. Baker, "Amerindian Power in the Early Modern Northeast: A Reappraisal" *WMQ* 61 (2004): 77–106; for the Wabanaki and their efforts to retain sovereignty see Saliha Belmessous, "Wabanaki versus French and English Claims in Northeastern North America, c. 1715," in *Native Claims: Indigenous Law against Empire, 1500–1920*, ed. Belmessous (New York: Oxford University Press, 2012); Colin G. Calloway, *The Western Abenakis of Vermont, 1600–1800: War, Migration, and the Survival of an Indian People* (Norman: University of Oklahoma Press, 1990); Geoffrey Plank, *An Unsettled Conquest: The British Campaign against the Peoples of Acadia*

(Philadelphia: University of Pennsylvania Press, 2000); and Alan S. Taylor, *American Colonies: The Settling of North America* (New York: Viking Press, 2001), esp. chap. 13.

7. *Mass. Acts*, 1;176, 530, 558, 594, 600.

8. "An Act to Encourage the Prosecution of the Indian Enemy and Rebels," and "Act for putting the inhabitant of the frontier towns within this province into a posture of defence," August 1722, *Mass. Acts*, 2:258–60.

9. MA, 28:240–43a; *Boston News-Letter*, August 28, 1724.

10. *Boston News-Letter*, August 20–27, 1724.

11. Order in Council, July 24, 1750, MA, 32:50.

12. Letter from Daniel Gookin, November 20, 1676, MA, 30:228; Order in Council, November 23, 1676, MA, 30:228a.

13. MA, 40:624; Denver Brunsman, *The Evil Necessity: British Naval Impressment in the Eighteenth Century* (Charlottesville: University of Virginia Press, 2003), 89.

14. La Tourasse to the Massachusetts Government, April 16, 1691, MA, 37:3–4.

15. Springfield, July 29, 1693, MA, 30:336.

16. *Boston News-Letter*, September 23–30, October 7–14, October 14–21, 1725.

17. "Petition from Peter Freeman, Indean of Narraganset," May 1685, *Mass. Recs.*, 5:477; "Petition from Jno. Paine to the Governors of Connecticut, Massachusetts, Plymouth, and the Commissioners of the United Colonies," October 1676, Photostats, Massachusetts Historical Society; Daniel Gookin, "Certificate for John Nemasittwas," November 20, 1676, Photostats, Massachusetts Historical Society.

18. Cromwell invoked the *leyenda negra* to justify the invasion of Jamaica. See *A Declaration of his Highness . . . Setting Forth . . . the Justice of their Course Against Spain* (London, 1655); for descriptions of theater performances reifying the theme of Indian aid to the English in the 1650s see Cynthia Lowenthal, *Performing Identities on the Restoration Stage* (Carbondale: Southern Illinois Press, 2003), 40–41.

19. See Commissions for Plantations to Lord Bellomont, April 29, 1701, MA, 40:689; also MA, 47:227; 5:496; 31:692–93.

20. *Boston News-Letter*, July 16–23 and July 23–30, 1724.

21. MA, 2:210, 210a, Treat to Governor Bradstreet, July 31, 1689.

22. Brett Rushforth, *Bonds of Alliance: Indigenous and Atlantic Slaveries in New France* (Chapel Hill: University of North Carolina Press, for the Omohundro Institute of Early American History and Culture, 2013).

23. See MA, 2:557, letters from Iberville and Villebon regarding Kennebec and Penobscot captives in Boston, 1696.

24. See Gregory Dowd, *War under Heaven: Pontiac, the Indian Nations, and the British Empire* (Baltimore: Johns Hopkins University Press, 2002), 40, 189, for references to Indian concerns about English enslavement of Indians, and R. David Edmunds, *The Shawnee Prophet* (Omaha: University of Nebraska Press, 1985), for similar expressions among the Shawnee confederacy.

25. MA, 2:557.

26. Regional accounts of this transition appear in Christina Snyder, *Slavery in Indian Country: The Changing Face of Captivity in Early America* (Cambridge, MA: Harvard University Press, 2010); Rushforth, *Bonds of Alliance*; Alan Gallay, *The Indian Slave Trade: The Rise of the English Empire in the South, 1670–1716* (New Haven, CT: Yale University Press, 2002); Juliana Barr, "From Captives to Slaves: Commodifying Indian Women in the Borderlands," *JAH* 92 (2005): 19–46; James F. Brooks, *Captives*

and Cousins: Slavery, Kinship, and Community in the Southwest Borderlands (Chapel Hill: University of North Carolina Press, for the Omohundro Institute of Early American History and Culture, 2002); and Nancy Van Deusen, "Seeing *Indios* in Sixteenth-Century Castile," *WMQ* 69 (October 2012).

27. [Samuel Vetch?], "The State of the Case of the English Prisoners at Canada," July 16, 1712, CO 5, box 9, Canada Expedition, PRO/NAUK.

28. For the northeastern wars see William Henry Foster, *The Captors' Narrative: Catholic Women and Their Puritan Men on the Early American Frontier* (Ithaca, NY: Cornell University Press, 2003); Ann Little, *Abraham in Arms: War and Gender in Colonial New England* (Philadelphia: University of Pennsylvania Press, 2006); Laurel Thatcher Ulrich, *Goodwives: Image and Reality in the Lives of Women in Northern New England* (New York: Alfred A. Knopf, 1980), esp. chap. 11. John Demos, *The Unredeemed Captive: A Family Story of Early New England* (New York: Alfred A. Knopf, 1994), suggests that Eunice Williams's conversion to Catholicism was more upsetting to her minister father than was her Indian identity. For Euro-American captives in general see June Namias, *White Captives: Gender and Ethnicity on the American Frontier* (Chapel Hill: University of North Carolina Press, 1993). Mary Beth Norton links the trauma of warfare on the northeastern frontier to the Salem witch crisis: Mary Beth Norton, *In the Devil's Snare: The Salem Witchcraft Crisis of 1692* (New York: Alfred A. Knopf, 2002).

29. For Native American soldiers see Richard R. Johnson, "The Search for a Usable Indian: An Aspect of the Defense of Colonial New England," *JAH* 64 (1977): 623–51.

30. MA, 30:317, 341a; MA, 36:162, 173a; MA, 100:465.

31. MA, 70:334.

32. MA, 31:7, 13, 112, 154.

33. Francis Nicholson and Samuel Vetch to the Lords of Trade, "Journal, March–June, 1709," CO 5, box 9, Canada Expedition, PRO/NAUK.

34. Ibid.

35. Ibid.

36. Ibid.

37. MA, 30:321, 322–22a, 322b, 323.

38. March 6, 1676/77, *RCNP,* 5:225.

39. MA, 2:252a.

40. MA, 31:686, 692.

41. MA, 5:496, 31:692–93.

42. "Letter to M. de la Jonquiere, Governor of Canada, from King Louis, pertaining to the release and exchange of prisoners from King George's War, February 28, 1750," MA, 32:110.

43. MA, 32:18, 50.

44. The Wabanaki never sought citizenship; they steadfastly rejected both French and English efforts to reduce them to subjects, as well as the boundaries both empires tried to impose on Wabanaki territory. See Belmessous, "Wabanaki."

45. Joshua Coffin and Joseph Bartlett, *A Sketch of the History of Newbury, Newburyport, and West Newbury, from 1635 to 1845* (Boston: S. G. Drake, 1845), 337.

46. Gallay, *Indian Slave Trade,* 135–43; Eric E. Brown, *The Westo Indians: Slave Traders of the Early Colonial South* (Tuscaloosa: University of Alabama Press, 2005).

Reports about the large numbers of Apalachee captives appeared in the *Boston News-Letter* April 24–May 1, 1704, about two years before the first notice of Carolina or Spanish Indians for sale.

47. Gary B. Nash, *Red, White, and Black: The Peoples of Early North America* (Englewood Cliffs, NJ: Prentice-Hall, 1992), 131–33, 136–37; Gallay, *Indian Slave Trade.*

48. *Boston News-Letter,* April 14–21, 22–29, 1706; March 24–31, July 28–August 4, 1707; March 29–April 4, April 12–19, November 15–22, 1708; August 13–20, 21–28, 1711; January 12–19, June 9–16, September 22–29, 1712; January 12–19, March 2–9, May 25–June 1, 1713; July 5–12, 1714; March 11–18, September 9–16, 1717; March 17–24, 1718.

49. MA, 9:169.

50. General Sessions and Inferior Court of Common Pleas, September 1701, in David T. Koenig, ed., *Plymouth Court Records, 1689–1859,* 3 vols. (Wilmington, DE: Michael Glazier Inc., 1978), 1:254.

51. *Boston News-Letter,* February 14–21, 1721.

52. *Boston News-Letter,* April 15–22, 1706.

53. *Boston News-Letter,* September 17–24, 1711; September 17–24, 1716.

54. *Boston News-Letter,* January 13–20, 1706.

55. *Boston News-Letter,* June 26–July 3, 1704.

56. *Boston News-Letter,* June 3–10, 1706.

57. *Boston News-Letter,* April 7–14, 1712. For more on the uprising see Walter Rucker, *The River Flows On: Black Resistance, Culture, and Identity Formation in Early America* (Baton Rouge: LSU Press, 2006), 34–36.

58. *Mass. Acts,* 1:634, 696; *RI Recs.,* 3:482–83, 4:131, 185–86.

59. *Boston News-Letter,* April 18–25, 1728.

60. Thomas Hunt to the Lords of Trade, June 23, 1712, in E. B. O'Callaghan, ed., *Documents Relative to the Colonial History of the State of New York* (1885), 5:341–42; E. G. Atkinson, ed., *Journals of the Board of Trade and Plantations,* vol. 2, *February 1709–March 1715* (London, 1925), 372–79.

61. *Connecticut Acts and Laws* (Hartford, 1715), 164–65.

Chapter 9

1. Daniel Mandell, *Behind the Frontier: Indians in Eighteenth-Century Eastern Massachusetts* (Lincoln: University of Nebraska Press, 1996), 29; Jean O'Brien, *Dispossession by Degrees: Indian Land and Identity in Natick, Massachusetts, 1650–1790* (New York: Cambridge University Press, 1997), 65–71; Order in Council, March 19, 1689/90, MA, 30:316.

2. MA, 69:115; see also Robert Roule, Deposition, MS 252, Edward E. Ayer Collection, Newberry Library, Chicago, reprinted in James Axtell, "The Vengeful Women of Marblehead: Robert Roule's Deposition of 1677," *WMQ* 31 (1974): 650–52.

3. March 19, 1689/90, "Letter from Council, signed I. Addington, MA, 30:316.

4. MA, 30:455.

5. Peter Mancall, *Deadly Medicine: Indians and Alcohol in Early America* (Ithaca, NY: Cornell University Press, 1995).

6. New London County Court Records, Trials, vol. 7, 77 (June 7, 1692), 330–61 (September 1702), 365 (June 1703), Microfilm 345/42 fc752t, Connecticut State Library, Hartford.

7. Ibid., 362 (April 1703).

8. Daniel Vickers coined this term, although he focuses on debt peonage, whereas accusations of criminality provided the majority of cases in my research. See Vickers, "The First Indian Whalemen of Nantucket," *WMQ* 40 (1983): 560–83.

9. David J. Silverman, "The Impact of Indentured Servitude on Southern New England Indian Society and Culture, 1680–1810," *NEQ* 74 (2001): 622–66.

10. *William Southmound v. Sassimmmin an Indian; Joseph Daggett v. Zackery Wonhosoott*, May 26, 1685, DCC.

11. "Spetiall Court at Edgartown January ye 14th [16]87/8," DCC.

12. "Declaration against James Covell and Keoiape two indian youths," September 11, 1693, DCC; Charles Banks, "unpublished notes re: Indian slavery," Banks Manuscripts, box 174a, folder 24, Martha's Vineyard Historical Society, Edgartown, MA.

13. J. Wickham Case, ed., *Records of the Town of Southold*, 2 vols. (Southold, NY, 1884) 2:74–75.

14. August 1690, DCC.

15. See the case of Ebeneezer Commoson and Isaac Solomon, January 19, 1704/5, BCC, vol. 2, 71–72.

16. Case of William Wannumpson, July 9, 1706, BCC, vol. 2:100.

17. *[Newport] Rhode Island General Court of Trials, 1671–1730*, transcribed by Jane Fletcher Fiske (Boxford, MA: self-published, 1998), 221.

18. James P. Ronda, "Red and White at the Bench: Indians and the Law in Plymouth Colony, 1620–1691," *Essex Institute Historical Collections* 110 (1974): 214; Yasuhide Kawashima, "Jurisdiction of the Colonial Courts over the Indians in Massachusetts, 1689–1763," *NEQ* 42 (1969): 542–44.

19. November 4, 1676, *RCNP*, 11: 242; March 6, 1676/7, *RCNP*, 5:225.

20. MA, 30:455.

21. See records of Benjamin and Thomas Church's justices court, among others, in Bristol Justices File, box 6, Massachusetts Judicial Records Collection, Massachusetts State Archives, Columbia Point, Boston.

22. Deposition of John Field of Providence, October 1732, Petitions to the General Assembly, vol. 2 (1728–33), 72, microfilm 947775, Rhode Island State Archives, Providence.

23. "Petition for Release of Grigory an Indian from indenture," ibid., 69.

24. "Trial of William [W]Right," March 4, 1693, New London County Court Records, Trials, Microfilm 345/42 fc752t, vol. 7:122, Connecticut State Archives, Hartford. John Rogers Bolles and Anna Bolles Williams, *The Rogerenes: Some Hitherto Unpublished Annals Belonging to the Colonial History of Connecticut* (Boston, 1904), 185–87, 219–20.

25. For Sarah Wright and John Prentiss see New London County Court Records, Trials, September 15, 1696, and September 16, 1701, Microfilm 345/42 fc752t, vol. 7:174, 330, Connecticut State Archives, Hartford; Barbara W. Brown and James M. Rose, *Black Roots in Southeastern Connecticut, 1650–1900* (Detroit: Gale Research, 1980), 201, 349, 452.

26. Joshua Hempstead, "The Diary of Joshua Hempstead, 1711–1758" [hereafter *Hempstead Diary*], in *New London County Historical Society, Collections* (Providence: Published by the Society, 1901), 1:1, 27.

27. Writ v. "A Certain Indian Commonly Called . . . Jo," November 1714; *Jonathan Rogers v. Jo.*; copy of Rogers's accounts with Jo, all in NLCC, RG003,

Native Americans, box 1, folder 5; Jo was still in servitude, and control of his labor was contested between John Rogers and Daniel Lester in 1722; see *Rogers v. Lester*, June–November 1722, NLCC, Native Americans, box 1, folder 7.

28. Jonathan Trumbull Papers, Account Books, Ledger F, 1739–57 (Pyras and Occatowit), and Ledger E, 1735–59, Connecticut Historical Society, Hartford.

29. Connecticut Historical Society *Collections* (Hartford, 1860), 9:87, 160.

30. December 23, 1760, and September 28, 1765, Lebanon Town Papers, cited in Brown and Rose, *Black Roots*, 560; see also Lebanon Selectmen's Records, 1710–84, Connecticut Historical Society, Hartford.

31. Debt cases involving John Quequoanon, Mamashacus, June 1714; Joseph Indian, November 1714; Indian Simon, August 1715; Indian Molly, February 1716; Wiams (February 1717); Mahawants Squaw, Peter Mashunkt, Mawhawent, and Wesamicus Squaw (August 1717); John Uncas, Caushunt (November 1717); Jo, Weebucks, June 1718; John Uncas, Haequit and sons Amos and Joshua, November 1718; Indians already indentured because of debt included Peter Way=a=may=hue, August 16; Trugo, November 1716; Ann and Ned, November 1717, folders 5–16; all NLCC, RG003, Native Americans, box 1.

32. Daniel Vickers, "The First Whalemen of Nantucket," in *After King Philip's War: Presence and Persistence in Indian New England*, ed. Colin Calloway (Hanover, NH: Dartmouth College Press, 1997), 90–113, 105–6.

33. Gideon Hawley to Andrew Oliver, December 9, 1760, Gideon Hawley Papers, Congregational Society, Boston.

34. See writ in the case of *Mason v. Fish*, May 28, 1716, NLCC, Native Americans, box 1, folder 9.

35. Edward Deake to Joseph Fish, mss. 77, frame 57, Indian Deeds/Indians Microfilm 80010, Connecticut Historical Society, Hartford.

36. *C. Champlin v. Betty Thompson*, Newport SCR, March 1733; also *Champlin v. Thompson*, WCC, June 1733–, and flat files nos. 1–3, Rhode Island Judicial Records Center, Pawtucket. Ann Marie Plane, *Colonial Intimacies: Indian Marriage in Early New England* (Ithaca, NY: Cornell University Press, 2000), 139–41, discusses the implications of Betty's case for legal definitions of Indian marriage in New England; see also John Wood Sweet, *Bodies Politic: Negotiating Race in the American North, 1730–1830* (Philadelphia: University of Pennsylvania Press, 2007), 36–38.

37. Depositions of Joseph Champlin and Ann Champlin, March 27, 1732, and Deposition of Pepewas Indian woman, August 30, 1733, *Champlin v. Thompson*, Newport SCR, March 1733; also *Champlin v. Thompson*, WCC, June 1733–, and flat files nos. 1–3.

38. PTP mss., vol. 1, p. 10, mss. 18, July 16, [1681?].

39. Jonathan Trumbull Account Book, Connecticut Historical Society, Hartford.

40. Examples include Phobe Crandall, March 30, 1706, Doroty and Jeny, April 1714, Newport Court of Trials, Newport SCR.

41. *Mass. Acts*, 2:182, 79. British officials found the pauper laws excessively harsh and recommended that imperial authorities disallow them. Richard West to the Lords of Trade and Plantations, May 14, 1725, *Mass. Acts*, 2:197, also CO 5, Board of Trade New England Papers, May 19, 1725, 23:133, PRO/NAUK.

42. Will of Mary Mecumpas, September 27, 1692, in Charles William Manwaring, *A Digest of the Early Connecticut Probate Records*, 3 vols. (Hartford, 1895–1904), 1:487–88.

43. Sarah Gardner tried to place her children in households without binding them for long-term indentures, only to be overruled by Warwick authorities. June 14, November 13, and December 13, 1762, Warwick Town Council Meetings, bound vol. 1 (actual vol. 4), 56, 62, 68.

44. "Petition to the Governor of Massachusetts from Simon Popmoney . . . on behalf of their neighbors asking to protect the Younger Indians," MA, 30:456. For the laws of 1718–19 and 1725–26 see *Mass. Acts*, 2:363–65.

45. MA, 30:460.

46. Susanah Osnanah complaint against Jonathan Bishop, January 24, 1710, Jack Burges petition against Samuel Snell, April 1719, BCC, vol. 1, 172, and vol. 2, 60.

47. *Mass. Acts*, 2:365, October–December 1725.

48. *Mass. Acts*, 2:364.

49. For abuses of Euro-American and African servants in the American context see Edmund Morgan, *American Slavery, American Freedom* (New York: W. W. Norton, 1973), and Kenneth Morgan, *Slavery and Servitude in Colonial North America* (New York: NYU Press, 2001).

50. Delores Bird Carpenter, *Early Encounters: Native Americans and Europeans in New England from the Papers of W. Sears Nickerson* (East Lansing: Michigan State University Press, 1984), traces the Quasson family sachemate and their property in Monamoy. Thomas Doughton, "Twenty Years in Plymouth County," paper presented at a National Endowment for the Humanities program on slavery in New England, Harriet Beecher Stowe Center/University of Hartford, Hartford, CT, July 2007; Joseph's own recounting of his childhood and crime appears in Samuel Moody, *Account of the Indian Executed at York, June 29, 1726* (Boston, 1726), 3–7.

51. "Petition of Phebee an Indian Maid," July 8, 1701, BCC, vol. 1, 67.

52. *Sarah [Chauqum] v. Robinson*, September 1724, Newport SCR, and South Kingstown Justices' Court, July 1733 prosecution bond, WCC. In earlier documents Sarah appears as "Sarah Mollatto."

53. John Sainsbury, "Indian Labor in Early Rhode Island," *NEQ* 47 (1974): 386; Jane Fletcher Fiske, *Gleanings from Newport Court Files, 1659–1783* (Boxford, MA, 1999), no. 658; *Boston News-Letter*, March 3–10, 1718.

54. Manwaring, *Connecticut Probate*, 3:318–20.

55. January 10, 1709/10, BCC, vol. 1, 171.

56. January 1718/19, April 1719, BCC, vol. 2, 55–56 and 60–62.

57. *RCNP*, 5:223, 253; *Mass. Acts*, 1:436, 2:104, 364.

58. Compare, for example, the indenture of Indian Ezekel Pomp, October 27, 1761, with that of an English child, Samuel Nichols, in March 1759. Nichols's clothing allowance, requirements concerning his education and training, and his freedom dues received much fuller treatment. Governor William Greene Collection, Mss. 468. See also indenture of Sarah, May 5, 1731, John Greene, Warwick, Mss. 9001-G, Rhode Island Historical Society, Providence. For other Indian and pauper indentures see PTP mss., vol. 1, ser. 1, July 16, 1681, p. 10, doc. 18; Will Lawrence indenture, January 11, 1747, p. 69, doc. 138, Will Drake indenture, p. 75, doc. 154; and Warwick Town Council Meetings, bound vol. 1 (actual vol. 4), Violet a "mustee apprentice," October 1759, p. 5; Rebecca Truck, January 1761, p. 31; Tim a "Mustee Child," September 14, 1761, p. 43.

59. Indenture, December 10, 1723, Shepley Papers, vol. 15, doc. 19, Rhode Island Historical Society, Providence. For a detailed comparative study of Rhode Island indentures across racial lines see John E. Murray and Ruth Wallis Herndon, "Markets for Children in Early America: A Political Economy of Pauper Apprenticeship," *Journal of Economic History* 62 (June 2002): 356–82, and Ruth Wallis Herdon and Ella Wilcox Sekatau, "Colonizing the Children: Indian Youngsters in Servitude in Early Rhode Island," in *Reinterpreting New England Indians and the Colonial Experience*, ed. Colin G. Calloway and Neal Salisbury (Boston: Colonial Society of Massachusetts, 2004), 137–62.

60. *Conn. Recs.*, 3:17 (October 1678).

61. *Mass. Acts*, 1:214, 240, 278, 714; CSA Misc., 2:48–49; *The Diary of Samuel Sewall*, ed. M. Halsey Thomas, 2 vols. (New York: Farrar, Straus and Giroux, 1973), 2:822.

62. *Records of the Suffolk County Court, 1671–1680*, ed. David Konig, 2 vols. (Boston: Colonial Society of Massachusetts, 1983), 1:89, 113, 258, 259, 521, 557; 2:869, 1015, 1016, 1157.

63. Ruth Wallis Herndon and Ella Wilcox Sekatau analyze officials' tendency to designate Narragansett Indian people as Negro or black, although they locate the shift in the post-Revolutionary period: "The Right to a Name: The Narragansett People and Rhode Island Officials in the Revolutionary Era," in Calloway, *After King Philip's War*, 114–43.

64. Daniel Mandell writes extensively about black–Indian relations; see his "Shifting Boundaries of Race and Ethnicity: Indian-Black Intermarriage in Southern New England, 1760–1880," *JAH* 85 (1998): 466–501, and "The Saga of Sara Muckamugg: Indian and African American Intermarriage in Colonial New England," in *Sex, Love, Race: Crossing Boundaries in North American History*, ed. Martha Hodes (New York: NYU Press, 1998), 72–90.

65. *Hempstead Diary*, 279.

66. Patience was sold and resold several times after being tried for infanticide and acquitted; she was finally convicted in 1738 of killing the grandchildren of her then master, a minister in Falmouth, Maine. See Samuel and Joseph Moody, *A Faithful Narrative of the Wicked Life and Remarkable Conversion of Patience Boston* (Boston, 1738), in Daniel A. Cohen, *Pillars of Salt, Monuments of Grace: New England Crime Literature and the Origins of American Popular Culture, 1674–1860* (New York: Oxford University Press, 1993), 72–74.

67. Brown and Rose, *Black Roots*, 491–92; *Hempstead Diary*, 580; New London Land Records, 6:2, 247; 11:146, Connecticut State Archives, Hartford.

68. MA, 8:185.

69. July 12, 1709, BCC, vol. 2, 161.

70. Ibid.

71. *Hempstead Diary*, 465.

Epilogue

1. For other interpretations of New England memory after the war see Jill Lepore, *The Name of War: King Philip's War and the Origins of American Identity* (New York: Alfred A. Knopf, 1998), chap. 8. While not focused on the slavery issue, Lepore and

Jean O'Brien trace the "whitening" of New England's history and present. O'Brien, *Firsting and Lasting: Writing Indians out of Existence in New England* (Minneapolis: University of Minnesota Press, 2010). For condemnation of Indian slavery in histories of King Philip's War see Samuel G. Drake, *History of the Great Indian War of 1675 and 1676, Commonly Called Philip's War; Also, the Old French and Indian Wars, from 1689 to 1704; By Thomas Church, Esq. with Numerous Notes and an Appendix* (New York, 1860); Herbert Milton Sylvester, *Indian Wars of New England*, 3 vols. (Boston, 1910); Benjamin Church and Thomas Church, *Church's Philip's War, or the History of King Philip's War*, introduction and notes by Henry Martin Dexter (Boston: J. K. Wilkins, 1865).

2. Drake, *History of the Great Indian War*, 95–96, n., and 51 n. Drake and Sylvester referred to Benjamin Church, John Mason, and indeed the entire Massachusetts government as finding to their "taste . . . the capture of Indians for the slave-market." Drake, *The Book of the Indians of North America* (Boston: Josiah Drake, 1833), 2:106–7, and Sylvester, *Indian Wars*, 1:293–94, n., 319–24, n.; 2:259, and n.2, 260 n.1, 325–26, 457.

3. Jean O'Brien, *Dispossession by Degrees: Indian Land and Identity in Natick, Massachusetts, 1650–1790* (New York: Cambridge University Press, 1997), 123; Ruth W. Herndon and Ella Sekatau, "The Right to a Name: The Narragansett People and Rhode Island Officials in the Revolutionary Era," *Ethnohistory* 44 (1997): 433–36.

4. *The Diary of Samuel Sewall*, ed. M. Halsey Thomas, 2 vols. (New York: Farrar, Straus and Giroux, 1973), 2:822, 1:260 [hereafter *Sewall Diary*].

5. *Sewall Diary*, 1:266.

6. *Sewall Diary*, 2:691.

7. *Sewall Diary*, 1:372–73.

8. *Sewall Diary*, 1:331.

9. Sewall to Rev. Samuel Treat, August 10, 1713, in *Letter-Book of Samuel Sewall*, Massachusetts Historical Society, *Collections*, 6th ser., vols. 1–2 (Boston: Massachusetts Historical Society, 1886), 2:23 [hereafter *Letter-Book*]; *The Diary of Samuel Sewall*, 3 vols., Massachusetts Historical Society, *Collections*, 5th ser. (Boston: Massachusetts Historical Society, 1878–).

10. *Sewall Diary*, 2:958, 966.

11. Sewall to Robert Ashurst, October 6, 1724, *Letter-Book*, 2:177.

12. *Martha Parke v Sam Indian*, July 20, 1685, Massachusetts Suffolk County Interior Court, *Abstract and Index of the Inferior Court of Pleas (Suffolk County), 1680–1698, Held at Boston* (Boston: Historical Records Survey, 1940), 230; *Sewall Diary*, 1:69.

13. *Sewall Diary*, 1:179, October 5, 1688.

14. *Sewall Diary*, 2:683–84, 691; also *Letter-Book*, 1:423.

15. *Sewall Diary*, 1:253–54.

16. *Sewall Diary*, 2:966.

17. *Sewall Diary*, 1:432.

18. *Sewall Diary*, 1:487.

19. *Conn. Recs.*, 3:17–18 (1678), *Mass. Acts*, 1:167 (1693); 199 (1695); 214 (1695); 240, 258 (1696); 615 (1707).

20. CSA Misc., 2:48–49.

21. *Sewall Diary*, 2:613.

22. *Sewall Diary*, 2:595.

23. Mohegans (Samson Occom, Henry Quaquaquod, Robert Ashpo, Samuell Ashpo, and John Coffer) to Richard Law of New London, December 5, 1789, Indian Deeds / Indians Microfilm 80010, frame 288–89, Connecticut Historical Society, Hartford.

24. "An act for the bringing up also Supporting the Children of Negro, and Molatos . . . ," May 1724, CSA Misc., 2, pt. 1, 38–39.

25. *Constitution of the Connecticut Society for the Promotion of Freedom* (New Haven, CT, 1799). Granville Sharp and other English abolitionists recognized the connection between African and Indian slavery. Granville Sharp to Lord North, February 18, 1772, quoted in Charles Stuart and Granville Sharp, *A Memoir of Granville Sharp* (New York, 1836), 12, 29n. For English, African, and transatlantic antislavery see Christopher Leslie Brown, *Moral Capital: Foundations of British Abolitionism* (Chapel Hill: University of North Carolina Press, 2006).

26. The Memorial of Peter Pratt of Hartford, May 1722, CSA Misc., 2:34.

27. May 1723, CSA Misc., 2:39.

28. *Richards v. Abda*, CSA Misc., 2:10–11, 12a, a 1/2, b, c, 13–21.

29. The Complaint of Thomas Richards of Hartford, May 11, 1704, CSA Misc., 2:15.

30. Curtiss had taken other Native American clients, notably Ben Uncas. He and Lee embraced paper money, a position associated with popular politics and proto-liberalism. They backed a private land bank run by the New London Society United for Trade and Commerce, which foundered in 1733. See *Conn. Recs.*, 5:448–52.

31. *Richard v. Cesar*, June Term 1739, NLCC, now RG003, Native Americans, box 1, folder 39; "Cezar" file.

32. Petition of William Marsh, October 1750, CSA Misc., 2:64a.

33. Testimony of Thomas Williams, CSA Misc., 2:71.

34. Eighteen years earlier, James's father William had faced a similar charge of helping a slave named Zaccheus escape service from John Clark's home. James Ely's brother Samuel later manumitted a family slave and showed a tendency toward back-country radicalism before, during, and after the Revolution. See Robert E. Moody, "Samuel Ely: Forerunner of Shays," *NEQ* 5 (January 1932): 105–34; also Manumission of Peter Freeman, 1781, Lyme Land Records, 16:22, Old Lyme Phoebe Griffin Noyes Library, Lyme, CT.

35. CSA Misc., 2:101; "Deposition of Thomas Halsey," *Richard Lord v. James Ely*, May 1757, NLCC, Native Americans, RG003, box 2, folder 5.

36. CSA Misc., 2:102–5; *Richard Lord v. James Ely*, May 1757, NLCC, Native Americans, RG003, box 2, folder 5; *John Clark v. William Ely*, June 1729, NLCC, box 1, folder 1.

37. William Williams, *Journal Kept by William Williams of the Proceedings of the Lower House of the Connecticut General Assembly, May 1757 Assembly*, ed. Sylvia J. Turner (Hartford: Connecticut Historical Society, 1975).

38. CSA Misc., 2:101; Williams, *Journal*, 44, 46–48.

39. Williams, *Journal*, 48, 50–51.

40. Dr. Ella Wilcox-Thomas Sekatau made these comments during a conversation following her presentation at a conference on "Reinterpreting New England Indian History and the Colonial Experience" sponsored by the Colonial Society of Massachusetts, Old Sturbridge Village, Sturbridge, MA, April 2001.

INDEX

Marlborough Indians, 144, 145, 146, 151
marriage: interracial, in New England, 233,
 235, 244, 252, 263n38; polygamy, among
 Indians, 40, 72
Marsh, William, 249–50
Martha's Vineyard Indians, 20; as day
 laborers, 121; intermarriage with English,
 244; judicial enslavement of, 214–15;
 kidnappings of, 19; Samuel Sewall on,
 241–42; and whaling, 224
Mashantucket Pequots, 10, 97, 101. *See also*
 Nameaug Pequots
Mashpee Indians: during King Philip's
 War, 137, 142, 154; labor relations with
 English, 207, 224, 227, 240; prosecution
 in colonial court, 122–23
Mason, Daniel, 224
Mason, John: Antinomian controversy and,
 68; expedition against Narragansetts, 111;
 Indian servants of, 63, 64, 99; in Pequot
 War, 25, 28, 30, 34, 41
Mason, Robert, 134
Mason, Thomas, 120
Massachusett Indians, 20; epidemics
 of 1616-19 and, 21; evangelization
 campaigns targeting, 87, 92; Pequot
 War captives and, 66; relationship with
 English settlements, 22
Massachusetts Bay Colony/Province:
 Antinomian controversy and, 36, 67–68;
 Christianization campaigns of, 88; client
 relationships with Indian groups, 22,
 64, 102, 126; establishment of, 9–10,
 22; and forcible resettlement of Indians,
 212; households with Indian captives in,
 63–69; hybrid society in, concerns about,
 112, 165–66; on Indian land purchases,
 114; and Indian trade, 23; before King
 Philip's War, 110–11, 138; during King
 Philip's War, 139, 141, 144–45, 150–51,
 152, 154, 156, 162; after King Philip's
 War, 132, 167, 168, 183, 185, 186, 212;
 labor regime in, 55–58; laws regulating
 Indians in, 116, 167, 168, 227; man-
 stealing law invoked by, 183, 185, 186,
 and northeastern wars, 191–92, 194; and
 Pequot War, 7, 25, 26, 33; revocation of
 charter of, 132, 187, 194; rival settlements
 of, 87–88; slave law in, 6, 44, 53, 108–9;
 slavery outlawed in, 16; Spanish and
 Carolina Indians in, 204–5, 207; on
 subjecthood of Indians, 58, 202. *See also*
 United Colonies; *specific settlements*
Massachusetts Body of Liberties, 53, 58

Massasoit (Wampanoag sachem), 125
Mather, Cotton, 204–5, 243
Mather, Increase, 150, 151
Mathews, John, 175, 177, 178
Maverick, Elias, 65, 87
Maverick, Samuel, 52, 64, 65, 69, 82–83, 180
Mayhew, Experience, 92, 93
Mayhew, Matthew, 215
Mayle, Jacob, 215
Mecumpas, Mary, 227
Mediterranean: enslaved New England
 Indians in, 14, 177; New England
 captives in, 288n48
menstrual seclusion, Indian custom of, 67
Metacom (Narragansett/Wampanoag
 sachem): defeat of, 182, 183; Indian
 alliance sought by, 137, 138, 140; and
 John Sassamon, 96, 138, 283n12; before
 King Philip's War, 133–34, 136–37, 138,
 139; land transfer to settlers, 184, 220;
 wife of, 150
Miantonomo (Narragansett sachem),
 79; death of, 110–11; grievances after
 Pequot War, 109–10; and high-status
 Pequot women, 40, 96; Indian alliance
 attempted by, 110; during Pequot War,
 79; reconstituted Pequot communities
 and, 97; runaway Indian servants/slaves and, 104–5
Micmac Indians: in King Philip's War,
 182–83; in Wabanaki alliance, 190
Minor, Thomas, 116
mixed-race identity, and enslavement, 1, 15,
 127, 234–35, 246, 252
mixed-race marriages: in 18th-century
 New England, 233, 235, 244, 252; in
 19th-century New England, 263n38
Moeallicke (Indian), 128
Mohawk Indians: enslavement of, 289n50;
 during Pequot War, 28, 41; relations with
 New England Indians, 79, 100, 110, 136,
 138, 187
Mohegan Indians: conflict with
 Narragansetts, 110–11, 113, 118, 137;
 Connecticut's alliance with 10, 99, 110;
 as day laborers, 120; judicial enslavement
 in 18th century, 214; in King Philip's
 War, 140, 140–47, 154–57, after King
 Philip's War, 214; Nameaug Pequots and,
 100; in northeastern wars, 198; in Pequot
 War, 7, 27, 31, 33, 38, 266n55; after
 Pequot War, 40, 97, 99–101, 109–11;
 racial awareness among, 245–46; runaway
 Indian servants/slaves and, 104, 105